INJUSTICE

GODS AMONG US: YEAR FIVE

VOLUME 1

INJU

GODS AMON

Brian Buccellato
Writer

Mike S. Miller Iban Coello Tom Derenick
Bruno Redondo Juan Albarran
Artists

J. Nanjan Rex Lokus
Colorists

Wes Abbott
Letterer

David Yardin
Collection Cover Artist

STICE

G US: YEAR FIVE

VOLUME 1

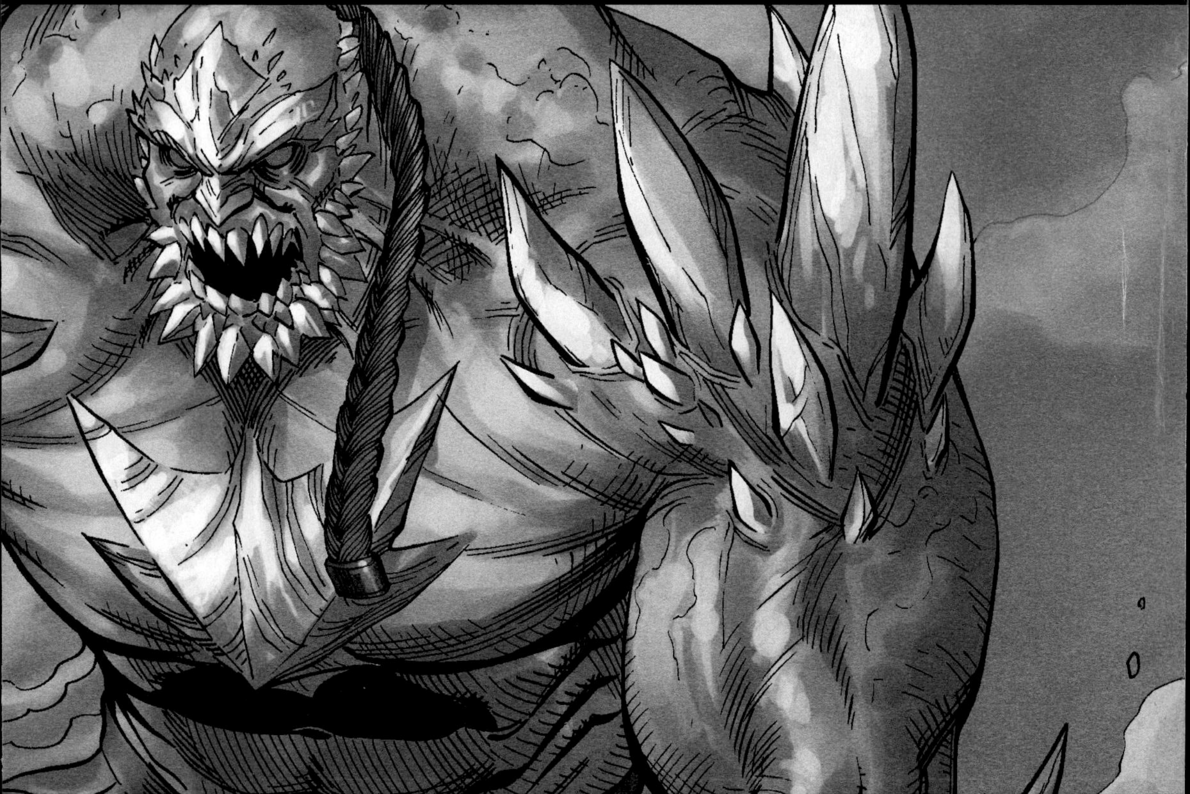

Jim Chadwick Editor – Original Series
David Piña Assistant Editor – Original Series
Jeb Woodard Group Editor – Collected Editions
Paul Santos Editor – Collected Edition
Steve Cook Design Director – Books
Louis Prandi Publication Design

Bob Harras Senior VP – Editor-in-Chief, DC Comics

Diane Nelson President
Dan DiDio Publisher
Jim Lee Publisher
Geoff Johns President & Chief Creative Officer
Amit Desai Executive VP – Business & Marketing Strategy,
    Direct to Consumer & Global Franchise Management
Sam Ades Senior VP – Direct to Consumer
Bobbie Chase VP – Talent Development
Mark Chiarello Senior VP – Art, Design & Collected Editions
John Cunningham Senior VP – Sales & Trade Marketing
Anne DePies Senior VP – Business Strategy, Finance & Administration
Don Falletti VP – Manufacturing Operations
Lawrence Ganem VP – Editorial Administration & Talent Relations
Alison Gill Senior VP – Manufacturing & Operations
Hank Kanalz Senior VP – Editorial Strategy & Administration
Jay Kogan VP – Legal Affairs
Thomas Loftus VP – Business Affairs
Jack Mahan VP – Business Affairs
Nick J. Napolitano VP – Manufacturing Administration
Eddie Scannell VP – Consumer Marketing
Courtney Simmons Senior VP – Publicity & Communications
Jim (Ski) Sokolowski VP – Comic Book Specialty Sales & Trade Marketing
Nancy Spears VP – Mass, Book, Digital Sales & Trade Marketing

INJUSTICE: GODS AMONG US YEAR FIVE #1
Variant cover by **Brett Booth, Norm Rapmund, & Andrew Dalhouse**

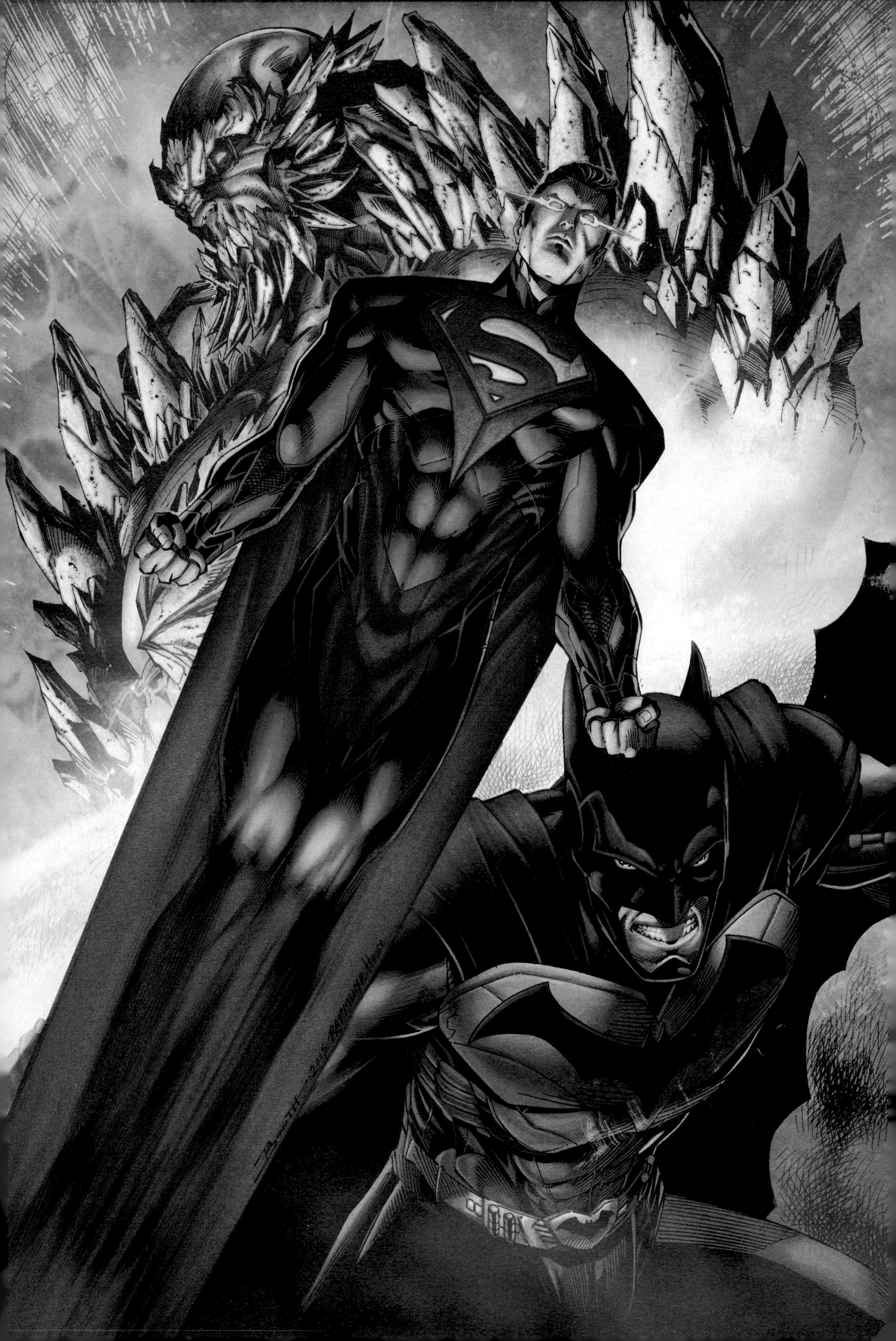

THE STORY SO FAR

This is not the world as you know it. This is a world where the Joker destroyed Metropolis in an atomic attack that claimed the lives of Lois Lane and her unborn child with Superman. This is a world where the Man of Steel, mad with grief, murdered the Joker in cold blood as Batman looked on in horror.

From that moment on, everything changed. Superman started going farther and farther to bring justice to the entire world. As Batman became concerned about Superman's increasing global power, the Justice League found themselves split between members loyal to Superman and those who share Batman's concerns. As Superman established his regime to help him keep world order, Batman's resistance team stole a supply of Kryptonite-powered pills that grants the user superpowers, evening the fight with Superman's superpowered troops.

Meanwhile, Superman found himself with an unexpected new ally: Sinestro, the former rogue Green Lantern who formed his own fear-powered Sinestro Corps. Sinestro recruited both Superman and Hal Jordan into the Sinestro Corps, and a huge war with the Green Lantern Corps and Batman's resistance followed, with casualties on both sides. Batman's team captured Raven, Flash and Robin from Batman's side and put Wonder Woman into a magical coma, but Superman now seemed unstoppable.

To combat a Superman empowered with a yellow power ring, Batman turned to the one force he knew could damage Superman—magic. Batman gathered an impressive array of magic users to his side and took to the Tower of Fate to plan an attack on Superman and his unexpected magical ally, the Spectre. But Batman's plan failed, and he found himself driven deep underground, his team reduced to just a handful of stalwarts. Superman's Justice League, however, was strengthened when Wonder Woman was awakened from her coma by her mother, Hippolyta, who made a deal with the goddess Hera.

But now the gods themselves were involved in the conflict between the two former friends. With both sides being manipulated by Ares, the god of war, Batman arranged for Zeus and Hera to intervene in the affairs of man and demand that Superman leave Earth. For an army, Hera cashed in on her deal with Hippolyta and arranged for the Amazons to stand against Superman's regime, with Wonder Woman caught in the middle. When Wonder Woman tried to avoid the bloodshed by calling for trial by combat, Batman shocked her by declaring her Olympus' champion to stand alone against Superman...to the death.

But the terms of the trial were violated when Sinestro attacked Wonder Woman, and the Greek gods stepped in and announced they were taking over as the ultimate authority on Earth and outlawing all other religions. The war quickly escalated, as Superman recruited Zeus' brother Poseidon to intervene, leading to a tidal wave that threatened to wipe out Themyscira and drawing Aquaman and Mera back into the battle. When Batman discovered that Ares was working with the new god Darkseid to create this war, Superman took off for Apokolips to confront Darkseid...seemingly leaving Earth unprotected.

With Superman gone, humanity got desperate. His supposed ally Lex Luthor worked to create a clone of Superman who could stand against him, but the clone escaped. And the representatives of Earth's governments used a stash of nuclear weapons that they had kept hidden from Superman to launch a strike against Themyscira in an attempt to wipe out the gods. The nuclear holocaust was averted by Wonder Woman and Superman, who returned from Apokolips just in time, but his discovery that the governments had betrayed him led him to fully disband their authority. Superman now truly rules Earth.

The war of the gods ended when Batman convinced the All-Father of New Genesis to intervene, leading Zeus and the gods to withdraw for all time. But now Batman was once again left with just a skeleton crew, looking for superpowered allies who could bolster his ranks.

At the same time, an anti-Superman protest led to the arrest of the shape-shifting son of Plastic Man. When the former Justice Leaguer staged a daring jailbreak at the underwater super-villain prison The Trench, he succeeded in not only breaking out his son but every villain and Green Lantern Corps member imprisoned there. After giving them their freedom, Plastic Man had just one request: if they had to do bad, try to do bad against Superman's regime...

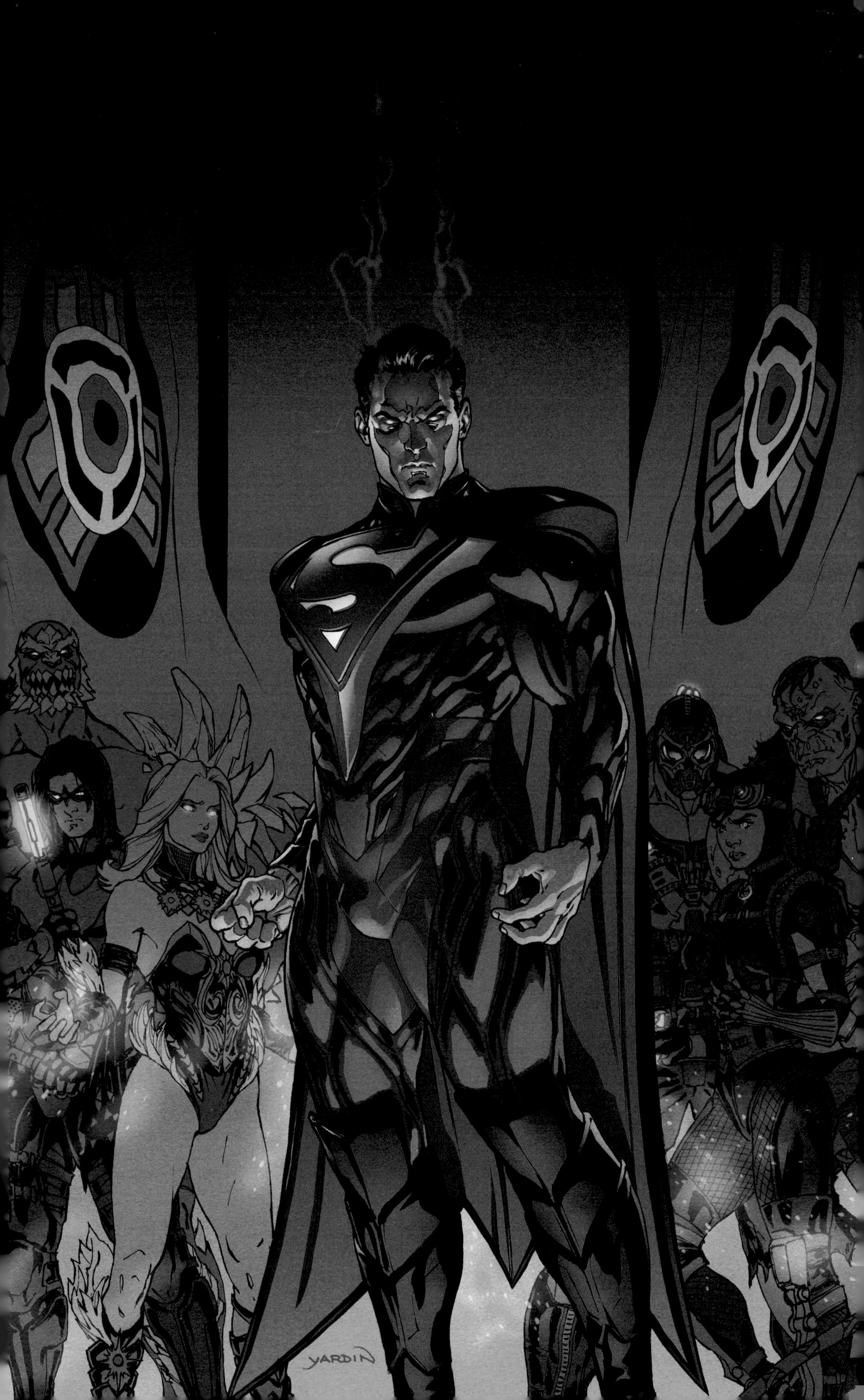
YARDIN

"Round Up" **Mike S. Miller** Artist **J. Nanjan** Colorist
"Doomsday" **Iban Coello** Artist **J. Nanjan** Colorist

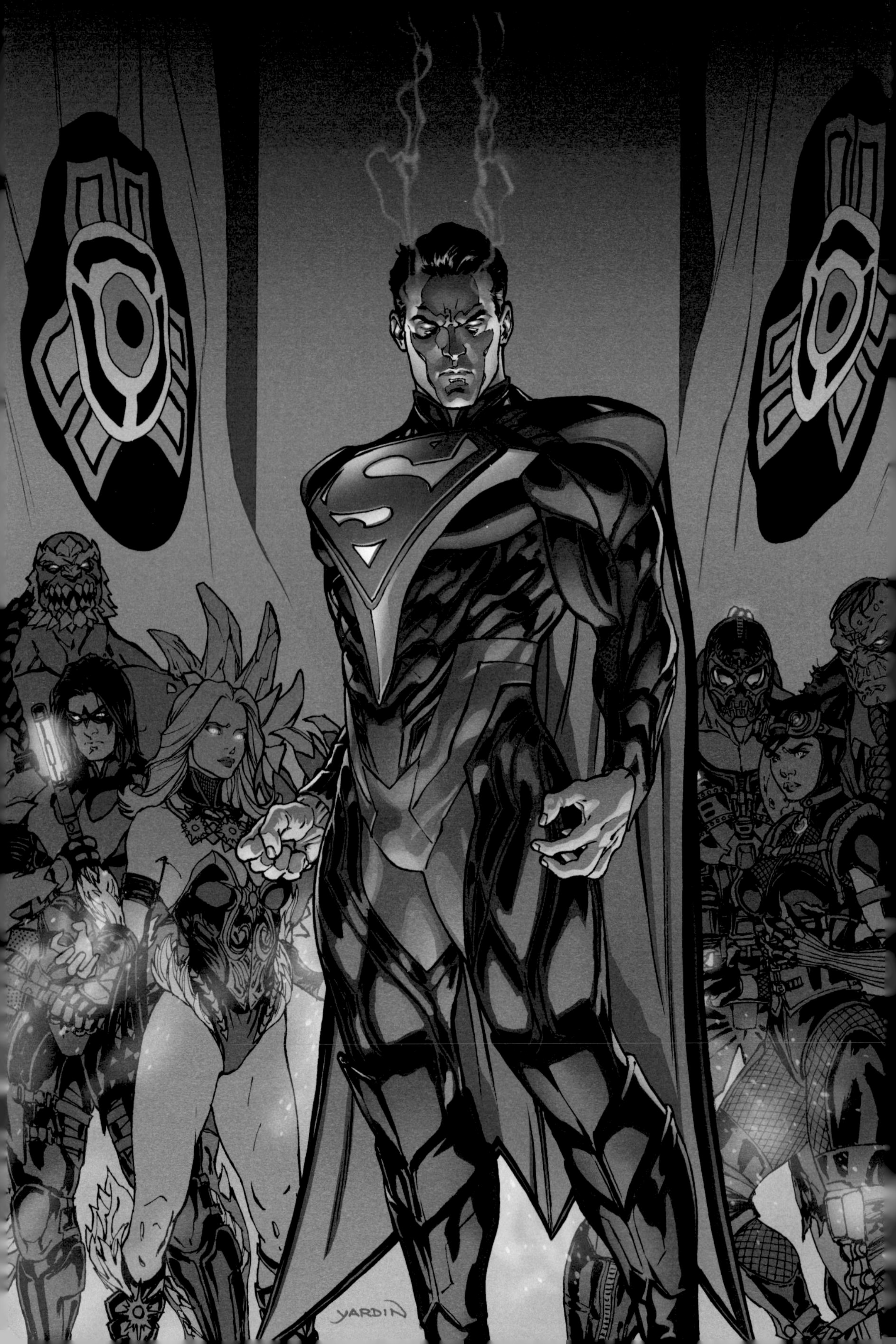
YARDIN

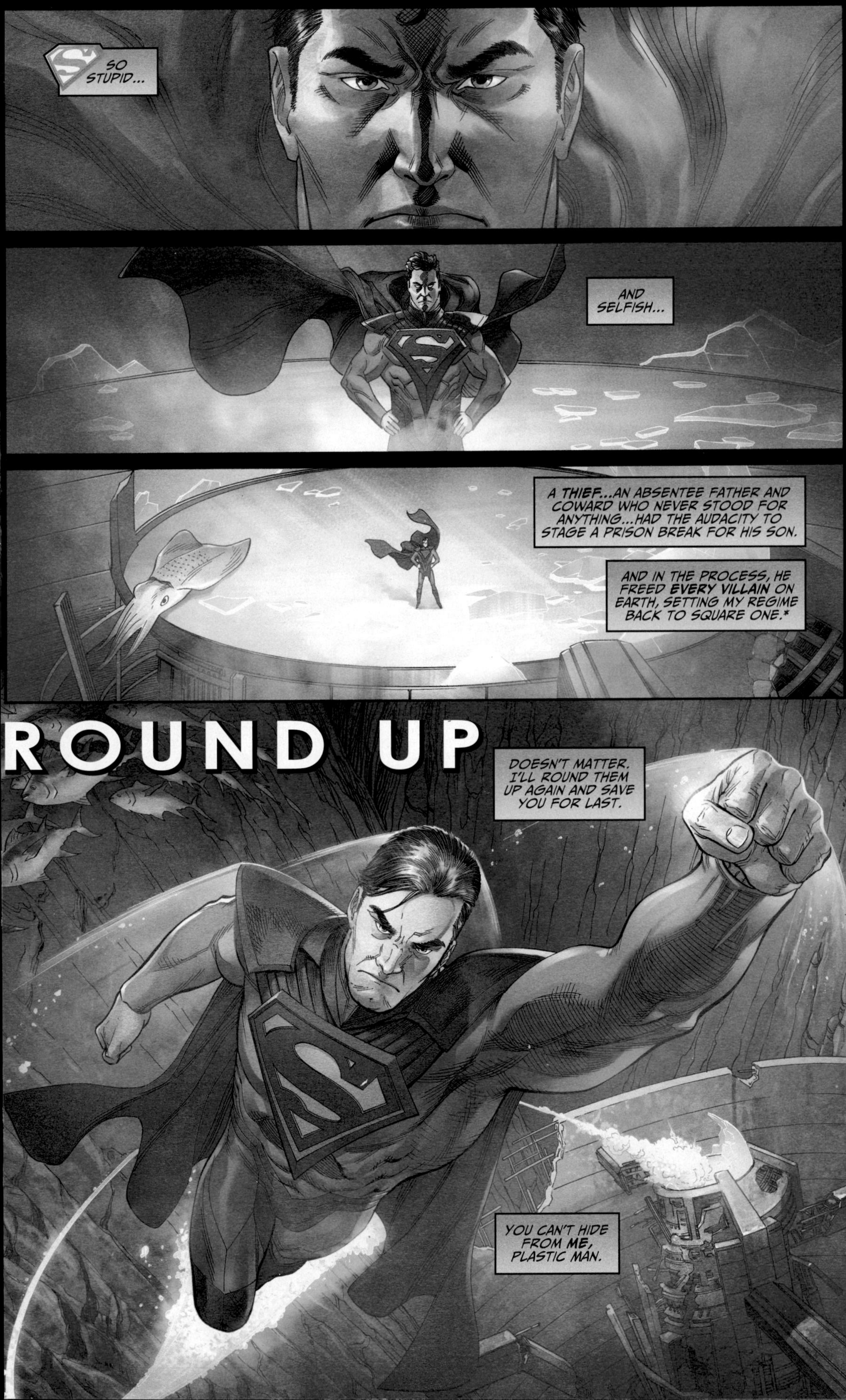
SO STUPID...
AND SELFISH...
A THIEF...AN ABSENTEE FATHER AND COWARD WHO NEVER STOOD FOR ANYTHING...HAD THE AUDACITY TO STAGE A PRISON BREAK FOR HIS SON.
AND IN THE PROCESS, HE FREED EVERY VILLAIN ON EARTH, SETTING MY REGIME BACK TO SQUARE ONE.*
ROUND UP
DOESN'T MATTER. I'LL ROUND THEM UP AGAIN AND SAVE YOU FOR LAST.
YOU CAN'T HIDE FROM ME, PLASTIC MAN.

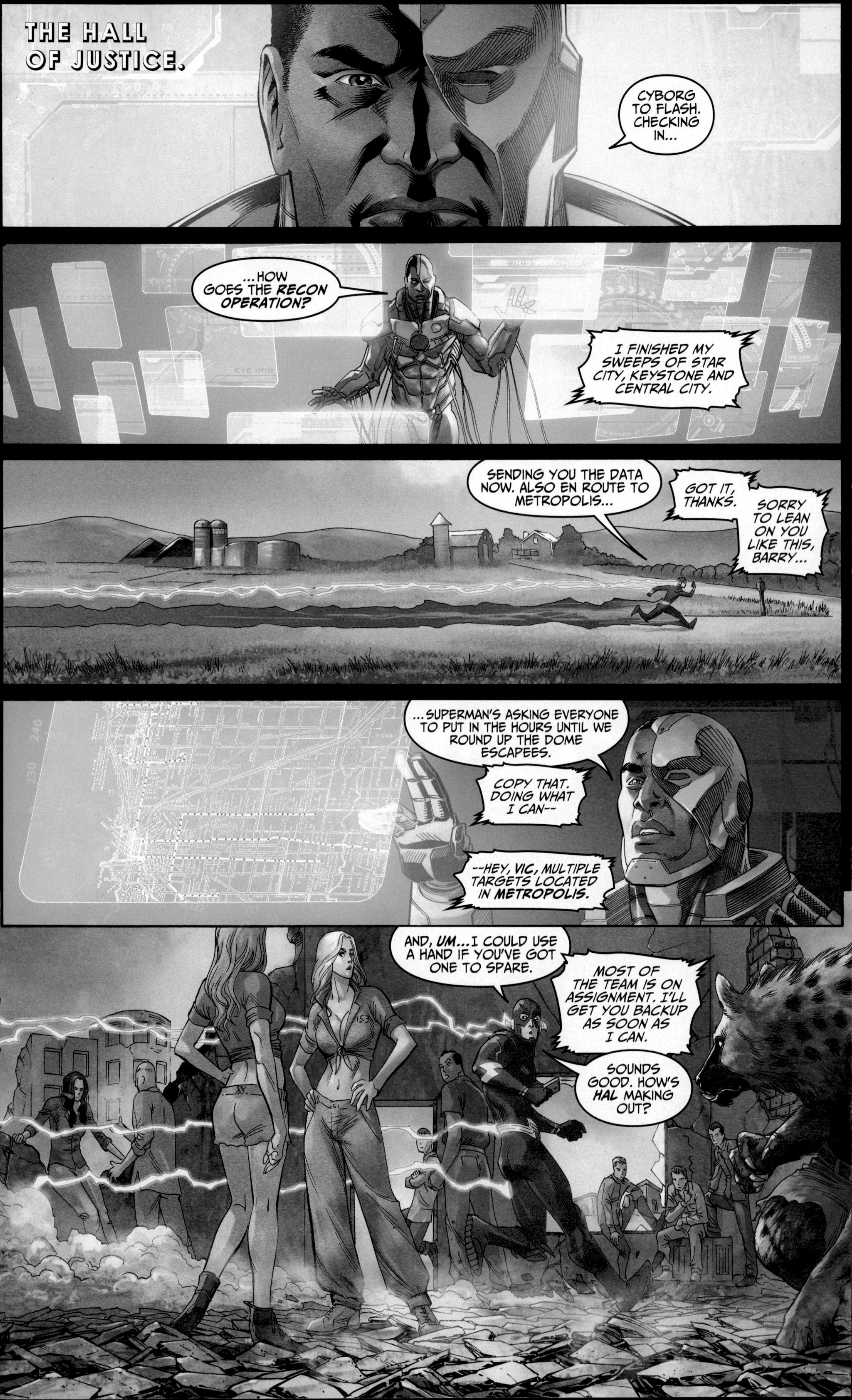
THE HALL OF JUSTICE.
CYBORG TO FLASH. CHECKING IN...
...HOW GOES THE RECON OPERATION?
I FINISHED MY SWEEPS OF STAR CITY, KEYSTONE AND CENTRAL CITY.
SENDING YOU THE DATA NOW. ALSO EN ROUTE TO METROPOLIS...
GOT IT, THANKS.
SORRY TO LEAN ON YOU LIKE THIS, BARRY...
...SUPERMAN'S ASKING EVERYONE TO PUT IN THE HOURS UNTIL WE ROUND UP THE DOME ESCAPEES.
COPY THAT. DOING WHAT I CAN--
--HEY, VIC, MULTIPLE TARGETS LOCATED IN METROPOLIS.
AND, UM...I COULD USE A HAND IF YOU'VE GOT ONE TO SPARE.
MOST OF THE TEAM IS ON ASSIGNMENT. I'LL GET YOU BACKUP AS SOON AS I CAN.
SOUNDS GOOD. HOW'S HAL MAKING OUT?

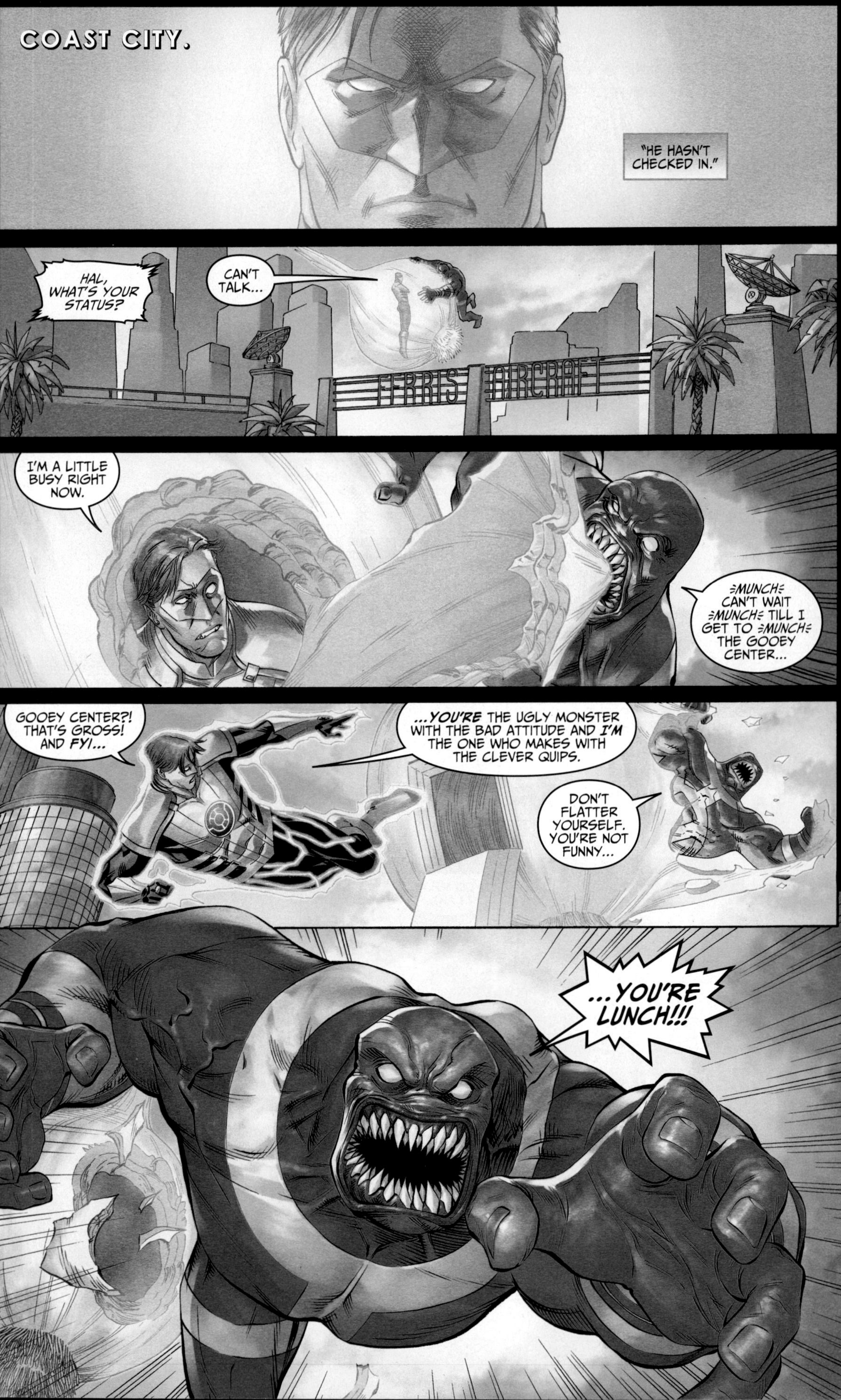
COAST CITY.
"HE HASN'T CHECKED IN."
HAL, WHAT'S YOUR STATUS?
CAN'T TALK...
FERRIS AIRCRAFT
I'M A LITTLE BUSY RIGHT NOW.
=MUNCH= CAN'T WAIT =MUNCH= TILL I GET TO =MUNCH= THE GOOEY CENTER...
GOOEY CENTER?! THAT'S GROSS! AND FYI...
...YOU'RE THE UGLY MONSTER WITH THE BAD ATTITUDE AND I'M THE ONE WHO MAKES WITH THE CLEVER QUIPS.
DON'T FLATTER YOURSELF. YOU'RE NOT FUNNY...
...YOU'RE LUNCH!!!

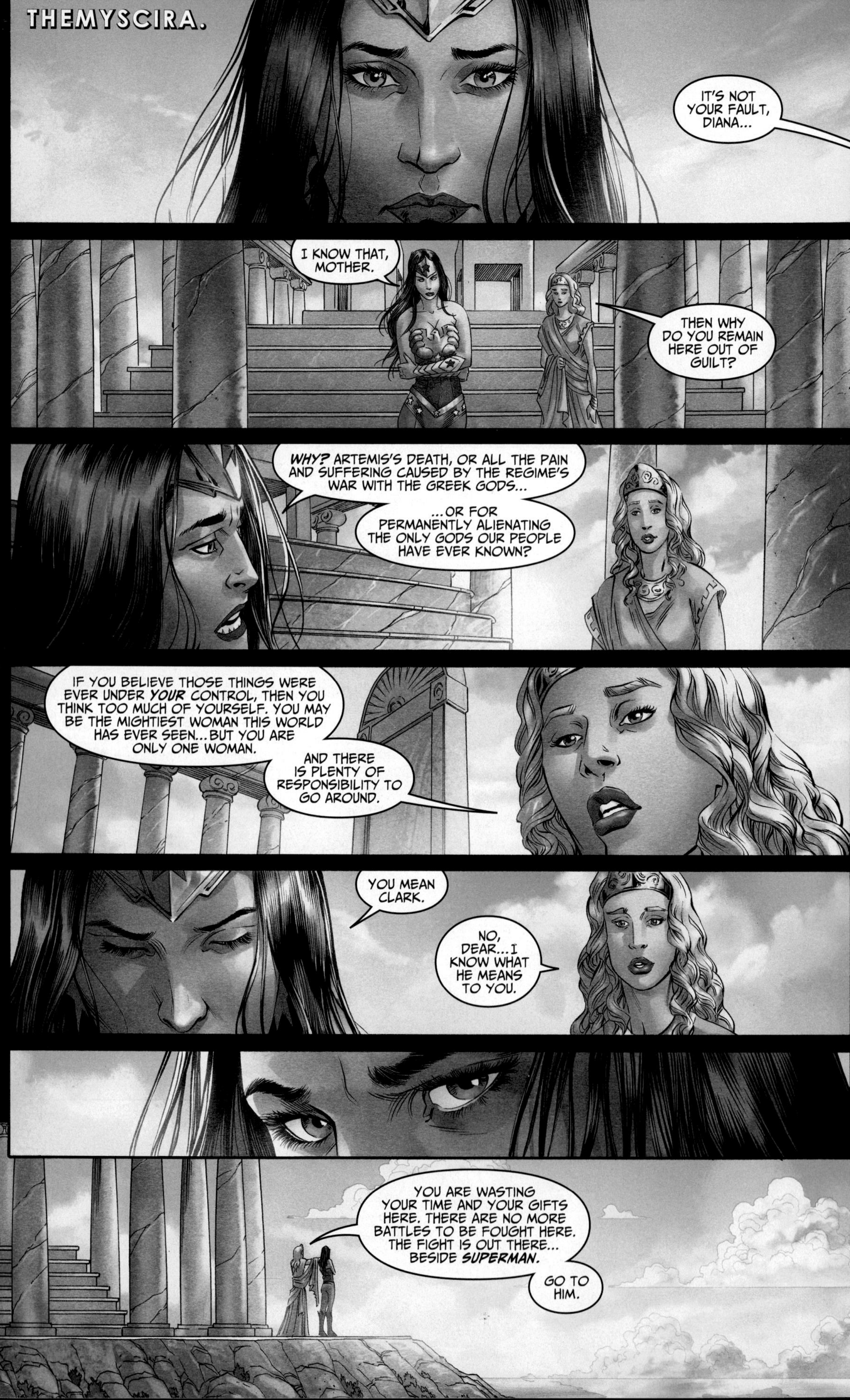
THEMYSCIRA.
IT'S NOT YOUR FAULT, DIANA...
I KNOW THAT, MOTHER.
THEN WHY DO YOU REMAIN HERE OUT OF GUILT?
WHY? ARTEMIS'S DEATH, OR ALL THE PAIN AND SUFFERING CAUSED BY THE REGIME'S WAR WITH THE GREEK GODS...
...OR FOR PERMANENTLY ALIENATING THE ONLY GODS OUR PEOPLE HAVE EVER KNOWN?
IF YOU BELIEVE THOSE THINGS WERE EVER UNDER YOUR CONTROL, THEN YOU THINK TOO MUCH OF YOURSELF. YOU MAY BE THE MIGHTIEST WOMAN THIS WORLD HAS EVER SEEN...BUT YOU ARE ONLY ONE WOMAN.
AND THERE IS PLENTY OF RESPONSIBILITY TO GO AROUND.
YOU MEAN CLARK.
NO, DEAR...I KNOW WHAT HE MEANS TO YOU.
YOU ARE WASTING YOUR TIME AND YOUR GIFTS HERE. THERE ARE NO MORE BATTLES TO BE FOUGHT HERE. THE FIGHT IS OUT THERE... BESIDE SUPERMAN.
GO TO HIM.

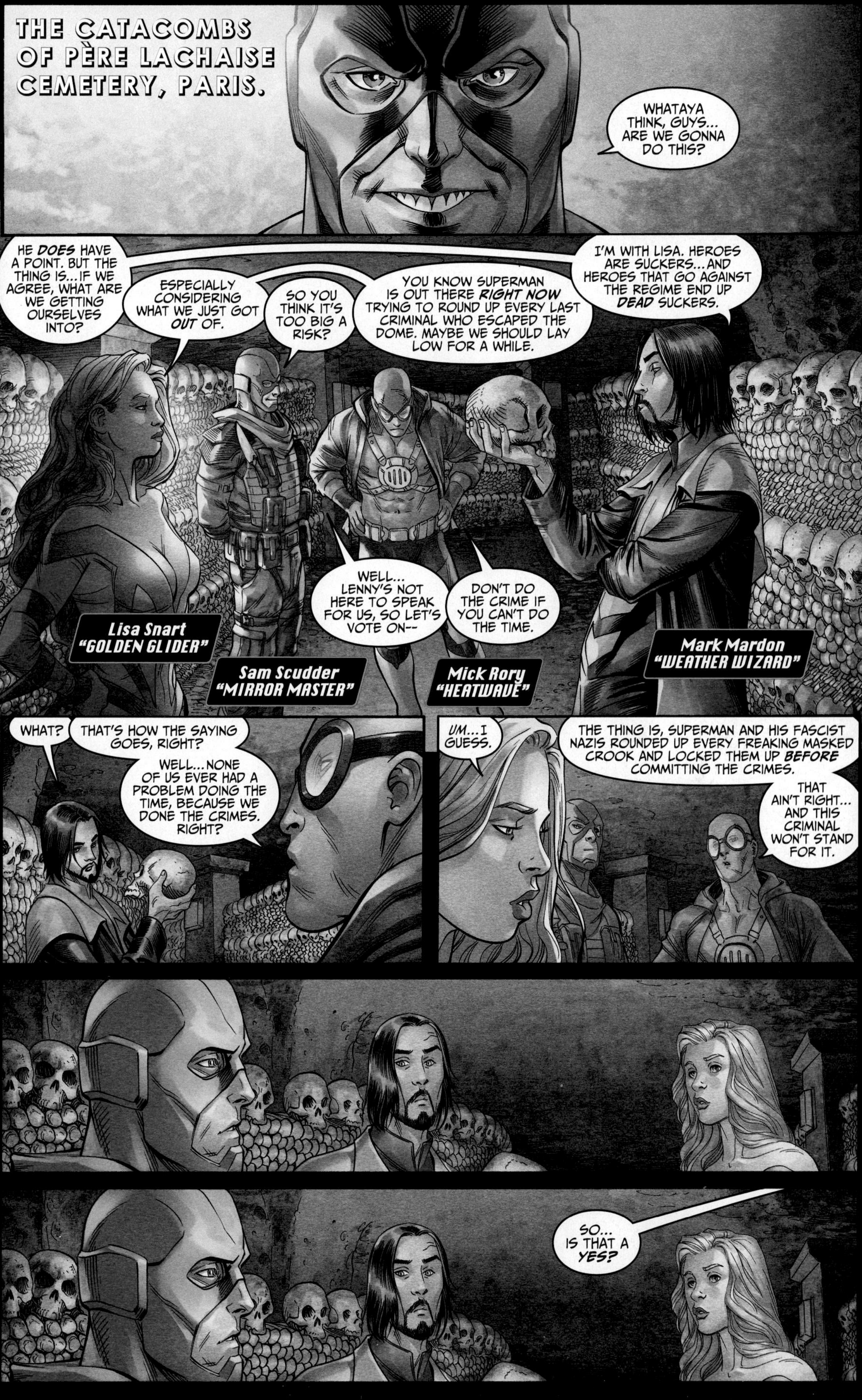
THE CATACOMBS OF PÈRE LACHAISE CEMETERY, PARIS.
WHATAYA THINK, GUYS... ARE WE GONNA DO THIS?
HE DOES HAVE A POINT. BUT THE THING IS...IF WE AGREE, WHAT ARE WE GETTING OURSELVES INTO?
ESPECIALLY CONSIDERING WHAT WE JUST GOT OUT OF.
SO YOU THINK IT'S TOO BIG A RISK?
YOU KNOW SUPERMAN IS OUT THERE RIGHT NOW TRYING TO ROUND UP EVERY LAST CRIMINAL WHO ESCAPED THE DOME. MAYBE WE SHOULD LAY LOW FOR A WHILE.
I'M WITH LISA. HEROES ARE SUCKERS...AND HEROES THAT GO AGAINST THE REGIME END UP DEAD SUCKERS.
WELL... LENNY'S NOT HERE TO SPEAK FOR US, SO LET'S VOTE ON--
DON'T DO THE CRIME IF YOU CAN'T DO THE TIME.
Lisa Snart "GOLDEN GLIDER"
Sam Scudder "MIRROR MASTER"
Mick Rory "HEATWAVE"
Mark Mardon "WEATHER WIZARD"
WHAT?
THAT'S HOW THE SAYING GOES, RIGHT?
WELL...NONE OF US EVER HAD A PROBLEM DOING THE TIME, BECAUSE WE DONE THE CRIMES. RIGHT?
UM...I GUESS.
THE THING IS, SUPERMAN AND HIS FASCIST NAZIS ROUNDED UP EVERY FREAKING MASKED CROOK AND LOCKED THEM UP BEFORE COMMITTING THE CRIMES.
THAT AIN'T RIGHT... AND THIS CRIMINAL WON'T STAND FOR IT.
SO... IS THAT A YES?

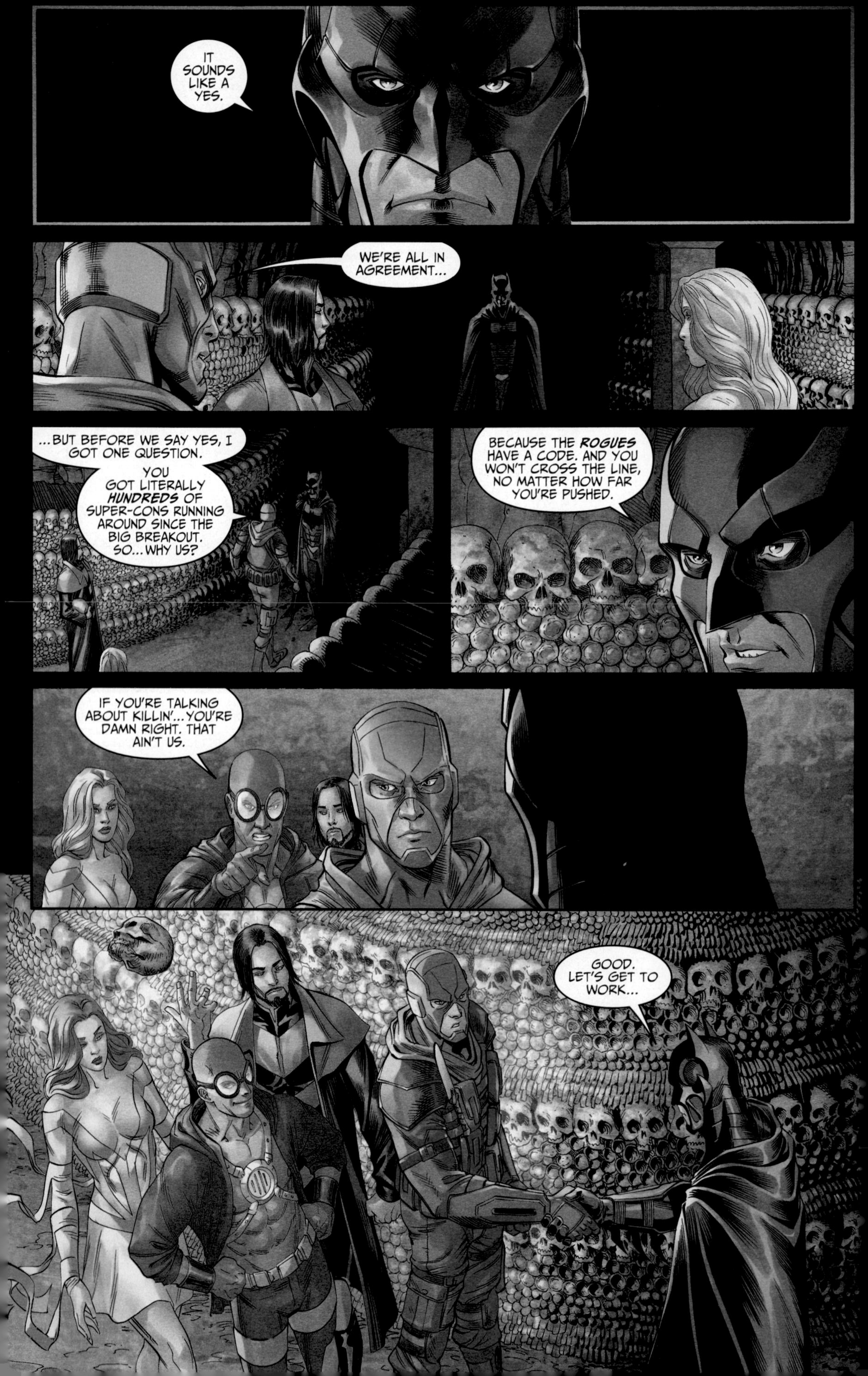
IT SOUNDS LIKE A YES.
WE'RE ALL IN AGREEMENT...
...BUT BEFORE WE SAY YES, I GOT ONE QUESTION.
YOU GOT LITERALLY HUNDREDS OF SUPER-CONS RUNNING AROUND SINCE THE BIG BREAKOUT. SO... WHY US?
BECAUSE THE ROGUES HAVE A CODE. AND YOU WON'T CROSS THE LINE, NO MATTER HOW FAR YOU'RE PUSHED.
IF YOU'RE TALKING ABOUT KILLIN'... YOU'RE DAMN RIGHT. THAT AIN'T US.
GOOD. LET'S GET TO WORK...

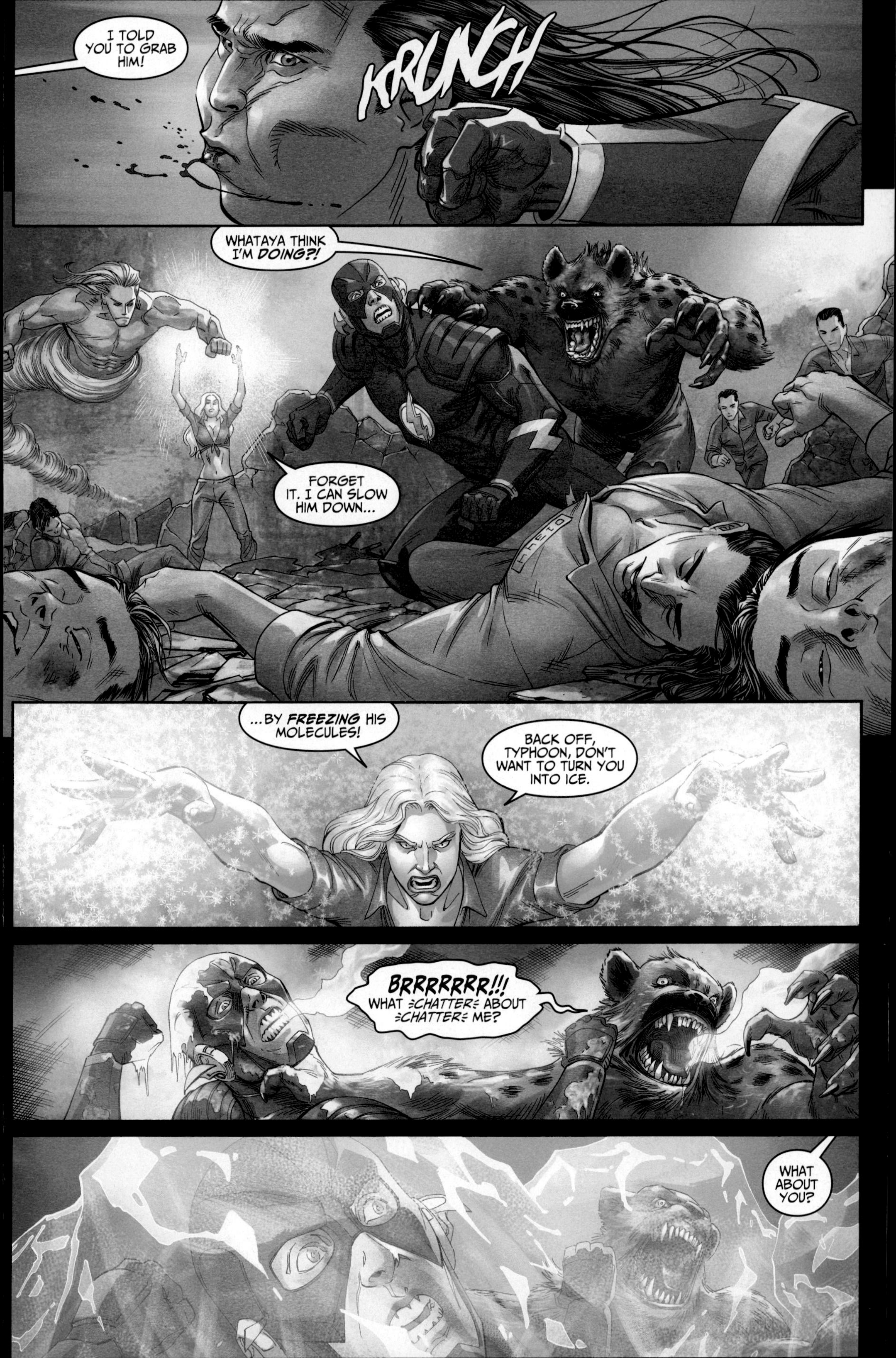
I TOLD YOU TO GRAB HIM!
KRUNCH
WHATAYA THINK I'M DOING?!
FORGET IT. I CAN SLOW HIM DOWN...
...BY FREEZING HIS MOLECULES!
BACK OFF, TYPHOON, DON'T WANT TO TURN YOU INTO ICE.
BRRRRRRR!!! WHAT =CHATTER= ABOUT =CHATTER= ME?
WHAT ABOUT YOU?

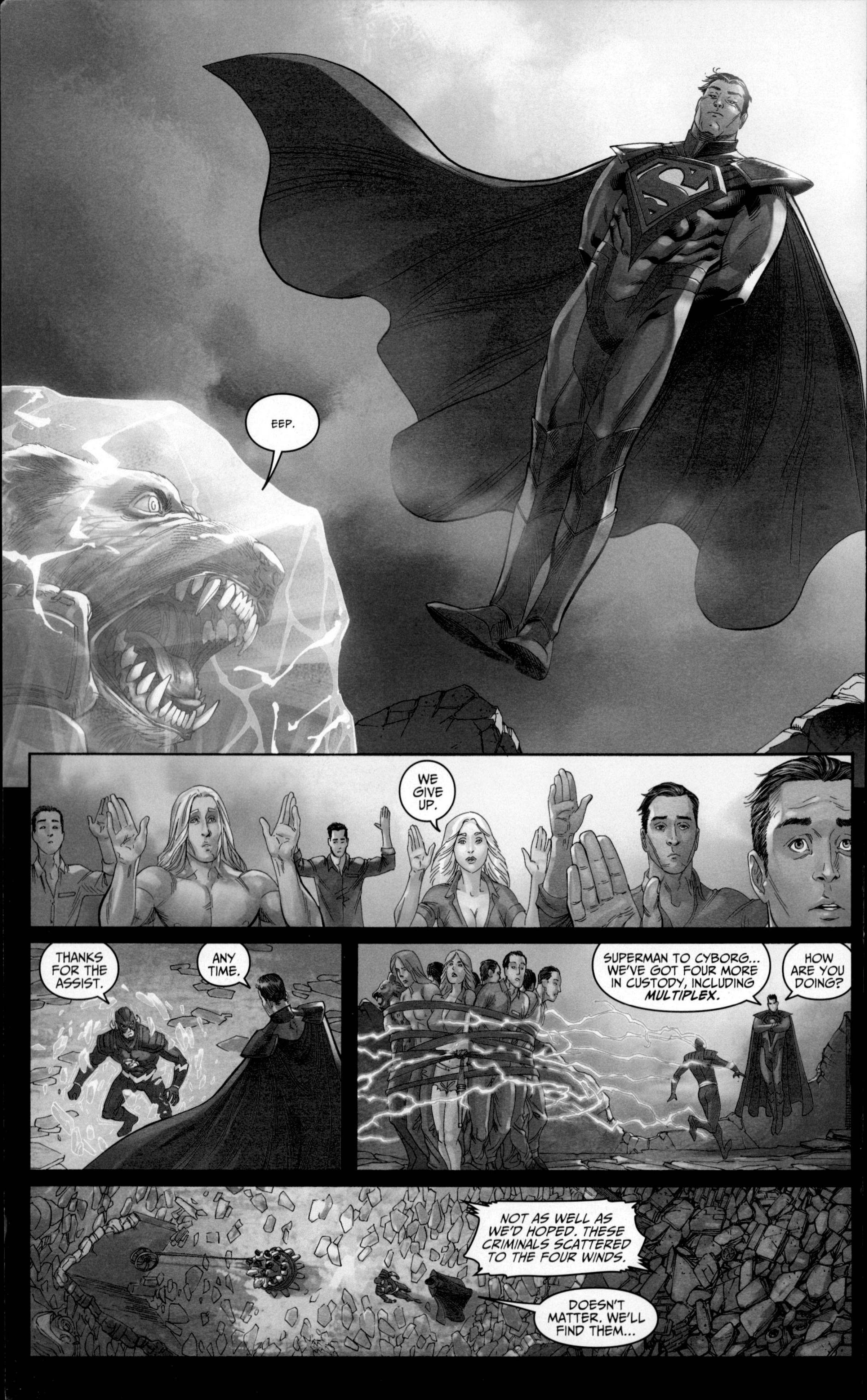
EEP.
WE GIVE UP.
THANKS FOR THE ASSIST.
ANY TIME.
SUPERMAN TO CYBORG... WE'VE GOT FOUR MORE IN CUSTODY, INCLUDING MULTIPLEX.
HOW ARE YOU DOING?
NOT AS WELL AS WE'D HOPED. THESE CRIMINALS SCATTERED TO THE FOUR WINDS.
DOESN'T MATTER. WE'LL FIND THEM...

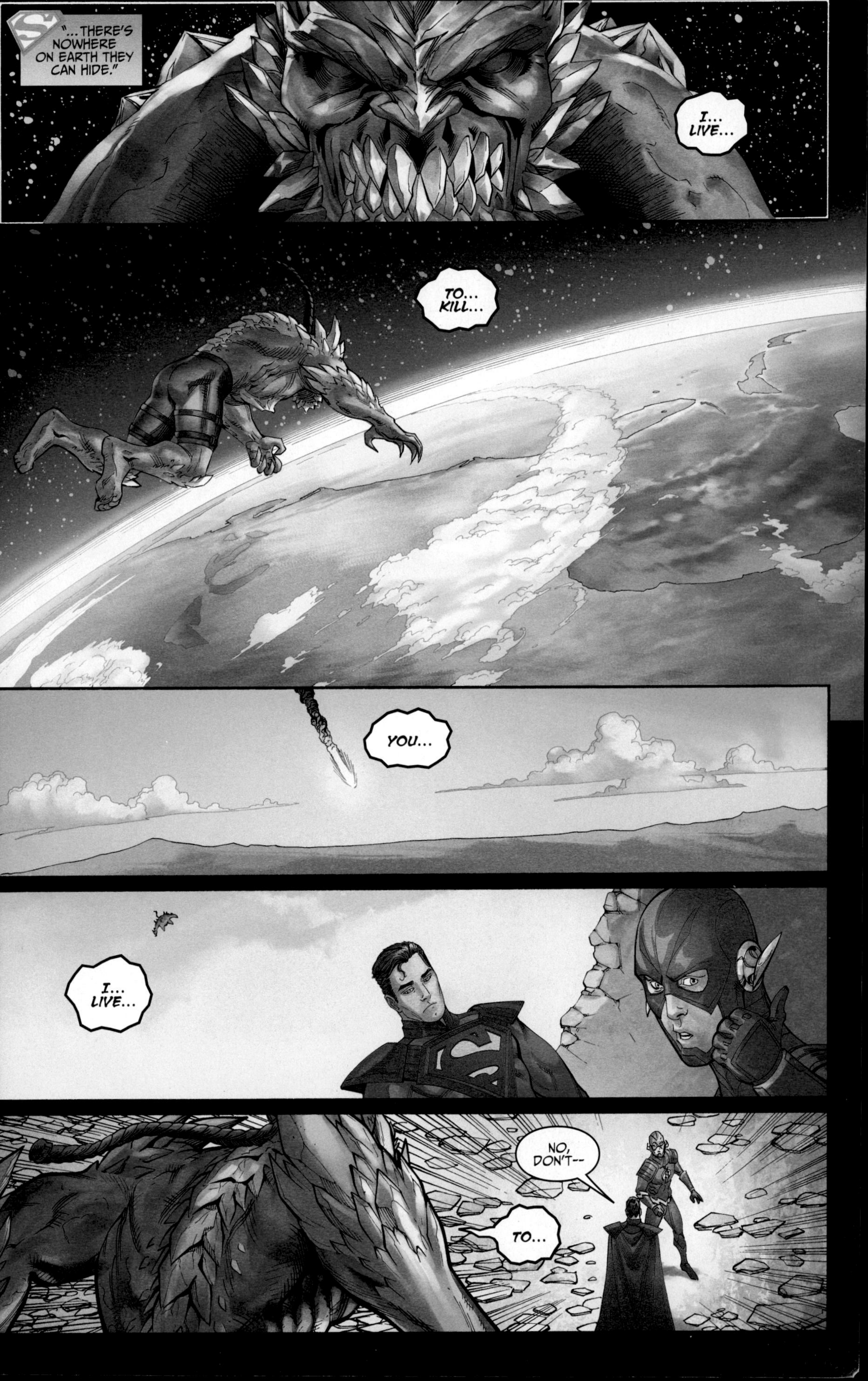
"...THERE'S NOWHERE ON EARTH THEY CAN HIDE."
I... LIVE...
TO... KILL...
YOU...
I... LIVE...
NO, DON'T--
TO...

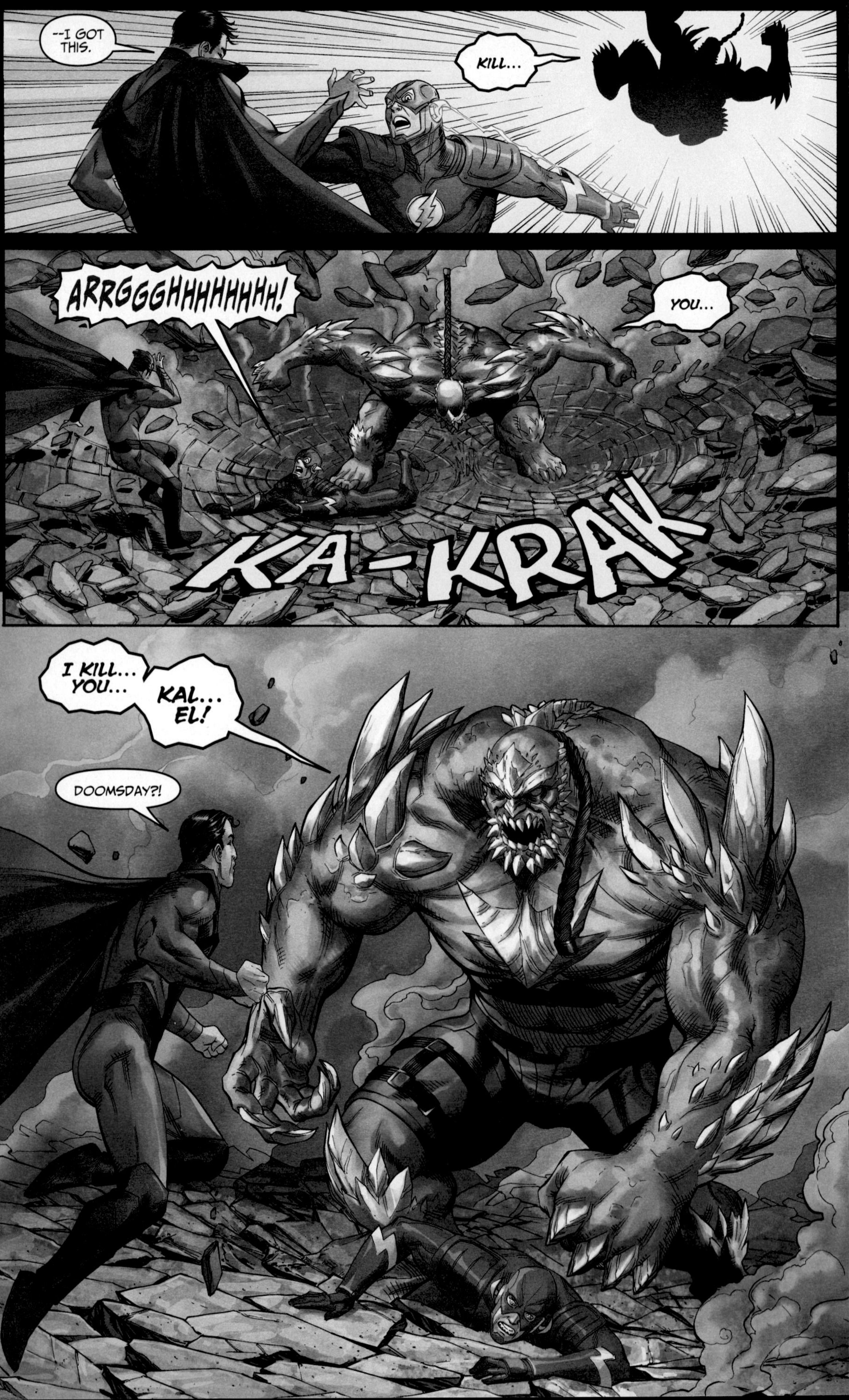
--I GOT THIS.
KILL...
ARRGGGHHHHHHHH!
YOU...
KA-KRAK
I KILL... YOU...
KAL... EL!
DOOMSDAY?!

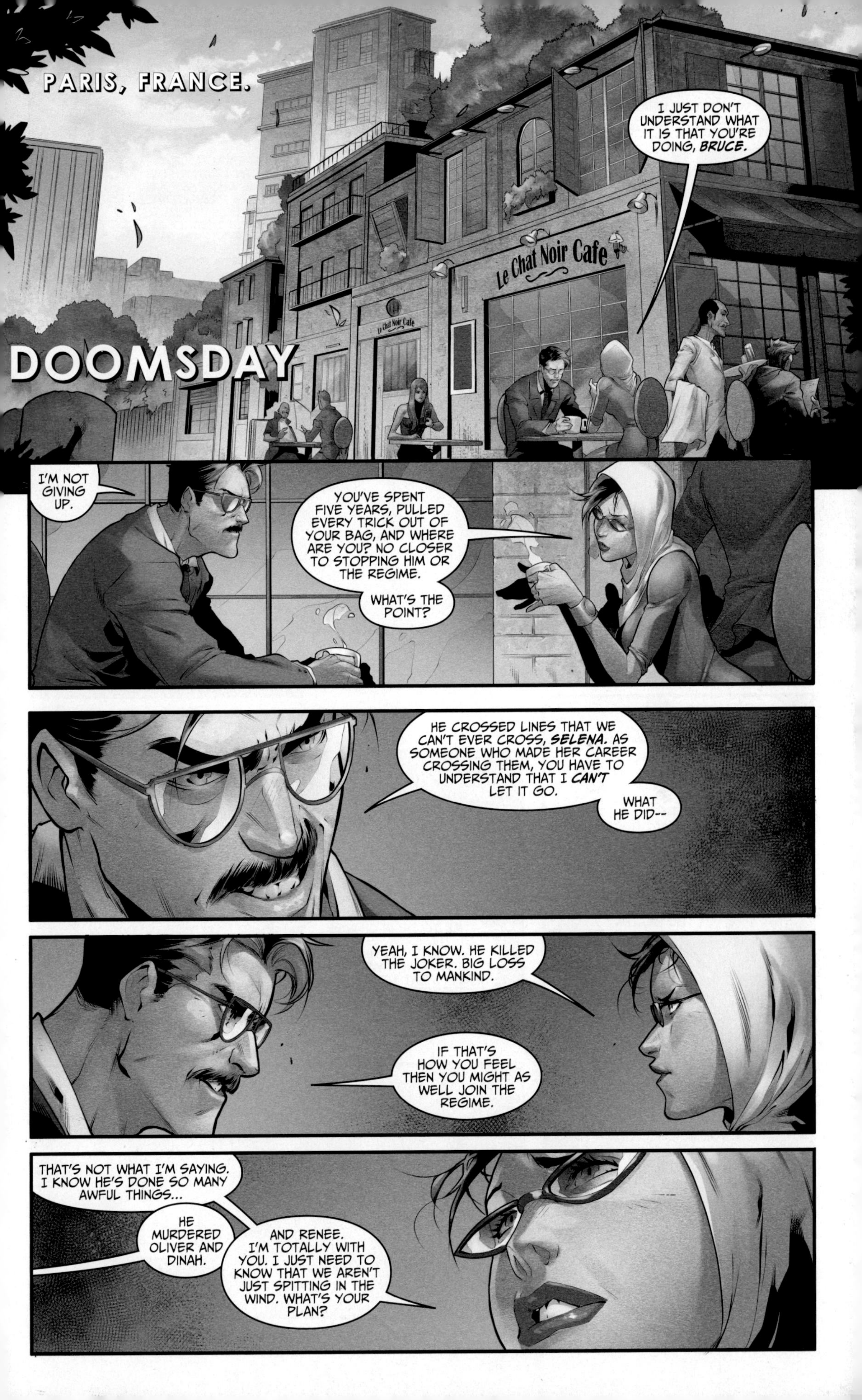
PARIS, FRANCE.
Le Chat Noir Cafe
Le Chat Noir Cafe
DOOMSDAY
I JUST DON'T UNDERSTAND WHAT IT IS THAT YOU'RE DOING, BRUCE.
I'M NOT GIVING UP.
YOU'VE SPENT FIVE YEARS, PULLED EVERY TRICK OUT OF YOUR BAG, AND WHERE ARE YOU? NO CLOSER TO STOPPING HIM OR THE REGIME.
WHAT'S THE POINT?
HE CROSSED LINES THAT WE CAN'T EVER CROSS, SELENA. AS SOMEONE WHO MADE HER CAREER CROSSING THEM, YOU HAVE TO UNDERSTAND THAT I CAN'T LET IT GO.
WHAT HE DID--
YEAH, I KNOW. HE KILLED THE JOKER. BIG LOSS TO MANKIND.
IF THAT'S HOW YOU FEEL THEN YOU MIGHT AS WELL JOIN THE REGIME.
THAT'S NOT WHAT I'M SAYING. I KNOW HE'S DONE SO MANY AWFUL THINGS...
HE MURDERED OLIVER AND DINAH.
AND RENEE. I'M TOTALLY WITH YOU. I JUST NEED TO KNOW THAT WE AREN'T JUST SPITTING IN THE WIND. WHAT'S YOUR PLAN?

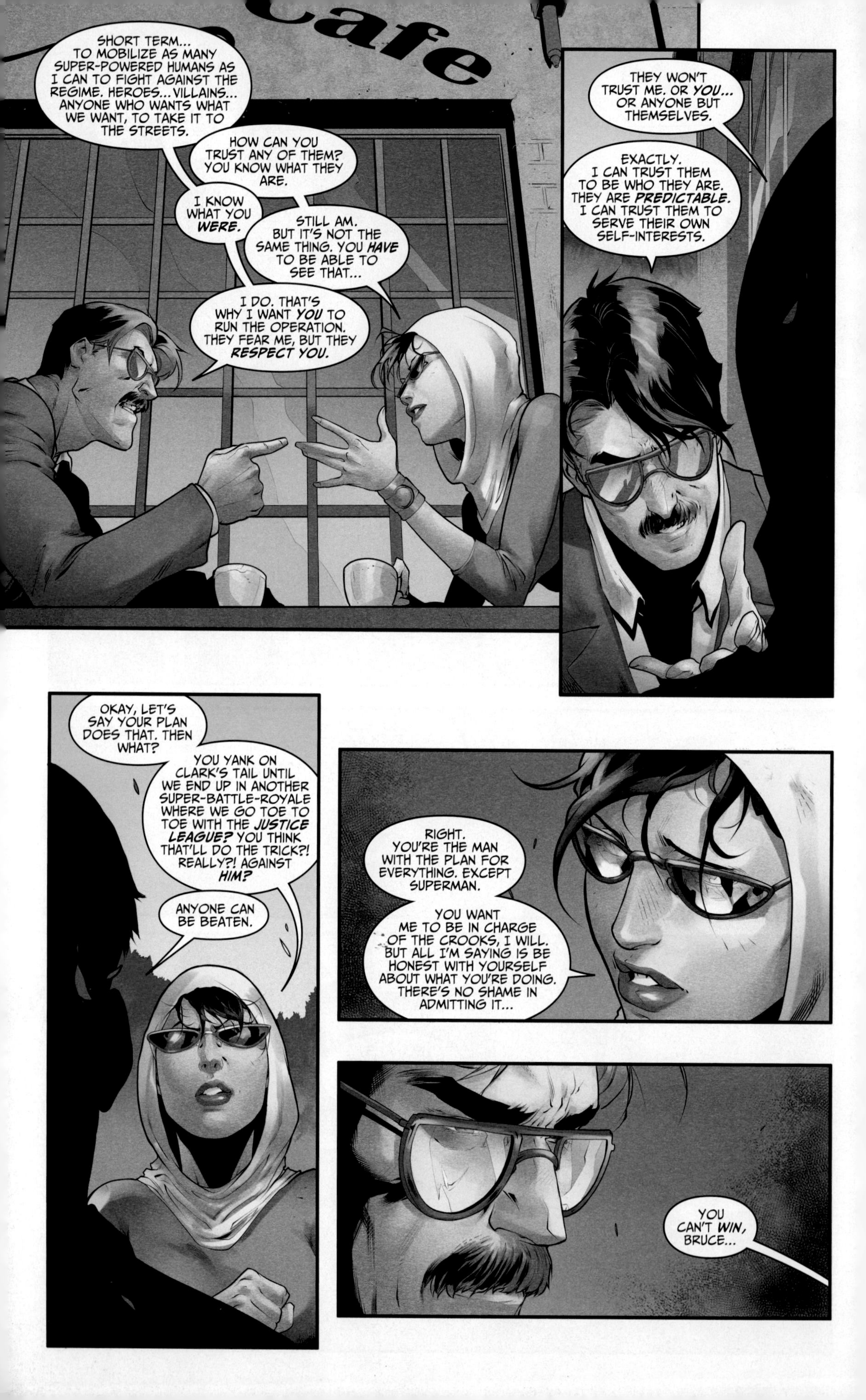
cafe
SHORT TERM... TO MOBILIZE AS MANY SUPER-POWERED HUMANS AS I CAN TO FIGHT AGAINST THE REGIME. HEROES... VILLAINS... ANYONE WHO WANTS WHAT WE WANT, TO TAKE IT TO THE STREETS.
HOW CAN YOU TRUST ANY OF THEM? YOU KNOW WHAT THEY ARE.
I KNOW WHAT YOU *WERE.*
STILL AM. BUT IT'S NOT THE SAME THING. YOU *HAVE* TO BE ABLE TO SEE THAT...
I DO. THAT'S WHY I WANT *YOU* TO RUN THE OPERATION. THEY FEAR ME, BUT THEY *RESPECT YOU.*
THEY WON'T TRUST ME. OR *YOU...* OR ANYONE BUT THEMSELVES.
EXACTLY. I CAN TRUST THEM TO BE WHO THEY ARE. THEY ARE *PREDICTABLE.* I CAN TRUST THEM TO SERVE THEIR OWN SELF-INTERESTS.
OKAY, LET'S SAY YOUR PLAN DOES THAT. THEN WHAT?
YOU YANK ON CLARK'S TAIL UNTIL WE END UP IN ANOTHER SUPER-BATTLE-ROYALE WHERE WE GO TOE TO TOE WITH THE *JUSTICE LEAGUE?* YOU THINK THAT'LL DO THE TRICK?! REALLY?! AGAINST *HIM?*
ANYONE CAN BE BEATEN.
RIGHT. YOU'RE THE MAN WITH THE PLAN FOR EVERYTHING. EXCEPT SUPERMAN.
YOU WANT ME TO BE IN CHARGE OF THE CROOKS, I WILL. BUT ALL I'M SAYING IS BE HONEST WITH YOURSELF ABOUT WHAT YOU'RE DOING. THERE'S NO SHAME IN ADMITTING IT...
YOU CAN'T *WIN,* BRUCE...

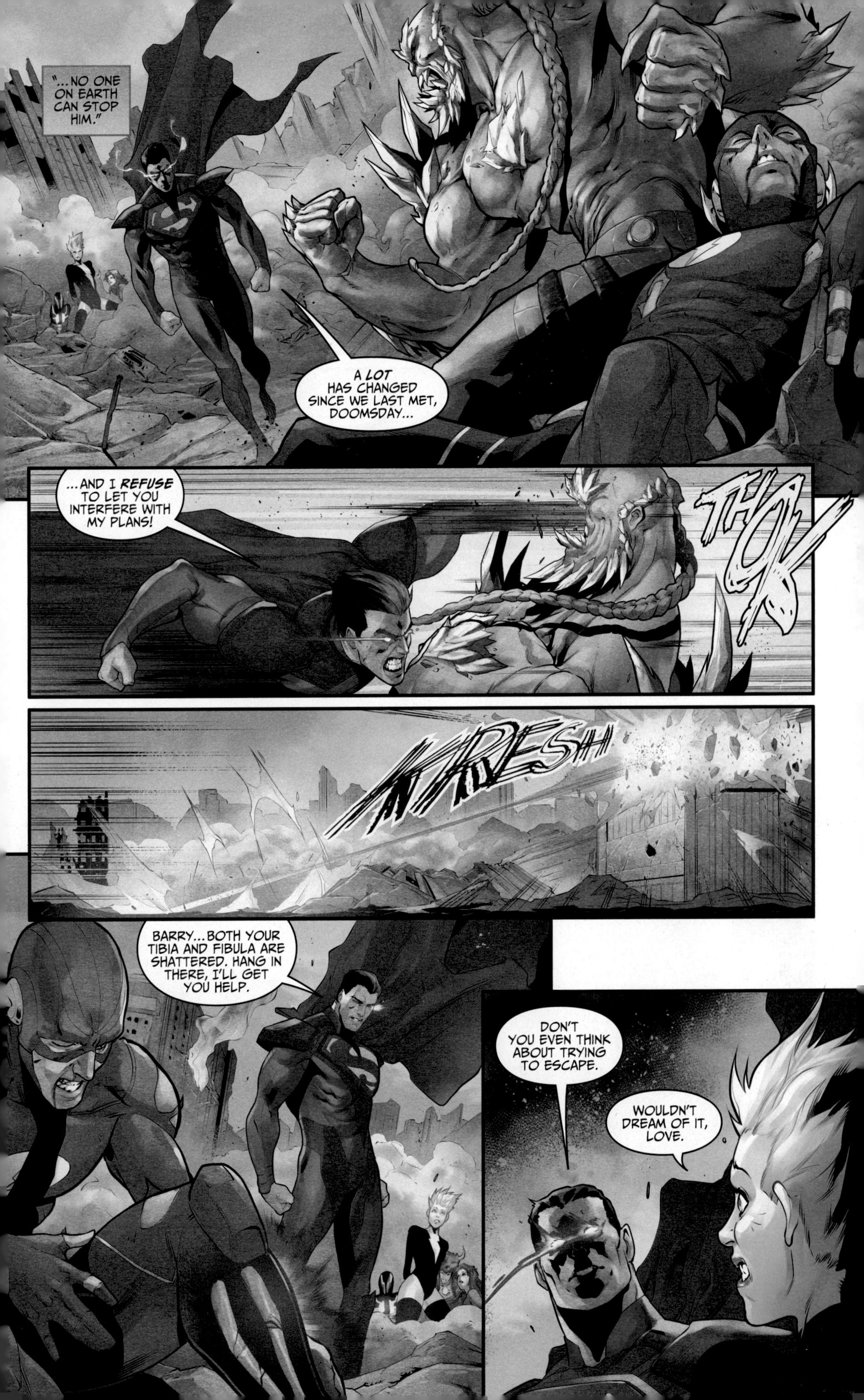
"...NO ONE ON EARTH CAN STOP HIM."
A LOT HAS CHANGED SINCE WE LAST MET, DOOMSDAY...
...AND I REFUSE TO LET YOU INTERFERE WITH MY PLANS!
THOK
KKRESSHH
BARRY...BOTH YOUR TIBIA AND FIBULA ARE SHATTERED. HANG IN THERE, I'LL GET YOU HELP.
DON'T YOU EVEN THINK ABOUT TRYING TO ESCAPE.
WOULDN'T DREAM OF IT, LOVE.

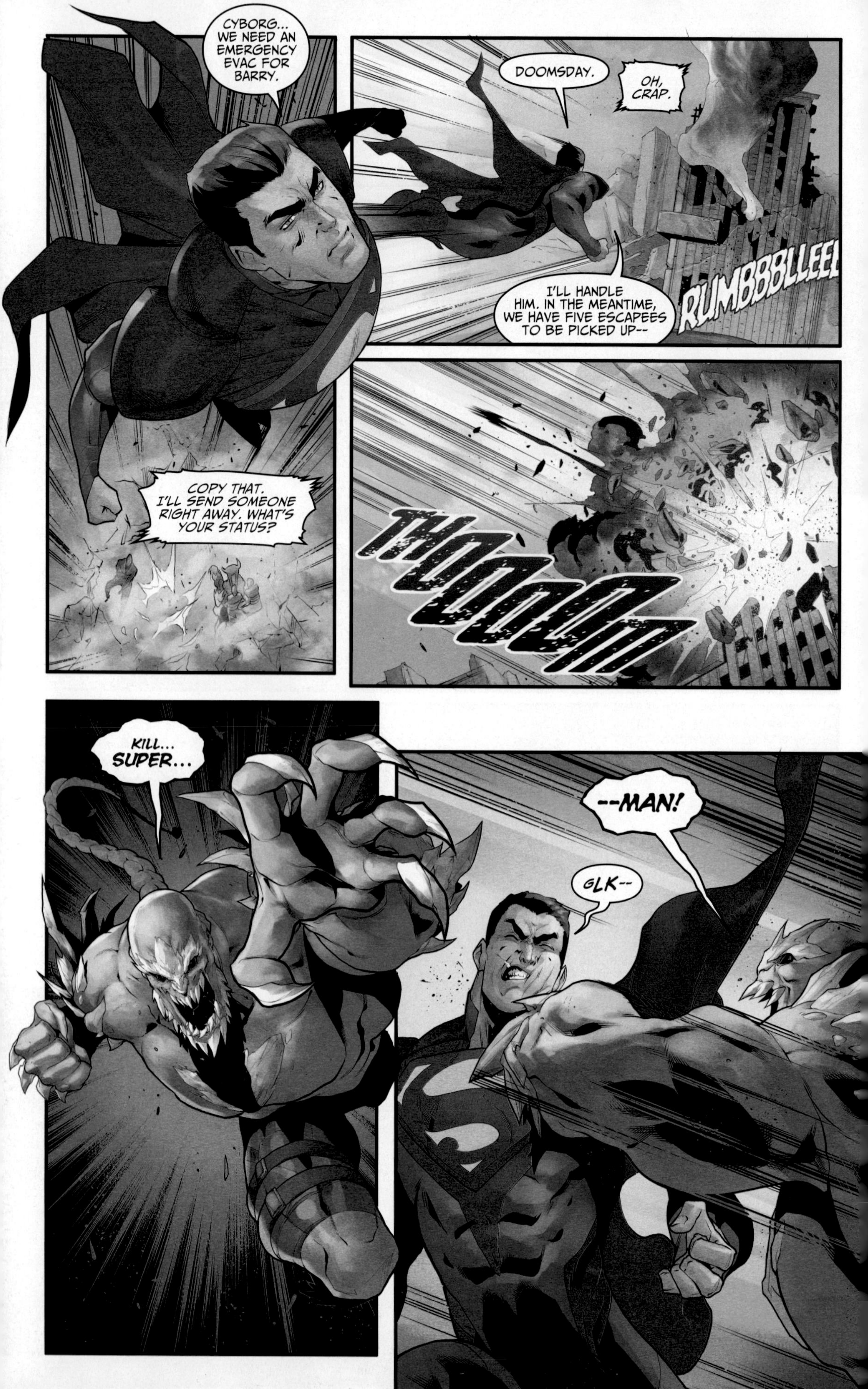
CYBORG... WE NEED AN EMERGENCY EVAC FOR BARRY.
DOOMSDAY.
OH, CRAP.
I'LL HANDLE HIM. IN THE MEANTIME, WE HAVE FIVE ESCAPEES TO BE PICKED UP--
RUMBBBLLEEE
COPY THAT. I'LL SEND SOMEONE RIGHT AWAY. WHAT'S YOUR STATUS?
THOOOM
KILL... SUPER...
--MAN!
GLK--

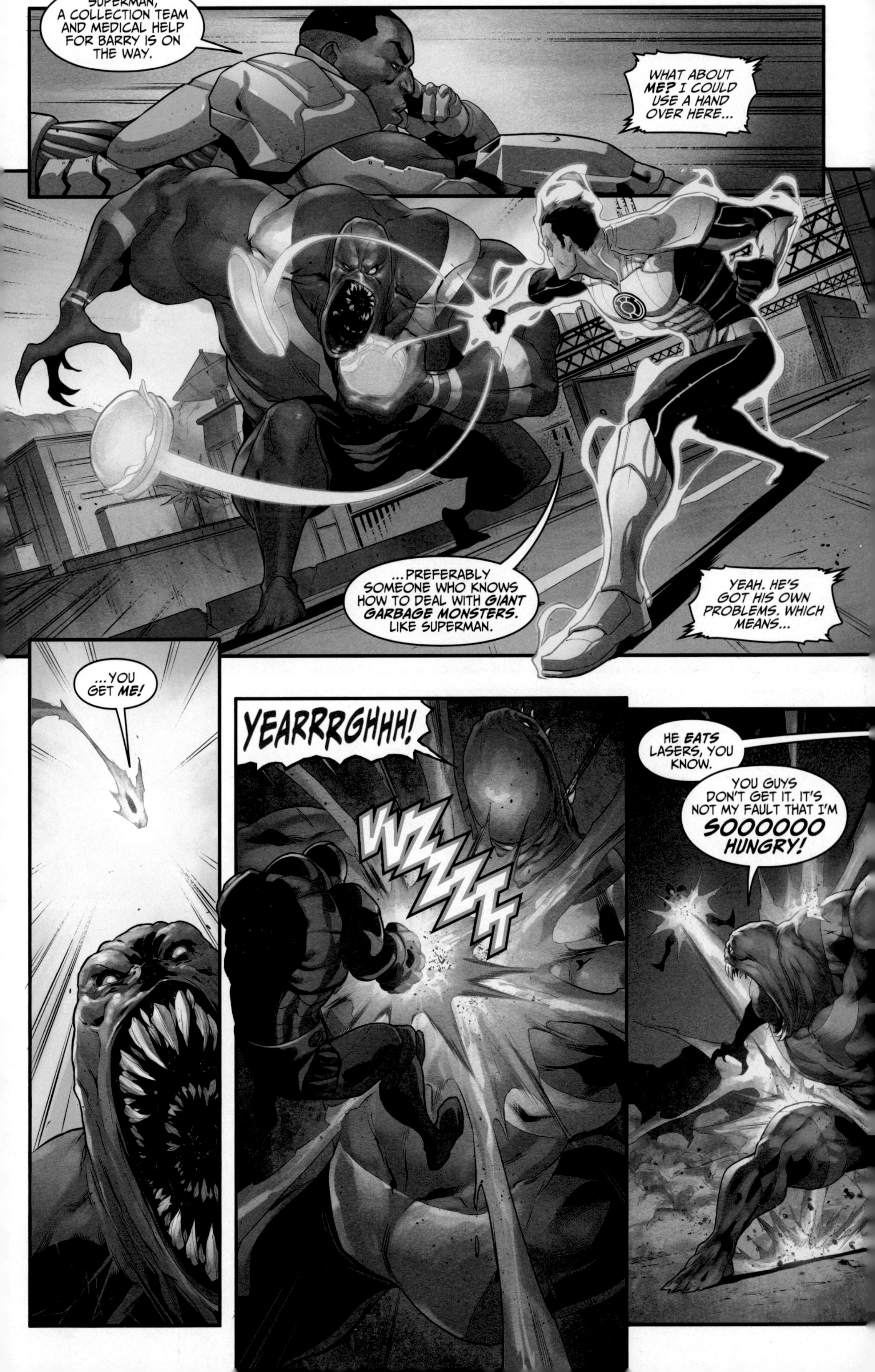
SUPERMAN, A COLLECTION TEAM AND MEDICAL HELP FOR BARRY IS ON THE WAY.
WHAT ABOUT ME? I COULD USE A HAND OVER HERE...
...PREFERABLY SOMEONE WHO KNOWS HOW TO DEAL WITH GIANT GARBAGE MONSTERS. LIKE SUPERMAN.
YEAH. HE'S GOT HIS OWN PROBLEMS. WHICH MEANS...
...YOU GET ME!
YEARRRGHHH!
VVZZZZT
HE EATS LASERS, YOU KNOW.
YOU GUYS DON'T GET IT. IT'S NOT MY FAULT THAT I'M SOOOOOO HUNGRY!

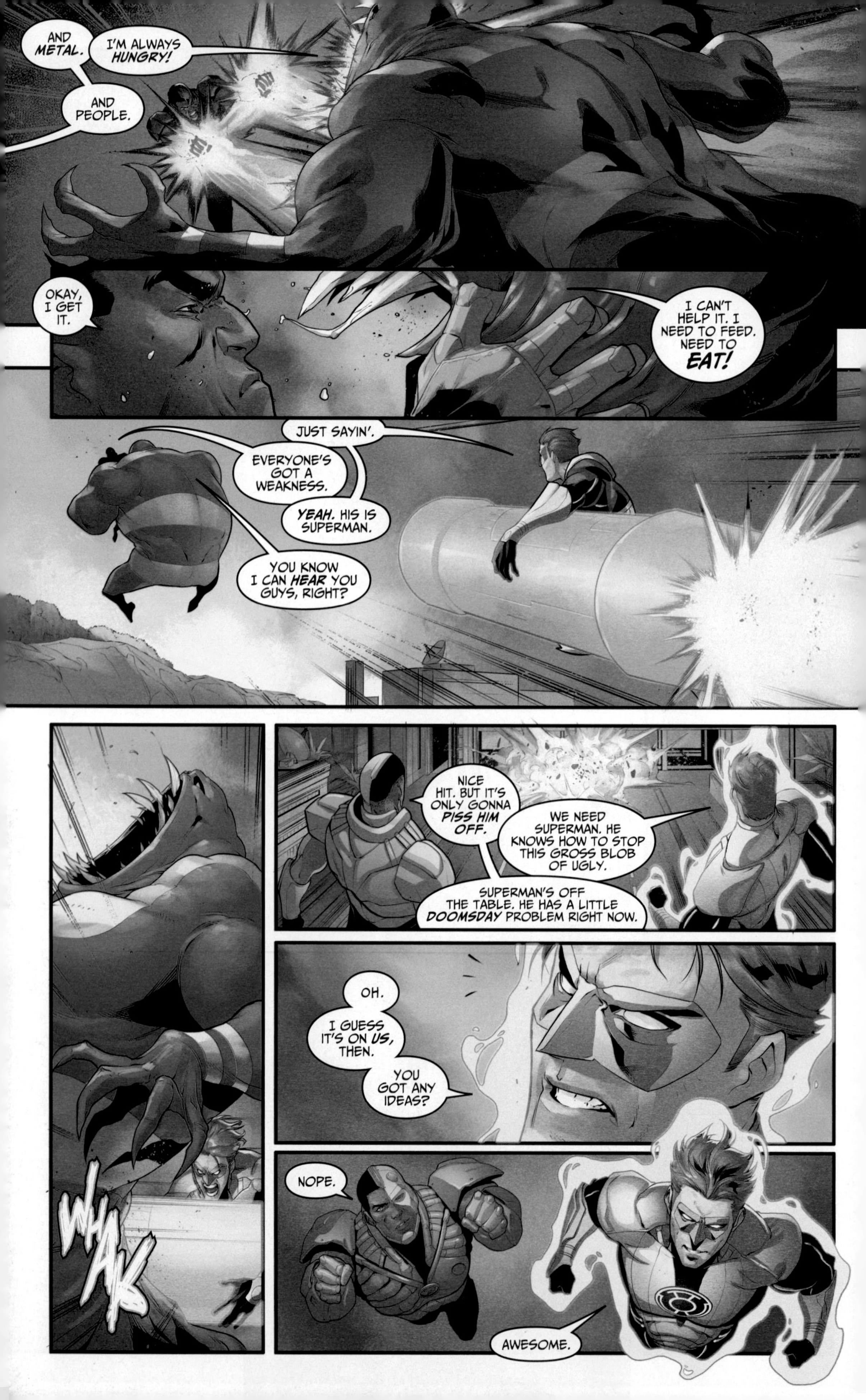

AND METAL.
I'M ALWAYS HUNGRY!
AND PEOPLE.
OKAY, I GET IT.
I CAN'T HELP IT. I NEED TO FEED. NEED TO EAT!
JUST SAYIN'.
EVERYONE'S GOT A WEAKNESS.
YEAH. HIS IS SUPERMAN.
YOU KNOW I CAN HEAR YOU GUYS, RIGHT?
WHAK
NICE HIT. BUT IT'S ONLY GONNA PISS HIM OFF.
WE NEED SUPERMAN. HE KNOWS HOW TO STOP THIS GROSS BLOB OF UGLY.
SUPERMAN'S OFF THE TABLE. HE HAS A LITTLE DOOMSDAY PROBLEM RIGHT NOW.
OH.
I GUESS IT'S ON US, THEN.
YOU GOT ANY IDEAS?
NOPE.
AWESOME.

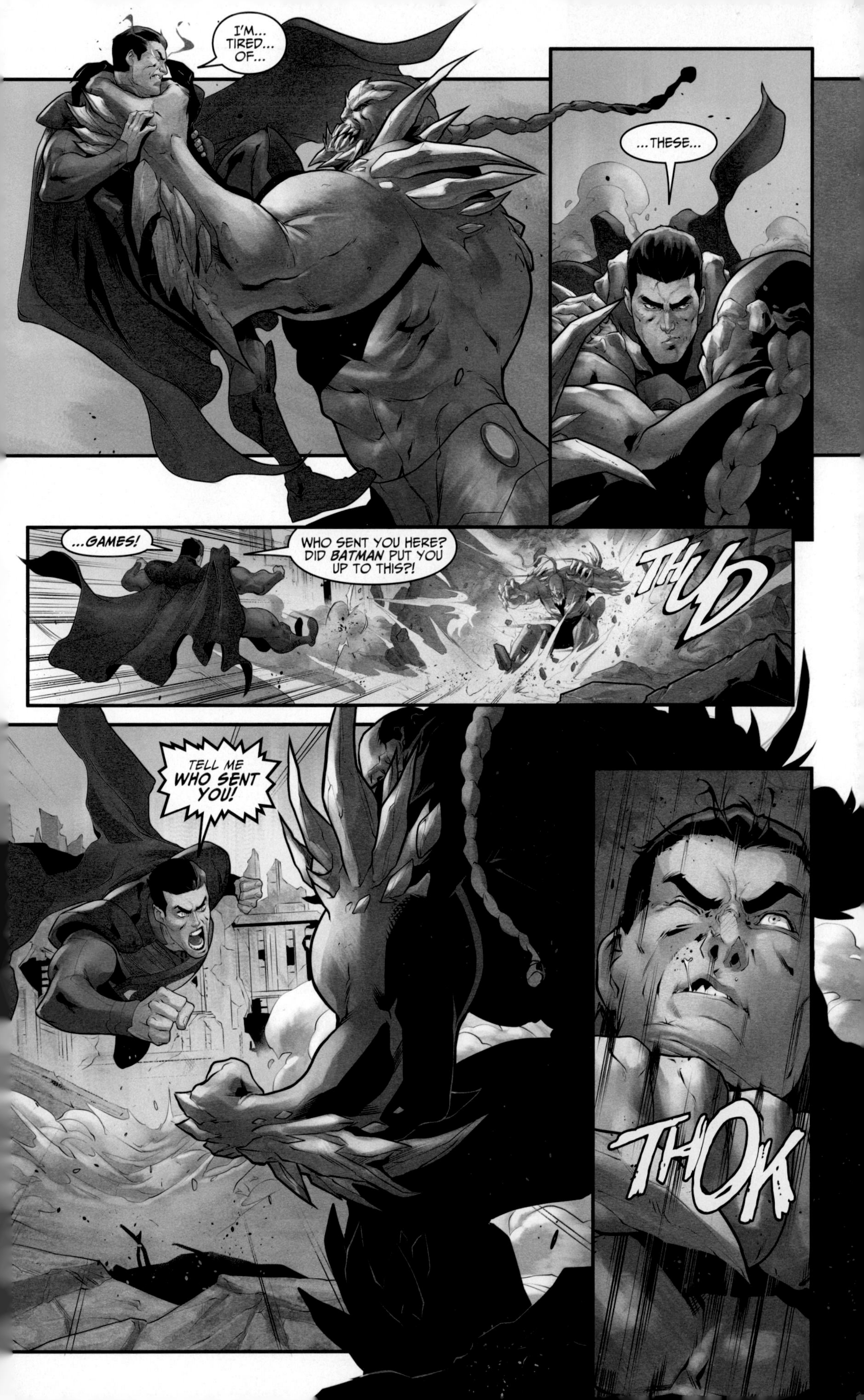
I'M... TIRED... OF...
...THESE...
...GAMES!
WHO SENT YOU HERE? DID BATMAN PUT YOU UP TO THIS?!
THUD
TELL ME WHO SENT YOU!
THOK

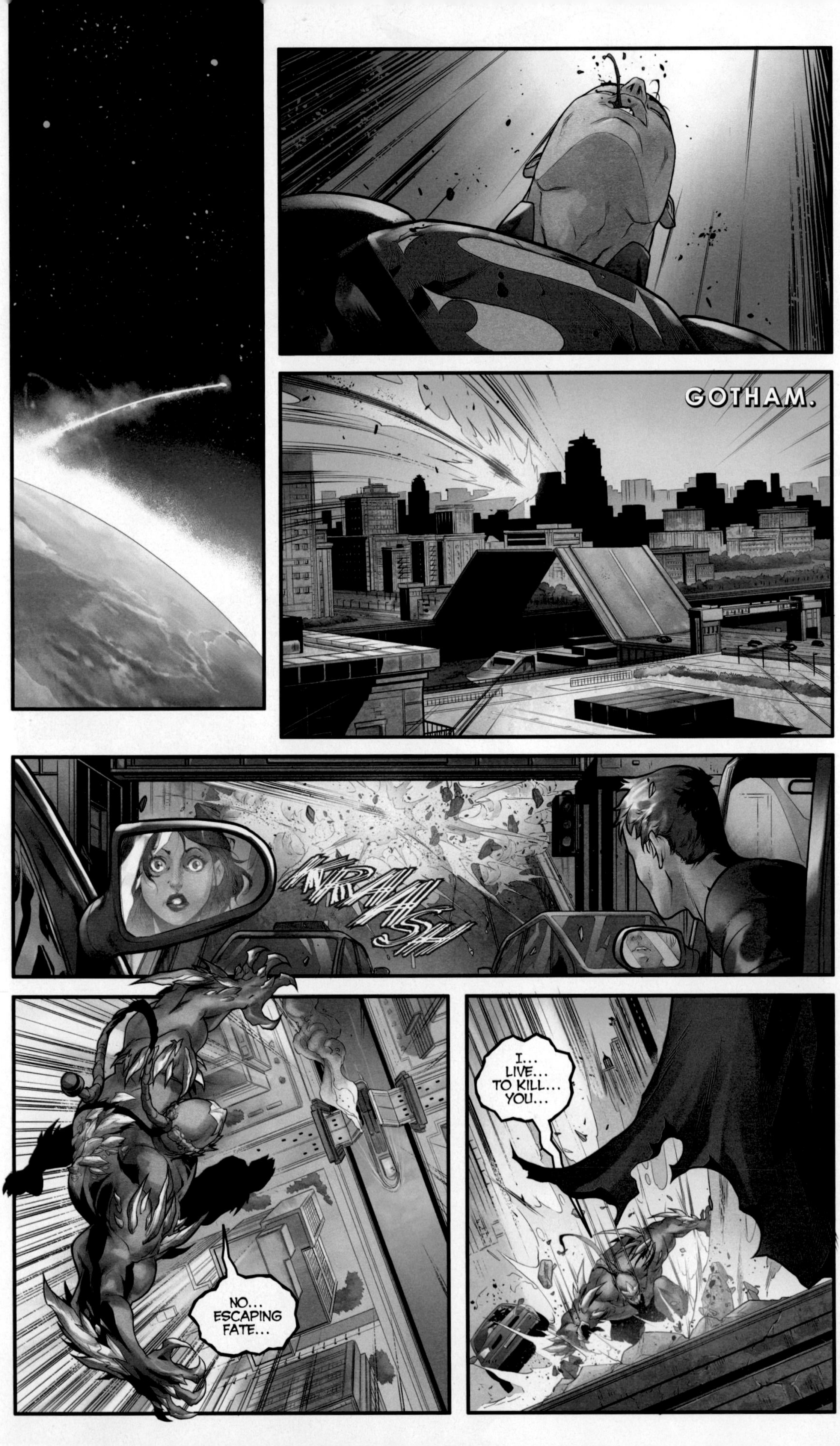
GOTHAM.
NO... ESCAPING FATE...
I... LIVE... TO KILL... YOU...

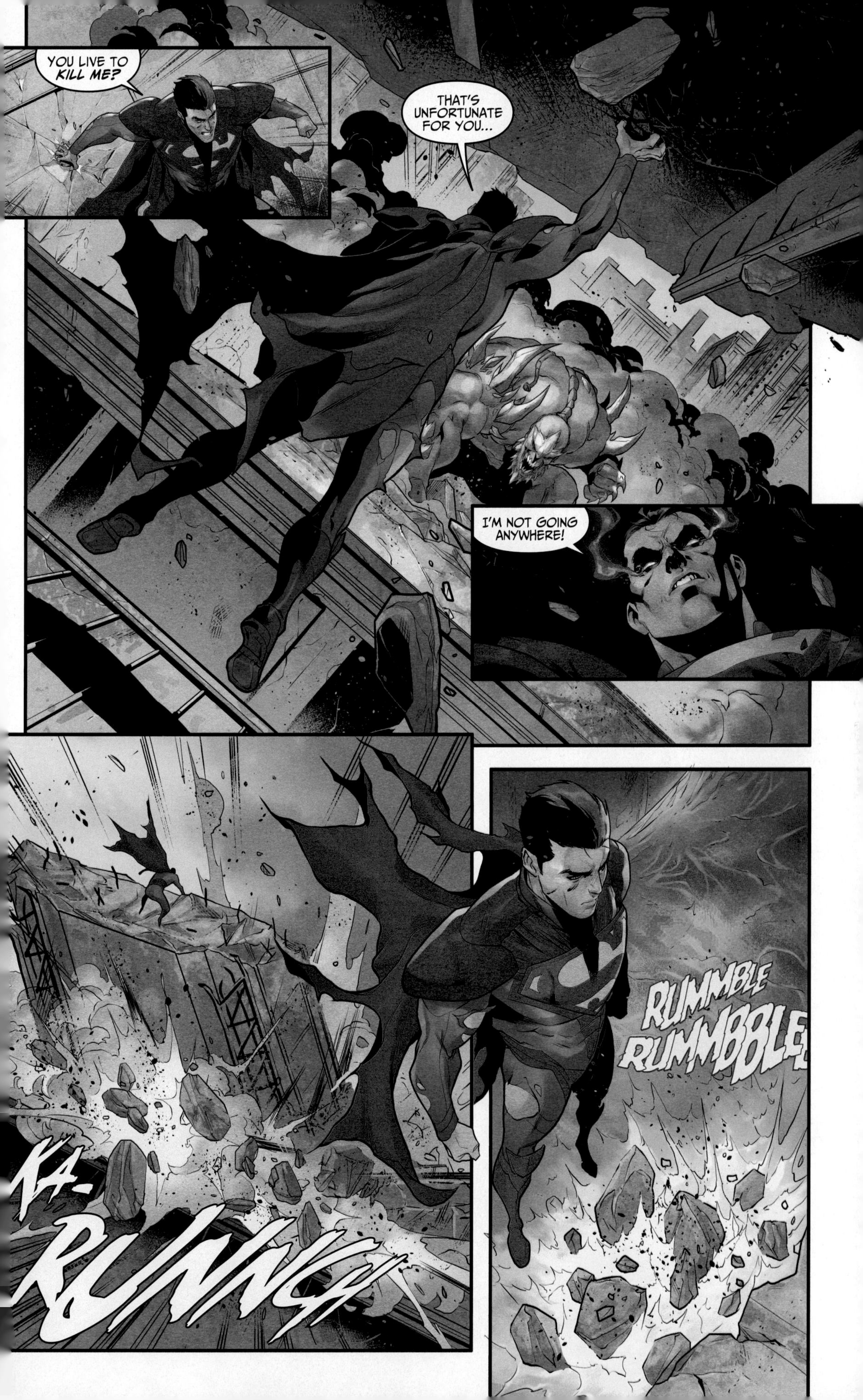
YOU LIVE TO KILL ME?
THAT'S UNFORTUNATE FOR YOU...
I'M NOT GOING ANYWHERE!
KA-RUNNCH
RUMMBLE
RUMMBBLE

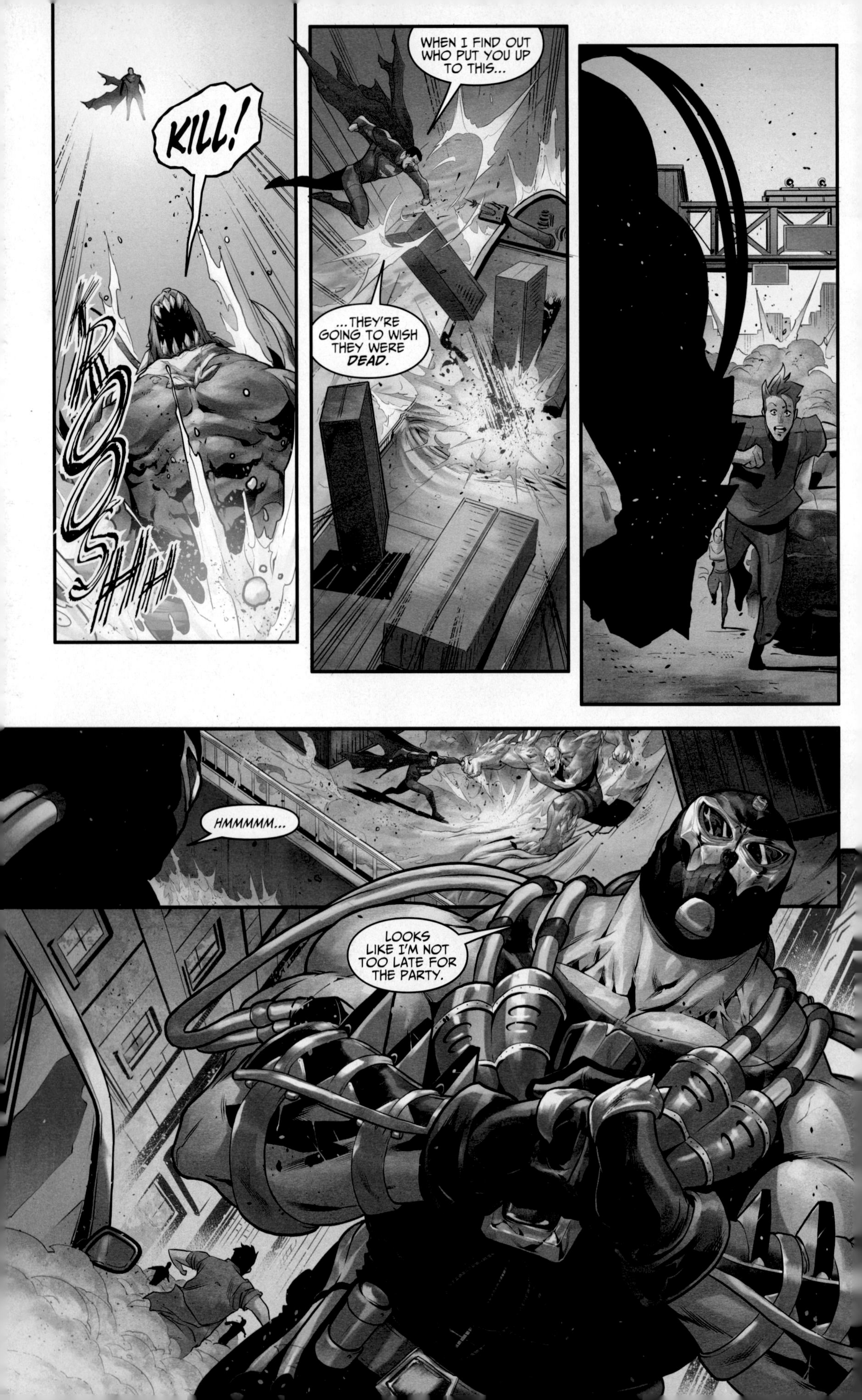
KILL!
KROOOSHHH
WHEN I FIND OUT WHO PUT YOU UP TO THIS...
...THEY'RE GOING TO WISH THEY WERE DEAD.
HMMMMM...
LOOKS LIKE I'M NOT TOO LATE FOR THE PARTY.

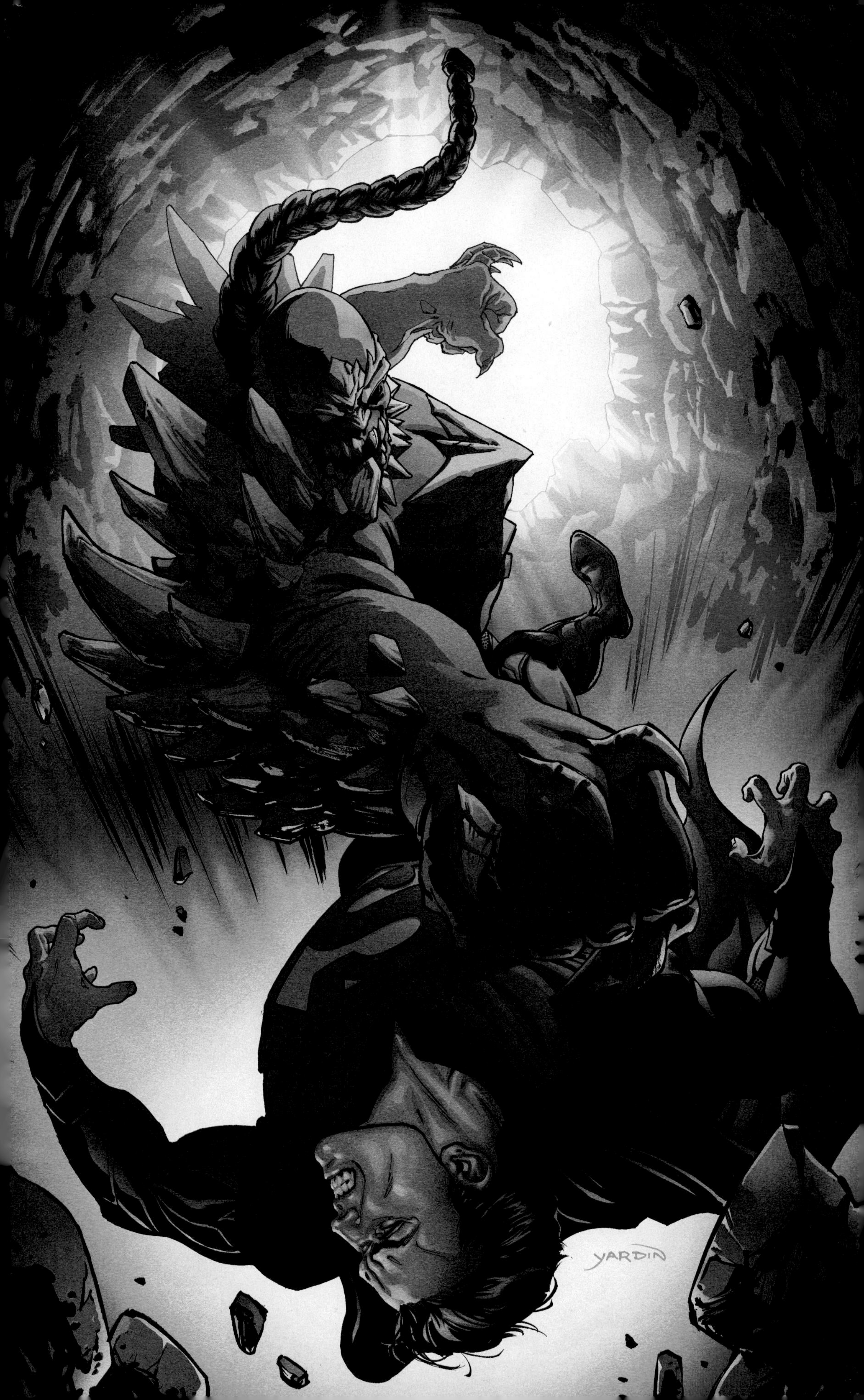
YARDIN

"The Enemy of My Enemy" **Tom Derenick** Artist **Rex Lokus** Colorist
"Dirty Work" **Mike S. Miller** Artist **J. Nanjan** Colorist

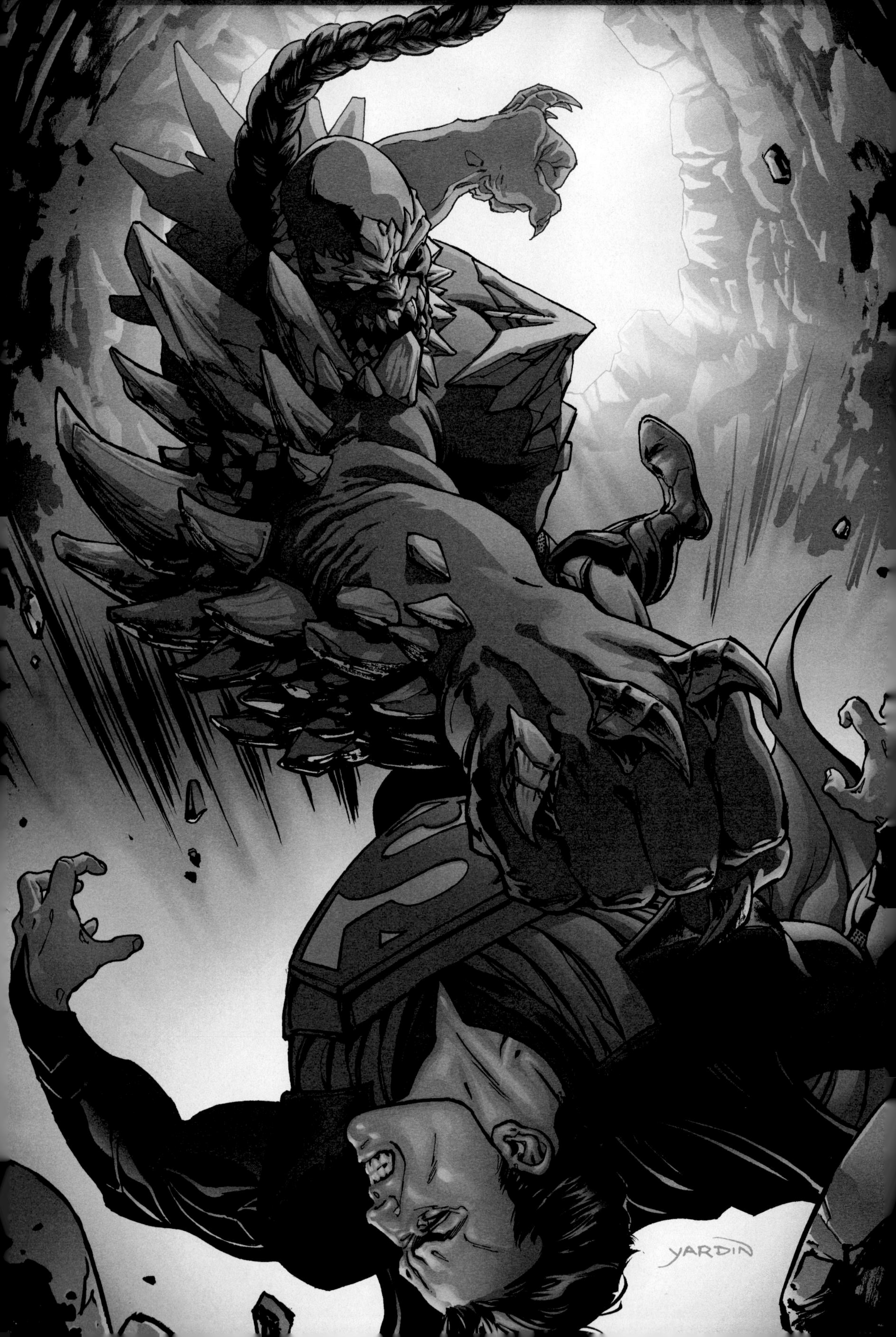
YARDIN

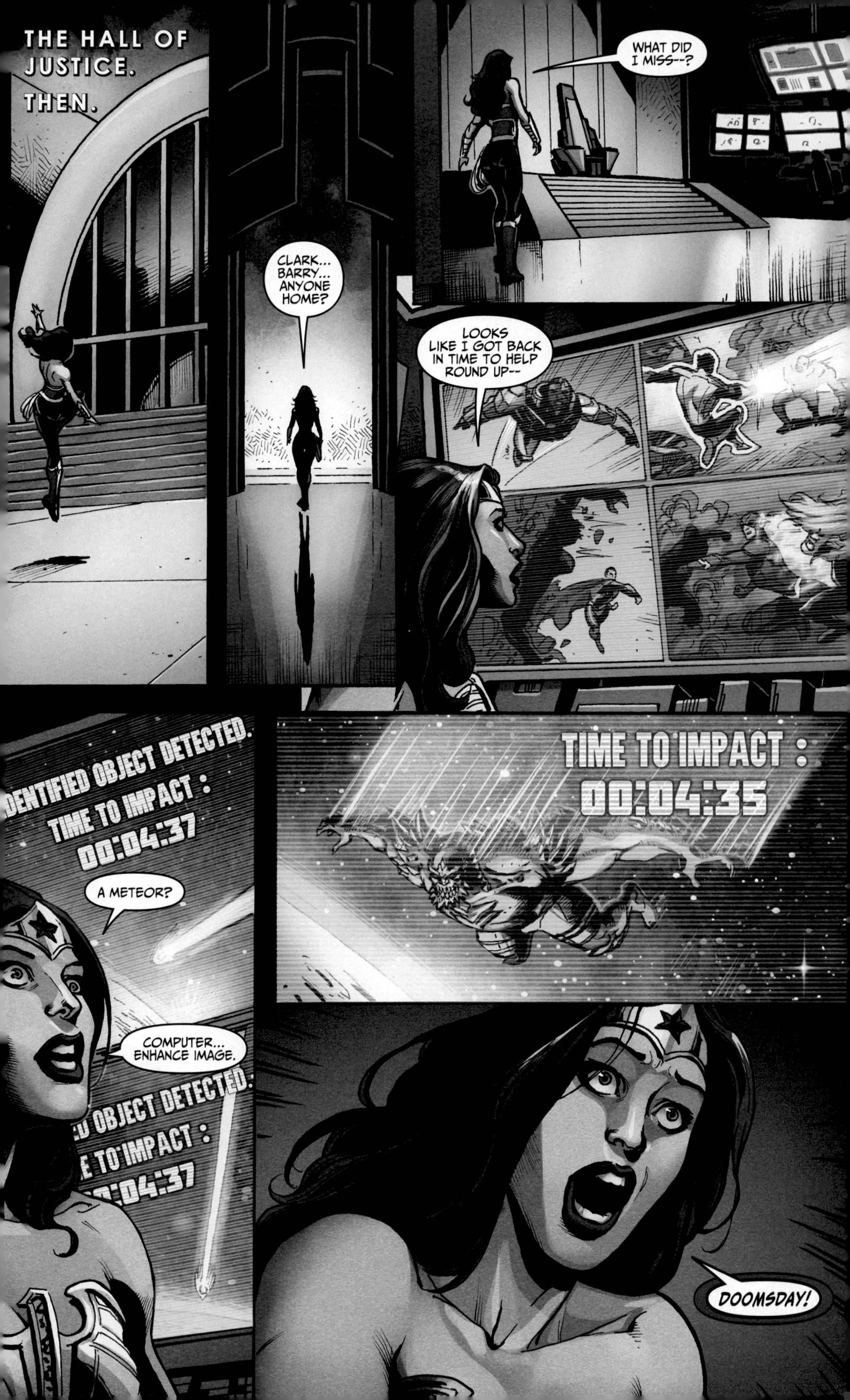
THE HALL OF JUSTICE.
THEN.
CLARK... BARRY... ANYONE HOME?
WHAT DID I MISS--?
LOOKS LIKE I GOT BACK IN TIME TO HELP ROUND UP--
DENTIFIED OBJECT DETECTED.
TIME TO IMPACT :
00:04:37
A METEOR?
COMPUTER... ENHANCE IMAGE.
ED OBJECT DETECTED.
E TO IMPACT :
0:04:37
TIME TO IMPACT :
00:04:35
DOOMSDAY!

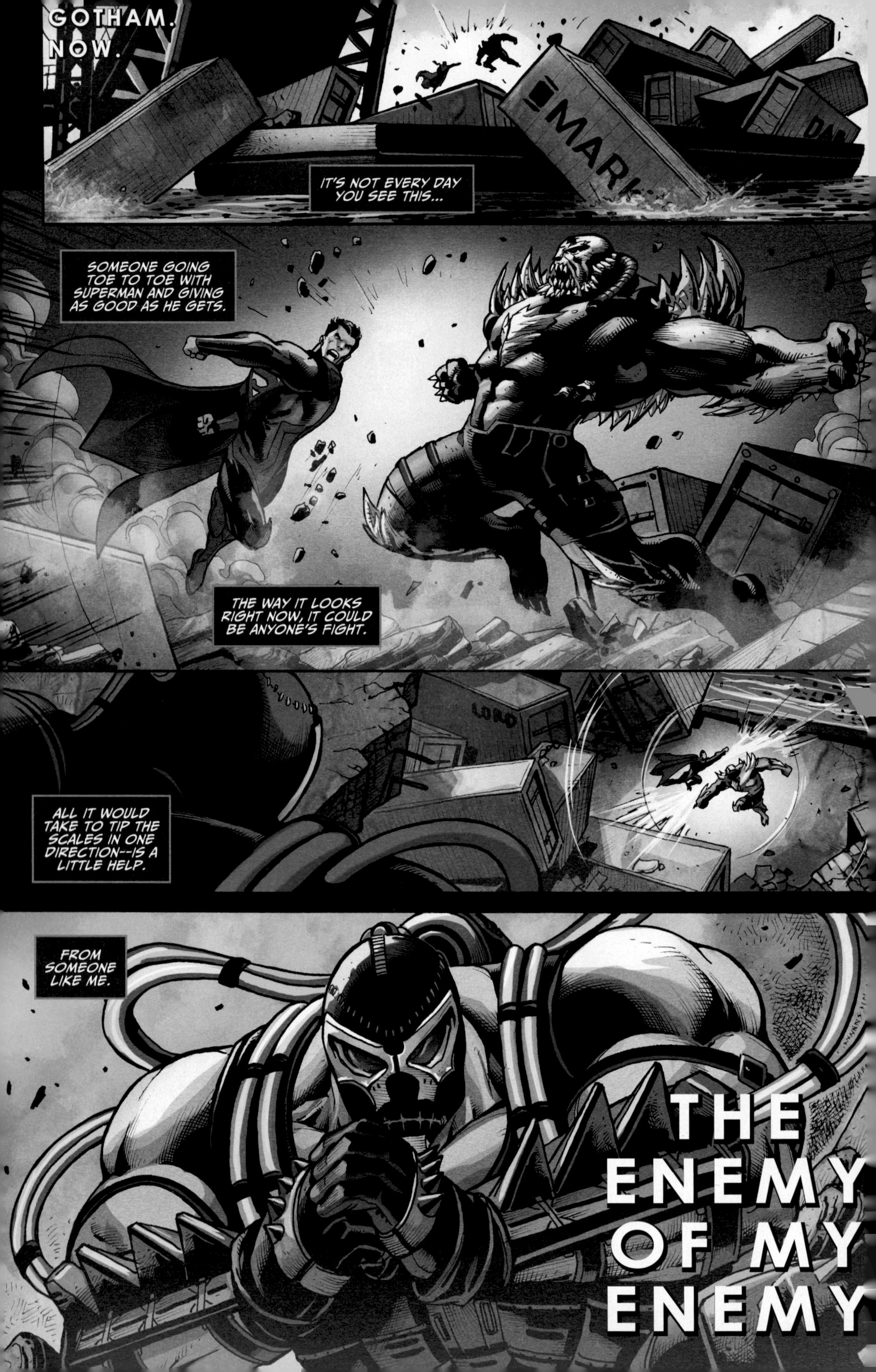
GOTHAM. NOW.
IT'S NOT EVERY DAY YOU SEE THIS...
SOMEONE GOING TOE TO TOE WITH SUPERMAN AND GIVING AS GOOD AS HE GETS.
THE WAY IT LOOKS RIGHT NOW, IT COULD BE ANYONE'S FIGHT.
ALL IT WOULD TAKE TO TIP THE SCALES IN ONE DIRECTION--IS A LITTLE HELP.
FROM SOMEONE LIKE ME.
THE ENEMY OF MY ENEMY

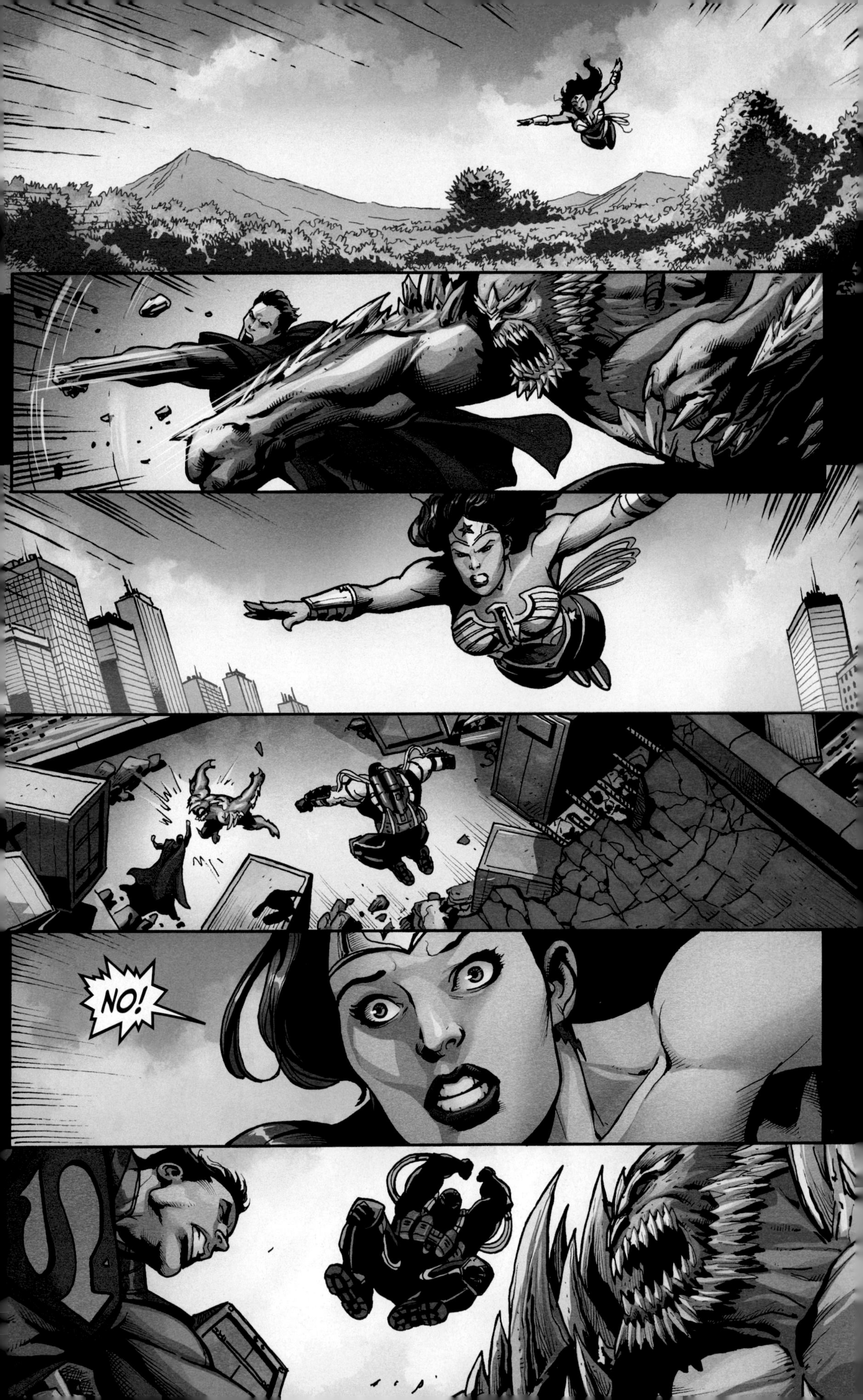
NO!

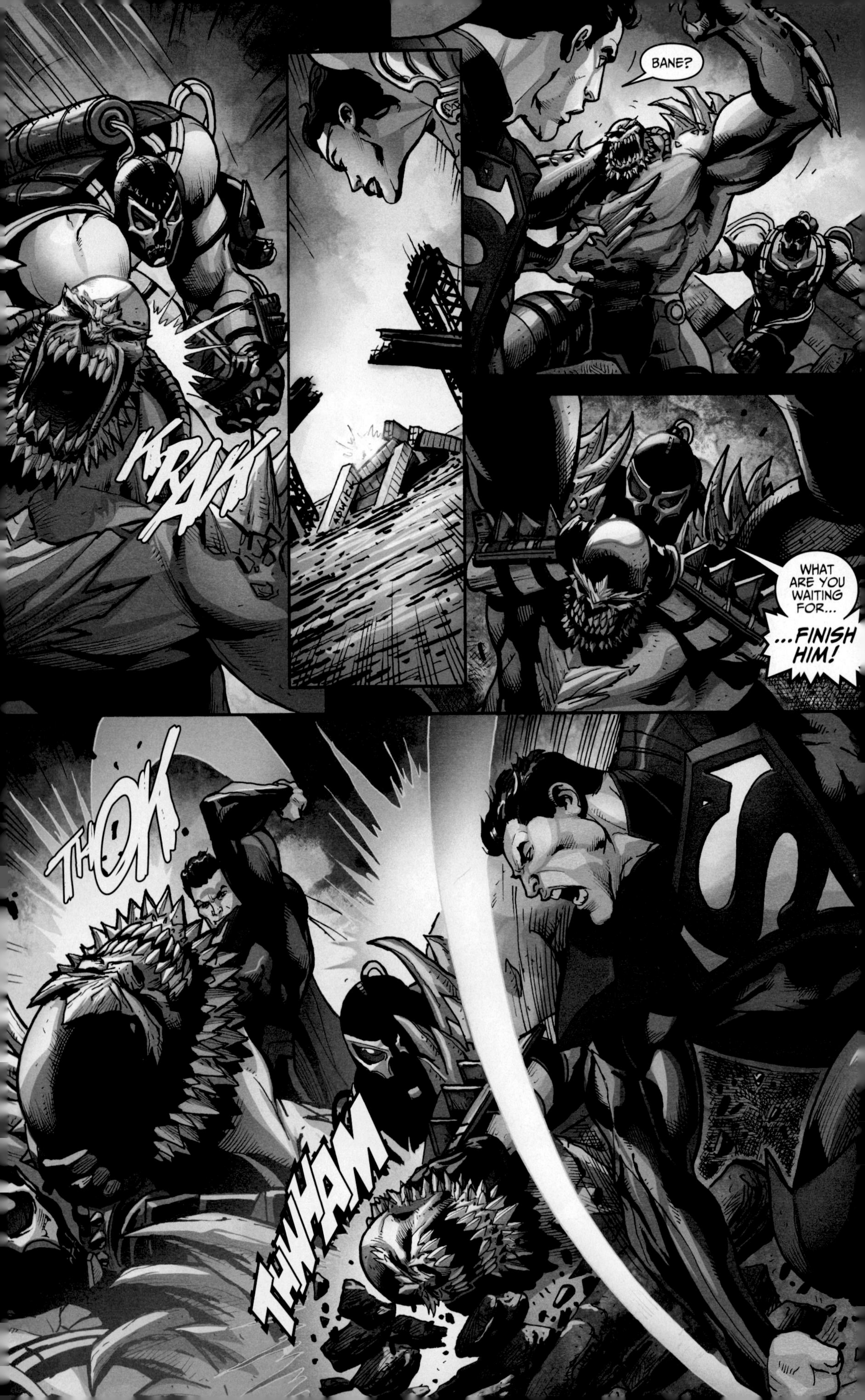
KRAKK
BANE?
WHAT ARE YOU WAITING FOR...
...FINISH HIM!
THOK
THWAM

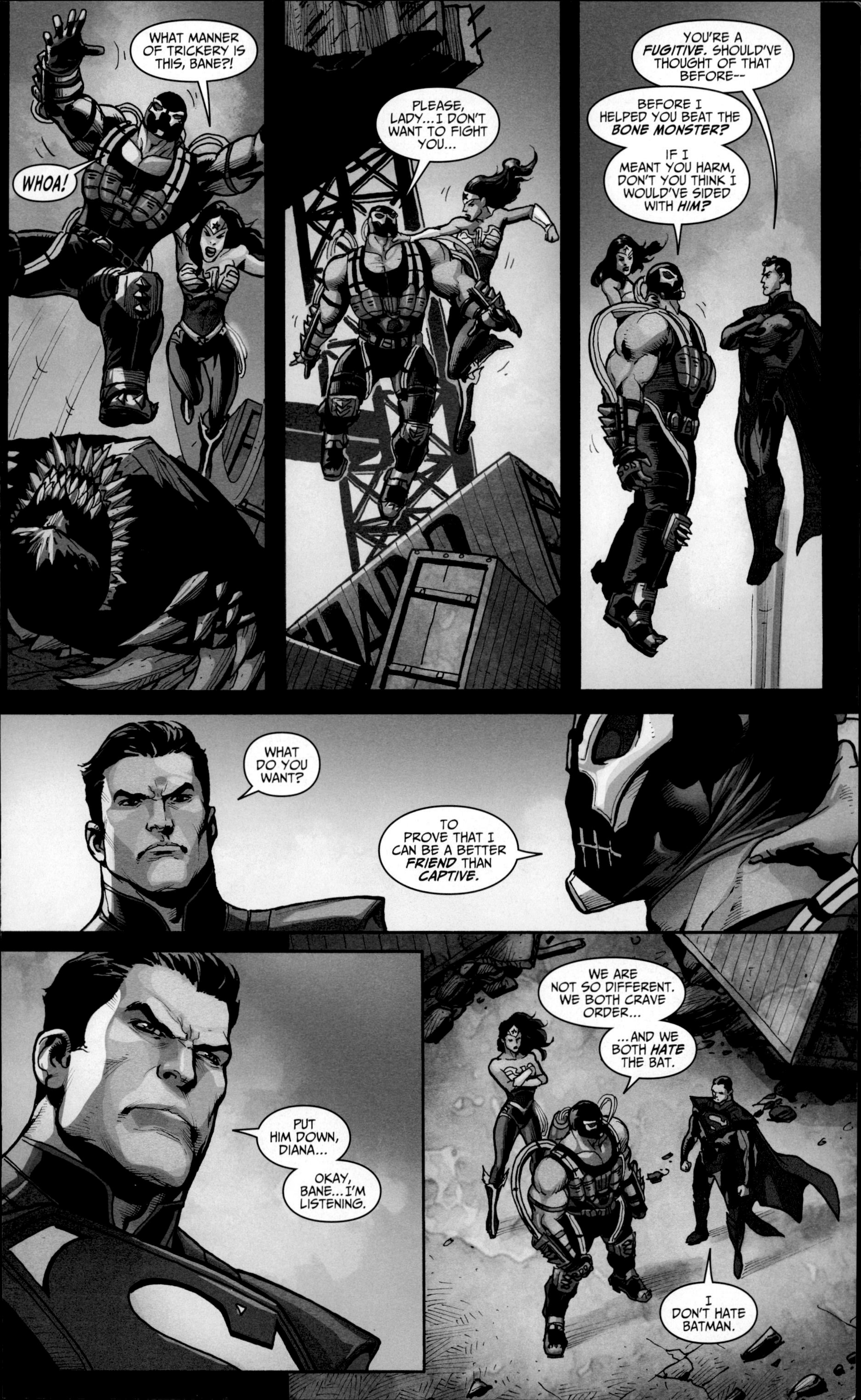
WHAT MANNER OF TRICKERY IS THIS, BANE?!
WHOA!
PLEASE, LADY... I DON'T WANT TO FIGHT YOU...
YOU'RE A FUGITIVE. SHOULD'VE THOUGHT OF THAT BEFORE--
BEFORE I HELPED YOU BEAT THE BONE MONSTER?
IF I MEANT YOU HARM, DON'T YOU THINK I WOULD'VE SIDED WITH HIM?
WHAT DO YOU WANT?
TO PROVE THAT I CAN BE A BETTER FRIEND THAN CAPTIVE.
PUT HIM DOWN, DIANA...
OKAY, BANE... I'M LISTENING.
WE ARE NOT SO DIFFERENT. WE BOTH CRAVE ORDER...
...AND WE BOTH HATE THE BAT.
I DON'T HATE BATMAN.

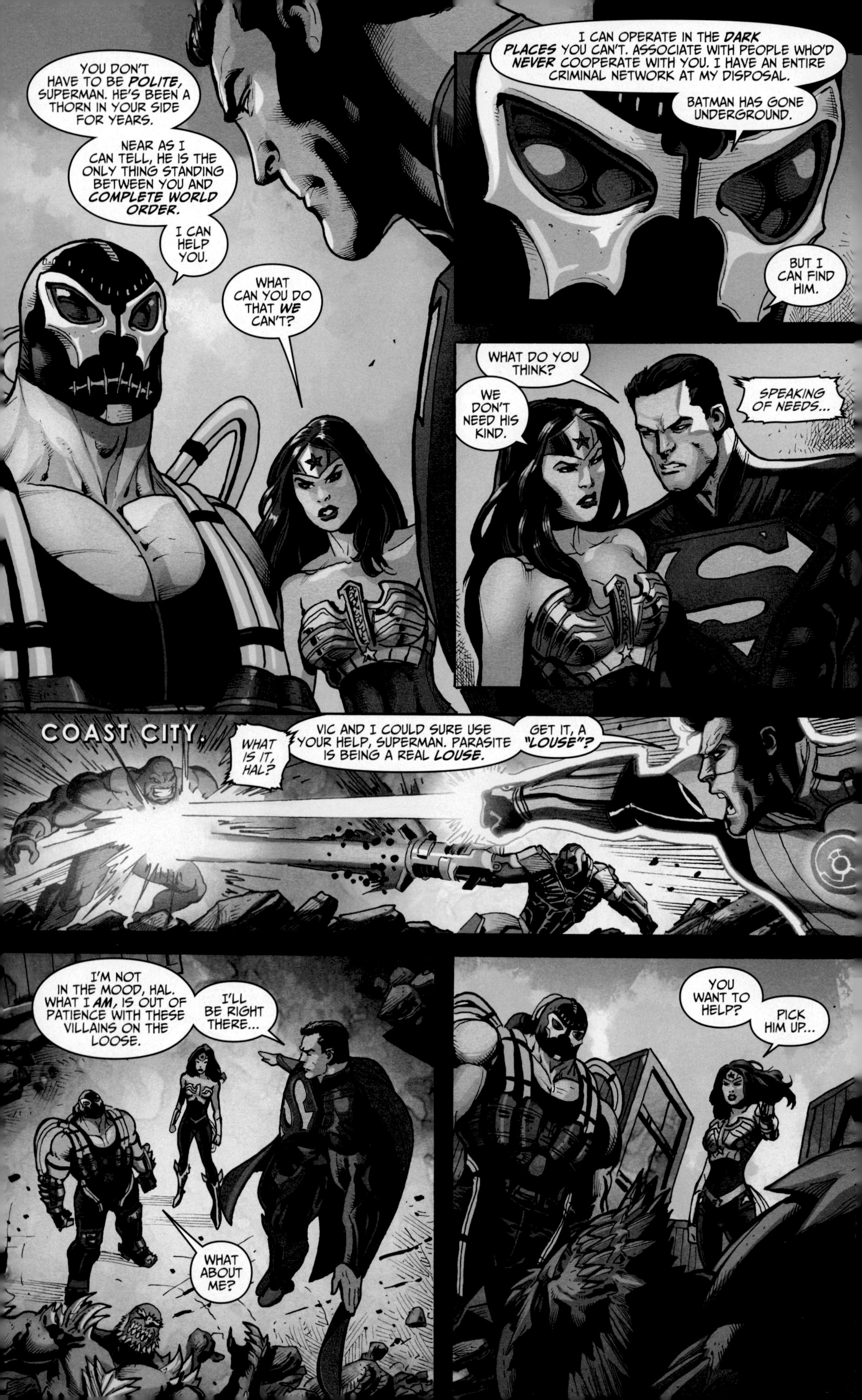
YOU DON'T HAVE TO BE POLITE, SUPERMAN. HE'S BEEN A THORN IN YOUR SIDE FOR YEARS.
NEAR AS I CAN TELL, HE IS THE ONLY THING STANDING BETWEEN YOU AND COMPLETE WORLD ORDER.
I CAN HELP YOU.
WHAT CAN YOU DO THAT WE CAN'T?
I CAN OPERATE IN THE DARK PLACES YOU CAN'T. ASSOCIATE WITH PEOPLE WHO'D NEVER COOPERATE WITH YOU. I HAVE AN ENTIRE CRIMINAL NETWORK AT MY DISPOSAL.
BATMAN HAS GONE UNDERGROUND.
BUT I CAN FIND HIM.
WHAT DO YOU THINK?
WE DON'T NEED HIS KIND.
SPEAKING OF NEEDS...
COAST CITY.
WHAT IS IT, HAL?
VIC AND I COULD SURE USE YOUR HELP, SUPERMAN. PARASITE IS BEING A REAL LOUSE.
GET IT, A "LOUSE"?
I'M NOT IN THE MOOD, HAL. WHAT I AM, IS OUT OF PATIENCE WITH THESE VILLAINS ON THE LOOSE.
I'LL BE RIGHT THERE...
WHAT ABOUT ME?
YOU WANT TO HELP?
PICK HIM UP...

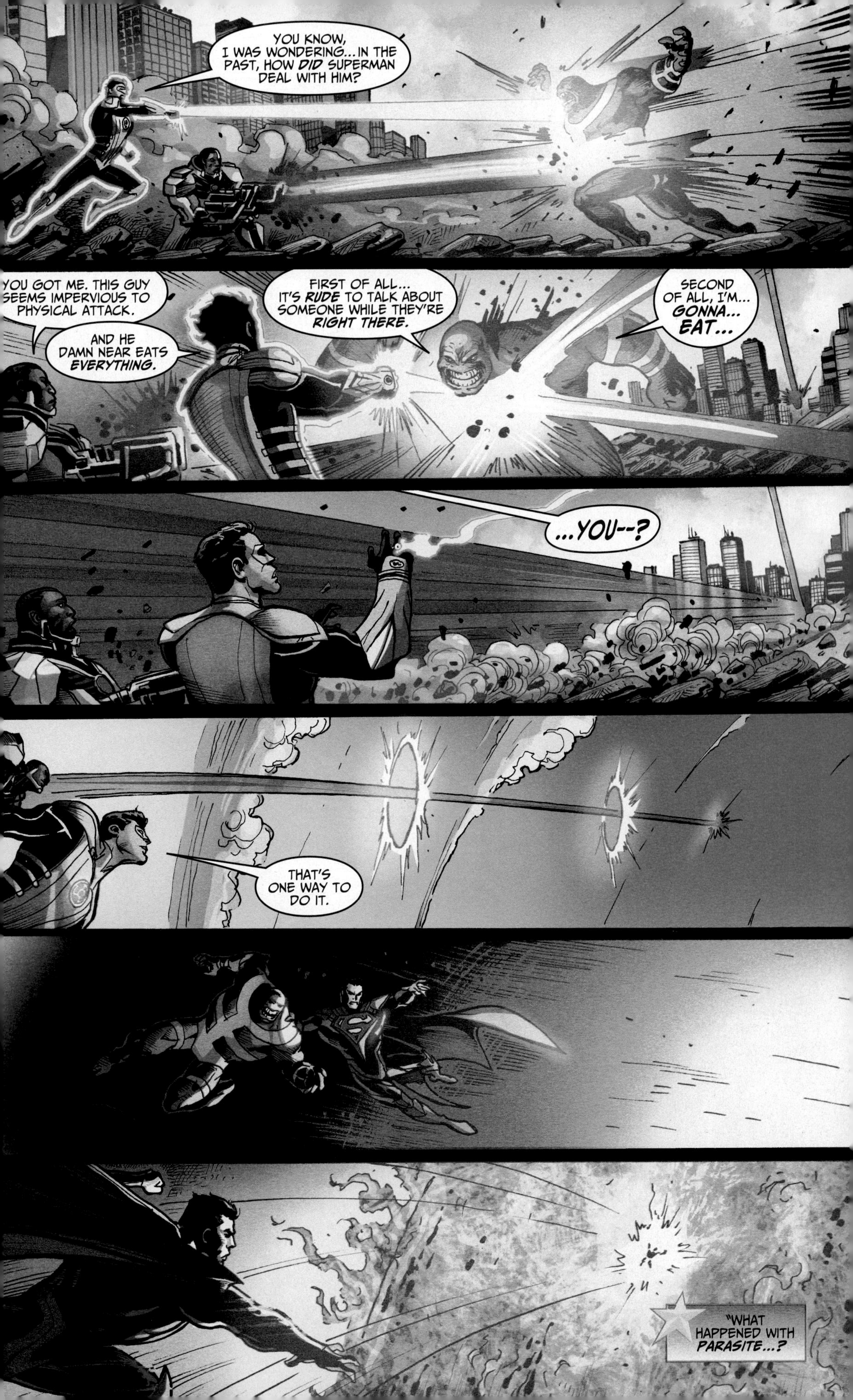
YOU KNOW, I WAS WONDERING... IN THE PAST, HOW *DID* SUPERMAN DEAL WITH HIM?
YOU GOT ME. THIS GUY SEEMS IMPERVIOUS TO PHYSICAL ATTACK.
AND HE DAMN NEAR EATS *EVERYTHING.*
FIRST OF ALL... IT'S *RUDE* TO TALK ABOUT SOMEONE WHILE THEY'RE *RIGHT THERE.*
SECOND OF ALL, I'M... *GONNA... EAT...*
...YOU--?
THAT'S ONE WAY TO DO IT.
"WHAT HAPPENED WITH *PARASITE*...?

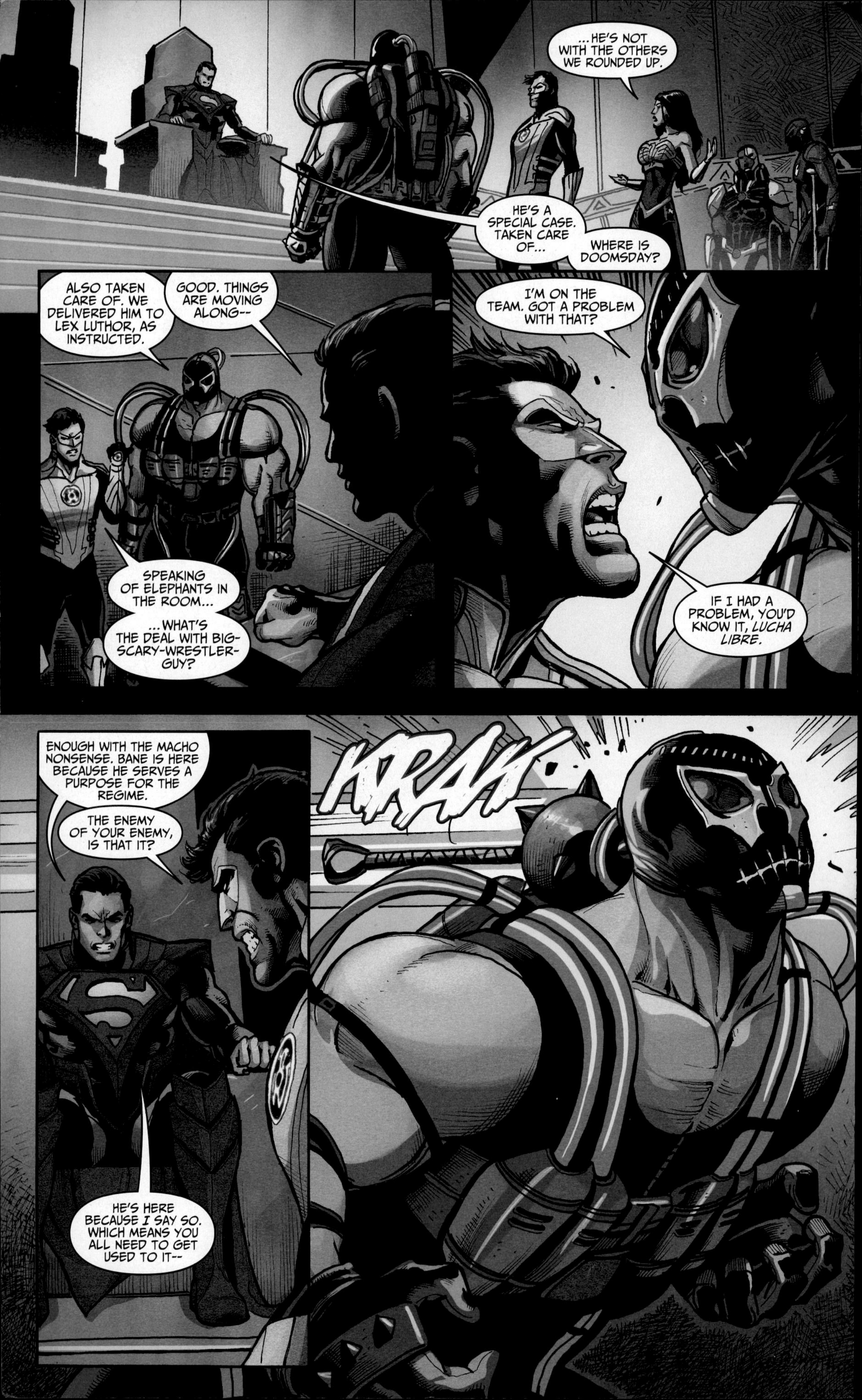
...HE'S NOT WITH THE OTHERS WE ROUNDED UP.
HE'S A SPECIAL CASE. TAKEN CARE OF...
WHERE IS DOOMSDAY?
ALSO TAKEN CARE OF. WE DELIVERED HIM TO LEX LUTHOR, AS INSTRUCTED.
GOOD. THINGS ARE MOVING ALONG--
SPEAKING OF ELEPHANTS IN THE ROOM...
...WHAT'S THE DEAL WITH BIG-SCARY-WRESTLER-GUY?
I'M ON THE TEAM. GOT A PROBLEM WITH THAT?
IF I HAD A PROBLEM, YOU'D KNOW IT, *LUCHA LIBRE*.
ENOUGH WITH THE MACHO NONSENSE. BANE IS HERE BECAUSE HE SERVES A PURPOSE FOR THE REGIME.
THE ENEMY OF YOUR ENEMY, IS THAT IT?
HE'S HERE BECAUSE *I* SAY SO. WHICH MEANS YOU ALL NEED TO GET USED TO IT--
KRAK

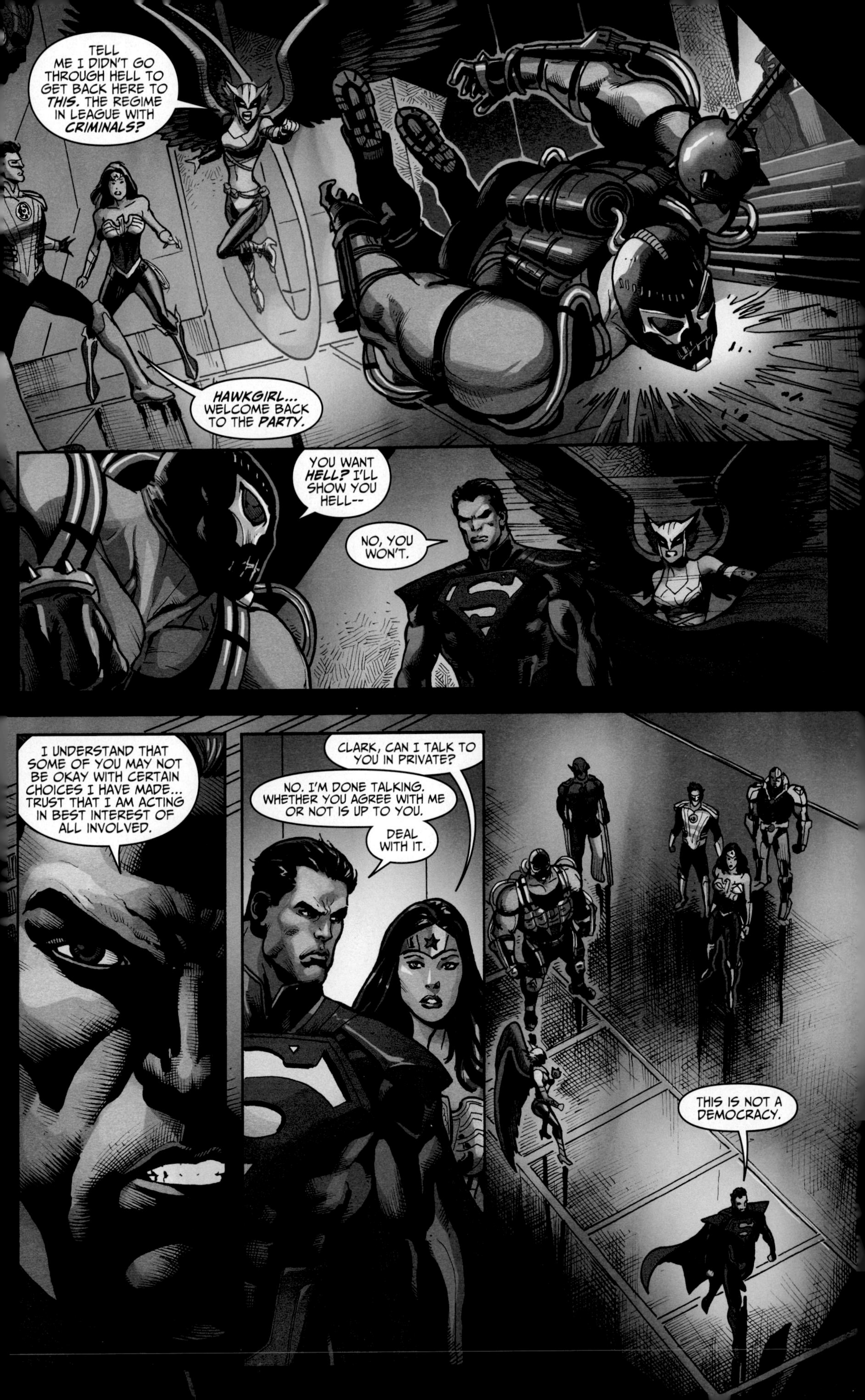
TELL ME I DIDN'T GO THROUGH HELL TO GET BACK HERE TO THIS. THE REGIME IN LEAGUE WITH CRIMINALS?
HAWKGIRL... WELCOME BACK TO THE PARTY.
YOU WANT HELL? I'LL SHOW YOU HELL--
NO, YOU WON'T.
I UNDERSTAND THAT SOME OF YOU MAY NOT BE OKAY WITH CERTAIN CHOICES I HAVE MADE... TRUST THAT I AM ACTING IN BEST INTEREST OF ALL INVOLVED.
CLARK, CAN I TALK TO YOU IN PRIVATE?
NO. I'M DONE TALKING. WHETHER YOU AGREE WITH ME OR NOT IS UP TO YOU.
DEAL WITH IT.
THIS IS NOT A DEMOCRACY.

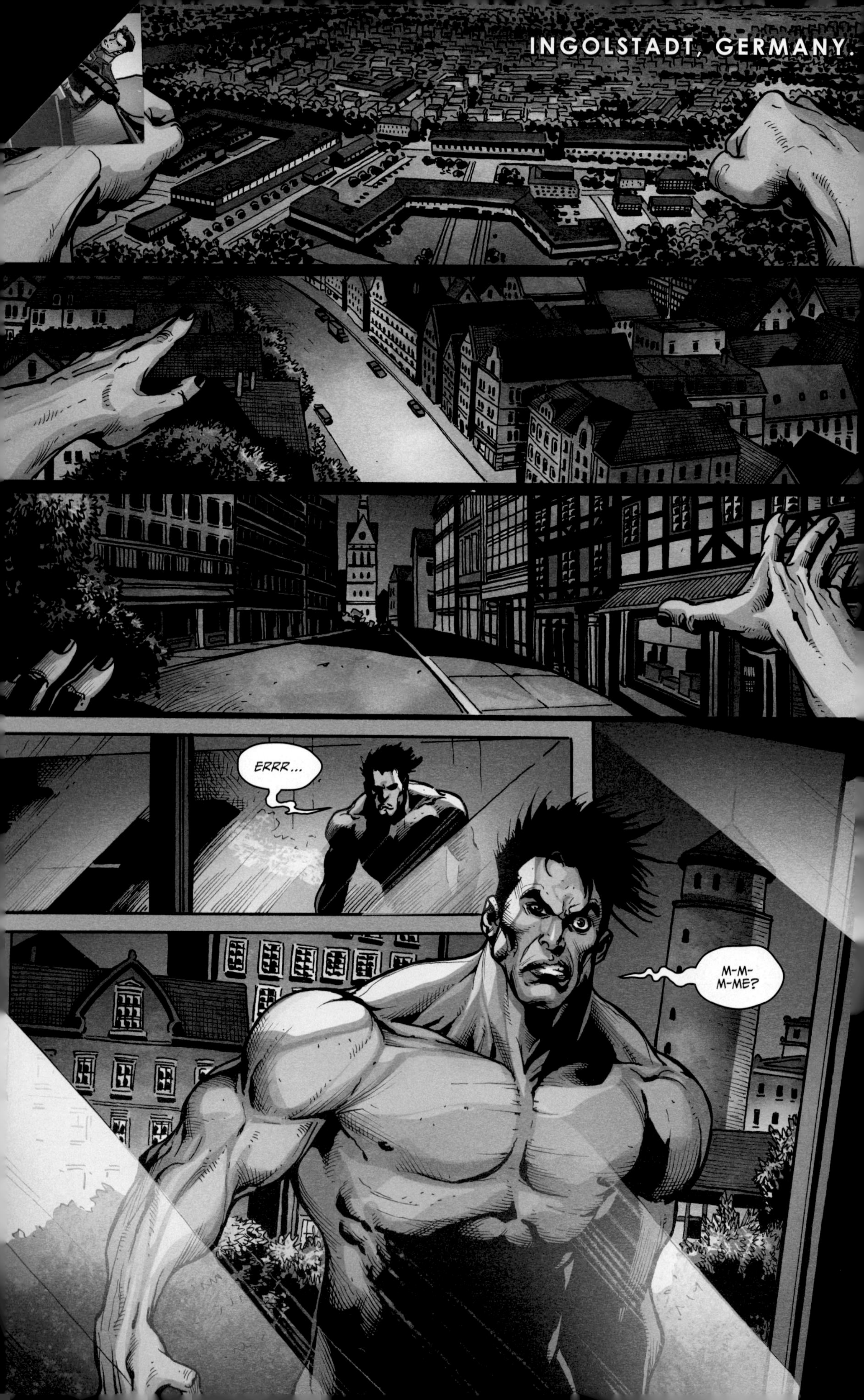
INGOLSTADT, GERMANY.
ERRR...
M-M-
M-ME?

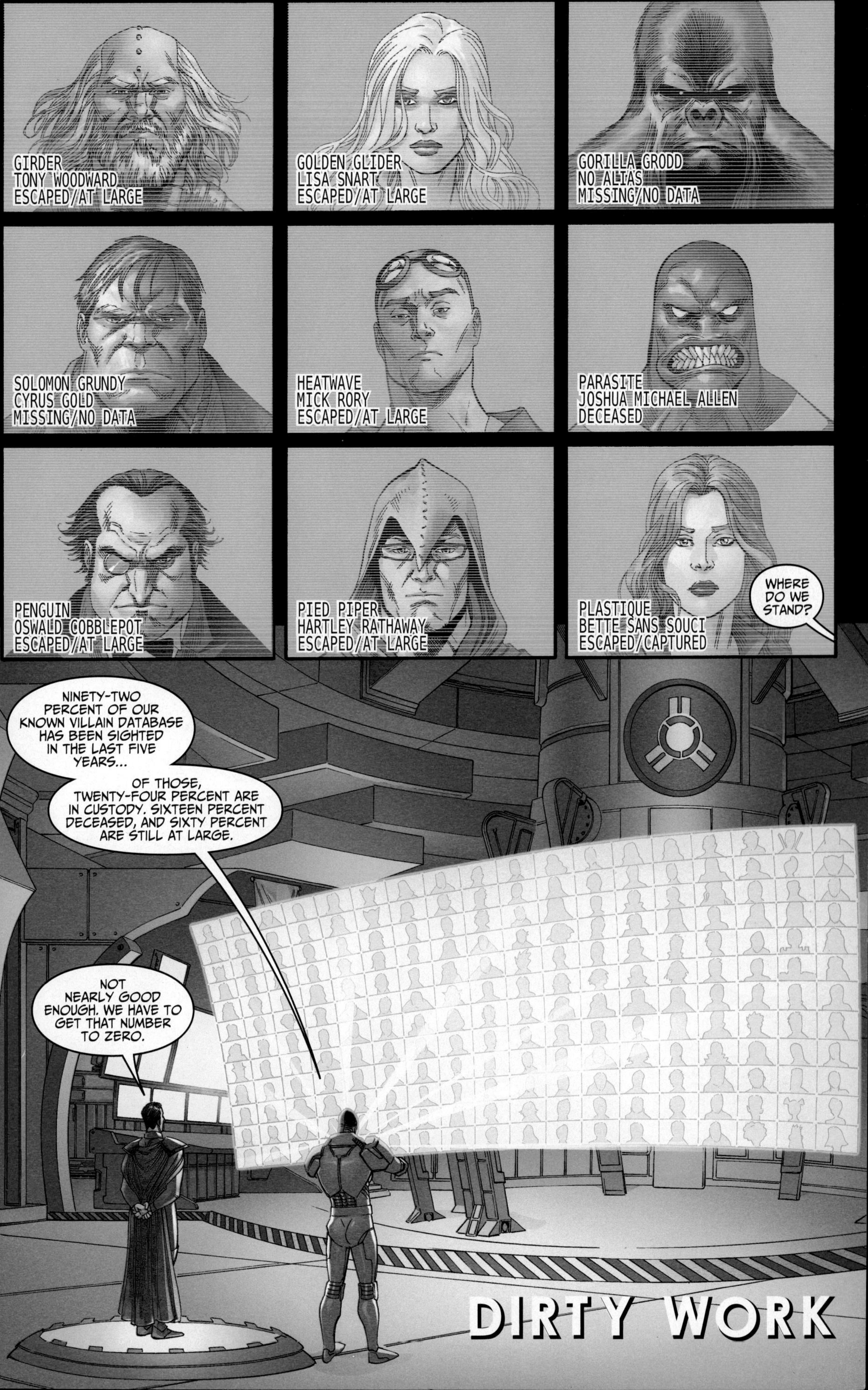
GIRDER
TONY WOODWARD
ESCAPED/AT LARGE
GOLDEN GLIDER
LISA SNART
ESCAPED/AT LARGE
GORILLA GRODD
NO ALIAS
MISSING/NO DATA
SOLOMON GRUNDY
CYRUS GOLD
MISSING/NO DATA
HEATWAVE
MICK RORY
ESCAPED/AT LARGE
PARASITE
JOSHUA MICHAEL ALLEN
DECEASED
PENGUIN
OSWALD COBBLEPOT
ESCAPED/AT LARGE
PIED PIPER
HARTLEY RATHAWAY
ESCAPED/AT LARGE
PLASTIQUE
BETTE SANS SOUCI
ESCAPED/CAPTURED
WHERE DO WE STAND?
NINETY-TWO PERCENT OF OUR KNOWN VILLAIN DATABASE HAS BEEN SIGHTED IN THE LAST FIVE YEARS...
OF THOSE, TWENTY-FOUR PERCENT ARE IN CUSTODY. SIXTEEN PERCENT DECEASED, AND SIXTY PERCENT ARE STILL AT LARGE.
NOT NEARLY GOOD ENOUGH. WE HAVE TO GET THAT NUMBER TO ZERO.
DIRTY WORK

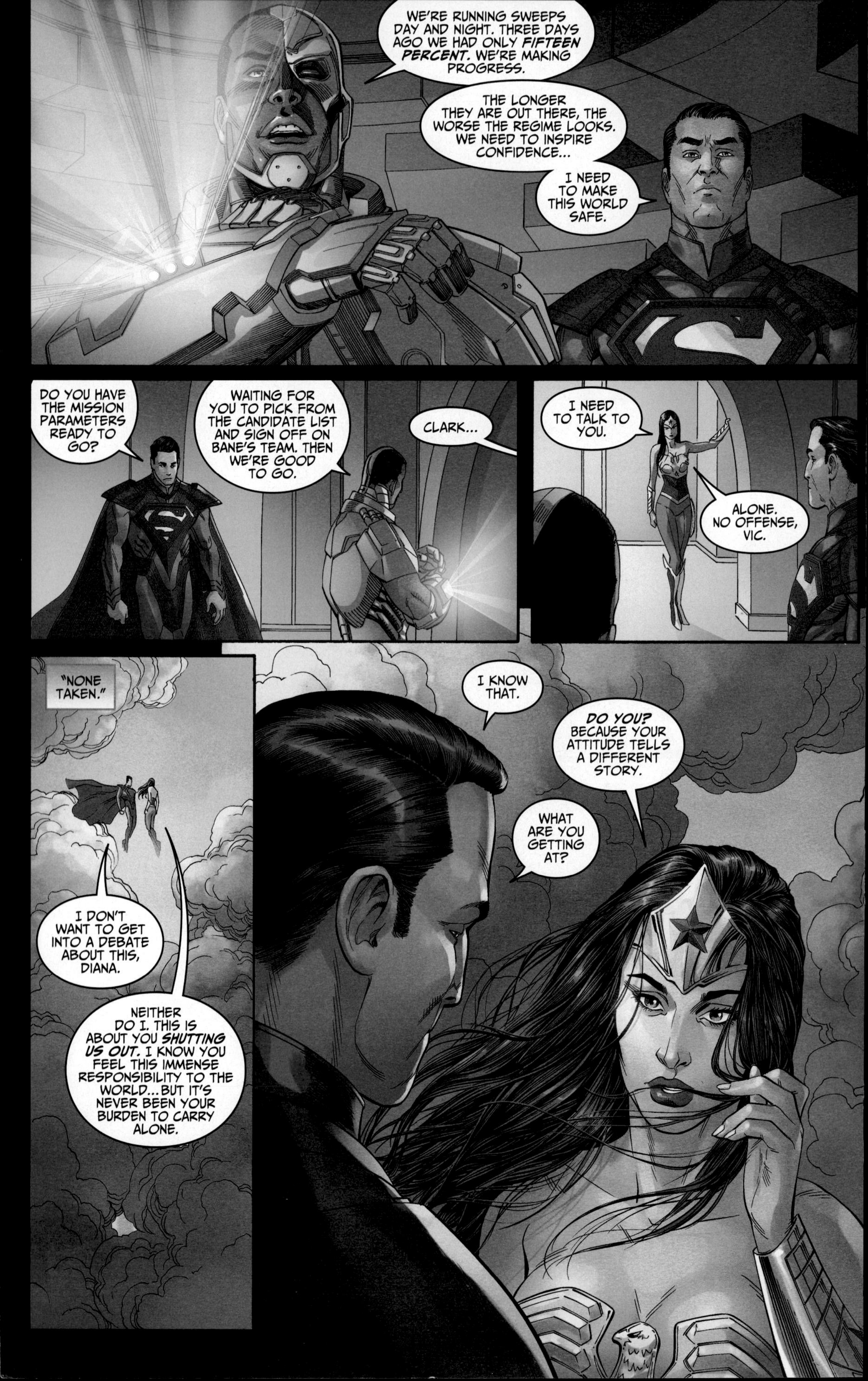
WE'RE RUNNING SWEEPS DAY AND NIGHT. THREE DAYS AGO WE HAD ONLY *FIFTEEN PERCENT*. WE'RE MAKING PROGRESS.
THE LONGER THEY ARE OUT THERE, THE WORSE THE REGIME LOOKS. WE NEED TO INSPIRE CONFIDENCE...
I NEED TO MAKE THIS WORLD SAFE.
DO YOU HAVE THE MISSION PARAMETERS READY TO GO?
WAITING FOR YOU TO PICK FROM THE CANDIDATE LIST AND SIGN OFF ON BANE'S TEAM. THEN WE'RE GOOD TO GO.
CLARK...
I NEED TO TALK TO YOU.
ALONE. NO OFFENSE, VIC.
"NONE TAKEN."
I DON'T WANT TO GET INTO A DEBATE ABOUT THIS, DIANA.
NEITHER DO I. THIS IS ABOUT YOU *SHUTTING US OUT*. I KNOW YOU FEEL THIS IMMENSE RESPONSIBILITY TO THE WORLD... BUT IT'S NEVER BEEN YOUR BURDEN TO CARRY ALONE.
I KNOW THAT.
DO YOU? BECAUSE YOUR ATTITUDE TELLS A DIFFERENT STORY.
WHAT ARE YOU GETTING AT?

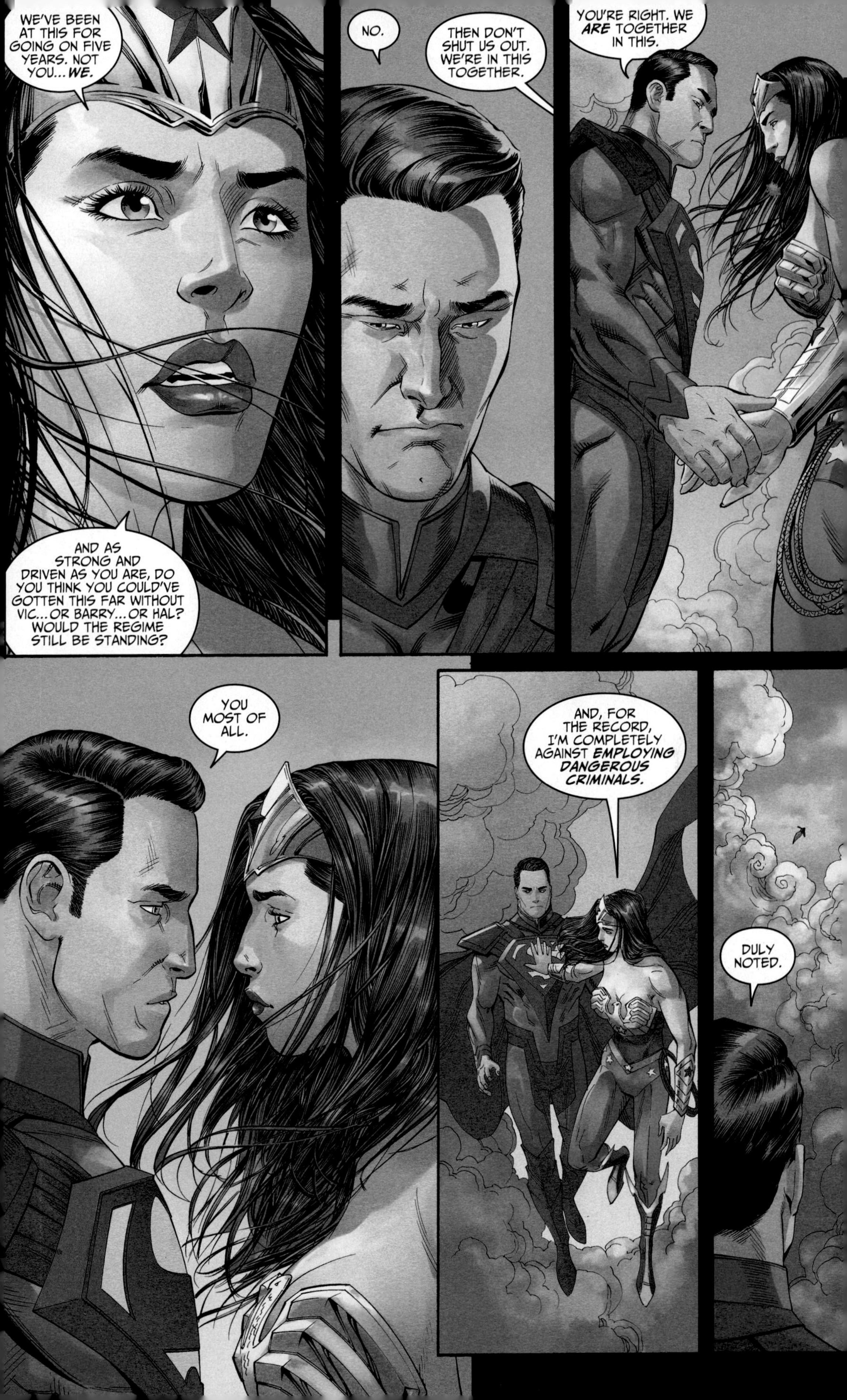
WE'VE BEEN AT THIS FOR GOING ON FIVE YEARS. NOT YOU... WE.
AND AS STRONG AND DRIVEN AS YOU ARE, DO YOU THINK YOU COULD'VE GOTTEN THIS FAR WITHOUT VIC...OR BARRY...OR HAL? WOULD THE REGIME STILL BE STANDING?
NO.
THEN DON'T SHUT US OUT. WE'RE IN THIS TOGETHER.
YOU'RE RIGHT. WE ARE TOGETHER IN THIS.
YOU MOST OF ALL.
AND, FOR THE RECORD, I'M COMPLETELY AGAINST EMPLOYING DANGEROUS CRIMINALS.
DULY NOTED.

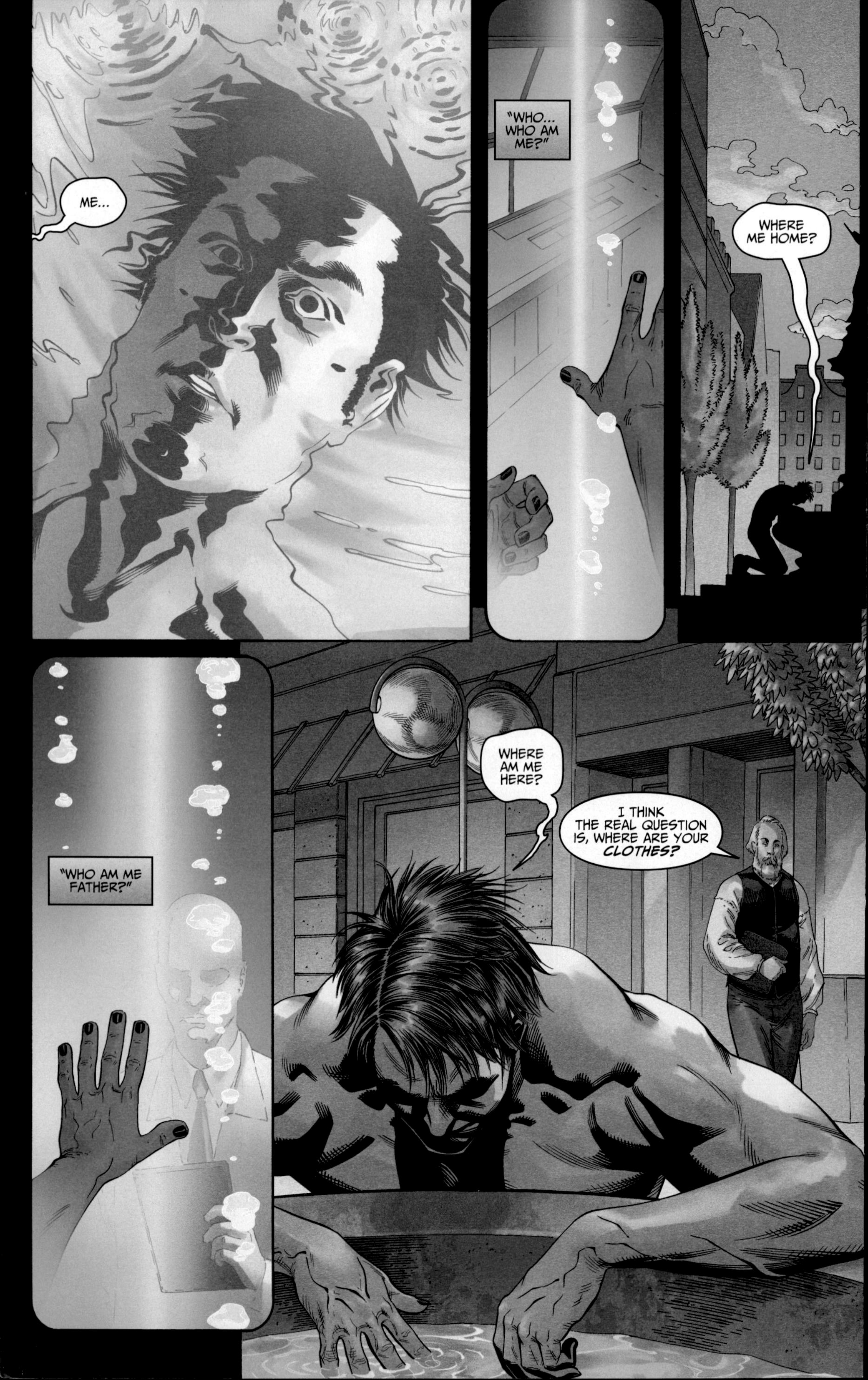
ME...
"WHO... WHO AM ME?"
WHERE ME HOME?
"WHO AM ME FATHER?"
WHERE AM ME HERE?
I THINK THE REAL QUESTION IS, WHERE ARE YOUR CLOTHES?

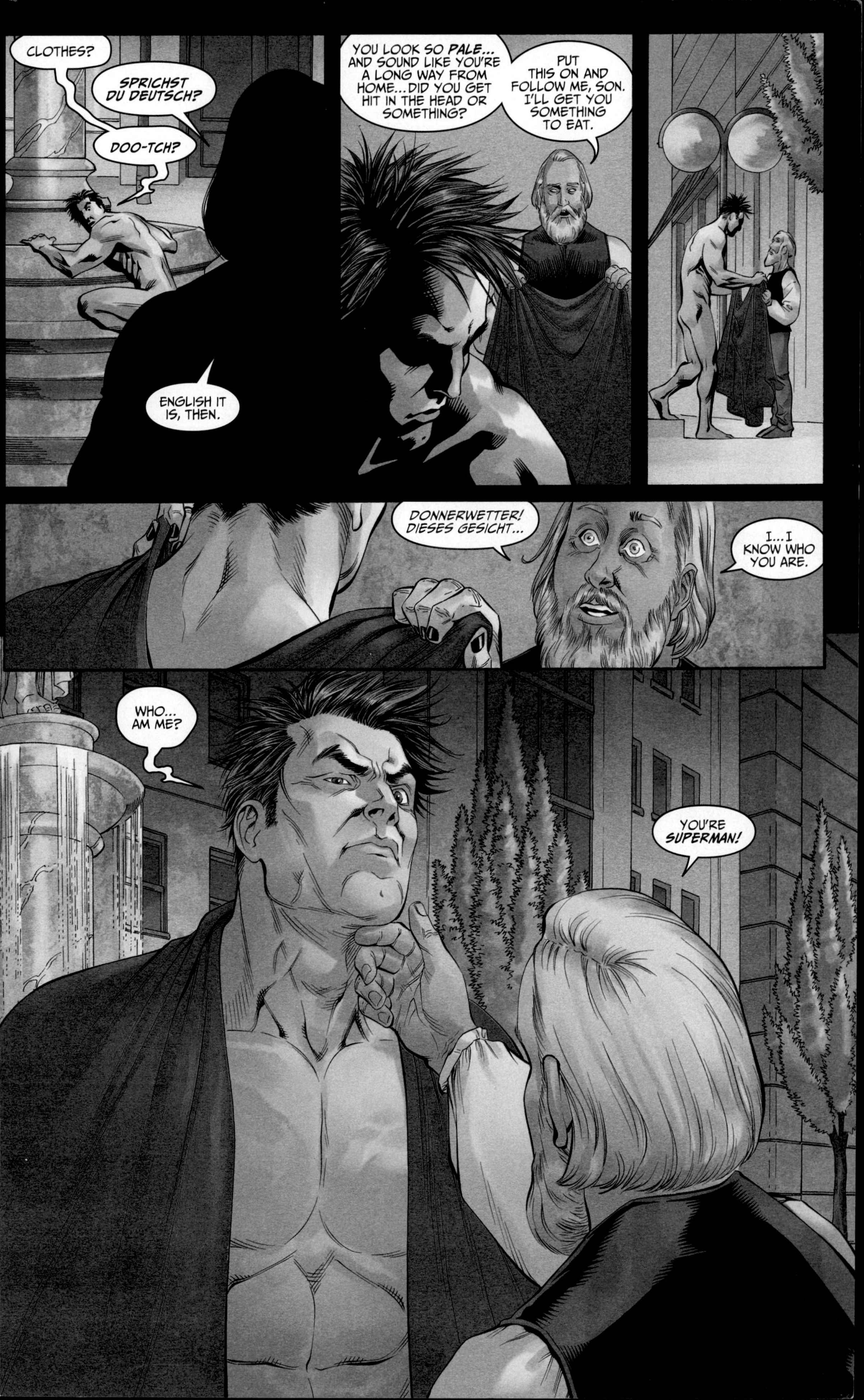

CLOTHES?
SPRICHST DU DEUTSCH?
DOO-TCH?
ENGLISH IT IS, THEN.
YOU LOOK SO PALE... AND SOUND LIKE YOU'RE A LONG WAY FROM HOME...DID YOU GET HIT IN THE HEAD OR SOMETHING?
PUT THIS ON AND FOLLOW ME, SON. I'LL GET YOU SOMETHING TO EAT.
DONNERWETTER! DIESES GESICHT...
I...I KNOW WHO YOU ARE.
WHO... AM ME?
YOU'RE SUPERMAN!

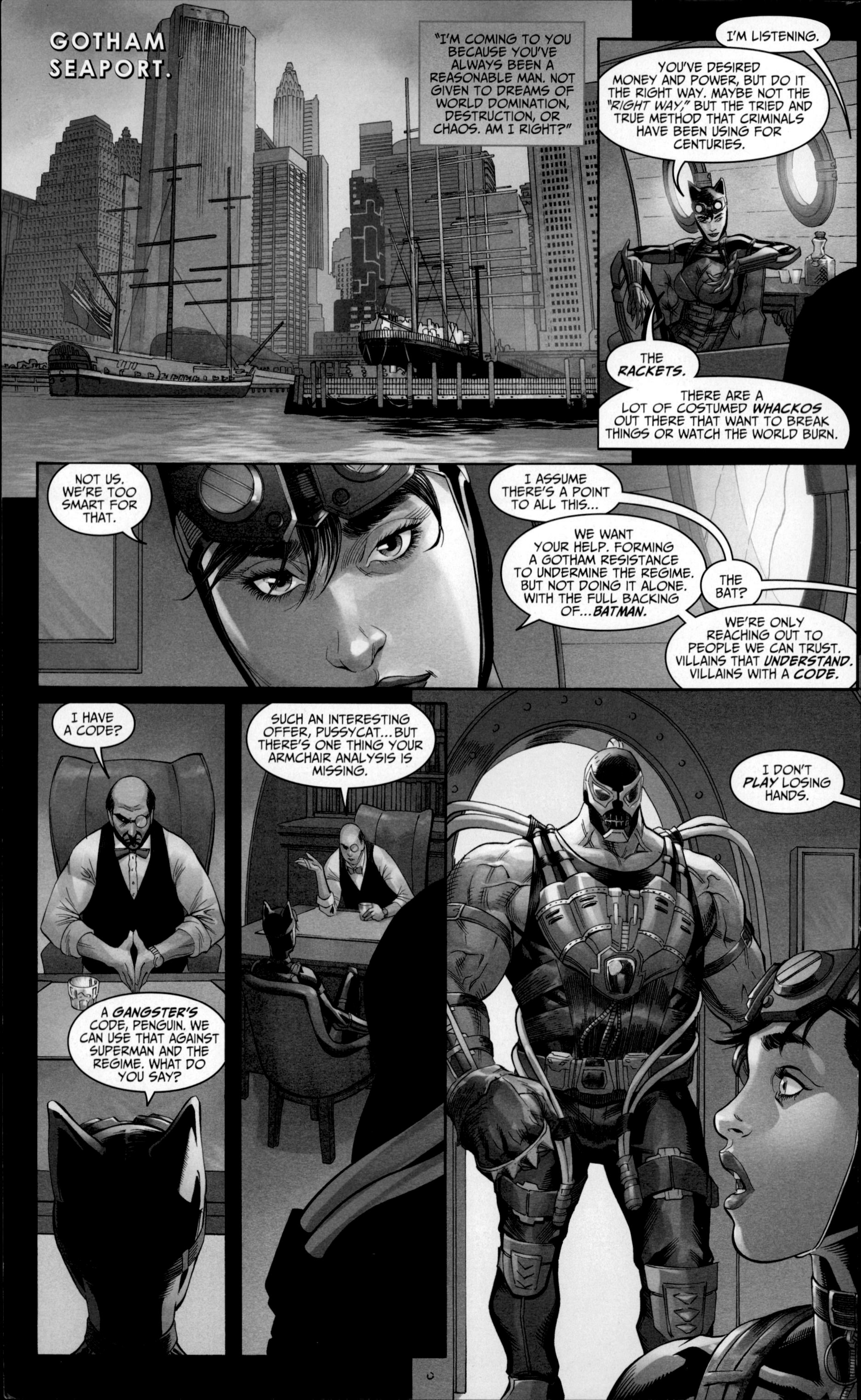
GOTHAM SEAPORT.
"I'M COMING TO YOU BECAUSE YOU'VE ALWAYS BEEN A REASONABLE MAN. NOT GIVEN TO DREAMS OF WORLD DOMINATION, DESTRUCTION, OR CHAOS. AM I RIGHT?"
I'M LISTENING.
YOU'VE DESIRED MONEY AND POWER, BUT DO IT THE RIGHT WAY. MAYBE NOT THE "RIGHT WAY," BUT THE TRIED AND TRUE METHOD THAT CRIMINALS HAVE BEEN USING FOR CENTURIES.
THE RACKETS.
THERE ARE A LOT OF COSTUMED WHACKOS OUT THERE THAT WANT TO BREAK THINGS OR WATCH THE WORLD BURN.
NOT US. WE'RE TOO SMART FOR THAT.
I ASSUME THERE'S A POINT TO ALL THIS...
WE WANT YOUR HELP. FORMING A GOTHAM RESISTANCE TO UNDERMINE THE REGIME. BUT NOT DOING IT ALONE. WITH THE FULL BACKING OF...BATMAN.
THE BAT?
WE'RE ONLY REACHING OUT TO PEOPLE WE CAN TRUST. VILLAINS THAT UNDERSTAND. VILLAINS WITH A CODE.
I HAVE A CODE?
A GANGSTER'S CODE, PENGUIN. WE CAN USE THAT AGAINST SUPERMAN AND THE REGIME. WHAT DO YOU SAY?
SUCH AN INTERESTING OFFER, PUSSYCAT...BUT THERE'S ONE THING YOUR ARMCHAIR ANALYSIS IS MISSING.
I DON'T PLAY LOSING HANDS.

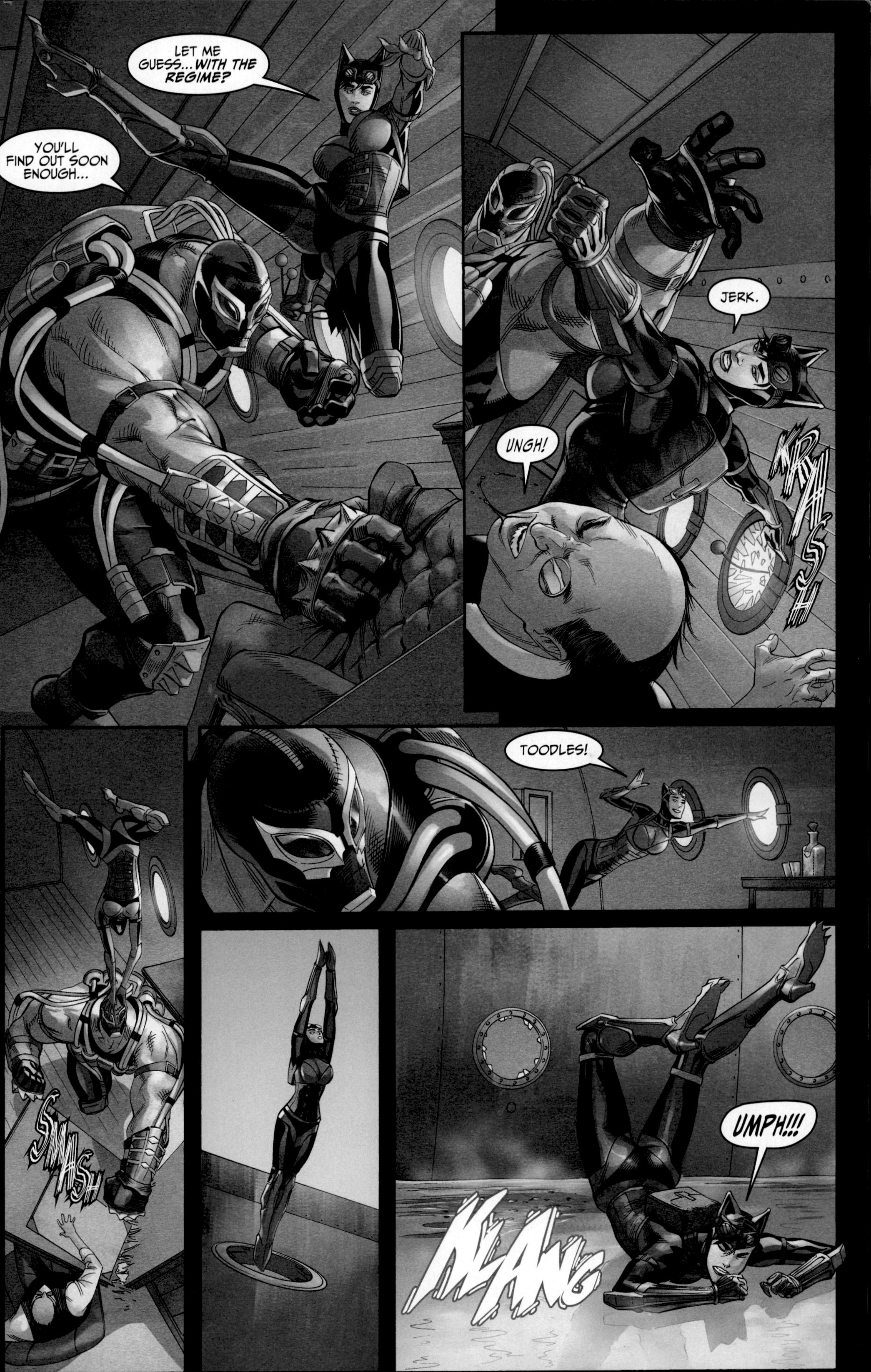
LET ME GUESS...WITH THE REGIME?
YOU'LL FIND OUT SOON ENOUGH...
JERK.
UNGH!
KRASH
TOODLES!
SMASH
UMPH!!!
KLANG

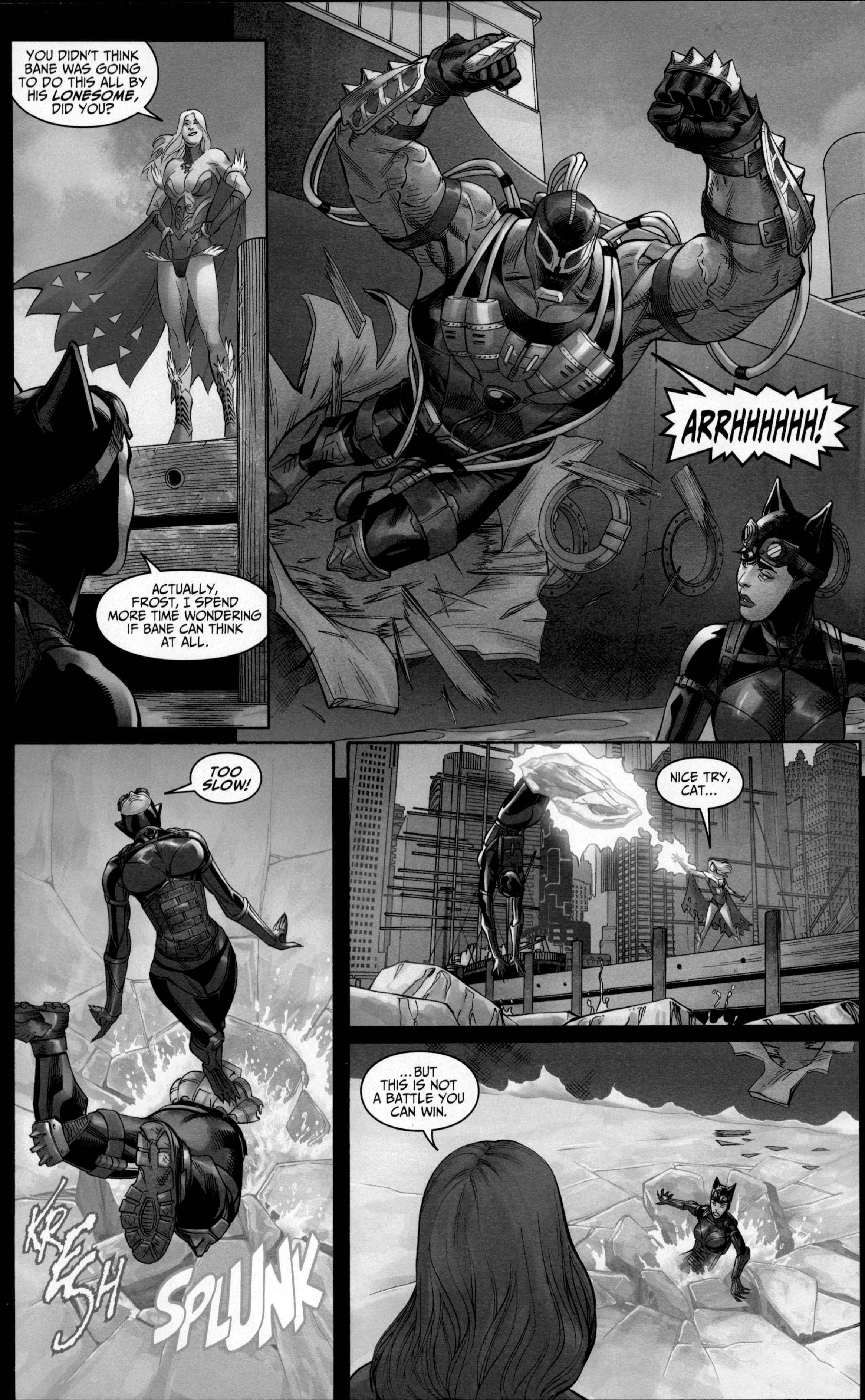

YOU DIDN'T THINK BANE WAS GOING TO DO THIS ALL BY HIS LONESOME, DID YOU?
ACTUALLY, FROST, I SPEND MORE TIME WONDERING IF BANE CAN THINK AT ALL.
ARRHHHHHH!
TOO SLOW!
KRESH
SPLUNK
NICE TRY, CAT...
...BUT THIS IS NOT A BATTLE YOU CAN WIN.

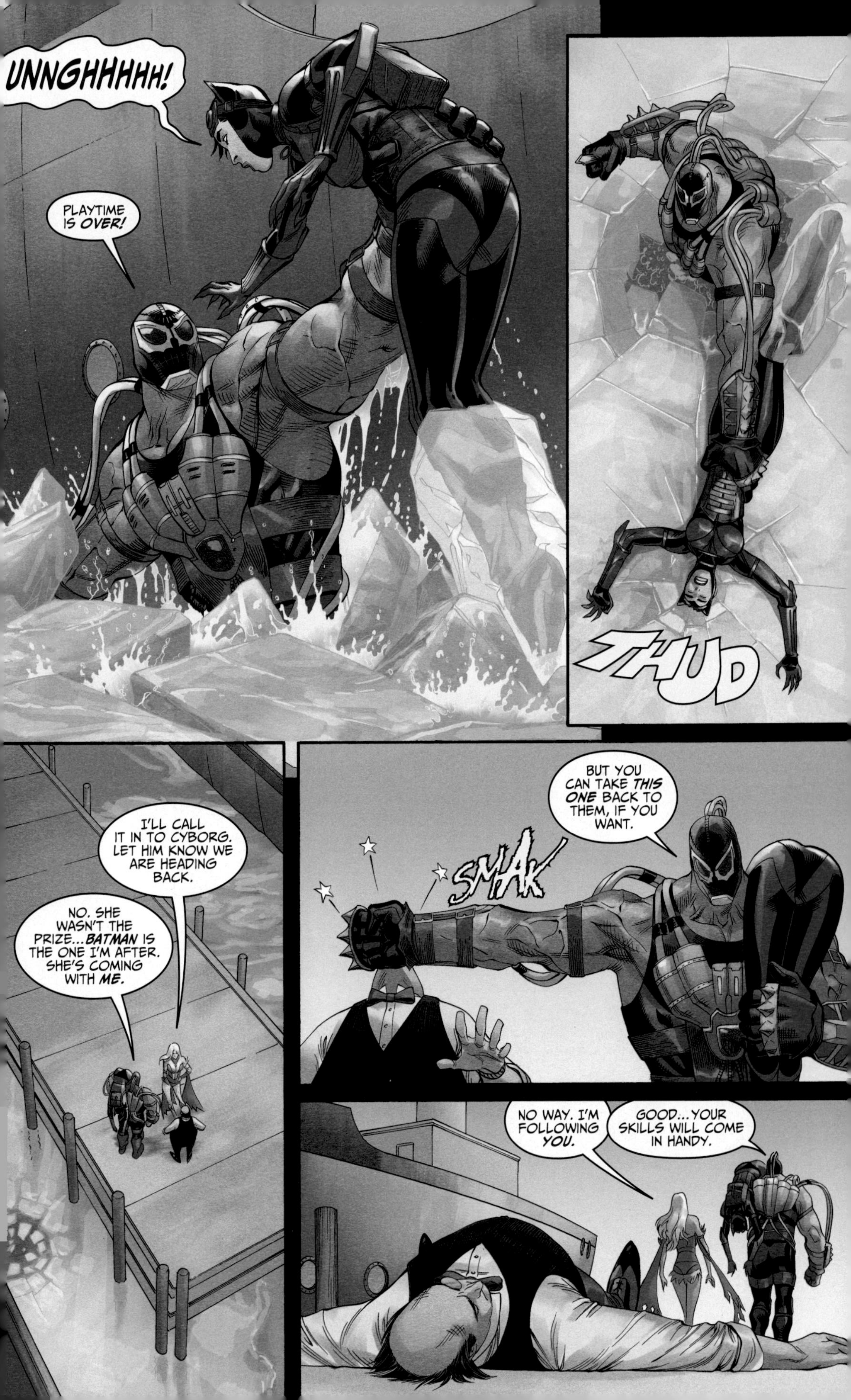
UNNGHHHHH!
PLAYTIME IS OVER!
THUD
I'LL CALL IT IN TO CYBORG. LET HIM KNOW WE ARE HEADING BACK.
NO. SHE WASN'T THE PRIZE...BATMAN IS THE ONE I'M AFTER. SHE'S COMING WITH ME.
BUT YOU CAN TAKE THIS ONE BACK TO THEM, IF YOU WANT.
SMAK
NO WAY. I'M FOLLOWING YOU.
GOOD...YOUR SKILLS WILL COME IN HANDY.

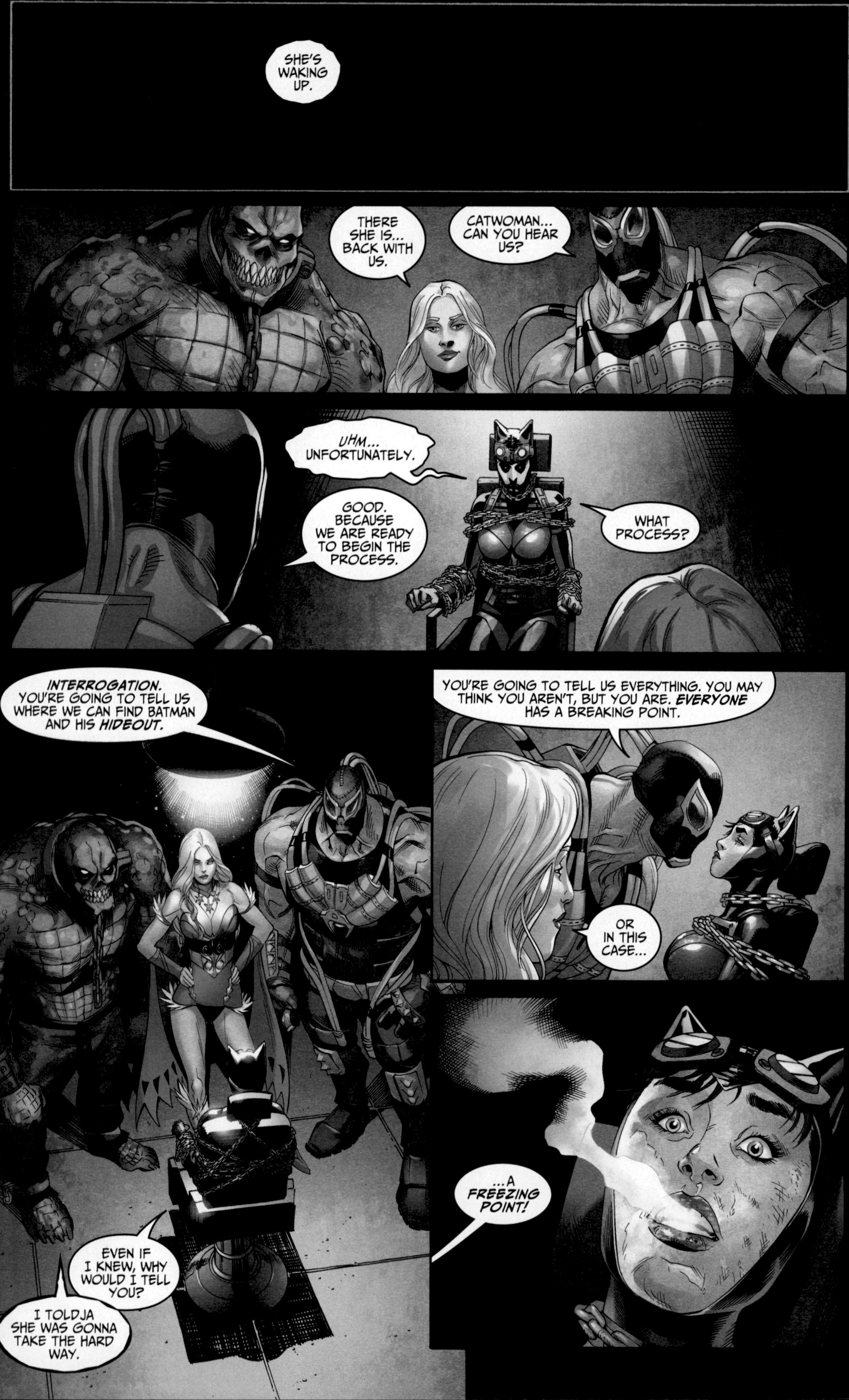
SHE'S WAKING UP.
THERE SHE IS... BACK WITH US.
CATWOMAN... CAN YOU HEAR US?
UHM... UNFORTUNATELY.
GOOD. BECAUSE WE ARE READY TO BEGIN THE PROCESS.
WHAT PROCESS?
INTERROGATION. YOU'RE GOING TO TELL US WHERE WE CAN FIND BATMAN AND HIS HIDEOUT.
EVEN IF I KNEW, WHY WOULD I TELL YOU?
I TOLDJA SHE WAS GONNA TAKE THE HARD WAY.
YOU'RE GOING TO TELL US EVERYTHING. YOU MAY THINK YOU AREN'T, BUT YOU ARE. EVERYONE HAS A BREAKING POINT.
OR IN THIS CASE...
...A FREEZING POINT!

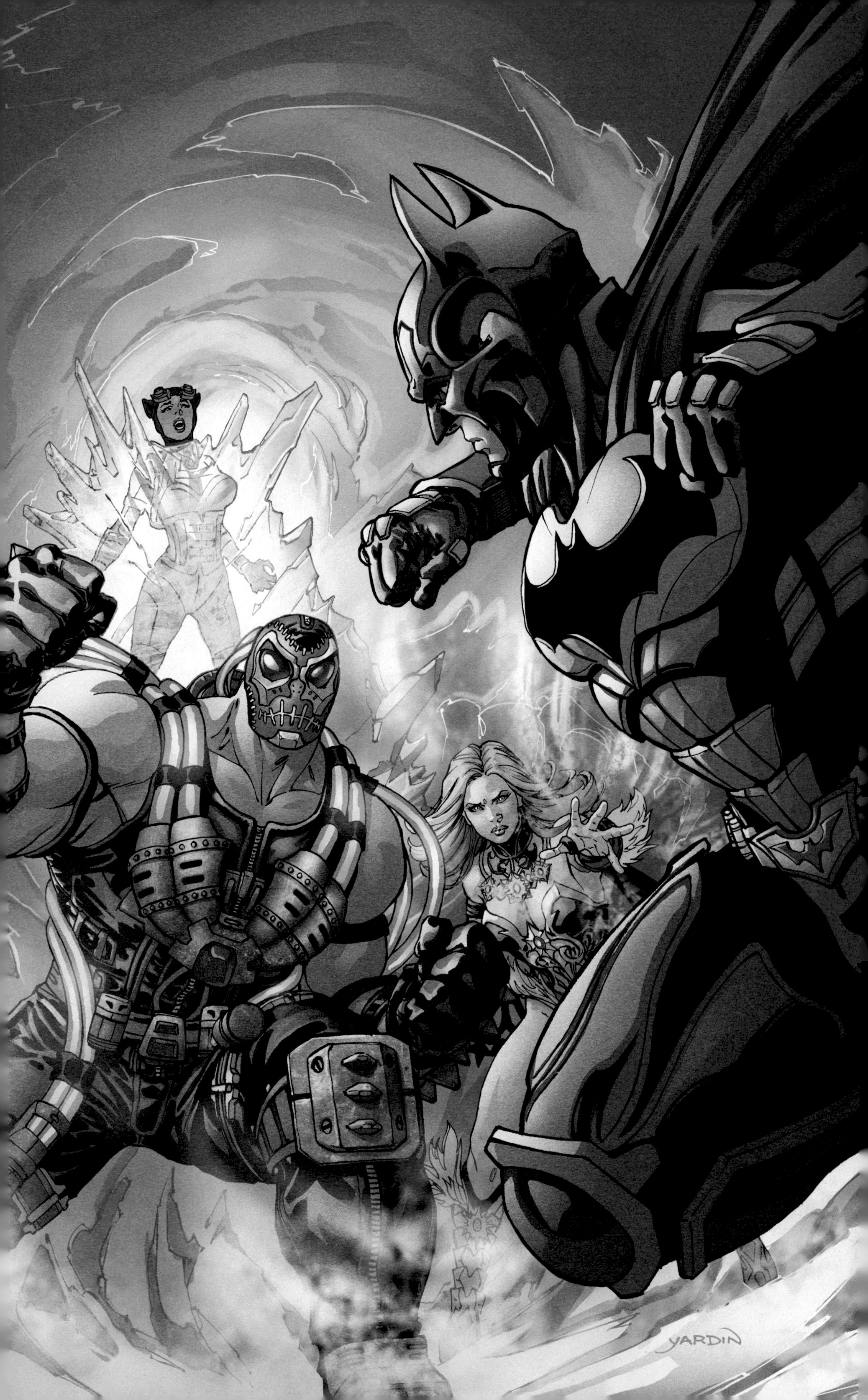
YARDIN

"Bait" **Bruno Redondo** Penciller **Juan Albarran** Inker **Rex Lokus** Colorist
"Decoy" **Bruno Redondo** Layouts **Juan Albarran** Finishes **Rex Lokus** Colorist

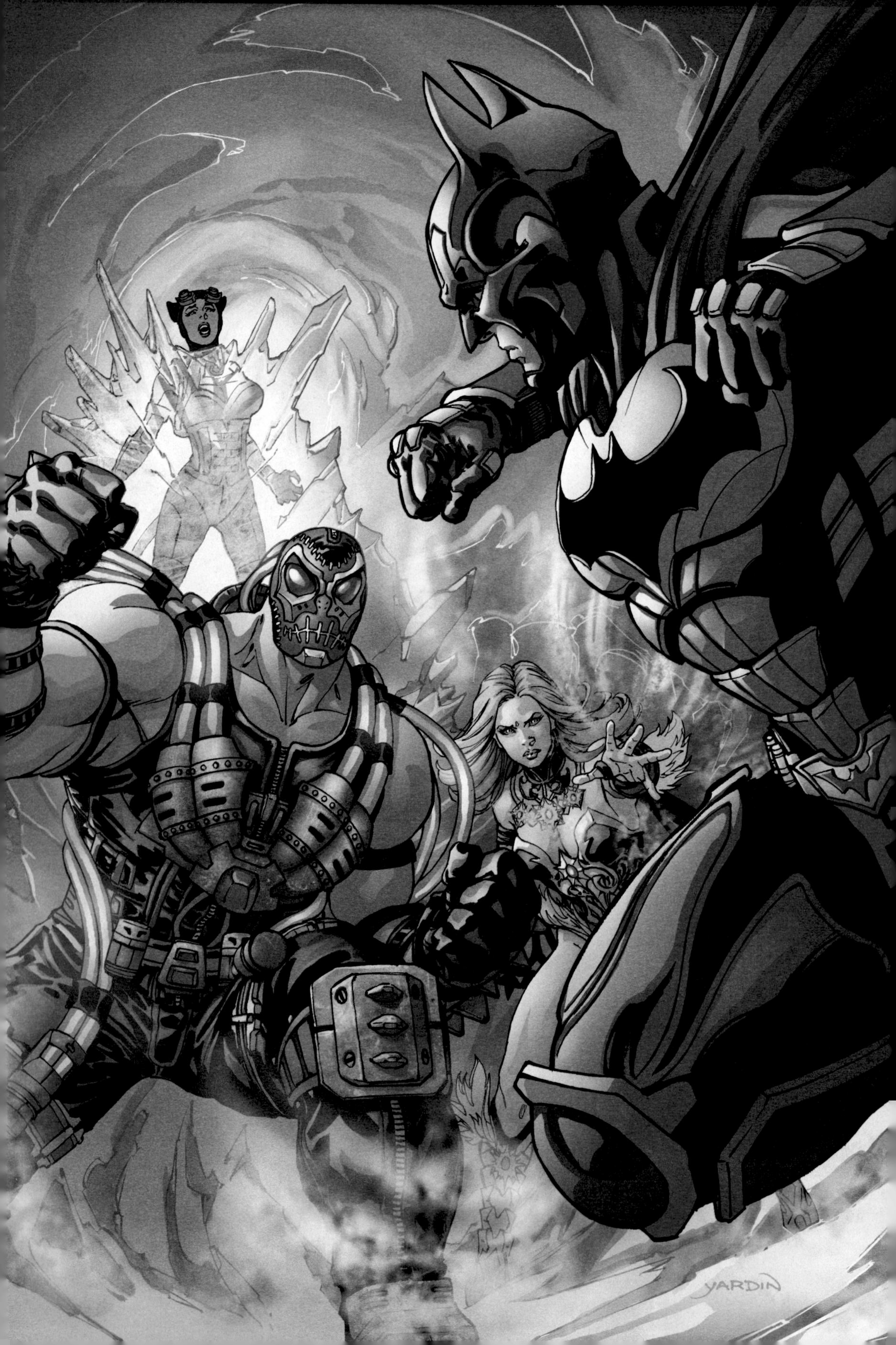
YARDIN

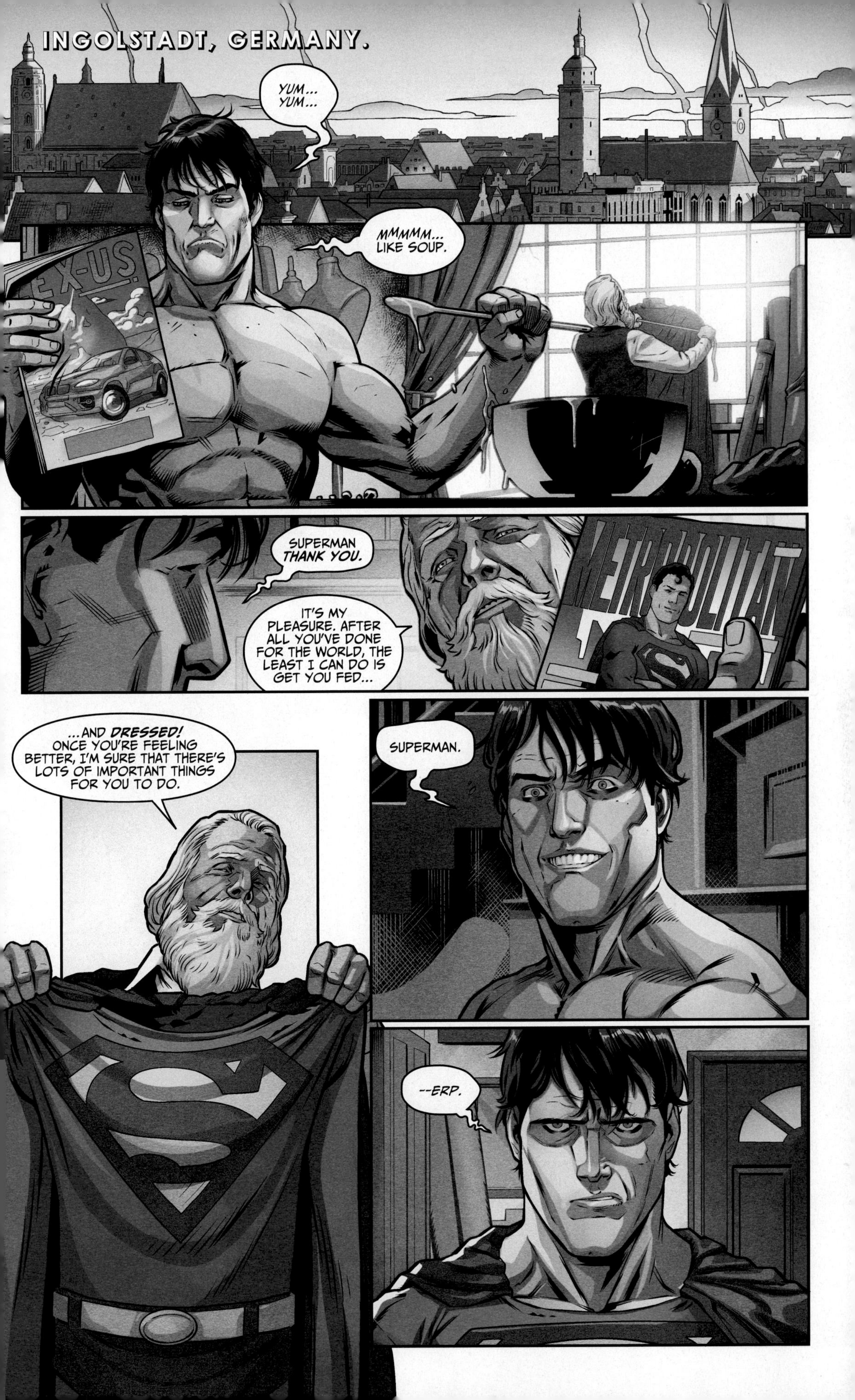
INGOLSTADT, GERMANY.
YUM... YUM...
MMMMM... LIKE SOUP.
SUPERMAN THANK YOU.
IT'S MY PLEASURE. AFTER ALL YOU'VE DONE FOR THE WORLD, THE LEAST I CAN DO IS GET YOU FED...
...AND DRESSED! ONCE YOU'RE FEELING BETTER, I'M SURE THAT THERE'S LOTS OF IMPORTANT THINGS FOR YOU TO DO.
SUPERMAN.
--ERP.

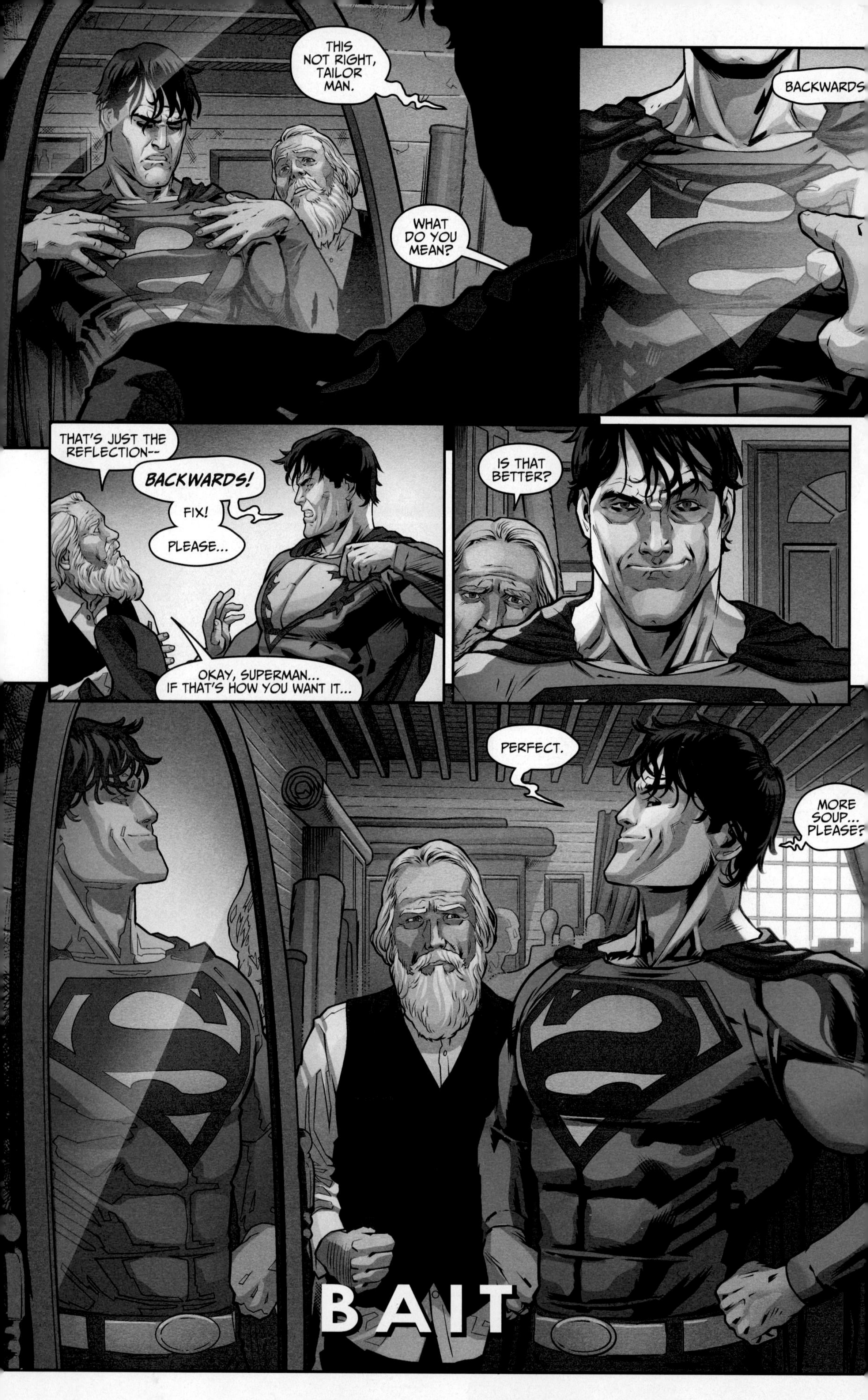
THIS NOT RIGHT, TAILOR MAN.
WHAT DO YOU MEAN?
BACKWARDS
THAT'S JUST THE REFLECTION--
BACKWARDS!
FIX!
PLEASE...
OKAY, SUPERMAN... IF THAT'S HOW YOU WANT IT...
IS THAT BETTER?
PERFECT.
MORE SOUP... PLEASE?
BAIT

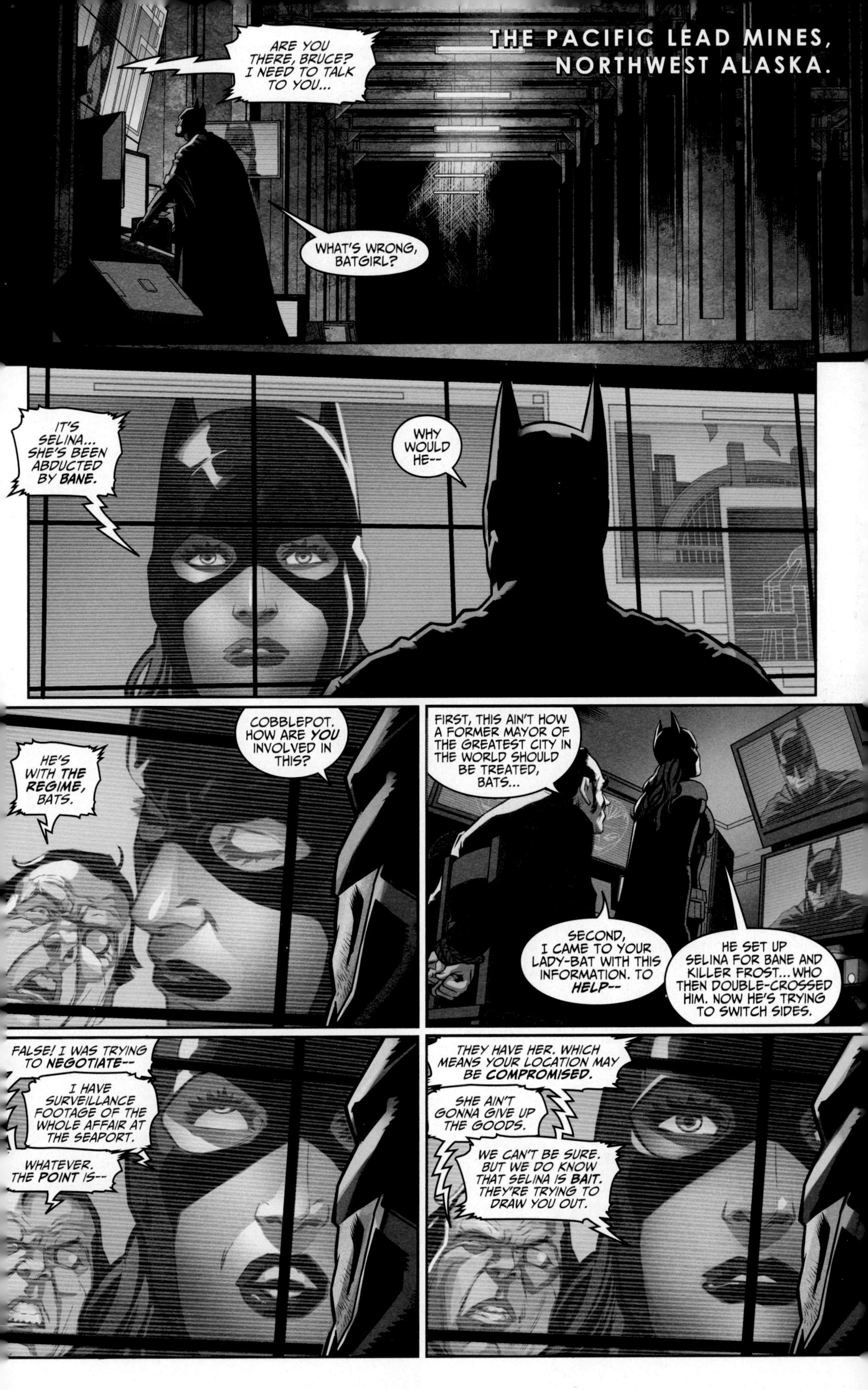
THE PACIFIC LEAD MINES, NORTHWEST ALASKA.
ARE YOU THERE, BRUCE? I NEED TO TALK TO YOU...
WHAT'S WRONG, BATGIRL?
IT'S SELINA... SHE'S BEEN ABDUCTED BY BANE.
WHY WOULD HE--
HE'S WITH THE REGIME, BATS.
COBBLEPOT. HOW ARE YOU INVOLVED IN THIS?
FIRST, THIS AIN'T HOW A FORMER MAYOR OF THE GREATEST CITY IN THE WORLD SHOULD BE TREATED, BATS...
SECOND, I CAME TO YOUR LADY-BAT WITH THIS INFORMATION. TO HELP--
HE SET UP SELINA FOR BANE AND KILLER FROST... WHO THEN DOUBLE-CROSSED HIM. NOW HE'S TRYING TO SWITCH SIDES.
FALSE! I WAS TRYING TO NEGOTIATE--
I HAVE SURVEILLANCE FOOTAGE OF THE WHOLE AFFAIR AT THE SEAPORT.
WHATEVER. THE POINT IS--
THEY HAVE HER. WHICH MEANS YOUR LOCATION MAY BE COMPROMISED.
SHE AIN'T GONNA GIVE UP THE GOODS.
WE CAN'T BE SURE. BUT WE DO KNOW THAT SELINA IS BAIT. THEY'RE TRYING TO DRAW YOU OUT.

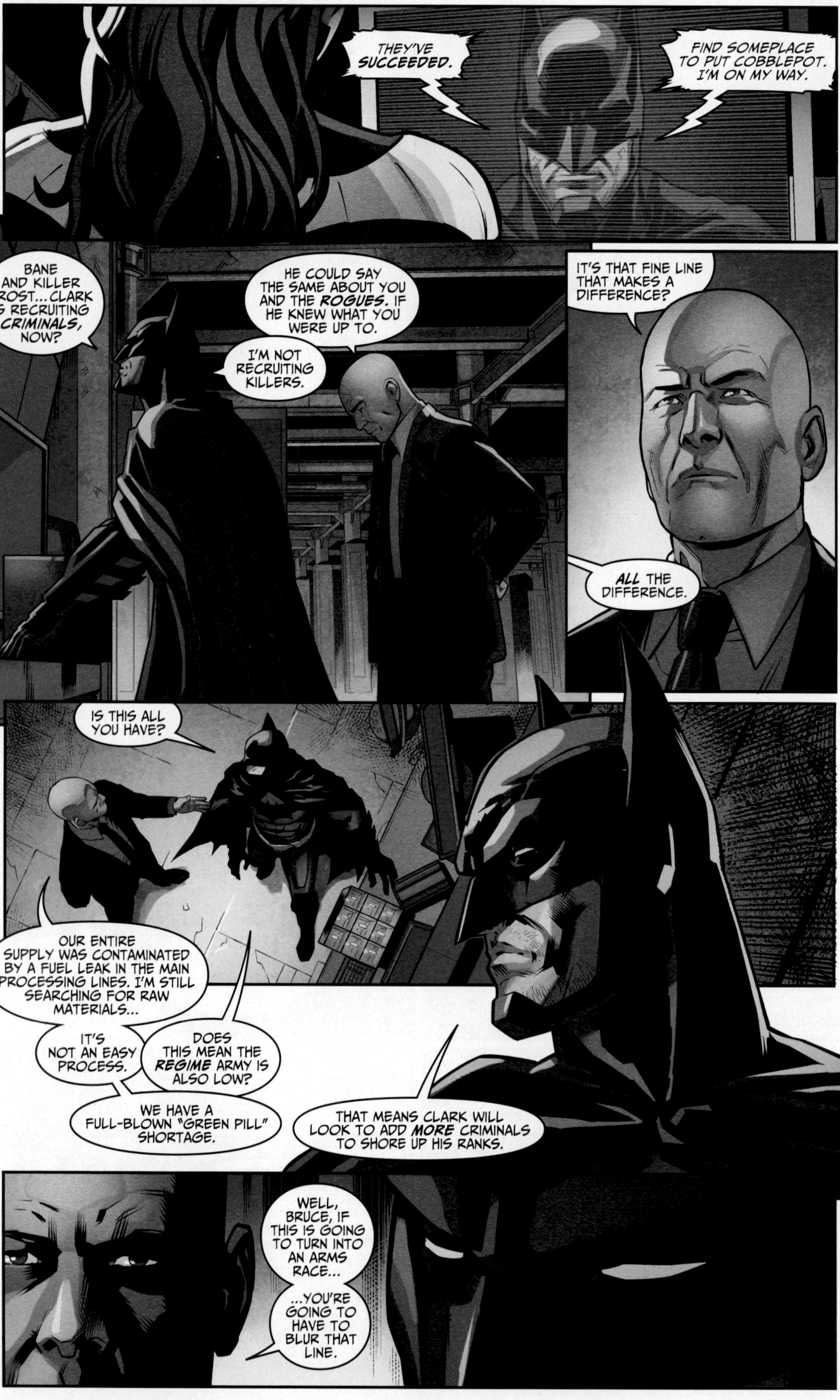
THEY'VE SUCCEEDED.
FIND SOMEPLACE TO PUT COBBLEPOT. I'M ON MY WAY.
BANE AND KILLER FROST...CLARK IS RECRUITING CRIMINALS, NOW?
HE COULD SAY THE SAME ABOUT YOU AND THE ROGUES. IF HE KNEW WHAT YOU WERE UP TO.
I'M NOT RECRUITING KILLERS.
IT'S THAT FINE LINE THAT MAKES A DIFFERENCE?
ALL THE DIFFERENCE.
IS THIS ALL YOU HAVE?
OUR ENTIRE SUPPLY WAS CONTAMINATED BY A FUEL LEAK IN THE MAIN PROCESSING LINES. I'M STILL SEARCHING FOR RAW MATERIALS...
IT'S NOT AN EASY PROCESS.
DOES THIS MEAN THE REGIME ARMY IS ALSO LOW?
WE HAVE A FULL-BLOWN "GREEN PILL" SHORTAGE.
THAT MEANS CLARK WILL LOOK TO ADD MORE CRIMINALS TO SHORE UP HIS RANKS.
WELL, BRUCE, IF THIS IS GOING TO TURN INTO AN ARMS RACE...
...YOU'RE GOING TO HAVE TO BLUR THAT LINE.

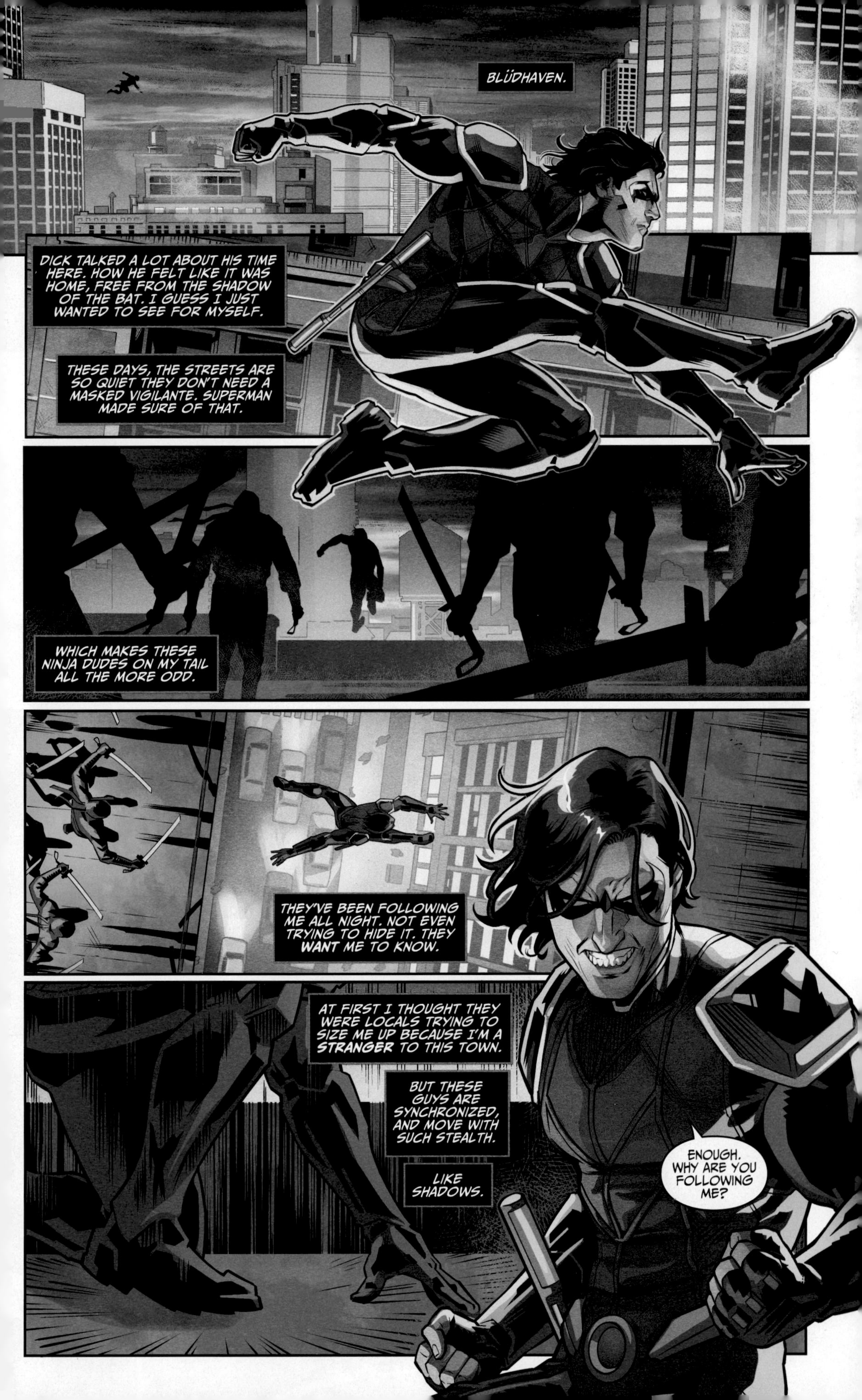
BLÜDHAVEN.
DICK TALKED A LOT ABOUT HIS TIME HERE. HOW HE FELT LIKE IT WAS HOME, FREE FROM THE SHADOW OF THE BAT. I GUESS I JUST WANTED TO SEE FOR MYSELF.
THESE DAYS, THE STREETS ARE SO QUIET THEY DON'T NEED A MASKED VIGILANTE. SUPERMAN MADE SURE OF THAT.
WHICH MAKES THESE NINJA DUDES ON MY TAIL ALL THE MORE ODD.
THEY'VE BEEN FOLLOWING ME ALL NIGHT. NOT EVEN TRYING TO HIDE IT. THEY WANT ME TO KNOW.
AT FIRST I THOUGHT THEY WERE LOCALS TRYING TO SIZE ME UP BECAUSE I'M A STRANGER TO THIS TOWN.
BUT THESE GUYS ARE SYNCHRONIZED, AND MOVE WITH SUCH STEALTH.
LIKE SHADOWS.
ENOUGH. WHY ARE YOU FOLLOWING ME?

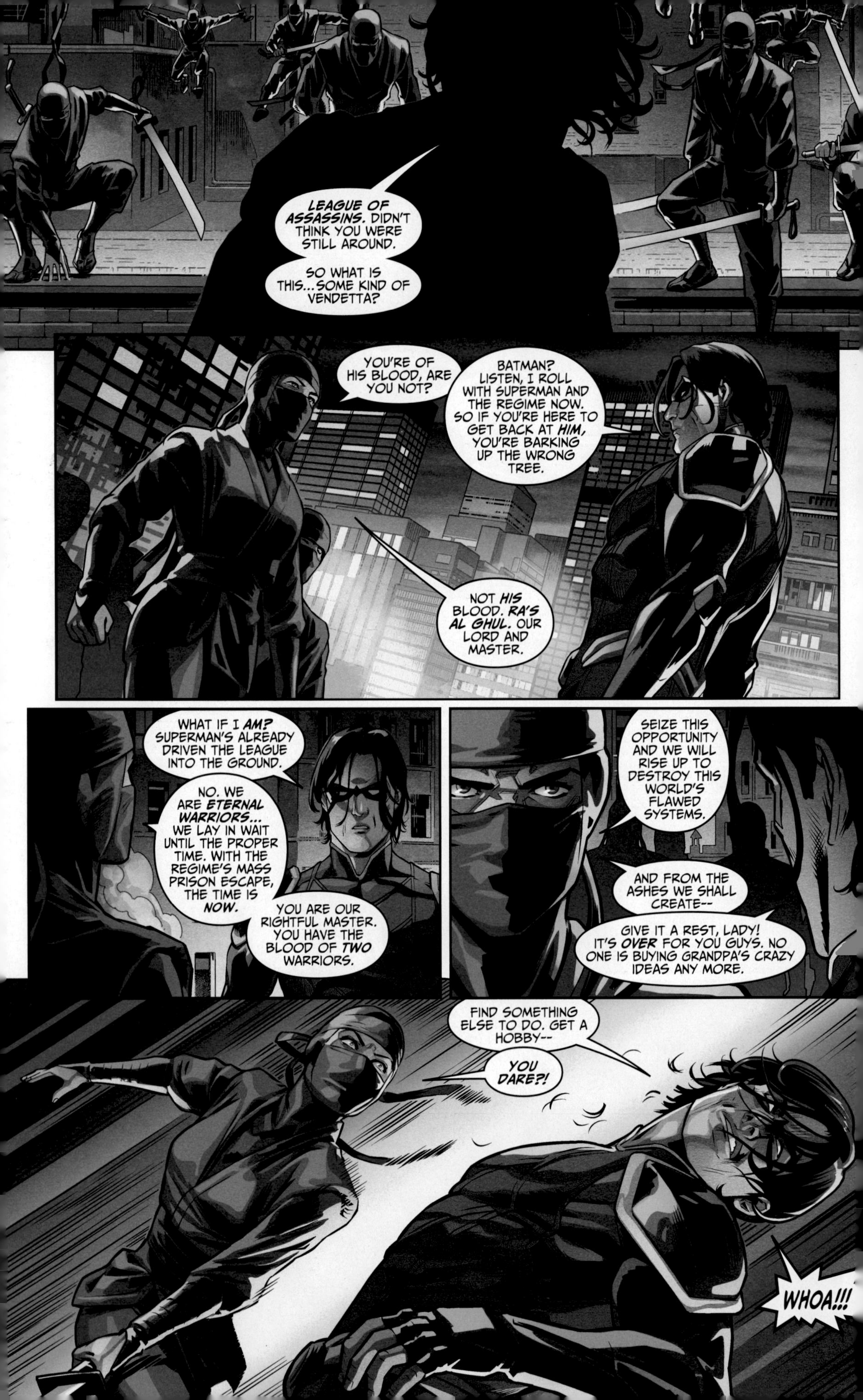

LEAGUE OF ASSASSINS. DIDN'T THINK YOU WERE STILL AROUND.
SO WHAT IS THIS...SOME KIND OF VENDETTA?
YOU'RE OF HIS BLOOD, ARE YOU NOT?
BATMAN? LISTEN, I ROLL WITH SUPERMAN AND THE REGIME NOW. SO IF YOU'RE HERE TO GET BACK AT HIM, YOU'RE BARKING UP THE WRONG TREE.
NOT HIS BLOOD. RA'S AL GHUL. OUR LORD AND MASTER.
WHAT IF I AM? SUPERMAN'S ALREADY DRIVEN THE LEAGUE INTO THE GROUND.
NO. WE ARE ETERNAL WARRIORS... WE LAY IN WAIT UNTIL THE PROPER TIME. WITH THE REGIME'S MASS PRISON ESCAPE, THE TIME IS NOW.
YOU ARE OUR RIGHTFUL MASTER. YOU HAVE THE BLOOD OF TWO WARRIORS.
SEIZE THIS OPPORTUNITY AND WE WILL RISE UP TO DESTROY THIS WORLD'S FLAWED SYSTEMS.
AND FROM THE ASHES WE SHALL CREATE--
GIVE IT A REST, LADY! IT'S OVER FOR YOU GUYS. NO ONE IS BUYING GRANDPA'S CRAZY IDEAS ANY MORE.
FIND SOMETHING ELSE TO DO. GET A HOBBY--
YOU DARE?!
WHOA!!!

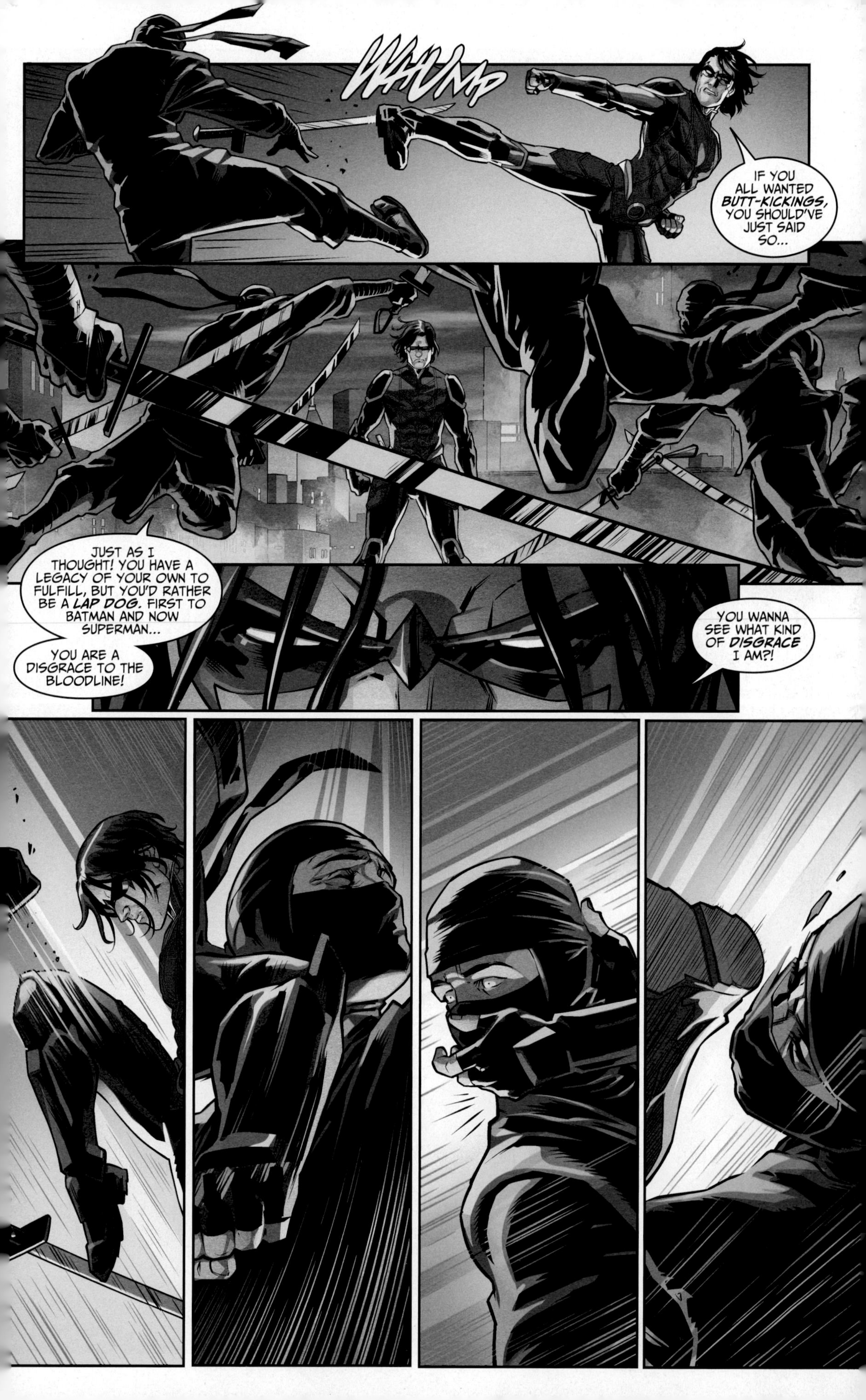
WHUMP
IF YOU ALL WANTED BUTT-KICKINGS, YOU SHOULD'VE JUST SAID SO...
JUST AS I THOUGHT! YOU HAVE A LEGACY OF YOUR OWN TO FULFILL, BUT YOU'D RATHER BE A LAP DOG. FIRST TO BATMAN AND NOW SUPERMAN...
YOU ARE A DISGRACE TO THE BLOODLINE!
YOU WANNA SEE WHAT KIND OF DISGRACE I AM?!

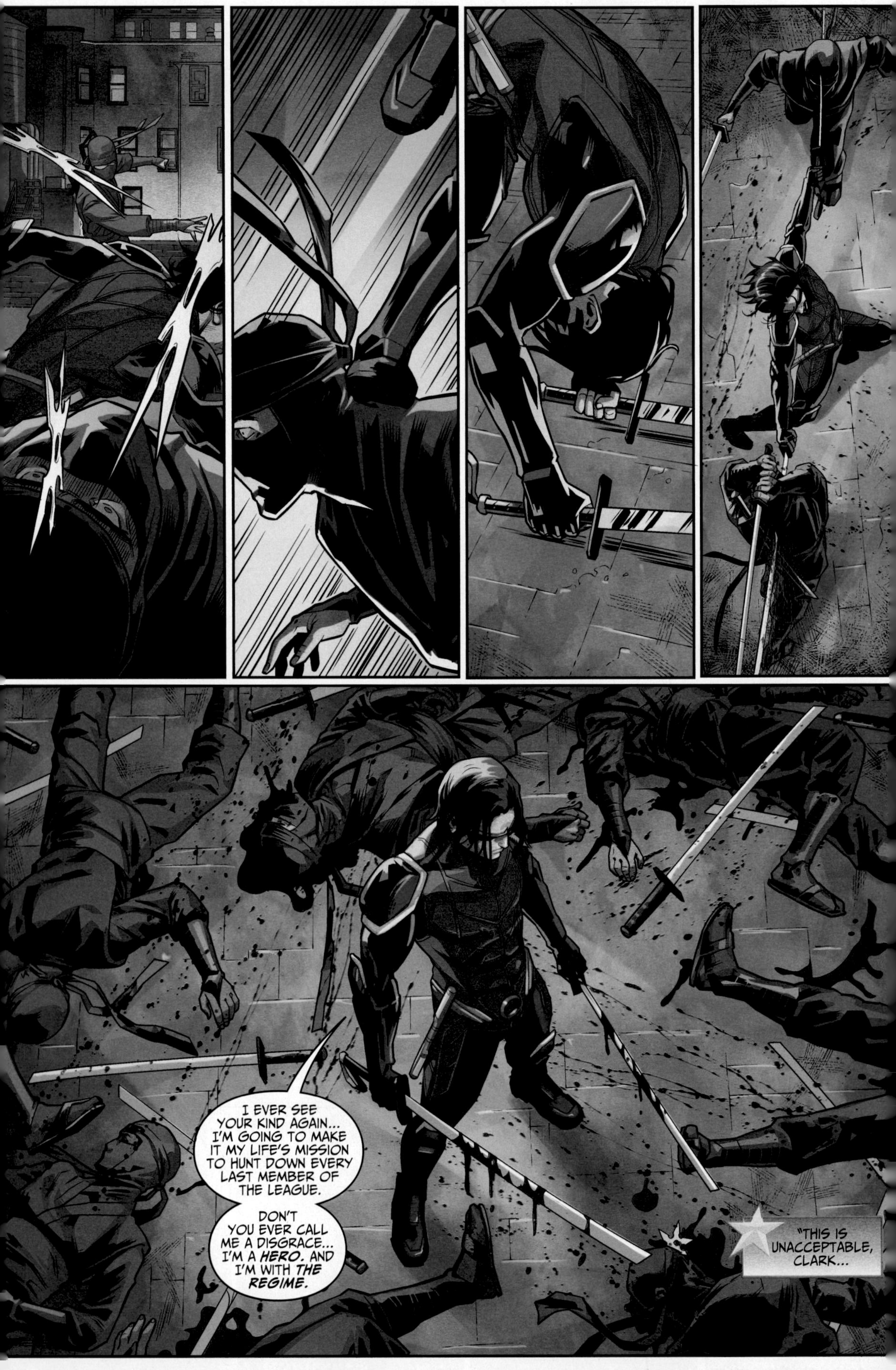
I EVER SEE YOUR KIND AGAIN... I'M GOING TO MAKE IT MY LIFE'S MISSION TO HUNT DOWN EVERY LAST MEMBER OF THE LEAGUE.
DON'T YOU EVER CALL ME A DISGRACE... I'M A *HERO.* AND I'M WITH *THE REGIME.*
"THIS IS UNACCEPTABLE, CLARK...

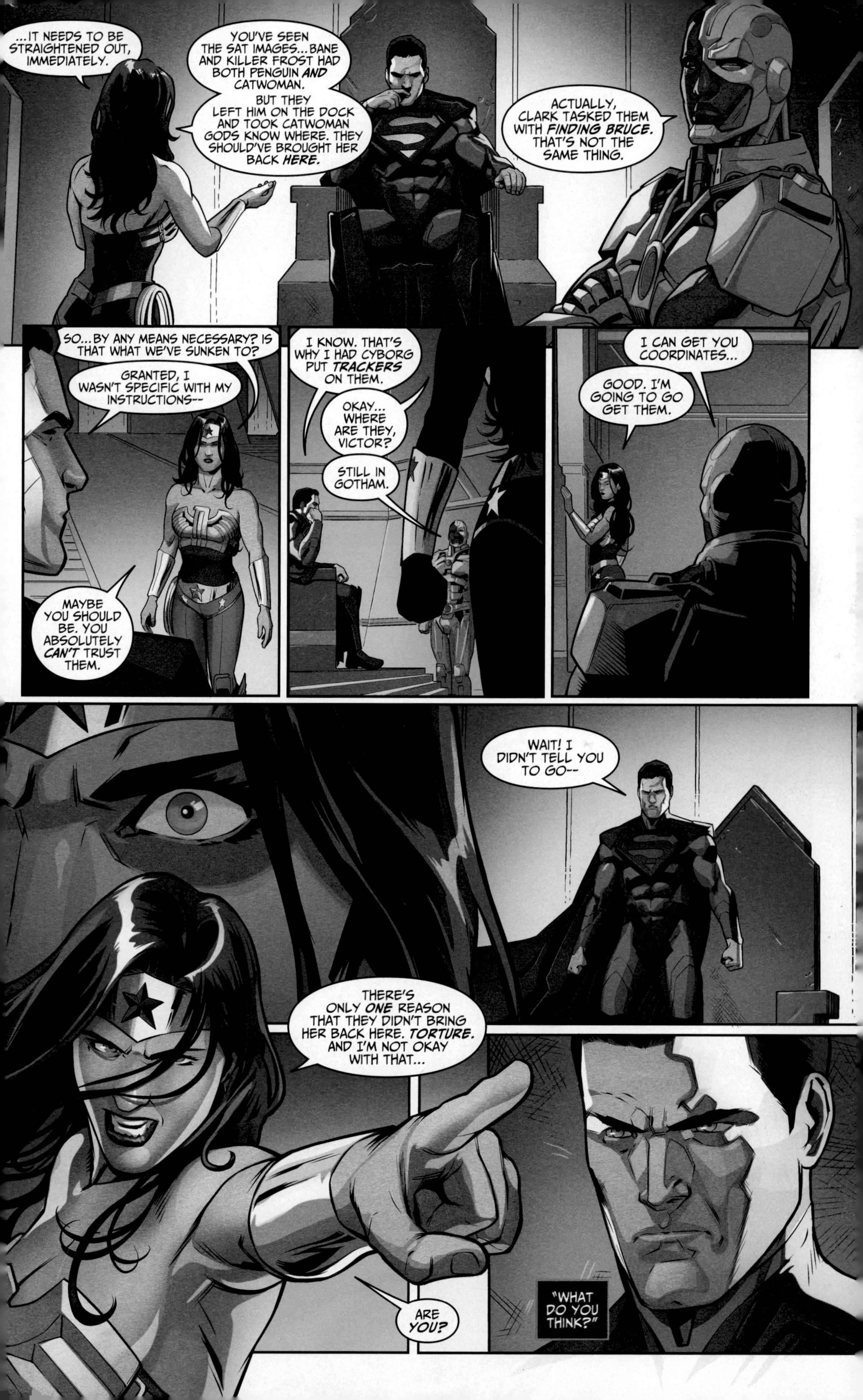
...IT NEEDS TO BE STRAIGHTENED OUT, IMMEDIATELY.
YOU'VE SEEN THE SAT IMAGES...BANE AND KILLER FROST HAD BOTH PENGUIN AND CATWOMAN.
BUT THEY LEFT HIM ON THE DOCK AND TOOK CATWOMAN GODS KNOW WHERE. THEY SHOULD'VE BROUGHT HER BACK HERE.
ACTUALLY, CLARK TASKED THEM WITH FINDING BRUCE. THAT'S NOT THE SAME THING.
SO...BY ANY MEANS NECESSARY? IS THAT WHAT WE'VE SUNKEN TO?
GRANTED, I WASN'T SPECIFIC WITH MY INSTRUCTIONS--
MAYBE YOU SHOULD BE. YOU ABSOLUTELY CAN'T TRUST THEM.
I KNOW. THAT'S WHY I HAD CYBORG PUT TRACKERS ON THEM.
OKAY... WHERE ARE THEY, VICTOR?
STILL IN GOTHAM.
I CAN GET YOU COORDINATES...
GOOD. I'M GOING TO GO GET THEM.
WAIT! I DIDN'T TELL YOU TO GO--
THERE'S ONLY ONE REASON THAT THEY DIDN'T BRING HER BACK HERE. TORTURE. AND I'M NOT OKAY WITH THAT...
ARE YOU?
"WHAT DO YOU THINK?"

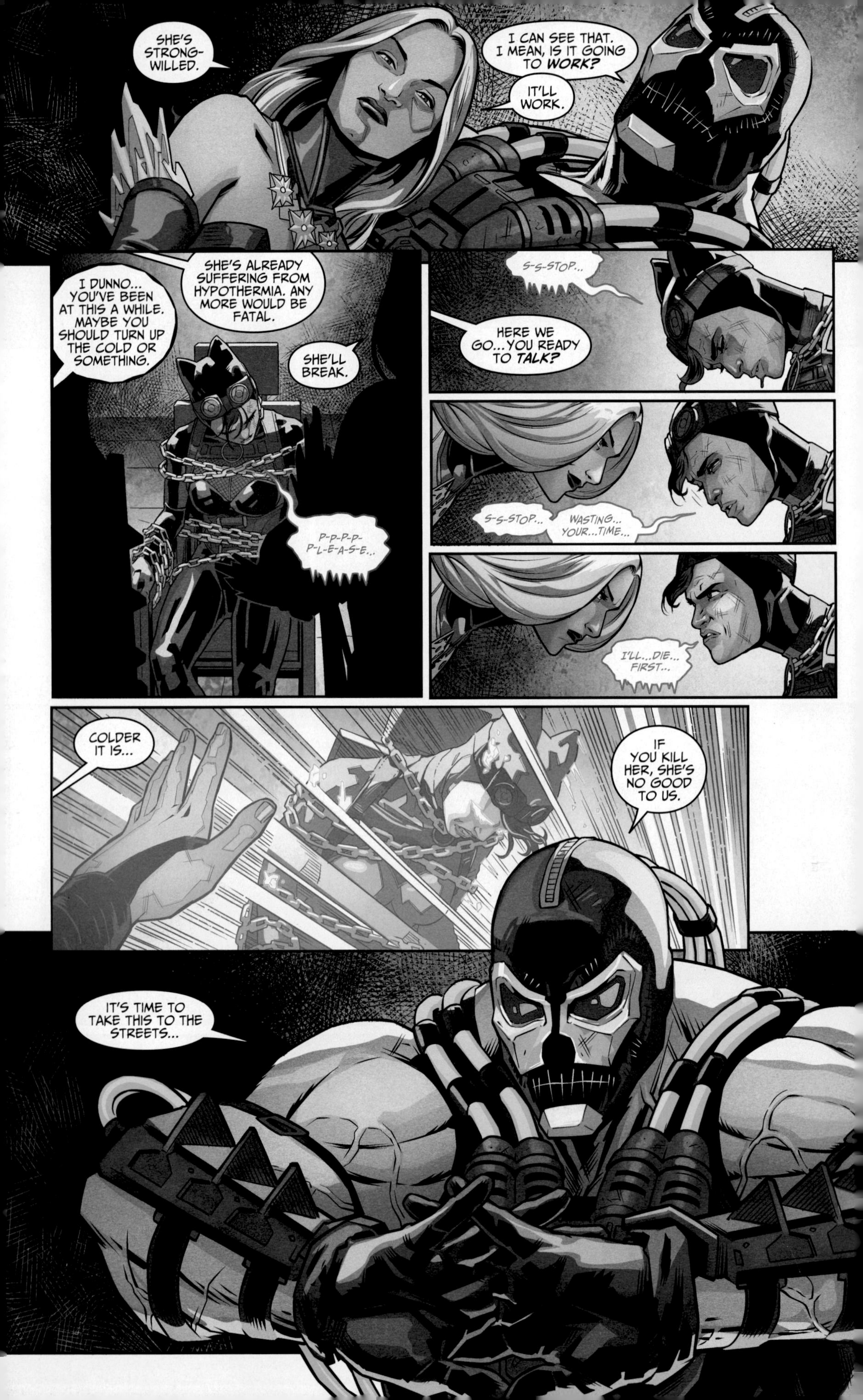

SHE'S STRONG-WILLED.
I CAN SEE THAT. I MEAN, IS IT GOING TO WORK?
IT'LL WORK.
I DUNNO... YOU'VE BEEN AT THIS A WHILE. MAYBE YOU SHOULD TURN UP THE COLD OR SOMETHING.
SHE'S ALREADY SUFFERING FROM HYPOTHERMIA. ANY MORE WOULD BE FATAL.
SHE'LL BREAK.
P-P-P-P P-L-E-A-S-E...
S-S-STOP...
HERE WE GO...YOU READY TO TALK?
S-S-STOP...
WASTING... YOUR...TIME...
I'LL...DIE... FIRST...
COLDER IT IS...
IF YOU KILL HER, SHE'S NO GOOD TO US.
IT'S TIME TO TAKE THIS TO THE STREETS...

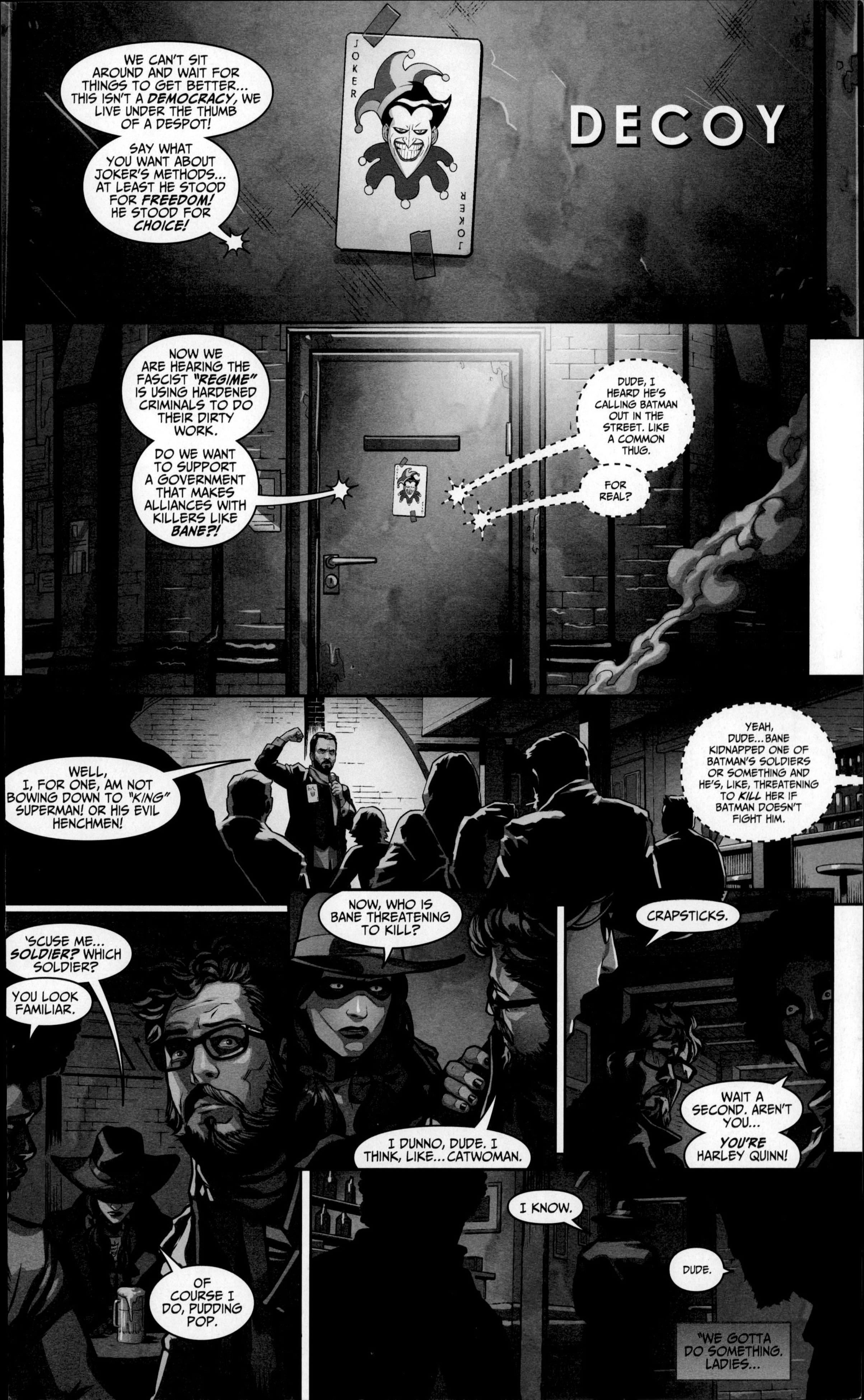
WE CAN'T SIT AROUND AND WAIT FOR THINGS TO GET BETTER... THIS ISN'T A DEMOCRACY, WE LIVE UNDER THE THUMB OF A DESPOT!
SAY WHAT YOU WANT ABOUT JOKER'S METHODS... AT LEAST HE STOOD FOR FREEDOM! HE STOOD FOR CHOICE!
JOKER
JOKER
DECOY
NOW WE ARE HEARING THE FASCIST "REGIME" IS USING HARDENED CRIMINALS TO DO THEIR DIRTY WORK.
DO WE WANT TO SUPPORT A GOVERNMENT THAT MAKES ALLIANCES WITH KILLERS LIKE BANE?!
DUDE, I HEARD HE'S CALLING BATMAN OUT IN THE STREET. LIKE A COMMON THUG.
FOR REAL?
WELL, I, FOR ONE, AM NOT BOWING DOWN TO "KING" SUPERMAN! OR HIS EVIL HENCHMEN!
YEAH, DUDE...BANE KIDNAPPED ONE OF BATMAN'S SOLDIERS OR SOMETHING AND HE'S, LIKE, THREATENING TO KILL HER IF BATMAN DOESN'T FIGHT HIM.
'SCUSE ME... SOLDIER? WHICH SOLDIER?
YOU LOOK FAMILIAR.
NOW, WHO IS BANE THREATENING TO KILL?
I DUNNO, DUDE. I THINK, LIKE...CATWOMAN.
CRAPSTICKS.
WAIT A SECOND. AREN'T YOU... YOU'RE HARLEY QUINN!
OF COURSE I DO, PUDDING POP.
I KNOW.
DUDE.
"WE GOTTA DO SOMETHING. LADIES...

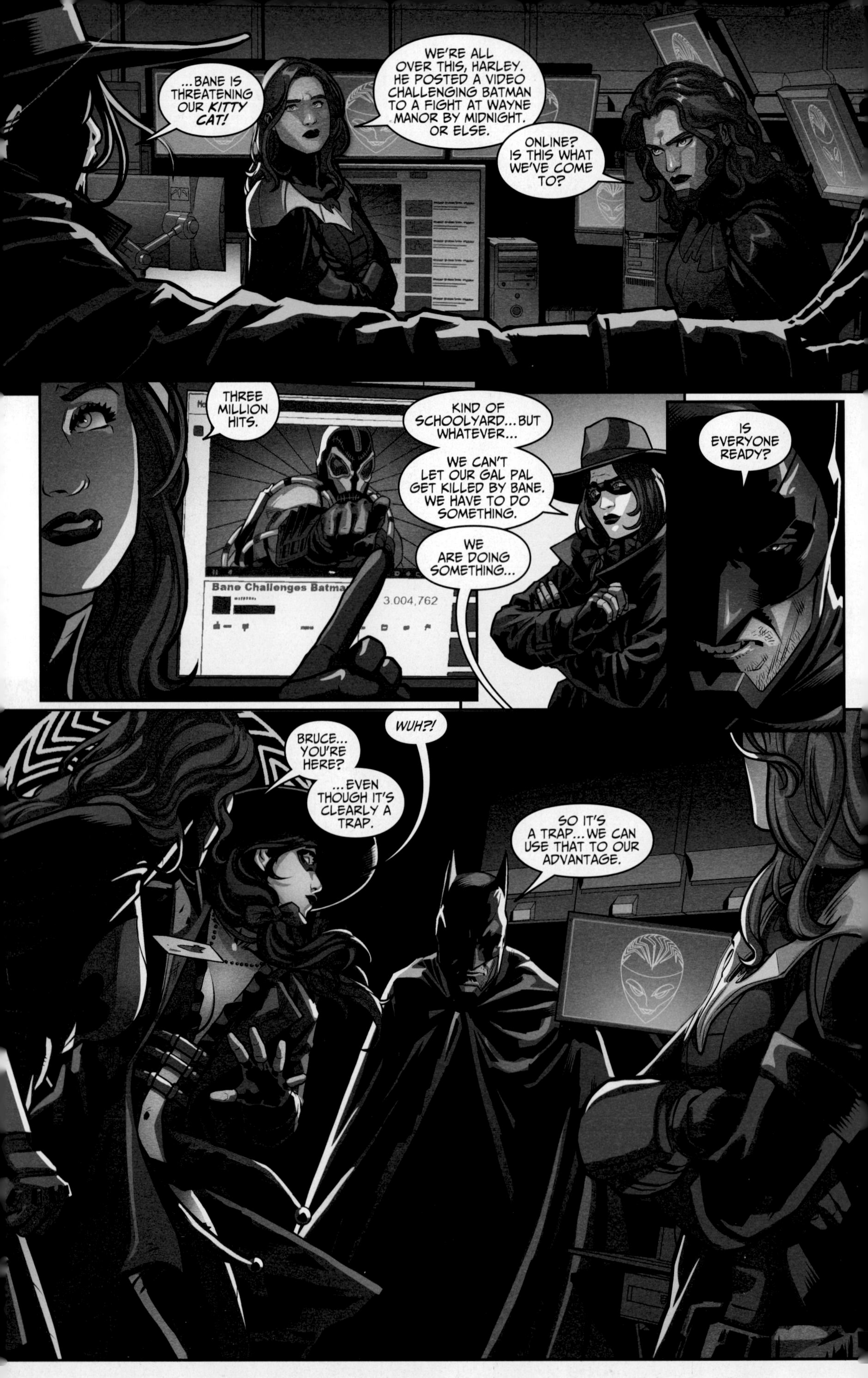
...BANE IS THREATENING OUR KITTY CAT!
WE'RE ALL OVER THIS, HARLEY. HE POSTED A VIDEO CHALLENGING BATMAN TO A FIGHT AT WAYNE MANOR BY MIDNIGHT. OR ELSE.
ONLINE? IS THIS WHAT WE'VE COME TO?
THREE MILLION HITS.
Bane Challenges Batma
3.004,762
KIND OF SCHOOLYARD...BUT WHATEVER...
WE CAN'T LET OUR GAL PAL GET KILLED BY BANE. WE HAVE TO DO SOMETHING.
WE ARE DOING SOMETHING...
IS EVERYONE READY?
BRUCE... YOU'RE HERE?
...EVEN THOUGH IT'S CLEARLY A TRAP.
WUH?!
SO IT'S A TRAP...WE CAN USE THAT TO OUR ADVANTAGE.

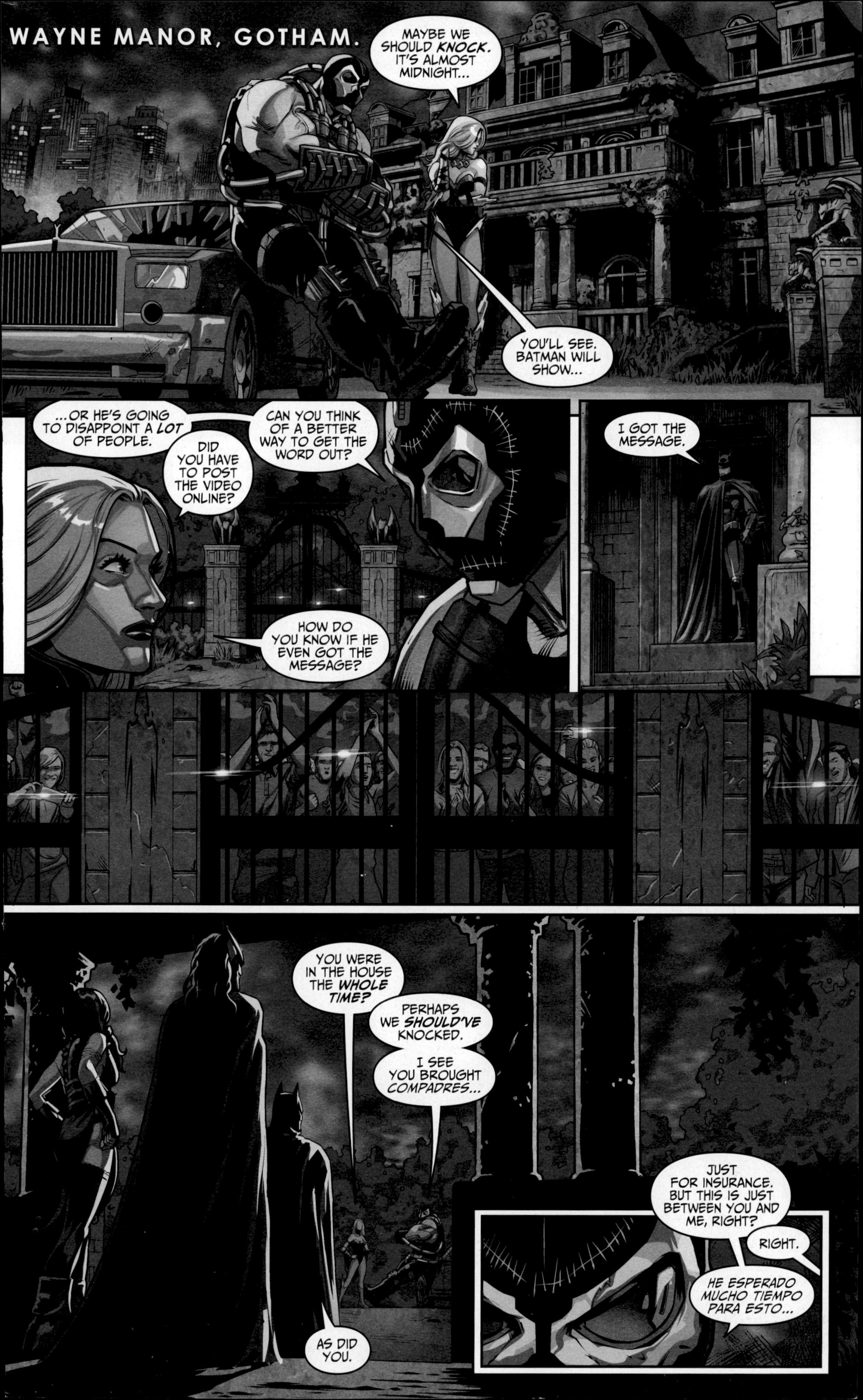
WAYNE MANOR, GOTHAM.
MAYBE WE SHOULD KNOCK. IT'S ALMOST MIDNIGHT...
YOU'LL SEE. BATMAN WILL SHOW...
...OR HE'S GOING TO DISAPPOINT A LOT OF PEOPLE.
DID YOU HAVE TO POST THE VIDEO ONLINE?
CAN YOU THINK OF A BETTER WAY TO GET THE WORD OUT?
HOW DO YOU KNOW IF HE EVEN GOT THE MESSAGE?
I GOT THE MESSAGE.
YOU WERE IN THE HOUSE THE WHOLE TIME?
PERHAPS WE SHOULD'VE KNOCKED.
I SEE YOU BROUGHT COMPADRES...
AS DID YOU.
JUST FOR INSURANCE. BUT THIS IS JUST BETWEEN YOU AND ME, RIGHT?
RIGHT.
HE ESPERADO MUCHO TIEMPO PARA ESTO...

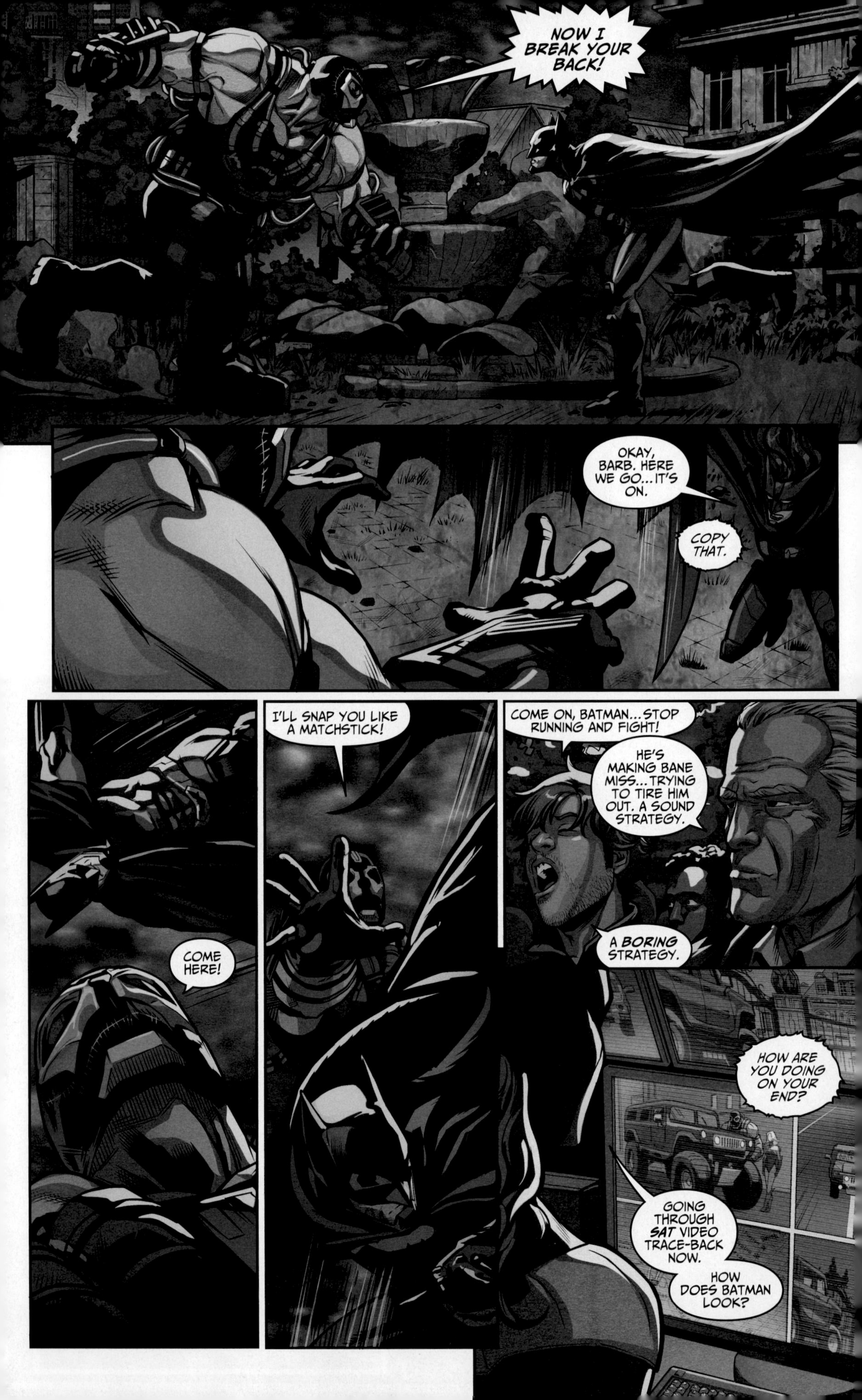
NOW I BREAK YOUR BACK!
OKAY, BARB. HERE WE GO...IT'S ON.
COPY THAT.
COME HERE!
I'LL SNAP YOU LIKE A MATCHSTICK!
COME ON, BATMAN...STOP RUNNING AND FIGHT!
HE'S MAKING BANE MISS...TRYING TO TIRE HIM OUT. A SOUND STRATEGY.
A BORING STRATEGY.
HOW ARE YOU DOING ON YOUR END?
GOING THROUGH SAT VIDEO TRACE-BACK NOW.
HOW DOES BATMAN LOOK?

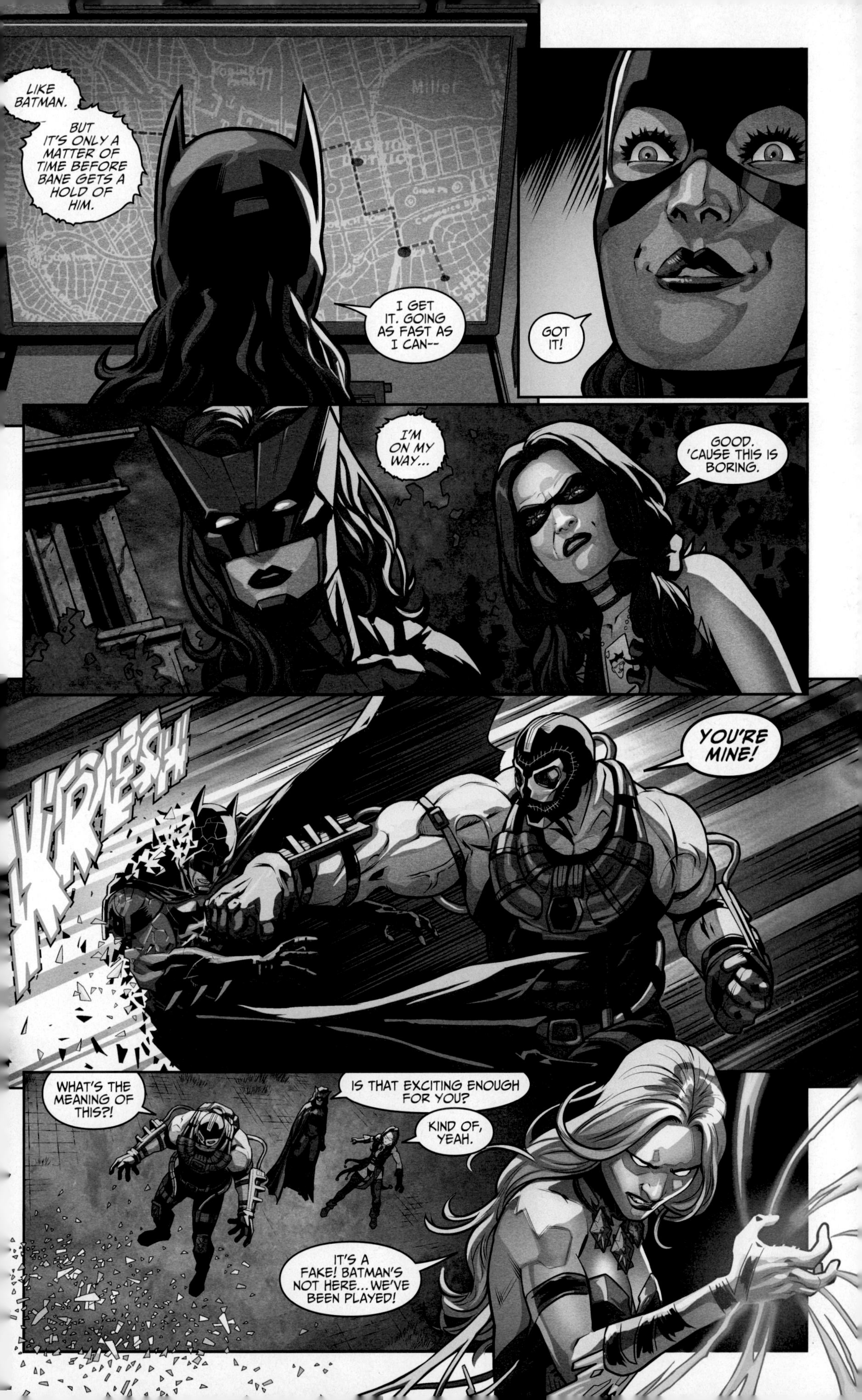
LIKE BATMAN.
BUT IT'S ONLY A MATTER OF TIME BEFORE BANE GETS A HOLD OF HIM.
I GET IT. GOING AS FAST AS I CAN--
GOT IT!
I'M ON MY WAY...
GOOD. 'CAUSE THIS IS BORING.
KRESH!
YOU'RE MINE!
WHAT'S THE MEANING OF THIS?!
IS THAT EXCITING ENOUGH FOR YOU?
KIND OF, YEAH.
IT'S A FAKE! BATMAN'S NOT HERE...WE'VE BEEN PLAYED!

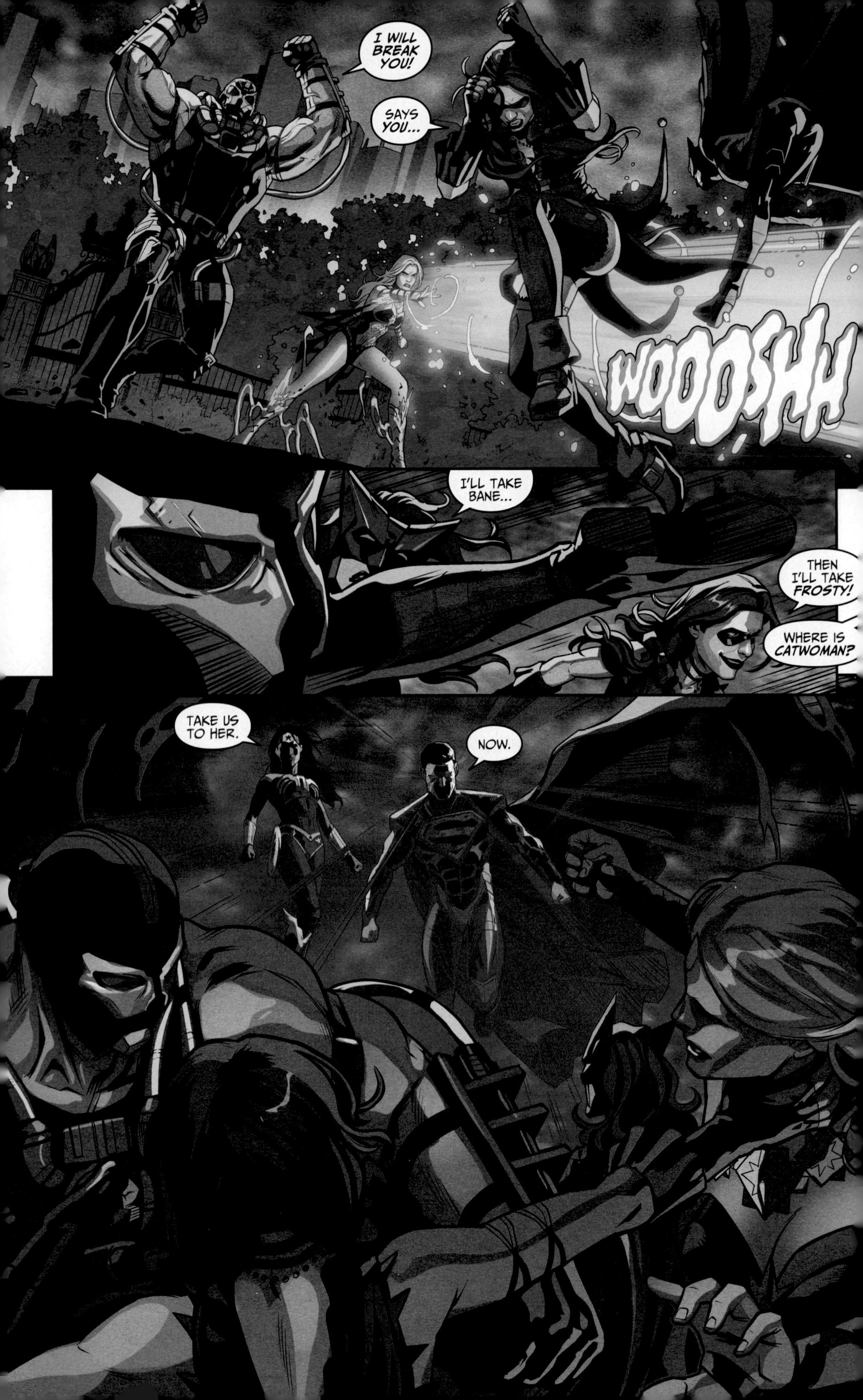
I WILL BREAK YOU!
SAYS YOU...
WOOOSHH
I'LL TAKE BANE...
THEN I'LL TAKE FROSTY!
WHERE IS CATWOMAN?
TAKE US TO HER.
NOW.

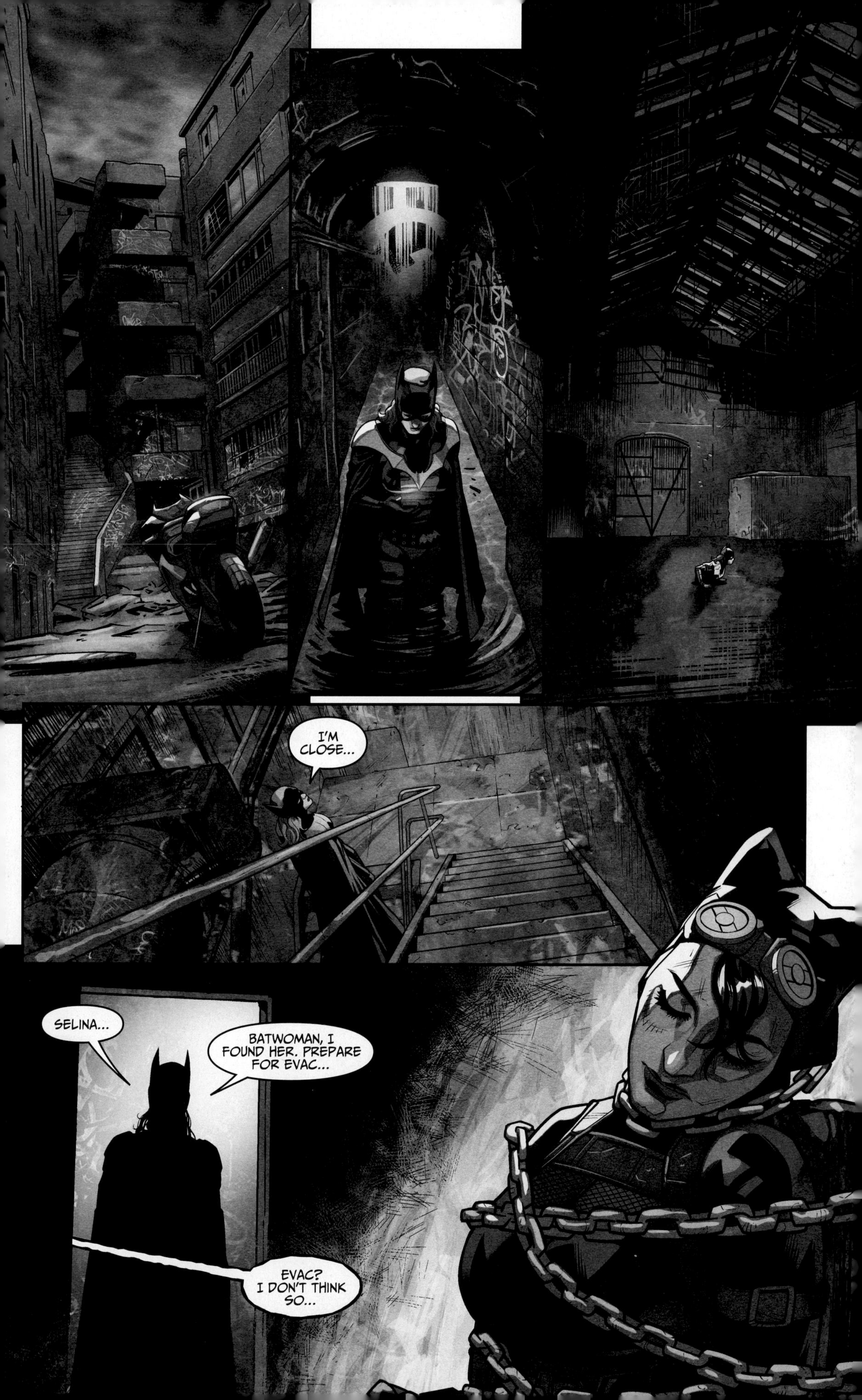
I'M CLOSE...
SELINA...
BATWOMAN, I FOUND HER. PREPARE FOR EVAC...
EVAC? I DON'T THINK SO...

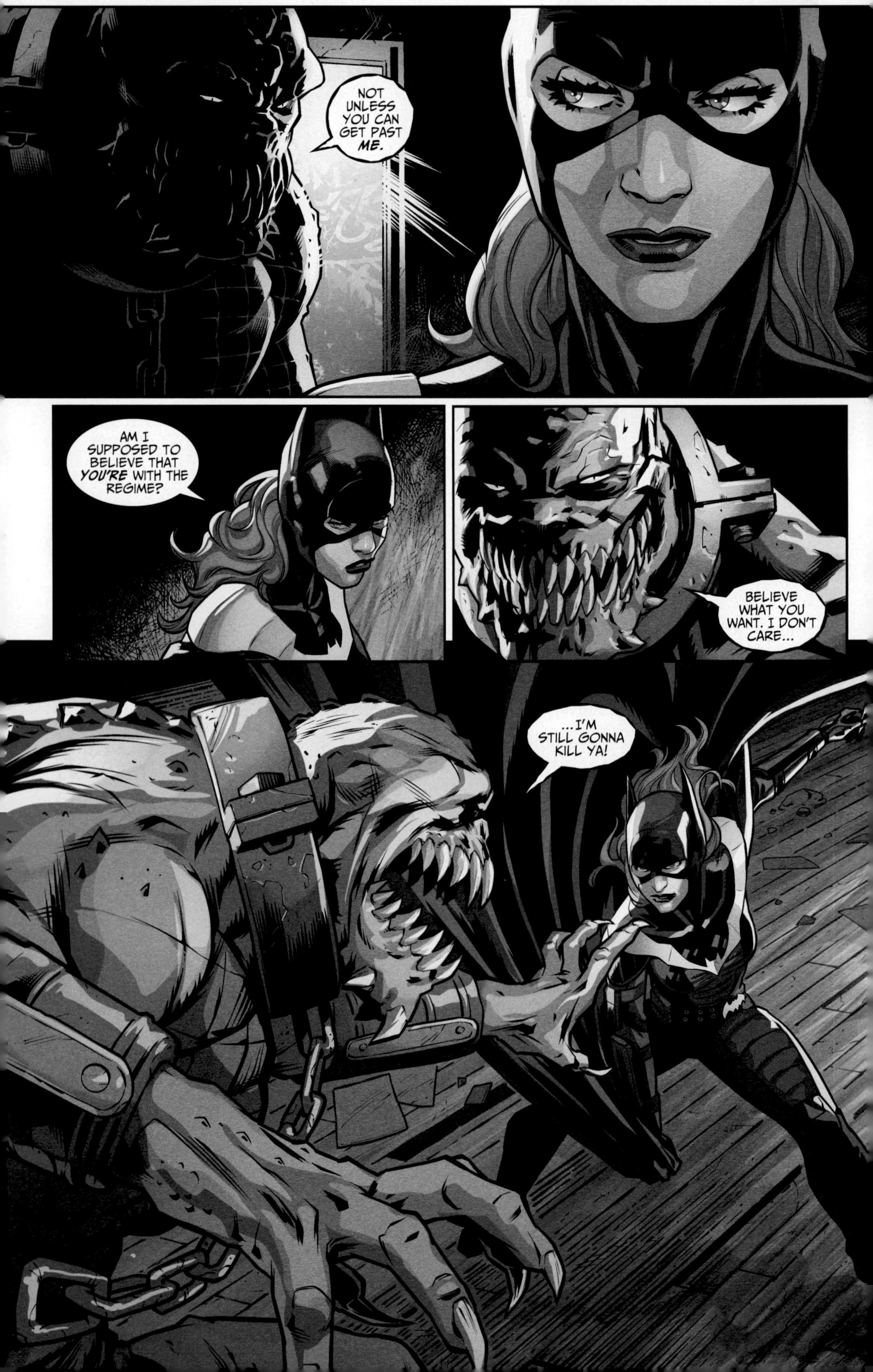
NOT UNLESS YOU CAN GET PAST *ME.*
AM I SUPPOSED TO BELIEVE THAT *YOU'RE* WITH THE REGIME?
BELIEVE WHAT YOU WANT. I DON'T CARE...
...I'M STILL GONNA KILL YA!

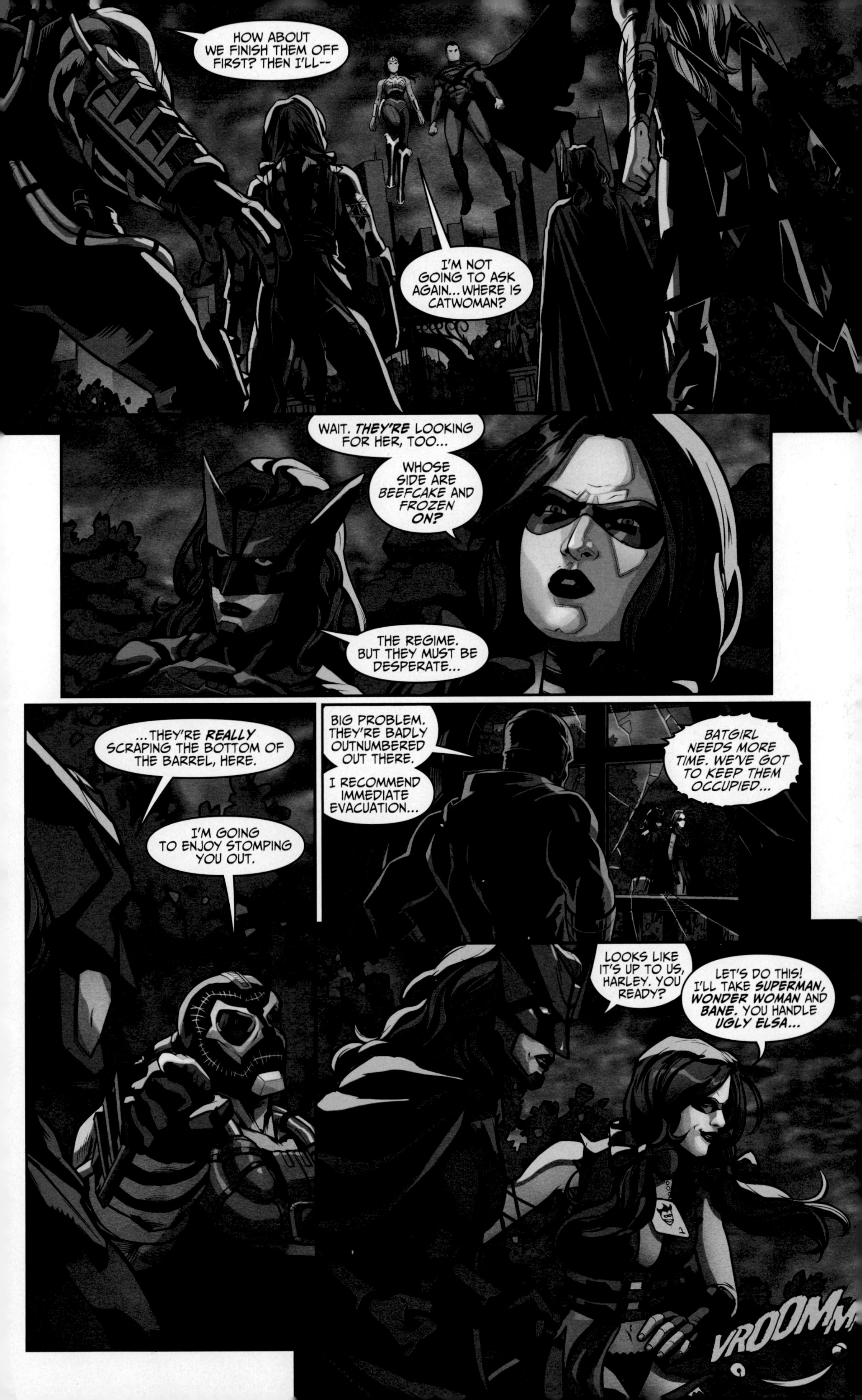
HOW ABOUT WE FINISH THEM OFF FIRST? THEN I'LL--
I'M NOT GOING TO ASK AGAIN...WHERE IS CATWOMAN?
WAIT. THEY'RE LOOKING FOR HER, TOO...
WHOSE SIDE ARE BEEFCAKE AND FROZEN ON?
THE REGIME. BUT THEY MUST BE DESPERATE...
...THEY'RE REALLY SCRAPING THE BOTTOM OF THE BARREL, HERE.
I'M GOING TO ENJOY STOMPING YOU OUT.
BIG PROBLEM. THEY'RE BADLY OUTNUMBERED OUT THERE.
I RECOMMEND IMMEDIATE EVACUATION...
BATGIRL NEEDS MORE TIME. WE'VE GOT TO KEEP THEM OCCUPIED...
LOOKS LIKE IT'S UP TO US, HARLEY. YOU READY?
LET'S DO THIS! I'LL TAKE SUPERMAN, WONDER WOMAN AND BANE. YOU HANDLE UGLY ELSA...
VROOMM

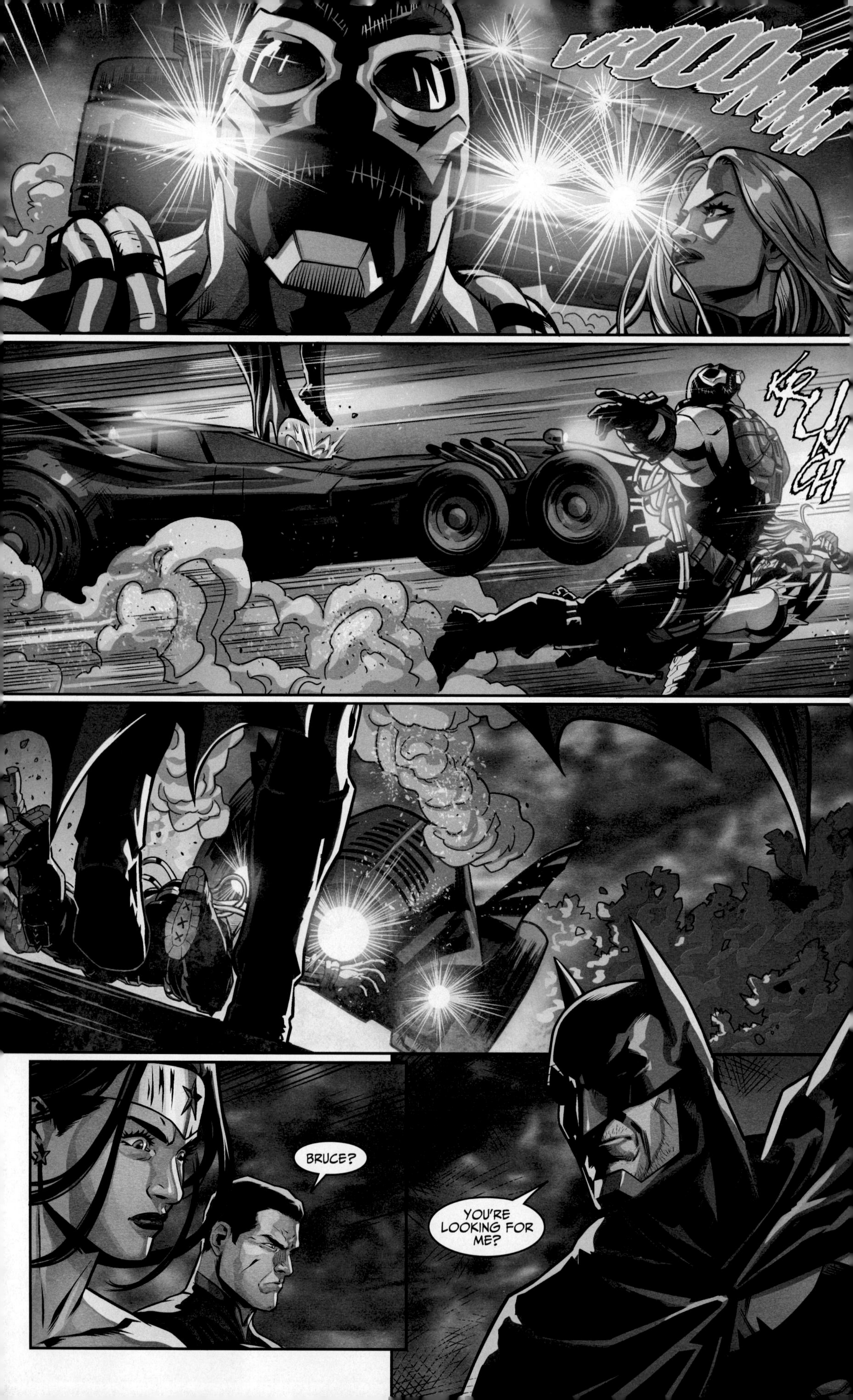
VROOOMM
KRUNCH
BRUCE?
YOU'RE LOOKING FOR ME?

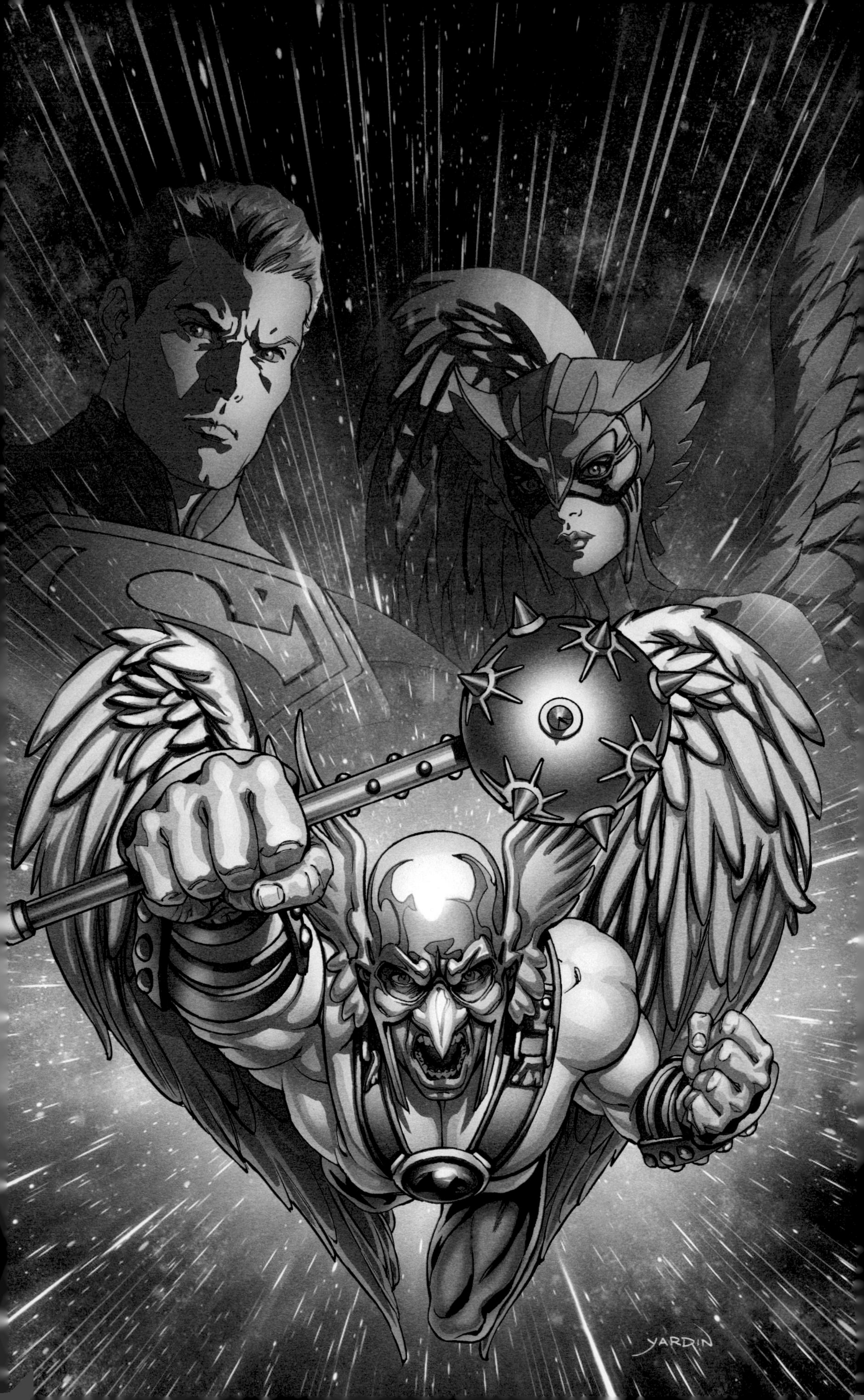
YARDIN

"Street Fight" **Mike S. Miller** Artist **J. Nanjan** Colorist
"Rage" **Iban Coello** Artist **J. Nanjan** Colorist

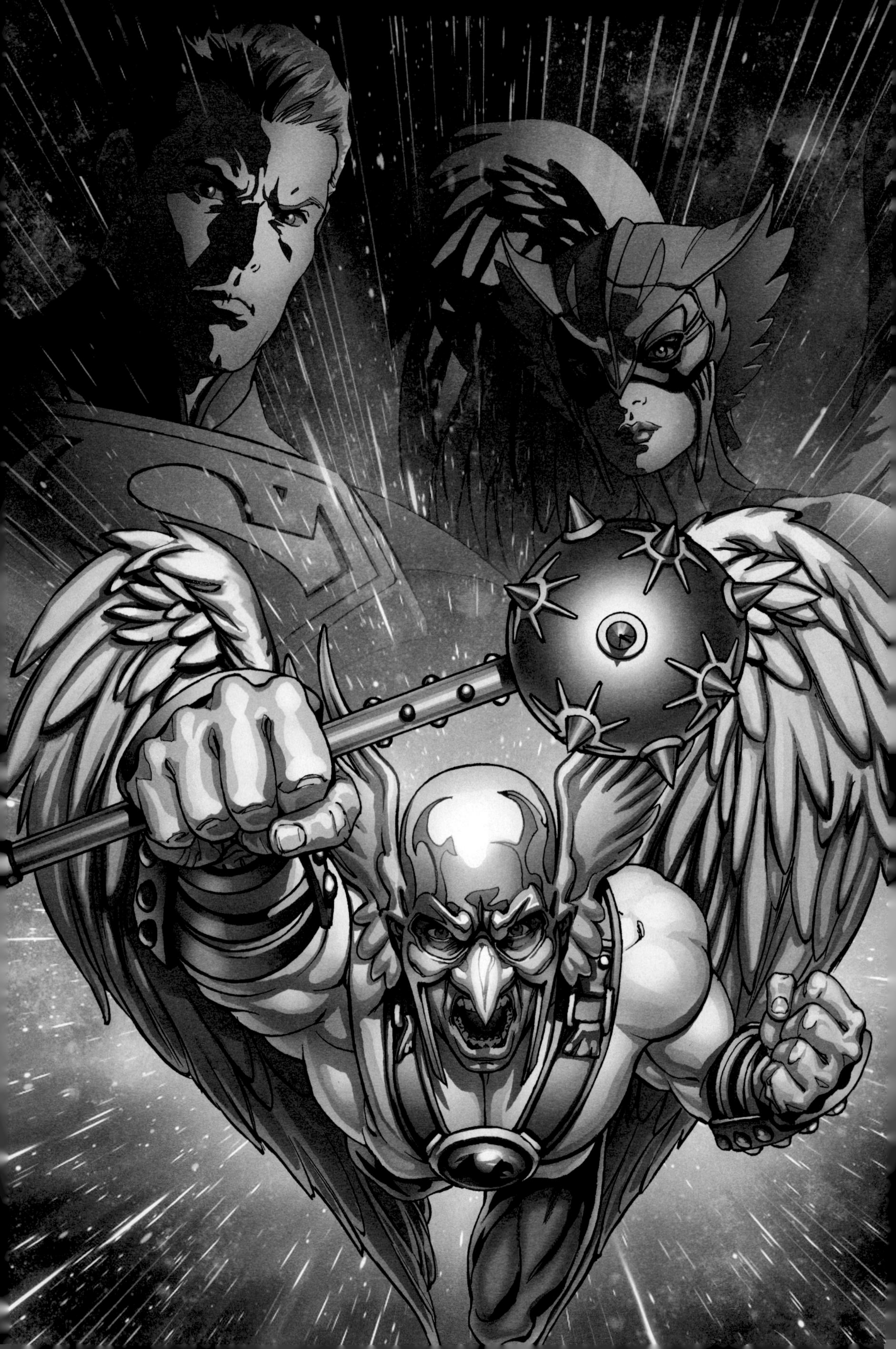

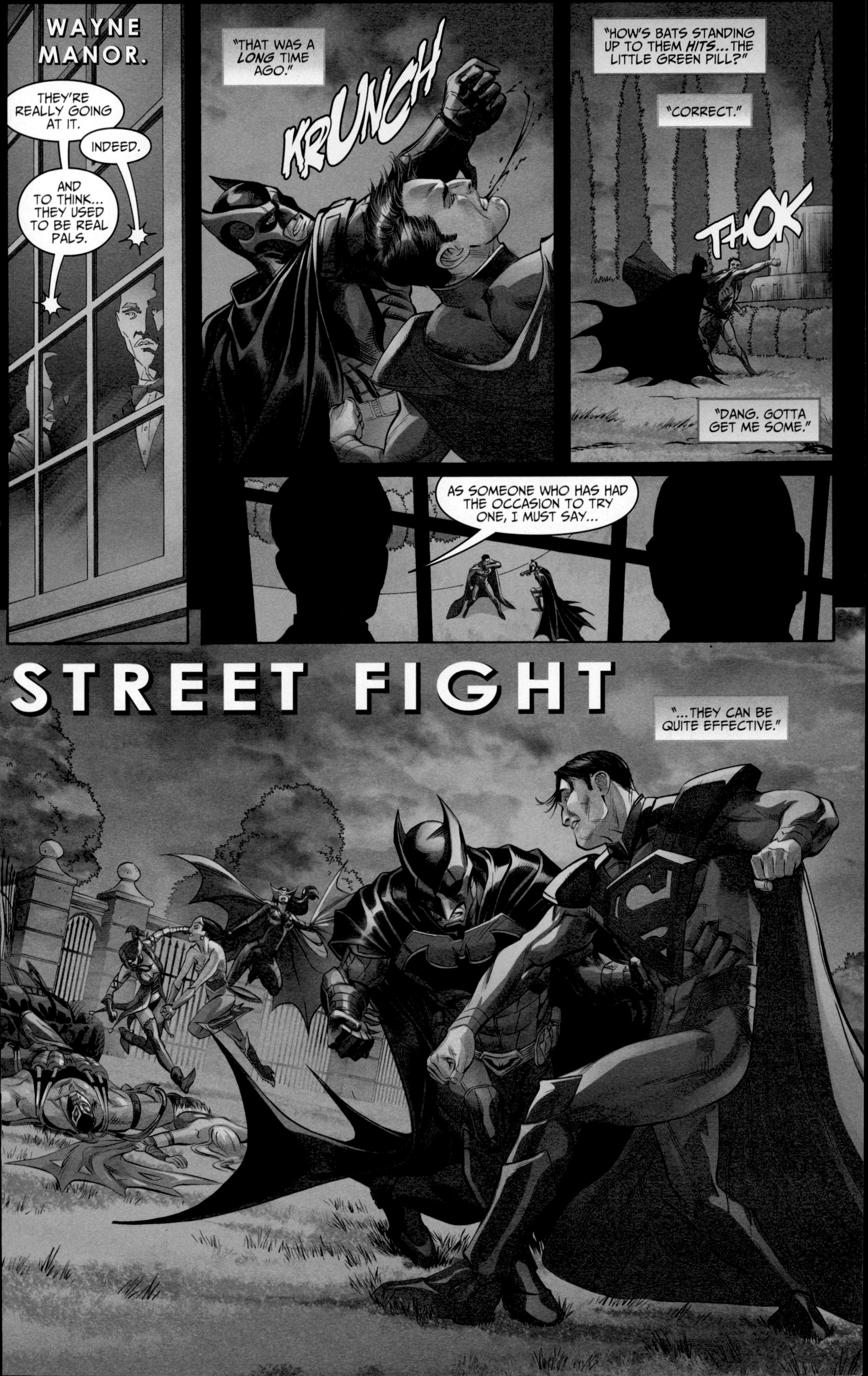

WAYNE MANOR.
THEY'RE REALLY GOING AT IT.
INDEED.
AND TO THINK... THEY USED TO BE REAL PALS.
"THAT WAS A LONG TIME AGO."
KRUNCH
"HOW'S BATS STANDING UP TO THEM HITS... THE LITTLE GREEN PILL?"
"CORRECT."
THOK
"DANG. GOTTA GET ME SOME."
AS SOMEONE WHO HAS HAD THE OCCASION TO TRY ONE, I MUST SAY...
STREET FIGHT
"...THEY CAN BE QUITE EFFECTIVE."

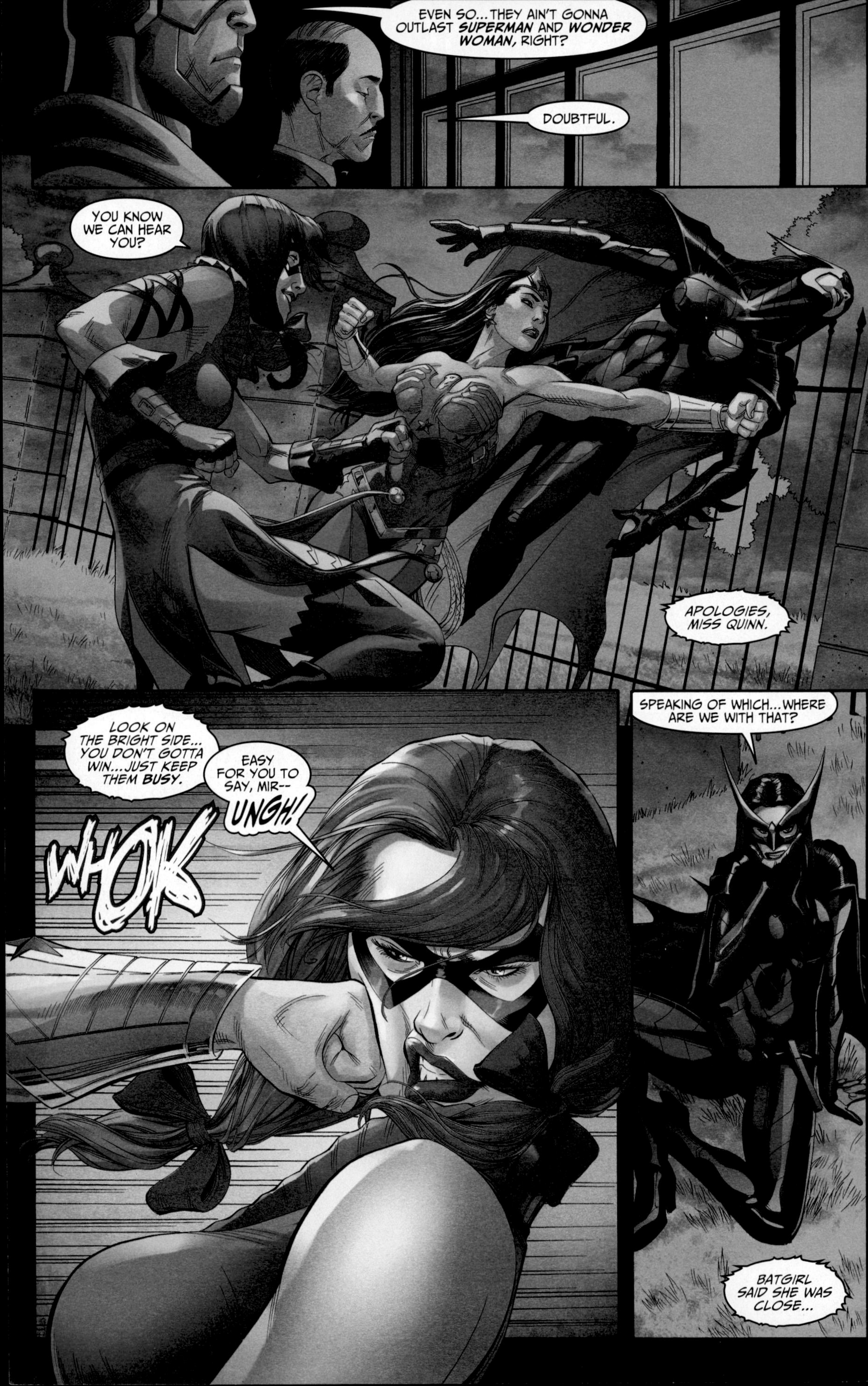
EVEN SO... THEY AIN'T GONNA OUTLAST **SUPERMAN** AND **WONDER WOMAN**, RIGHT?
DOUBTFUL.
YOU KNOW WE CAN HEAR YOU?
APOLOGIES, MISS QUINN.
LOOK ON THE BRIGHT SIDE... YOU DON'T GOTTA WIN... JUST KEEP THEM **BUSY**.
EASY FOR YOU TO SAY, MIR--
UNGH!
WHOK
SPEAKING OF WHICH... WHERE ARE WE WITH THAT?
BATGIRL SAID SHE WAS CLOSE...

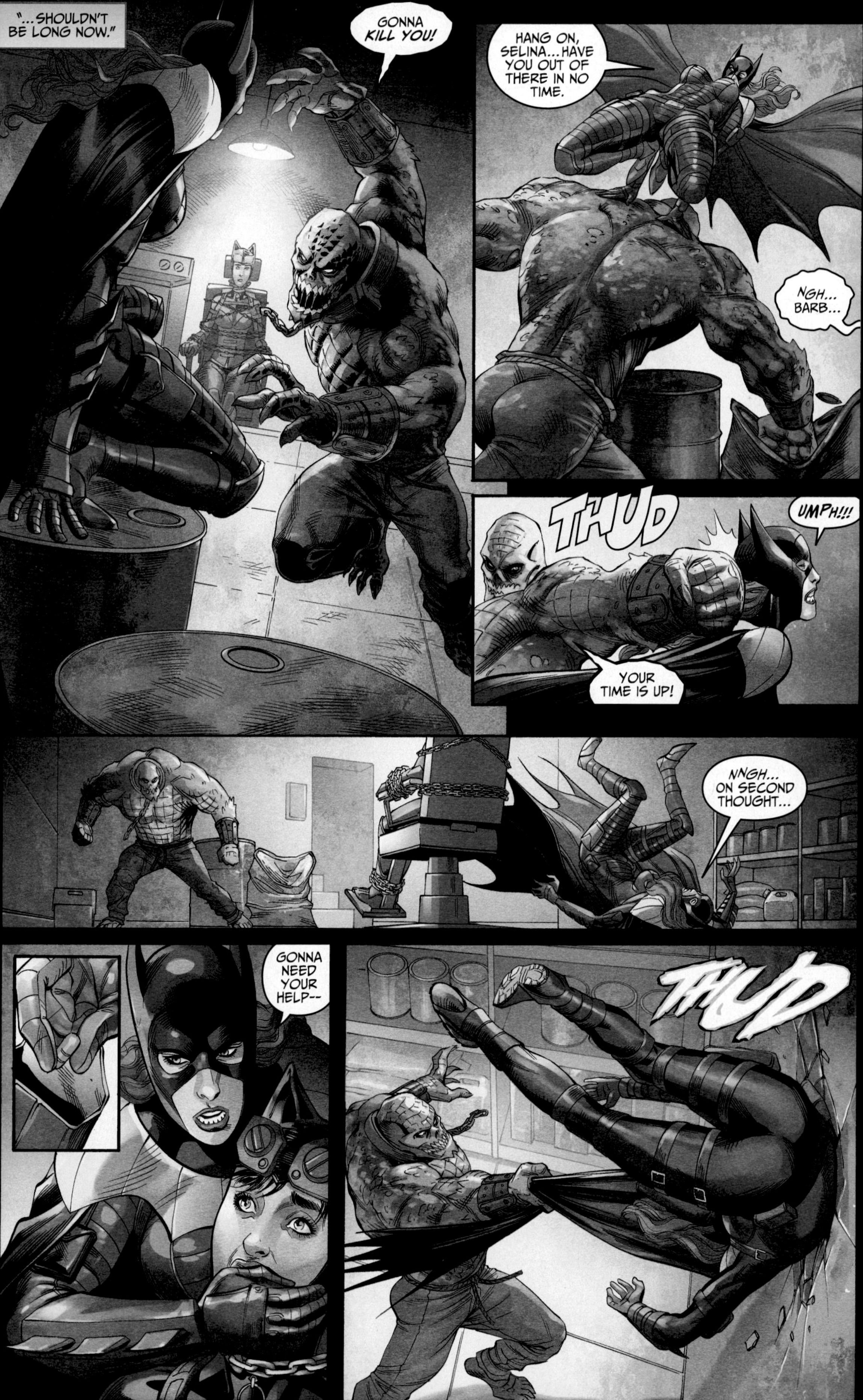
"...SHOULDN'T BE LONG NOW."
GONNA KILL YOU!
HANG ON, SELINA...HAVE YOU OUT OF THERE IN NO TIME.
NGH... BARB...
THUD
UMPH!!!
YOUR TIME IS UP!
NNGH... ON SECOND THOUGHT...
GONNA NEED YOUR HELP--
THUD

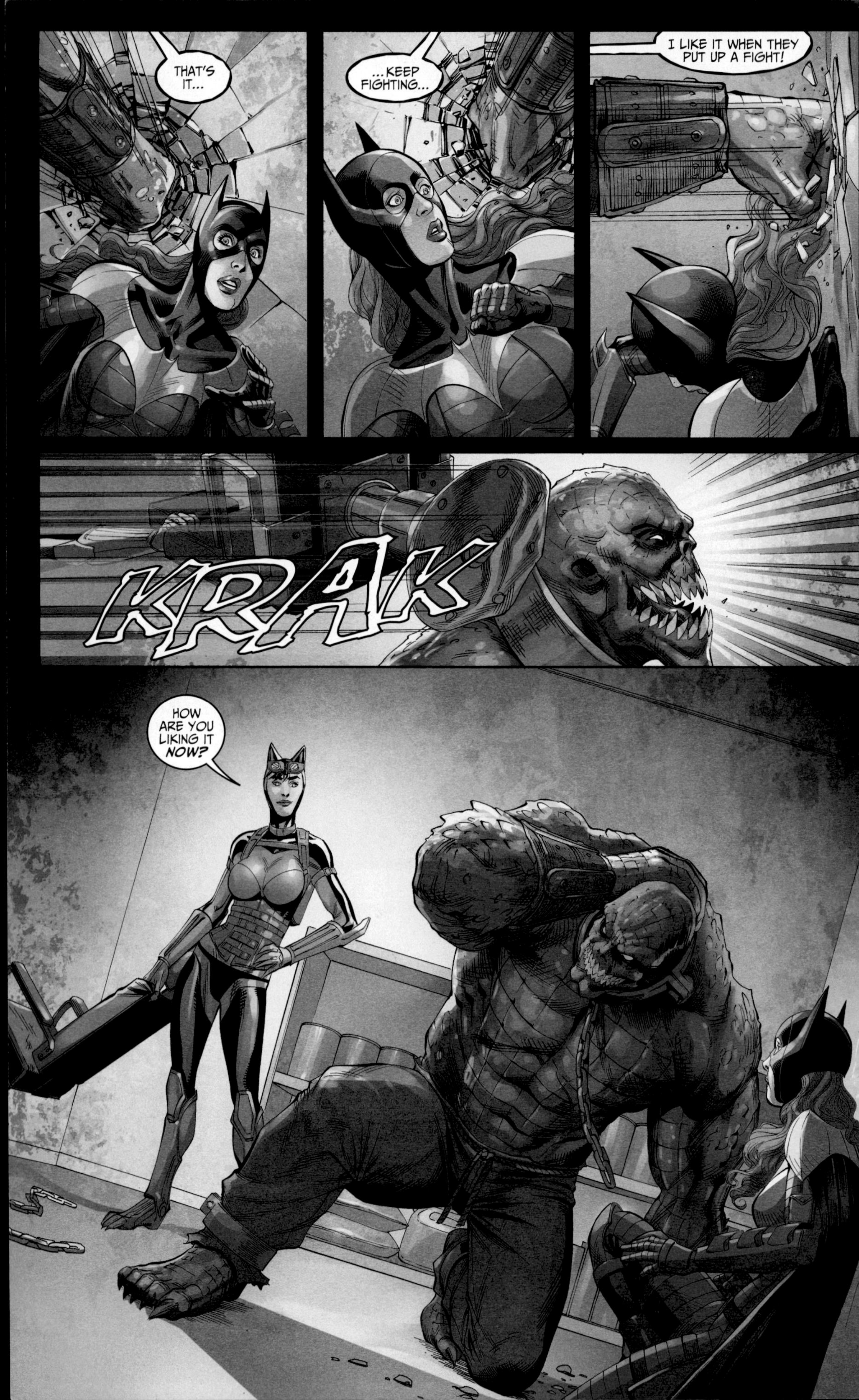
THAT'S IT...
...KEEP FIGHTING...
I LIKE IT WHEN THEY PUT UP A FIGHT!
KRAK
HOW ARE YOU LIKING IT *NOW?*

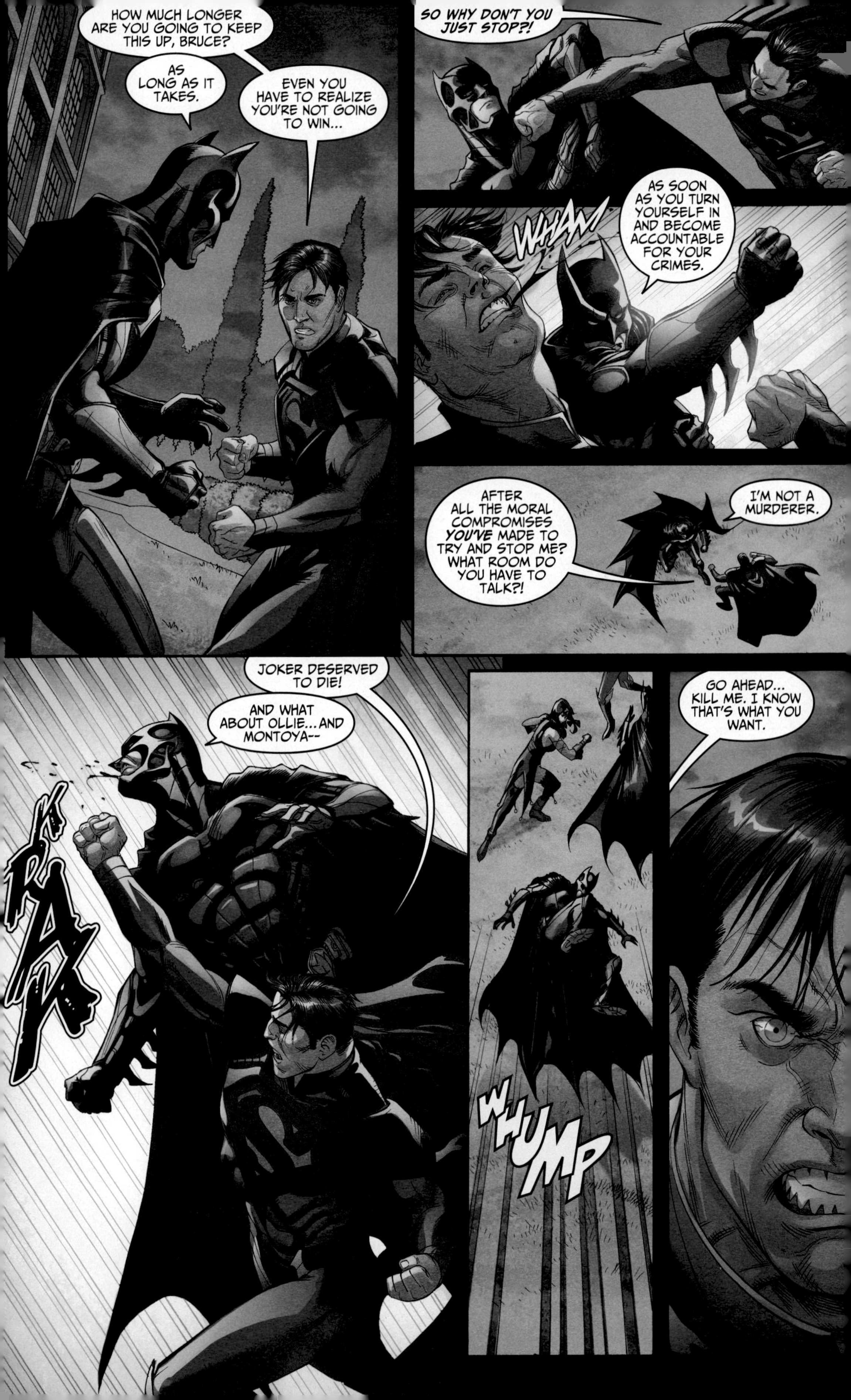
HOW MUCH LONGER ARE YOU GOING TO KEEP THIS UP, BRUCE?
AS LONG AS IT TAKES.
EVEN YOU HAVE TO REALIZE YOU'RE NOT GOING TO WIN...
SO WHY DON'T YOU JUST STOP?!
WHAM
AS SOON AS YOU TURN YOURSELF IN AND BECOME ACCOUNTABLE FOR YOUR CRIMES.
AFTER ALL THE MORAL COMPROMISES YOU'VE MADE TO TRY AND STOP ME? WHAT ROOM DO YOU HAVE TO TALK?!
I'M NOT A MURDERER.
JOKER DESERVED TO DIE!
AND WHAT ABOUT OLLIE...AND MONTOYA--
KRAK
WHUMP
GO AHEAD... KILL ME. I KNOW THAT'S WHAT YOU WANT.

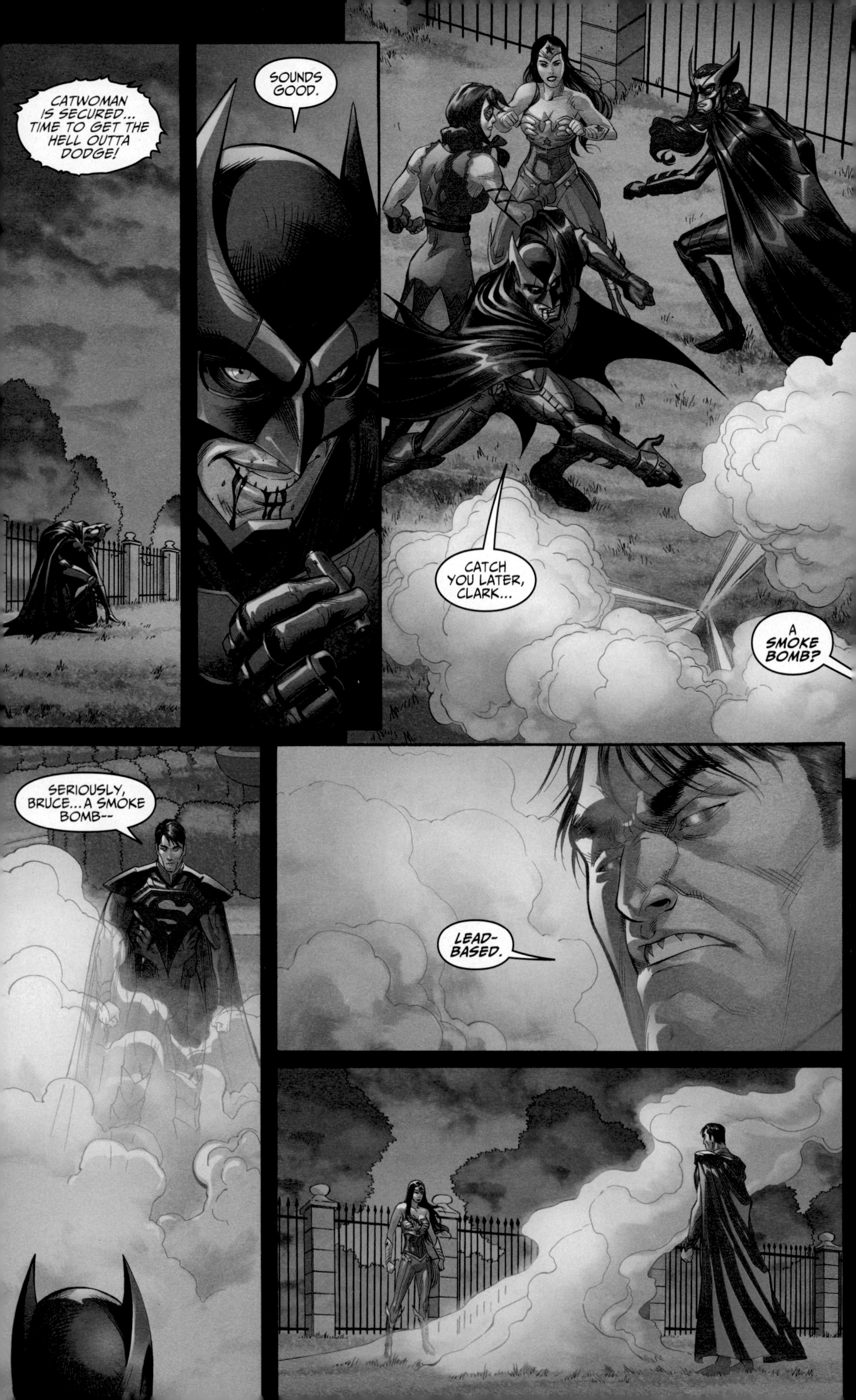
CATWOMAN IS SECURED... TIME TO GET THE HELL OUTTA DODGE!
SOUNDS GOOD.
CATCH YOU LATER, CLARK...
A SMOKE BOMB?
SERIOUSLY, BRUCE...A SMOKE BOMB--
LEAD-BASED.

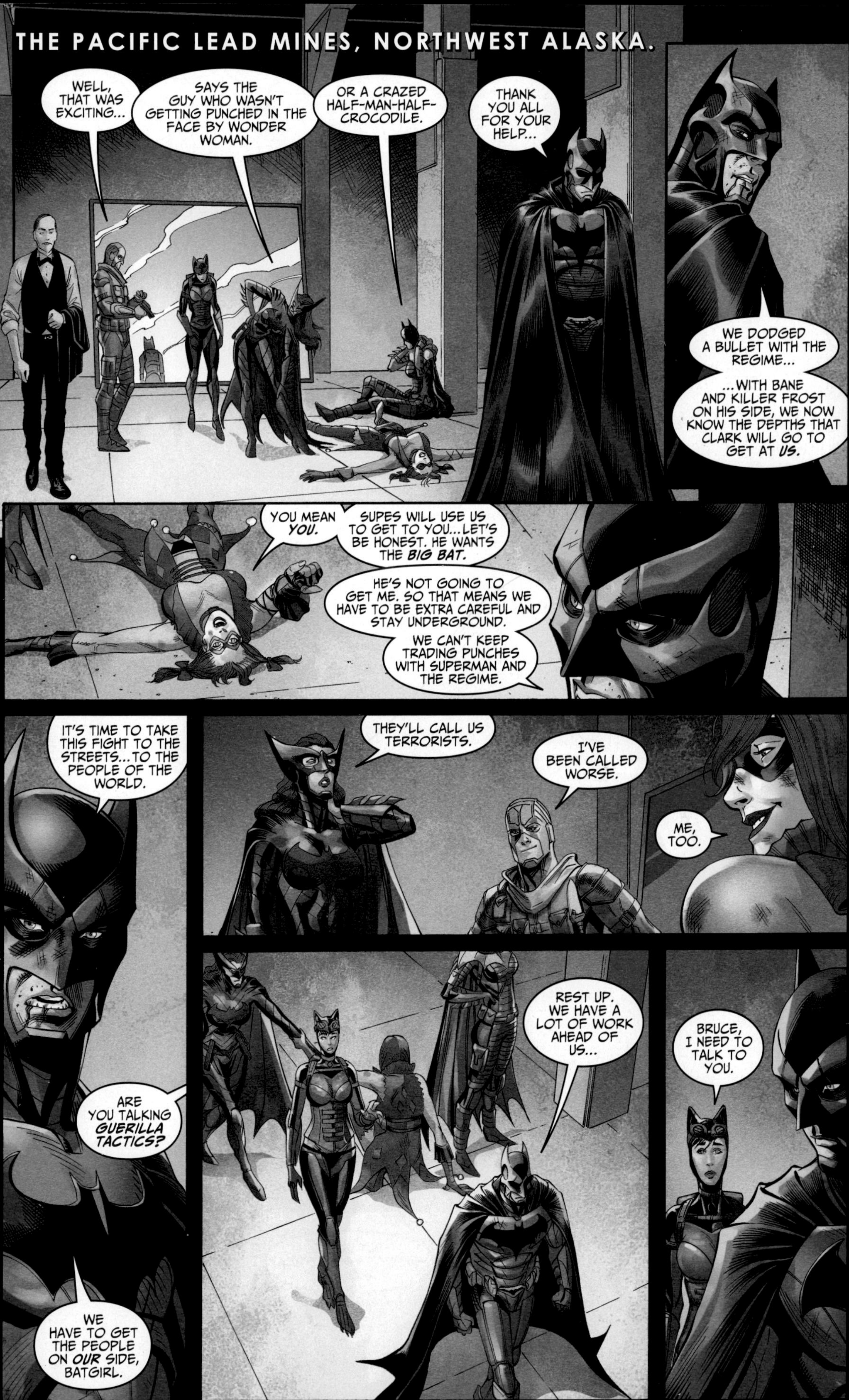
THE PACIFIC LEAD MINES, NORTHWEST ALASKA.
WELL, THAT WAS EXCITING...
SAYS THE GUY WHO WASN'T GETTING PUNCHED IN THE FACE BY WONDER WOMAN.
OR A CRAZED HALF-MAN-HALF-CROCODILE.
THANK YOU ALL FOR YOUR HELP...
WE DODGED A BULLET WITH THE REGIME...
...WITH BANE AND KILLER FROST ON HIS SIDE, WE NOW KNOW THE DEPTHS THAT CLARK WILL GO TO GET AT US.
YOU MEAN YOU.
SUPES WILL USE US TO GET TO YOU...LET'S BE HONEST. HE WANTS THE BIG BAT.
HE'S NOT GOING TO GET ME. SO THAT MEANS WE HAVE TO BE EXTRA CAREFUL AND STAY UNDERGROUND.
WE CAN'T KEEP TRADING PUNCHES WITH SUPERMAN AND THE REGIME.
IT'S TIME TO TAKE THIS FIGHT TO THE STREETS...TO THE PEOPLE OF THE WORLD.
ARE YOU TALKING GUERILLA TACTICS?
WE HAVE TO GET THE PEOPLE ON OUR SIDE, BATGIRL.
THEY'LL CALL US TERRORISTS.
I'VE BEEN CALLED WORSE.
ME, TOO.
REST UP. WE HAVE A LOT OF WORK AHEAD OF US...
BRUCE, I NEED TO TALK TO YOU.

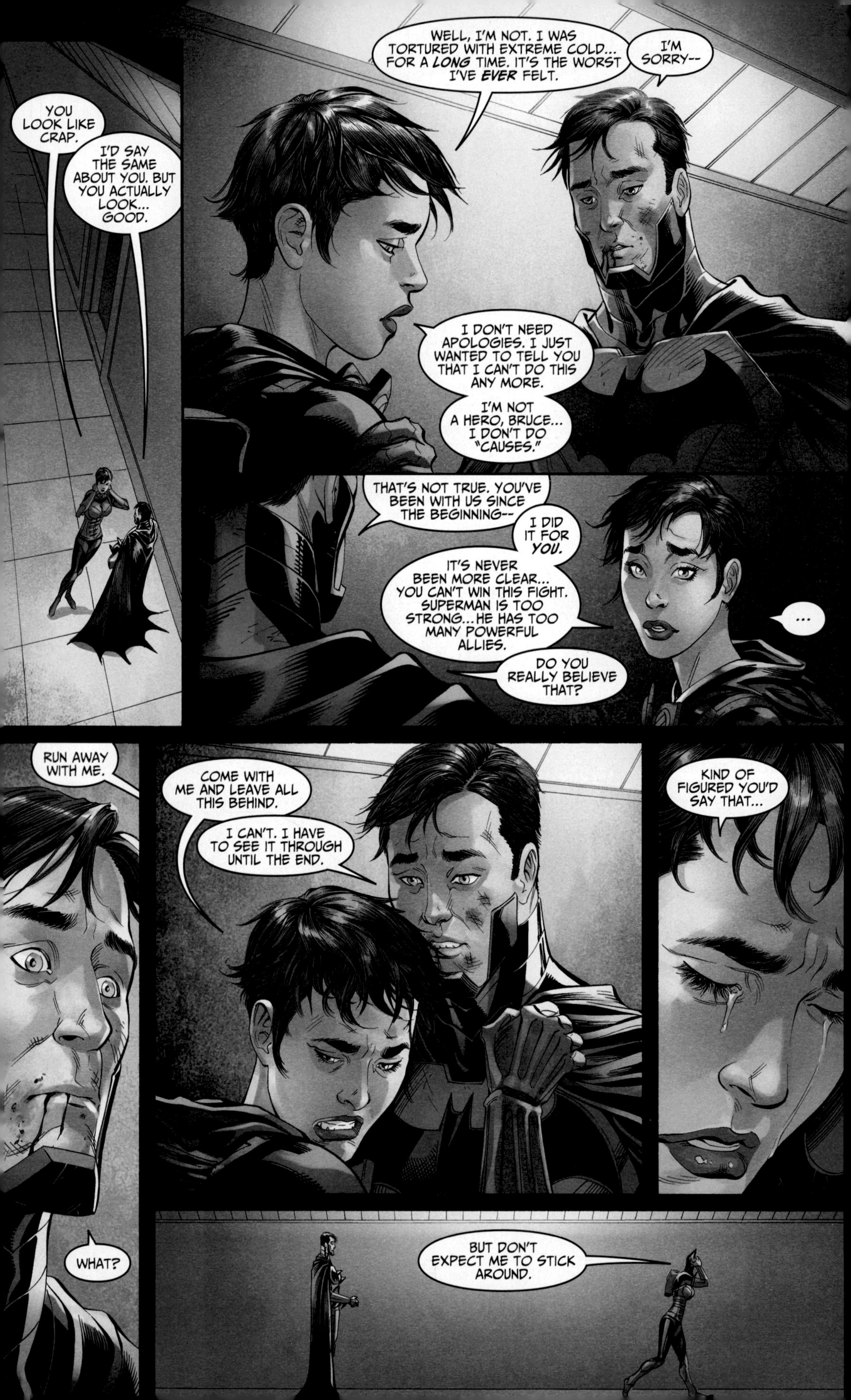
YOU LOOK LIKE CRAP.
I'D SAY THE SAME ABOUT YOU. BUT YOU ACTUALLY LOOK... GOOD.
WELL, I'M NOT. I WAS TORTURED WITH EXTREME COLD... FOR A LONG TIME. IT'S THE WORST I'VE EVER FELT.
I'M SORRY--
I DON'T NEED APOLOGIES. I JUST WANTED TO TELL YOU THAT I CAN'T DO THIS ANY MORE.
I'M NOT A HERO, BRUCE... I DON'T DO "CAUSES."
THAT'S NOT TRUE. YOU'VE BEEN WITH US SINCE THE BEGINNING--
I DID IT FOR YOU.
IT'S NEVER BEEN MORE CLEAR... YOU CAN'T WIN THIS FIGHT. SUPERMAN IS TOO STRONG...HE HAS TOO MANY POWERFUL ALLIES.
DO YOU REALLY BELIEVE THAT?
...
RUN AWAY WITH ME.
WHAT?
COME WITH ME AND LEAVE ALL THIS BEHIND.
I CAN'T. I HAVE TO SEE IT THROUGH UNTIL THE END.
KIND OF FIGURED YOU'D SAY THAT...
BUT DON'T EXPECT ME TO STICK AROUND.

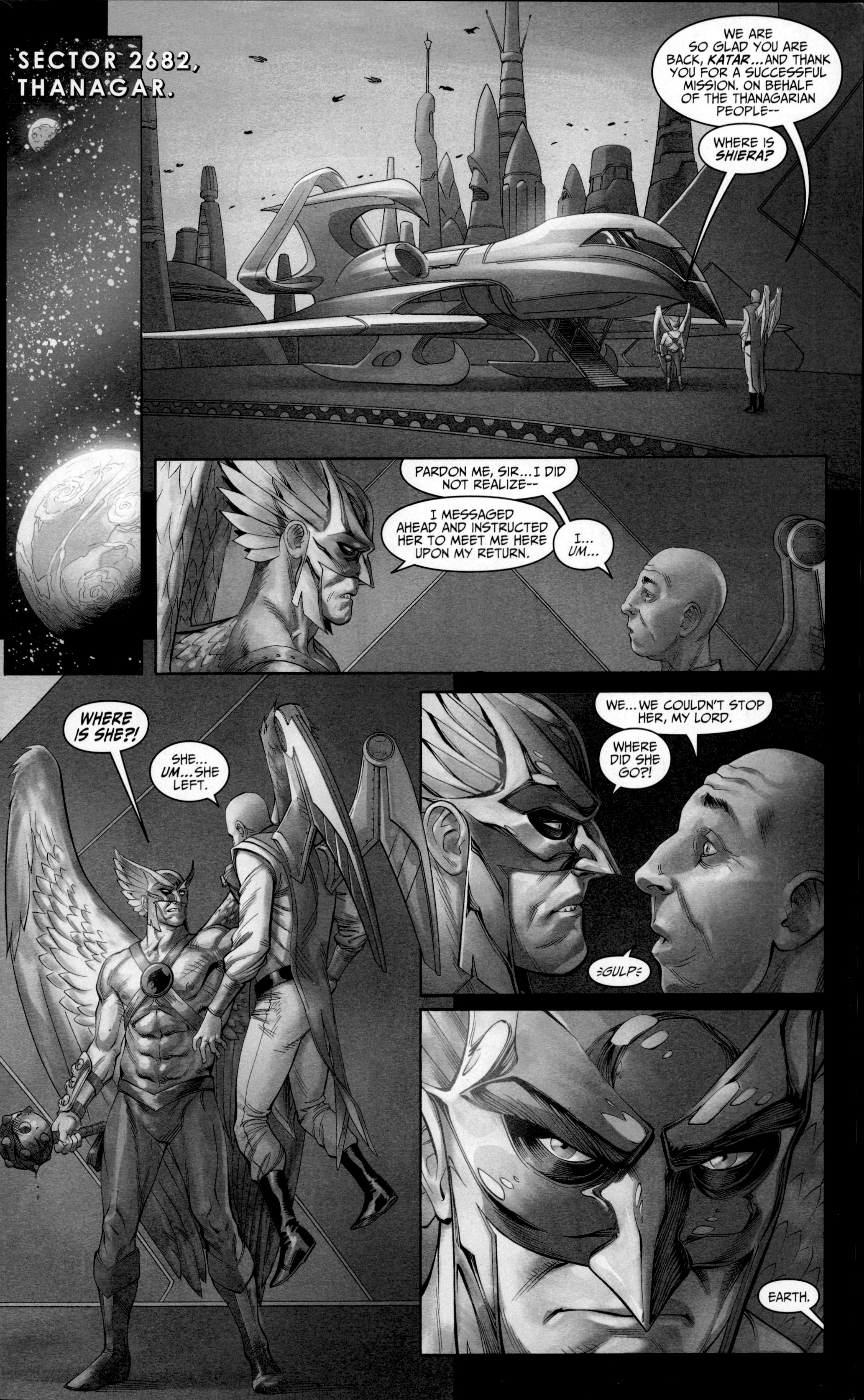
SECTOR 2682, THANAGAR.
WE ARE SO GLAD YOU ARE BACK, KATAR...AND THANK YOU FOR A SUCCESSFUL MISSION. ON BEHALF OF THE THANAGARIAN PEOPLE--
WHERE IS SHIERA?
PARDON ME, SIR...I DID NOT REALIZE--
I MESSAGED AHEAD AND INSTRUCTED HER TO MEET ME HERE UPON MY RETURN.
I... UM...
WHERE IS SHE?!
SHE... UM...SHE LEFT.
WE...WE COULDN'T STOP HER, MY LORD.
WHERE DID SHE GO?!
GULP
EARTH.

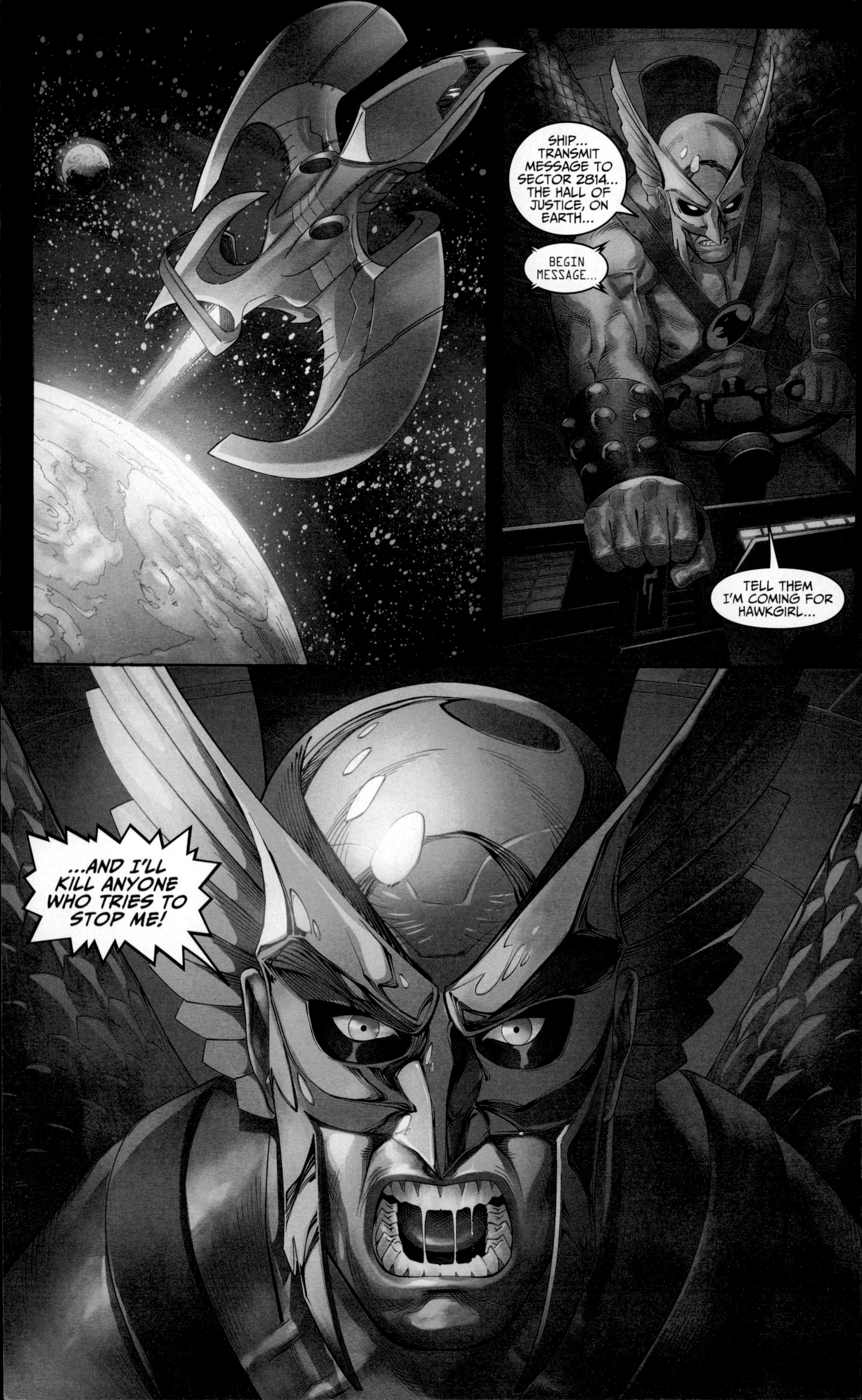
SHIP... TRANSMIT MESSAGE TO SECTOR 2814... THE HALL OF JUSTICE, ON EARTH...
BEGIN MESSAGE...
TELL THEM I'M COMING FOR HAWKGIRL...
...AND I'LL KILL ANYONE WHO TRIES TO STOP ME!

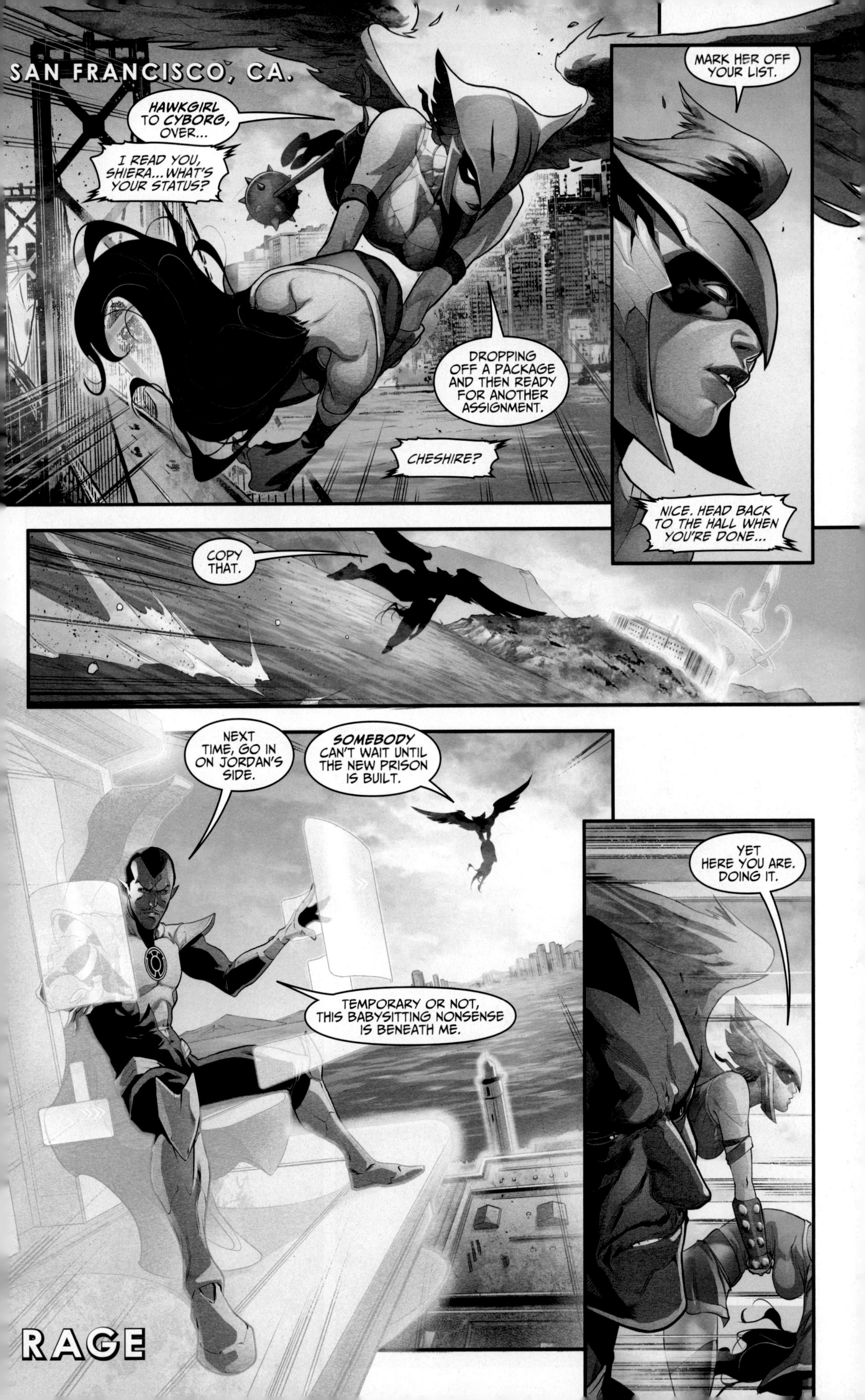
SAN FRANCISCO, CA.
HAWKGIRL TO CYBORG, OVER...
I READ YOU, SHIERA...WHAT'S YOUR STATUS?
DROPPING OFF A PACKAGE AND THEN READY FOR ANOTHER ASSIGNMENT.
CHESHIRE?
MARK HER OFF YOUR LIST.
NICE. HEAD BACK TO THE HALL WHEN YOU'RE DONE...
COPY THAT.
NEXT TIME, GO IN ON JORDAN'S SIDE.
SOMEBODY CAN'T WAIT UNTIL THE NEW PRISON IS BUILT.
TEMPORARY OR NOT, THIS BABYSITTING NONSENSE IS BENEATH ME.
YET HERE YOU ARE. DOING IT.
RAGE

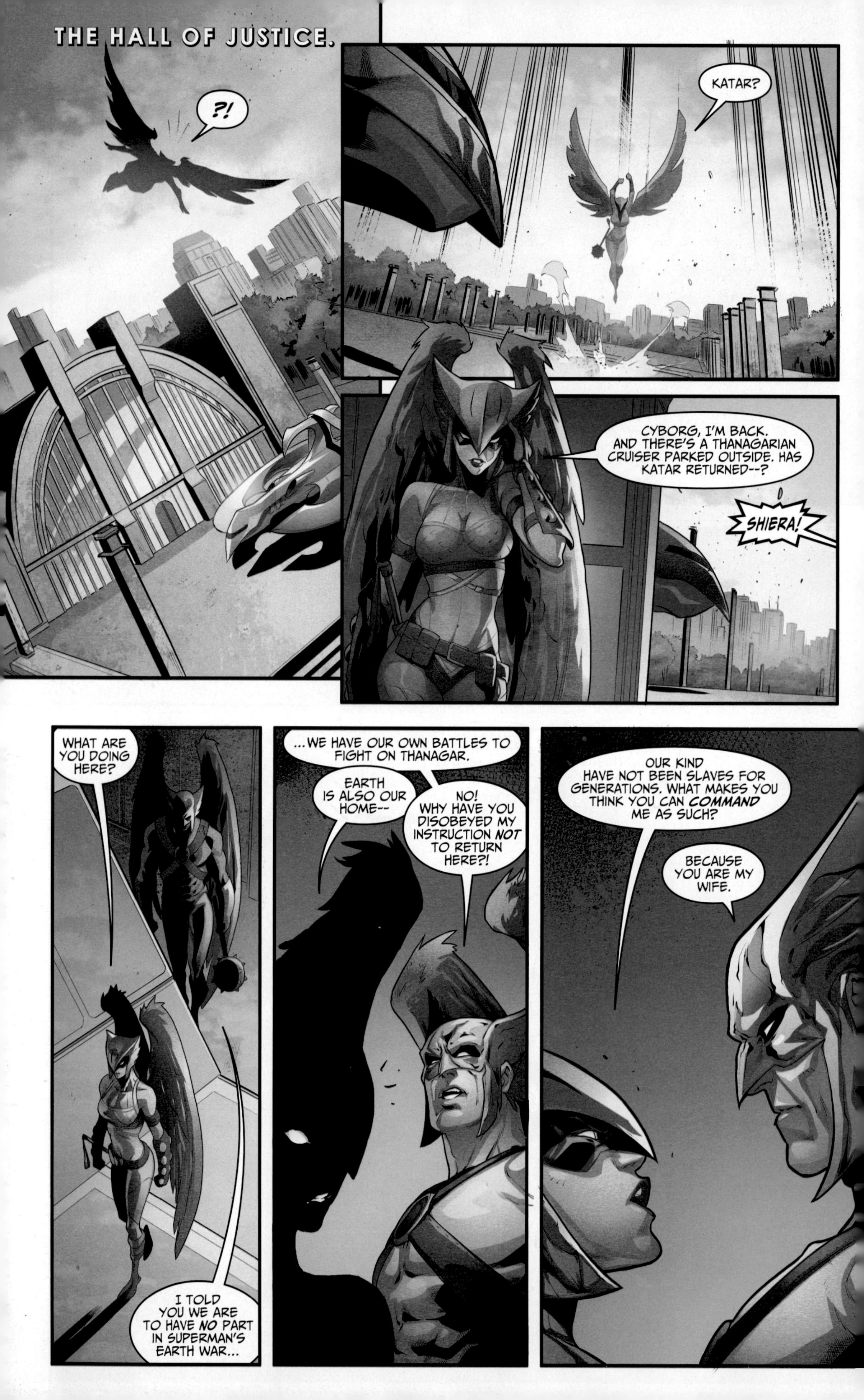
THE HALL OF JUSTICE.
?!
KATAR?
CYBORG, I'M BACK. AND THERE'S A THANAGARIAN CRUISER PARKED OUTSIDE. HAS KATAR RETURNED--?
SHIERA!
WHAT ARE YOU DOING HERE?
I TOLD YOU WE ARE TO HAVE NO PART IN SUPERMAN'S EARTH WAR...
...WE HAVE OUR OWN BATTLES TO FIGHT ON THANAGAR.
EARTH IS ALSO OUR HOME--
NO! WHY HAVE YOU DISOBEYED MY INSTRUCTION NOT TO RETURN HERE?!
OUR KIND HAVE NOT BEEN SLAVES FOR GENERATIONS. WHAT MAKES YOU THINK YOU CAN COMMAND ME AS SUCH?
BECAUSE YOU ARE MY WIFE.

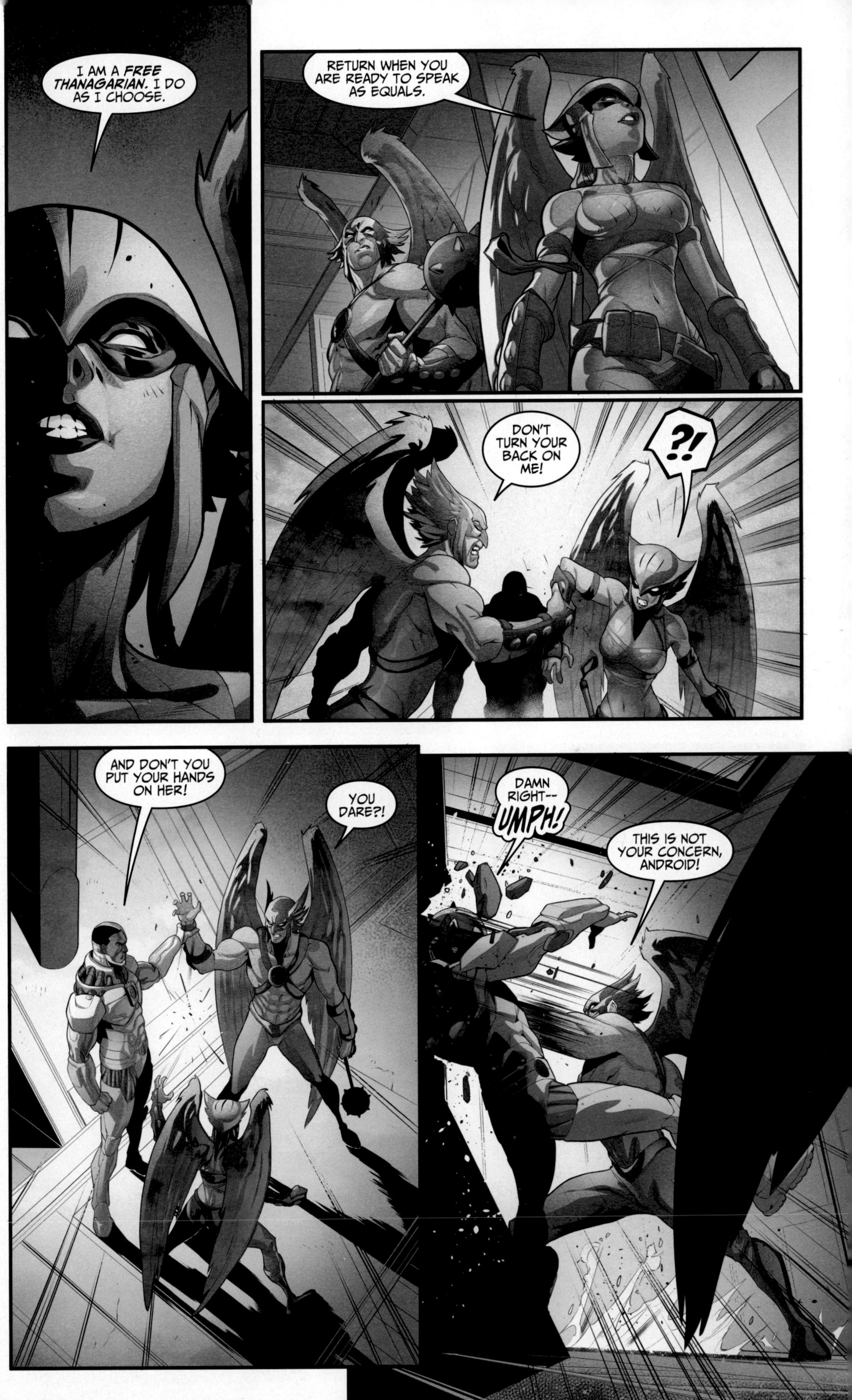
I AM A FREE THANAGARIAN. I DO AS I CHOOSE.
RETURN WHEN YOU ARE READY TO SPEAK AS EQUALS.
DON'T TURN YOUR BACK ON ME!
?!
AND DON'T YOU PUT YOUR HANDS ON HER!
YOU DARE?!
DAMN RIGHT--
UMPH!
THIS IS NOT YOUR CONCERN, ANDROID!

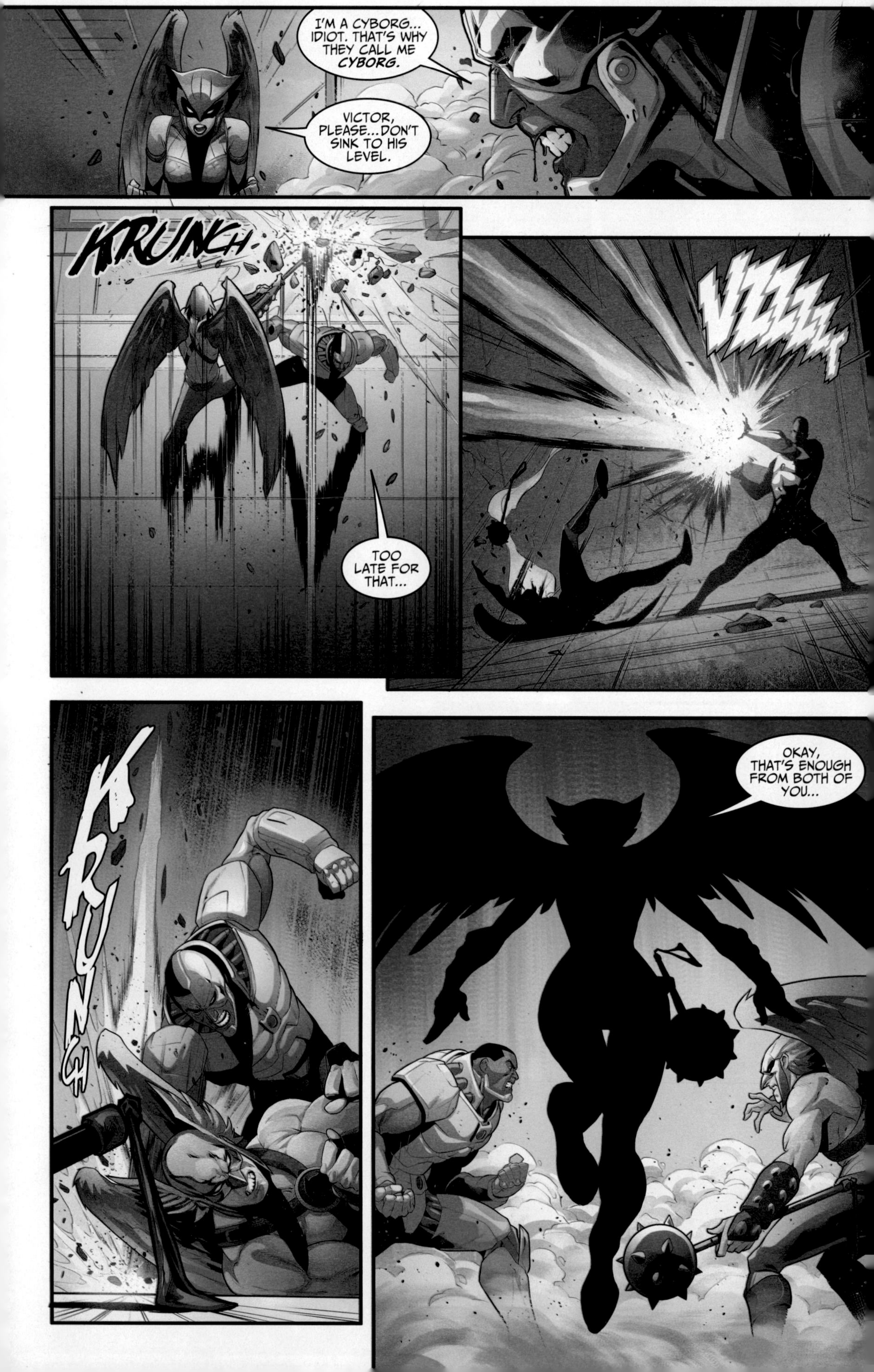
I'M A CYBORG... IDIOT. THAT'S WHY THEY CALL ME CYBORG.
VICTOR, PLEASE...DON'T SINK TO HIS LEVEL.
KRUNCH
TOO LATE FOR THAT...
VZZZZT
KRUNCH
OKAY, THAT'S ENOUGH FROM BOTH OF YOU...

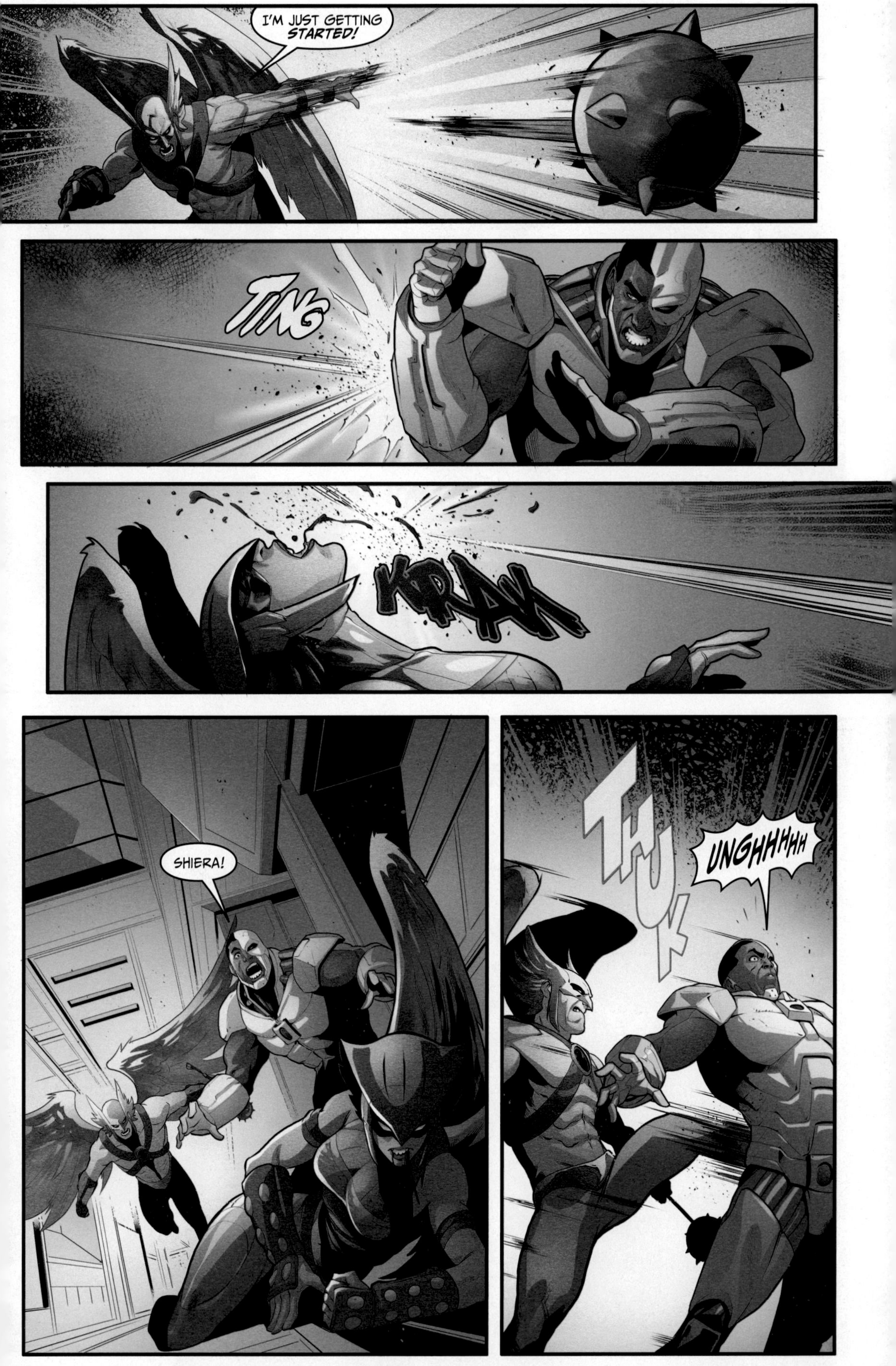
I'M JUST GETTING STARTED!
TING
KRAK
SHIERA!
THUK
UNGHHHHH

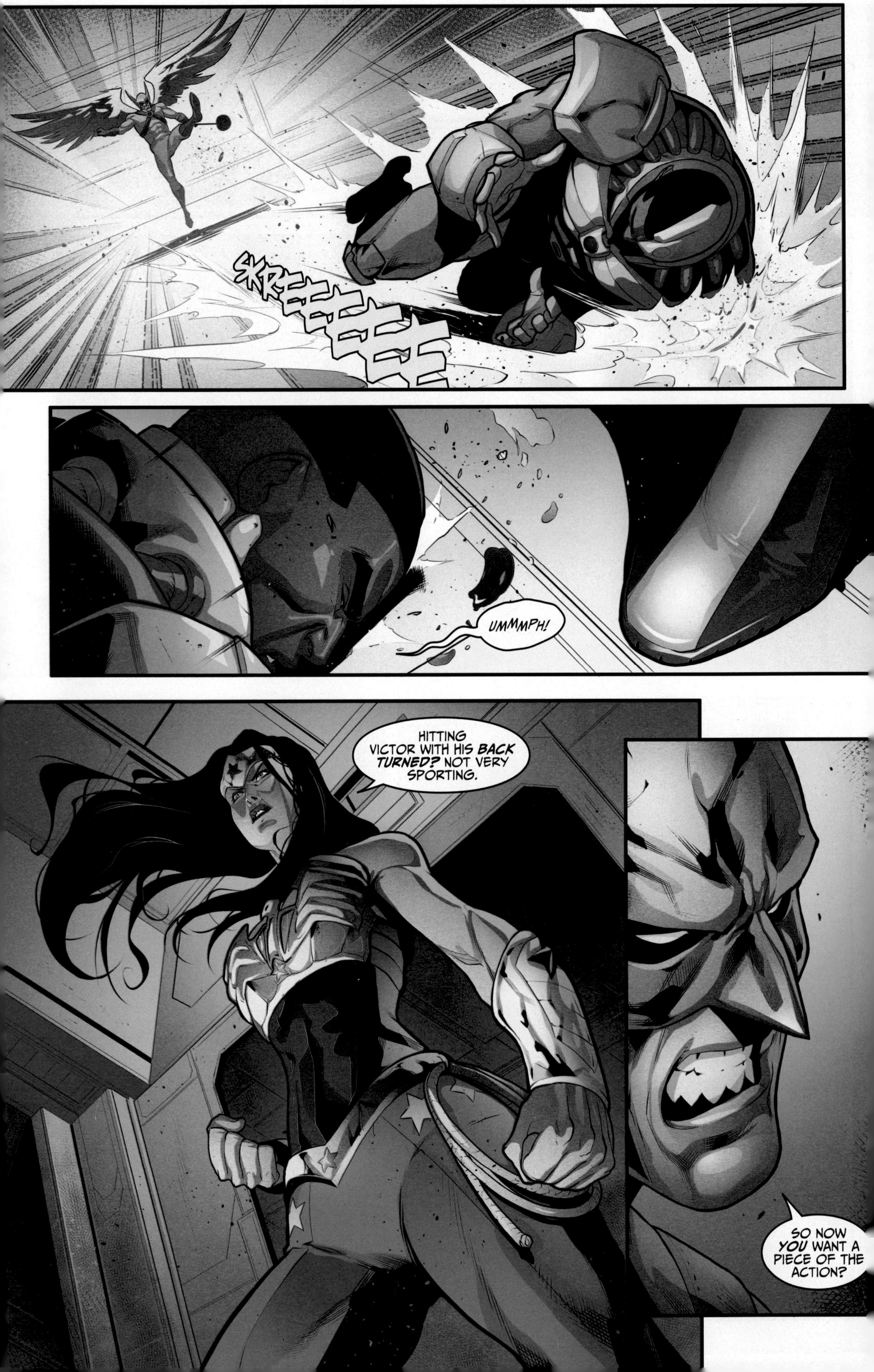
SKREEEEEEE
UMMMPH!
HITTING VICTOR WITH HIS BACK TURNED? NOT VERY SPORTING.
SO NOW YOU WANT A PIECE OF THE ACTION?

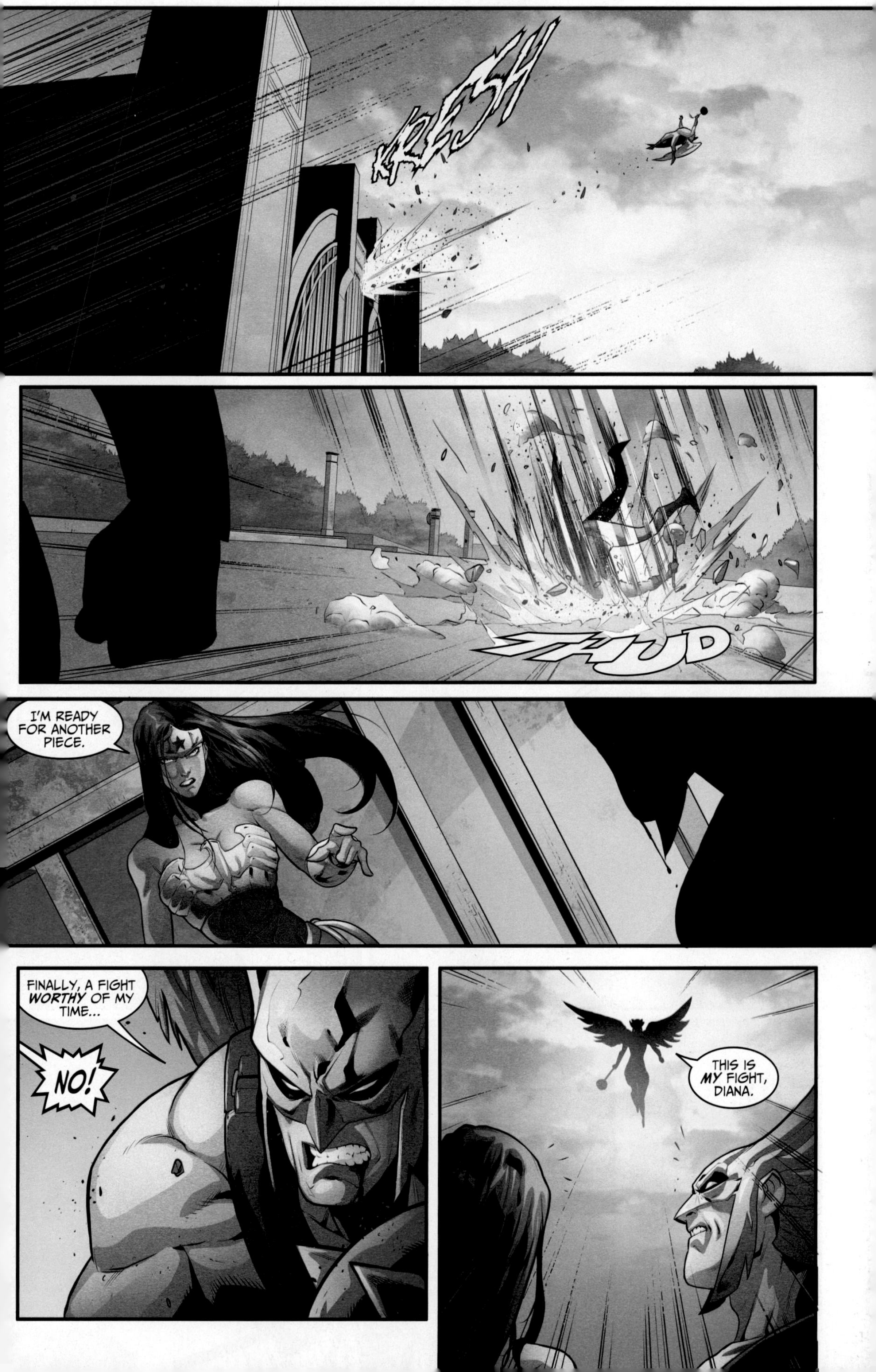
KRESH
THUD
I'M READY FOR ANOTHER PIECE.
FINALLY, A FIGHT WORTHY OF MY TIME...
NO!
THIS IS MY FIGHT, DIANA.

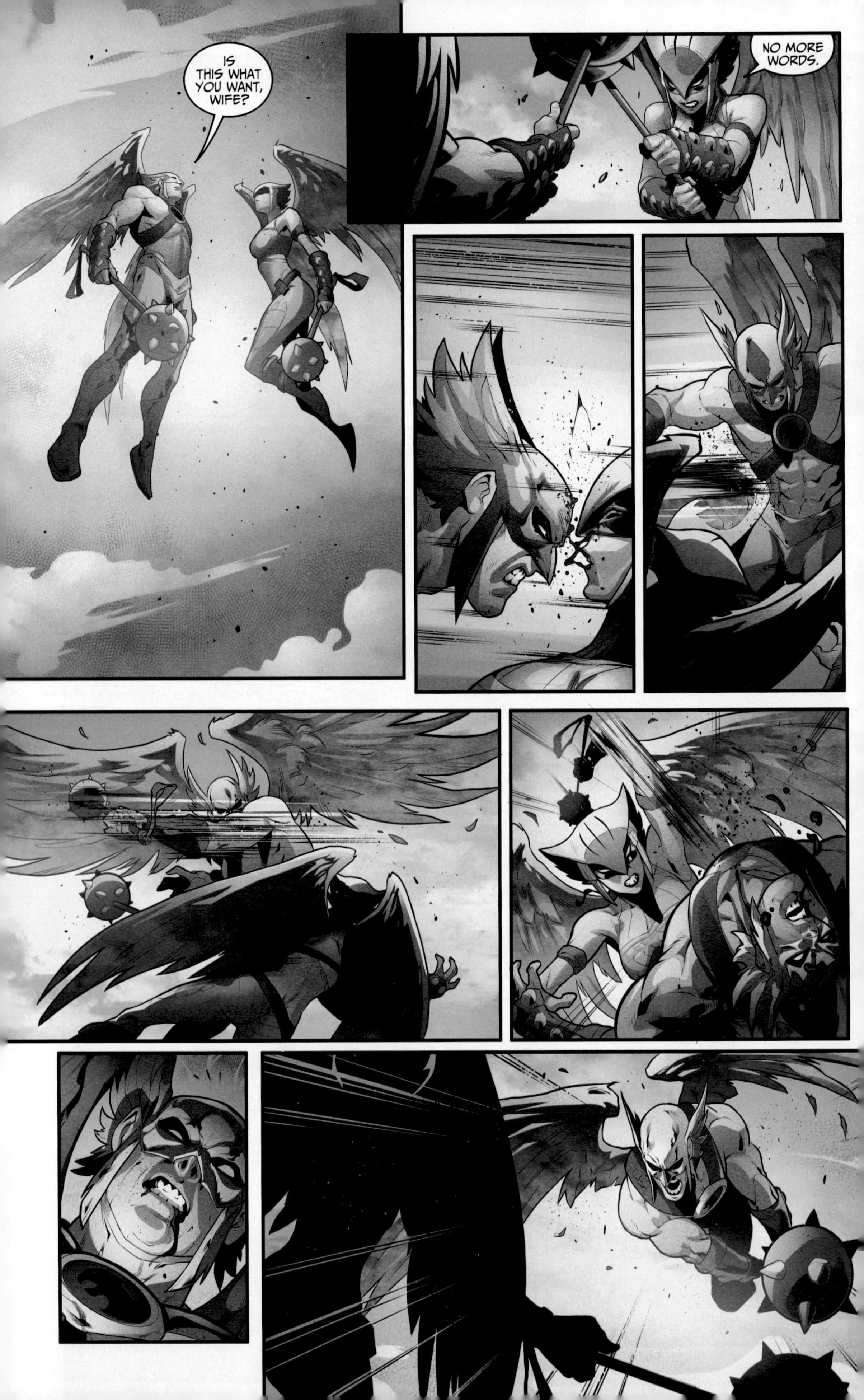
IS THIS WHAT YOU WANT, WIFE?
NO MORE WORDS.

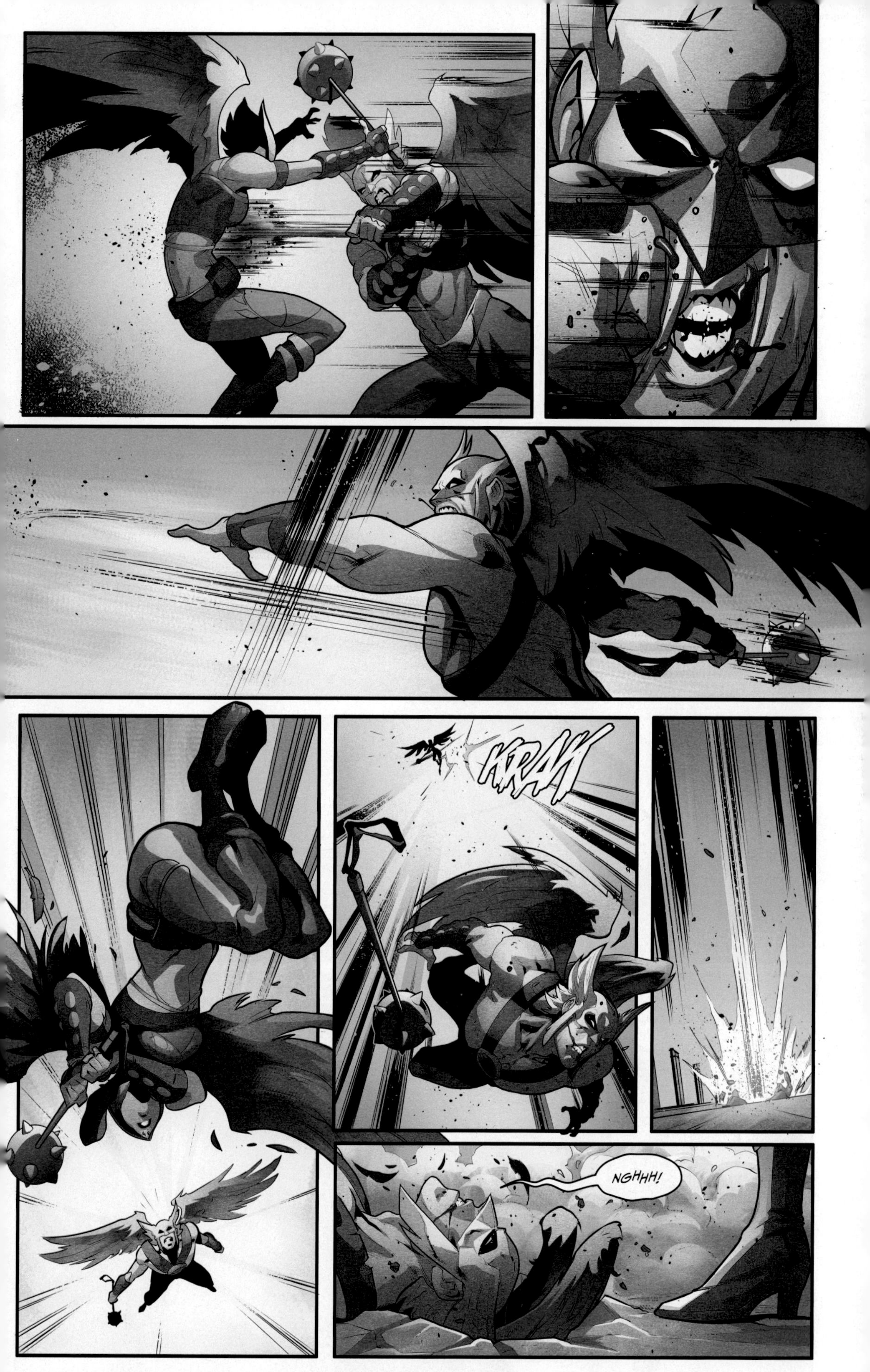
KRAK
NGHHH!

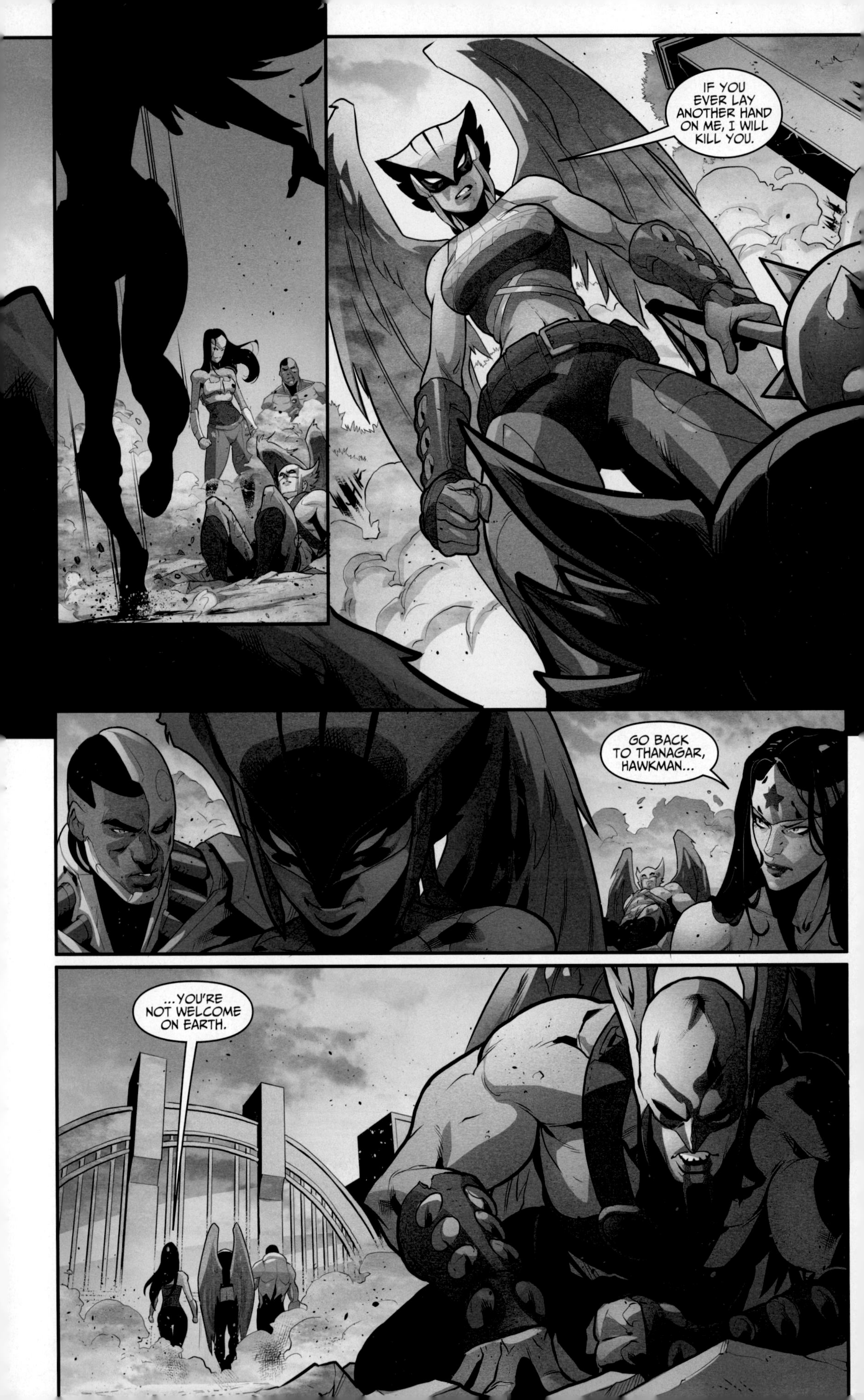
IF YOU EVER LAY ANOTHER HAND ON ME, I WILL KILL YOU.
GO BACK TO THANAGAR, HAWKMAN...
...YOU'RE NOT WELCOME ON EARTH.

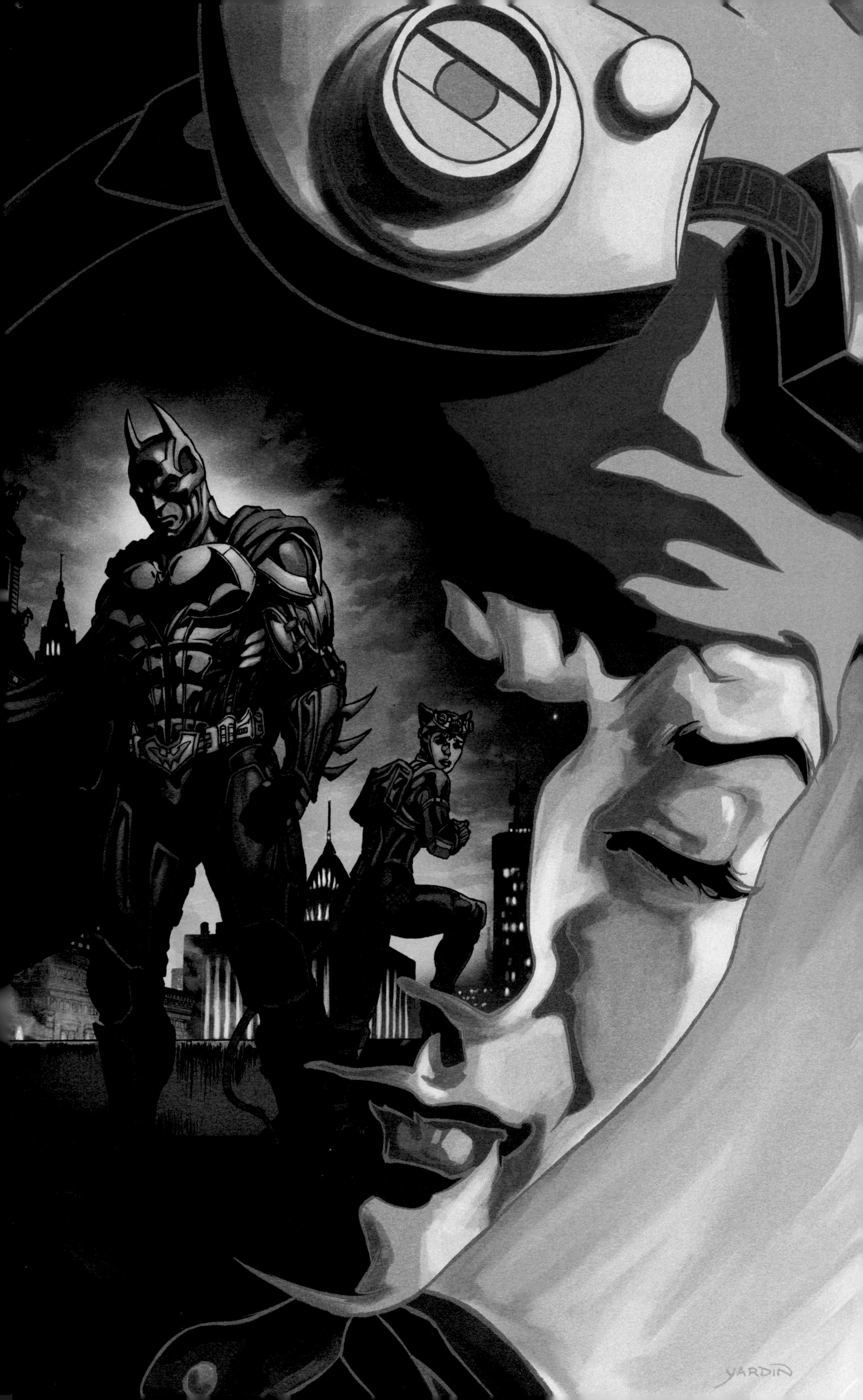
YARDIN

"Objects in Mirror..." **Bruno Redondo** Penciller **Juan Albarran** Inker **Rex Lokus** Colorist
"The Curious Case of Bizarro Superman" **Bruno Redondo** Penciller **Juan Albarran** Inker **Rex Lokus** Colorist

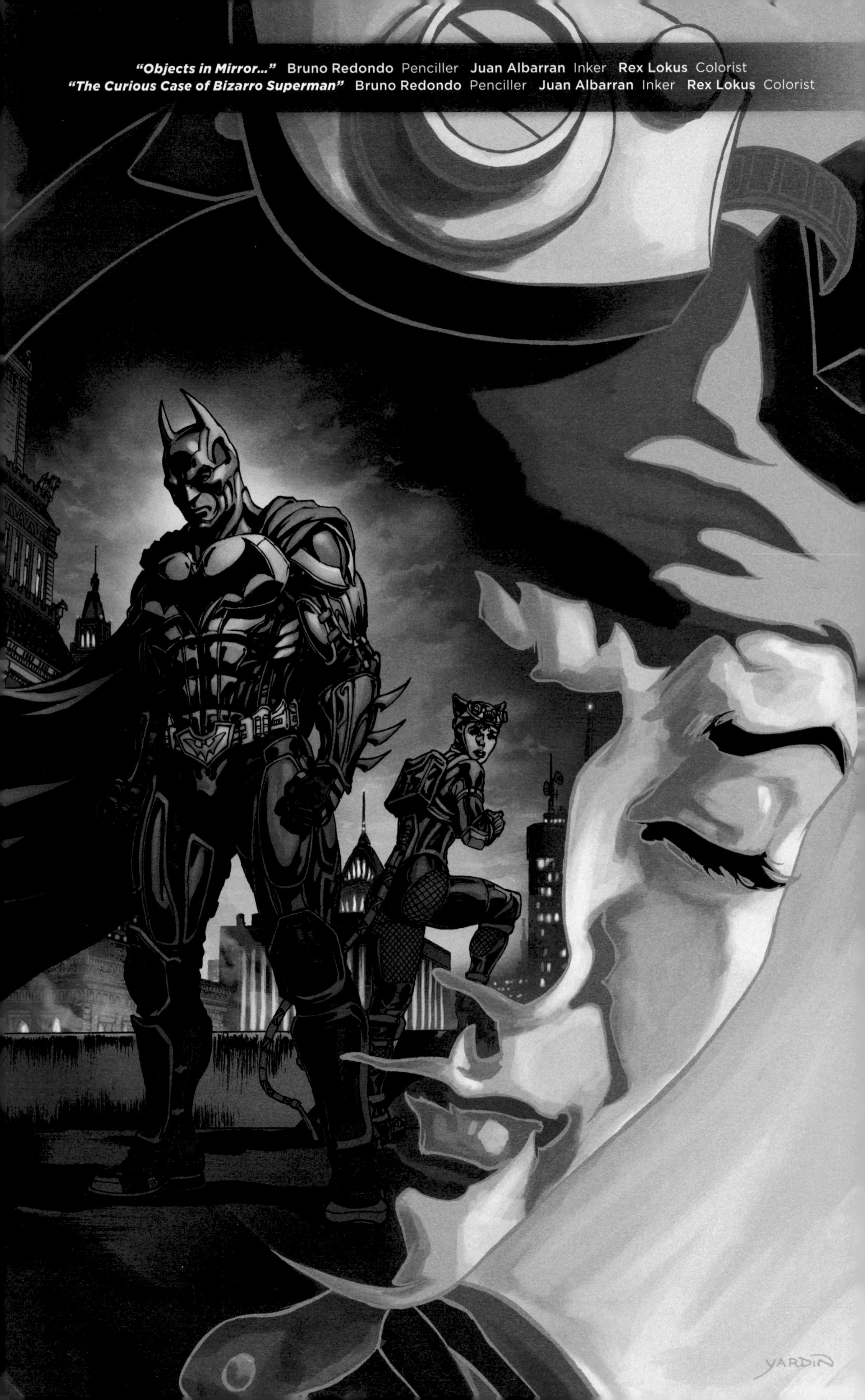
YARDIN

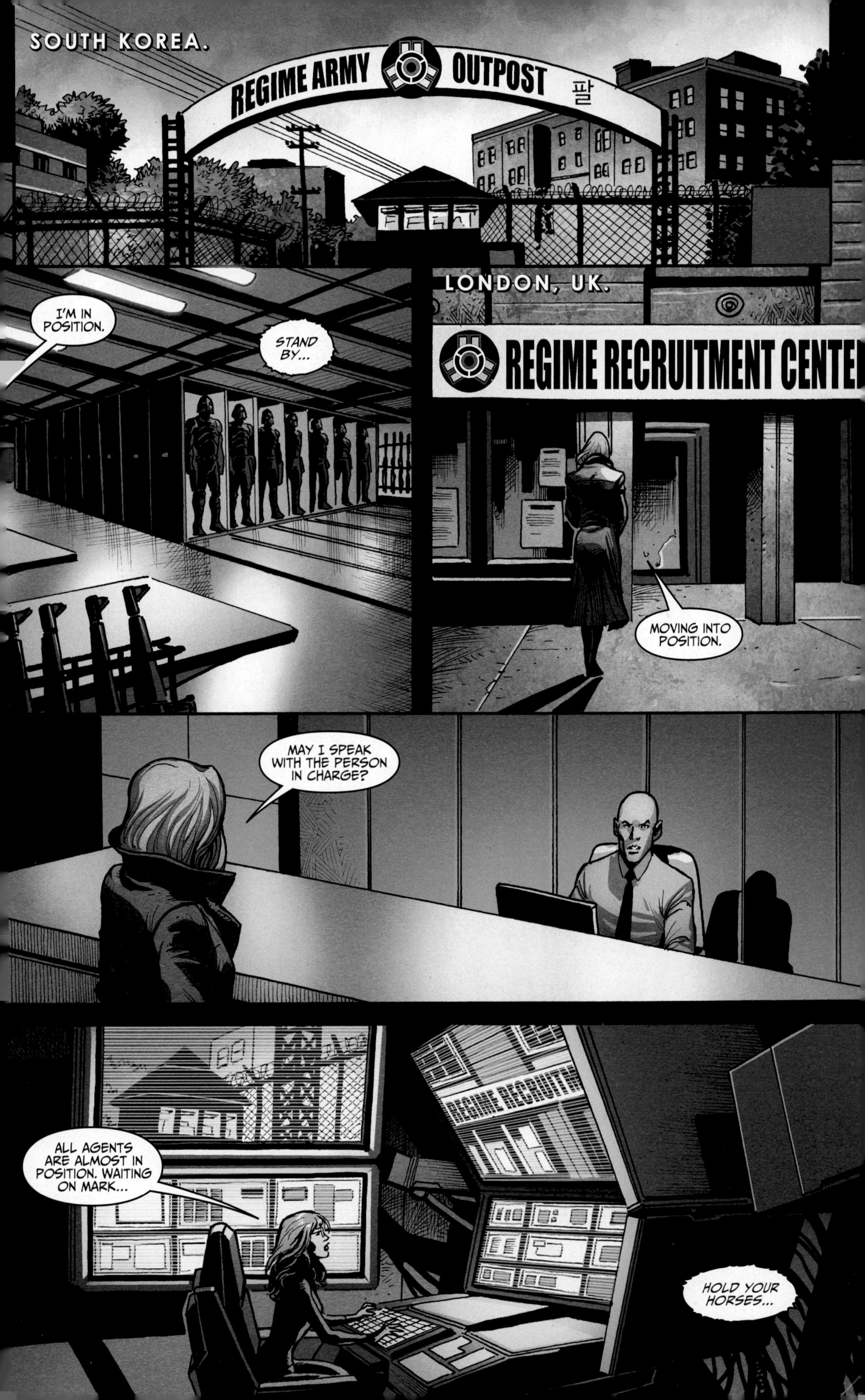
SOUTH KOREA.
REGIME ARMY OUTPOST 팔
I'M IN POSITION.
STAND BY...
LONDON, UK.
REGIME RECRUITMENT CENTE
MOVING INTO POSITION.
MAY I SPEAK WITH THE PERSON IN CHARGE?
ALL AGENTS ARE ALMOST IN POSITION. WAITING ON MARK...
HOLD YOUR HORSES...

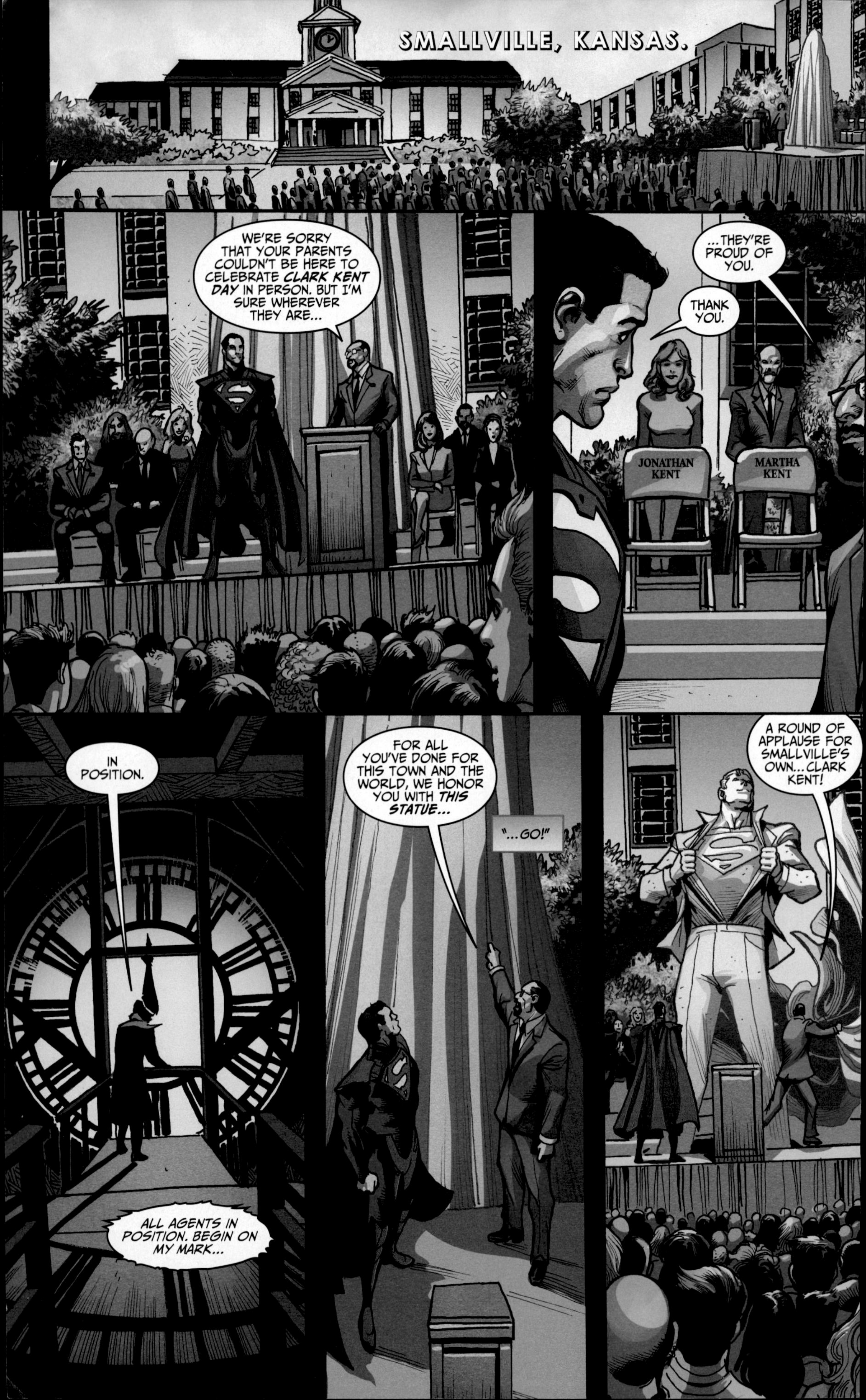
SMALLVILLE, KANSAS.
WE'RE SORRY THAT YOUR PARENTS COULDN'T BE HERE TO CELEBRATE CLARK KENT DAY IN PERSON. BUT I'M SURE WHEREVER THEY ARE...
...THEY'RE PROUD OF YOU.
THANK YOU.
JONATHAN KENT
MARTHA KENT
IN POSITION.
ALL AGENTS IN POSITION. BEGIN ON MY MARK...
FOR ALL YOU'VE DONE FOR THIS TOWN AND THE WORLD, WE HONOR YOU WITH THIS STATUE...
"...GO!"
A ROUND OF APPLAUSE FOR SMALLVILLE'S OWN...CLARK KENT!

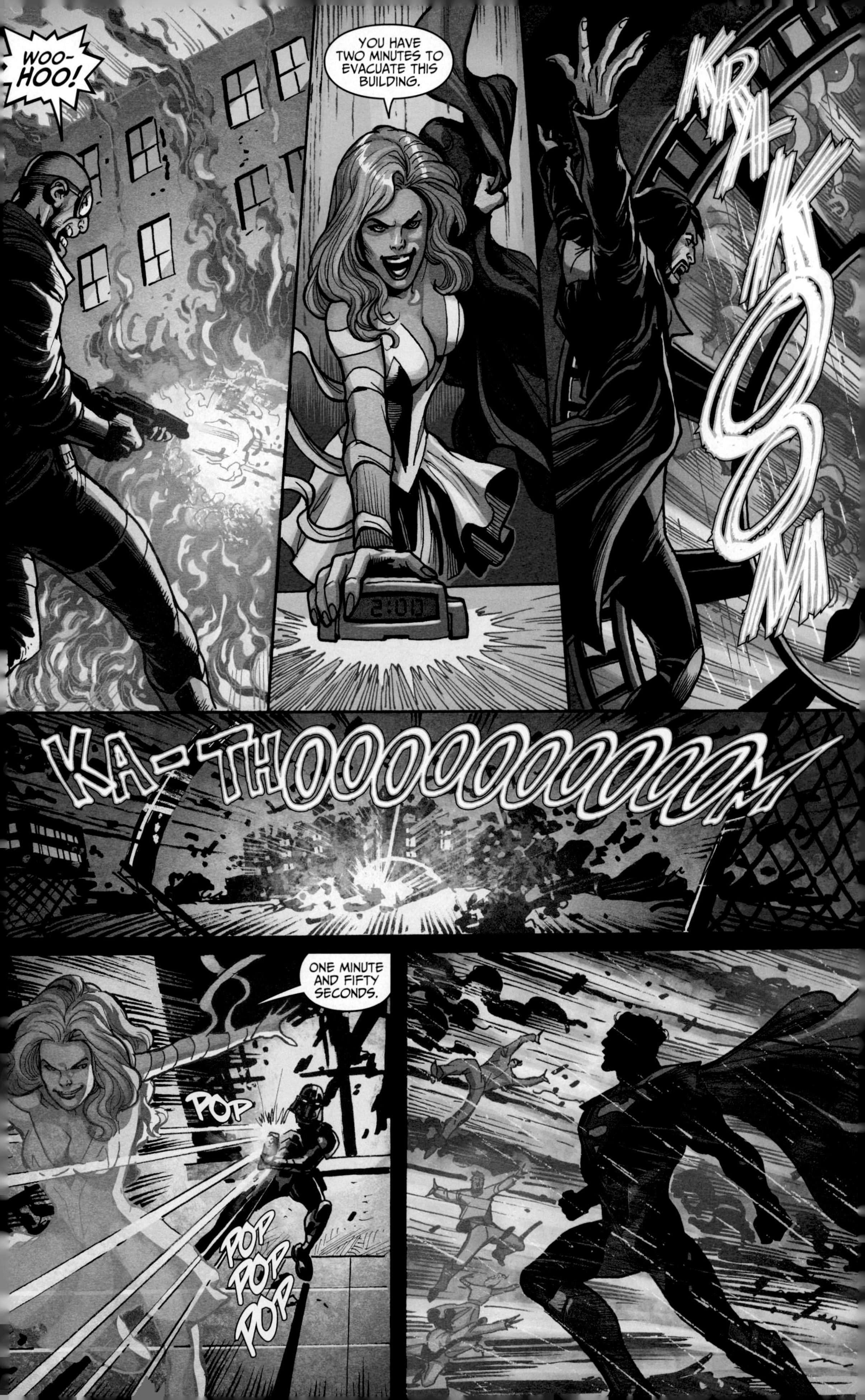
WOO-HOO!
YOU HAVE TWO MINUTES TO EVACUATE THIS BUILDING.
KRAKOOM
KA-THOOOOOOOOOM
ONE MINUTE AND FIFTY SECONDS.
POP
POP POP POP

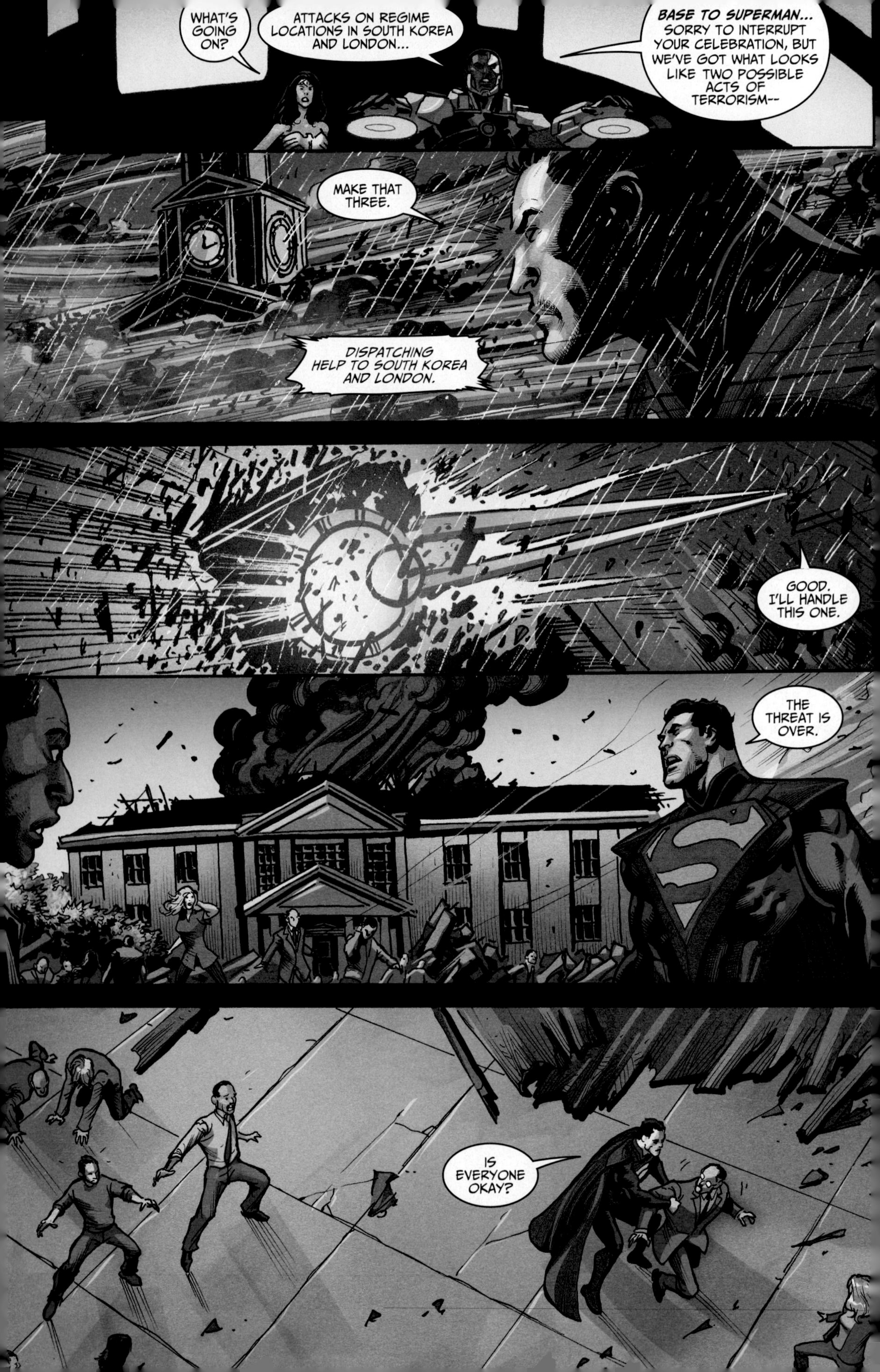
WHAT'S GOING ON?
ATTACKS ON REGIME LOCATIONS IN SOUTH KOREA AND LONDON...
BASE TO SUPERMAN... SORRY TO INTERRUPT YOUR CELEBRATION, BUT WE'VE GOT WHAT LOOKS LIKE TWO POSSIBLE ACTS OF TERRORISM--
MAKE THAT THREE.
DISPATCHING HELP TO SOUTH KOREA AND LONDON.
GOOD. I'LL HANDLE THIS ONE.
THE THREAT IS OVER.
IS EVERYONE OKAY?

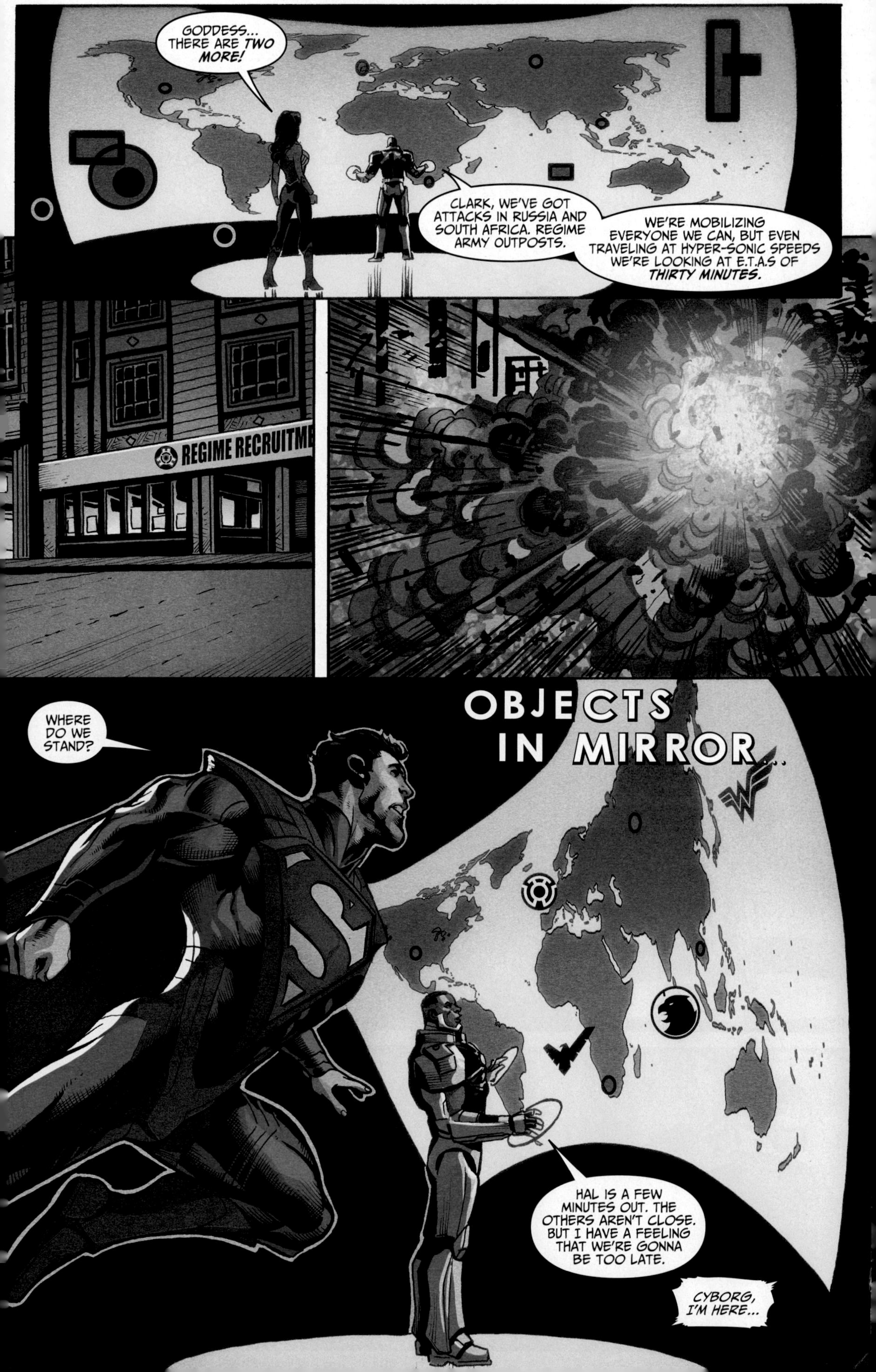
GODDESS... THERE ARE TWO MORE!
CLARK, WE'VE GOT ATTACKS IN RUSSIA AND SOUTH AFRICA. REGIME ARMY OUTPOSTS.
WE'RE MOBILIZING EVERYONE WE CAN, BUT EVEN TRAVELING AT HYPER-SONIC SPEEDS WE'RE LOOKING AT E.T.A.S OF THIRTY MINUTES.
REGIME RECRUITME
OBJECTS IN MIRROR...
WHERE DO WE STAND?
HAL IS A FEW MINUTES OUT. THE OTHERS AREN'T CLOSE. BUT I HAVE A FEELING THAT WE'RE GONNA BE TOO LATE.
CYBORG, I'M HERE...

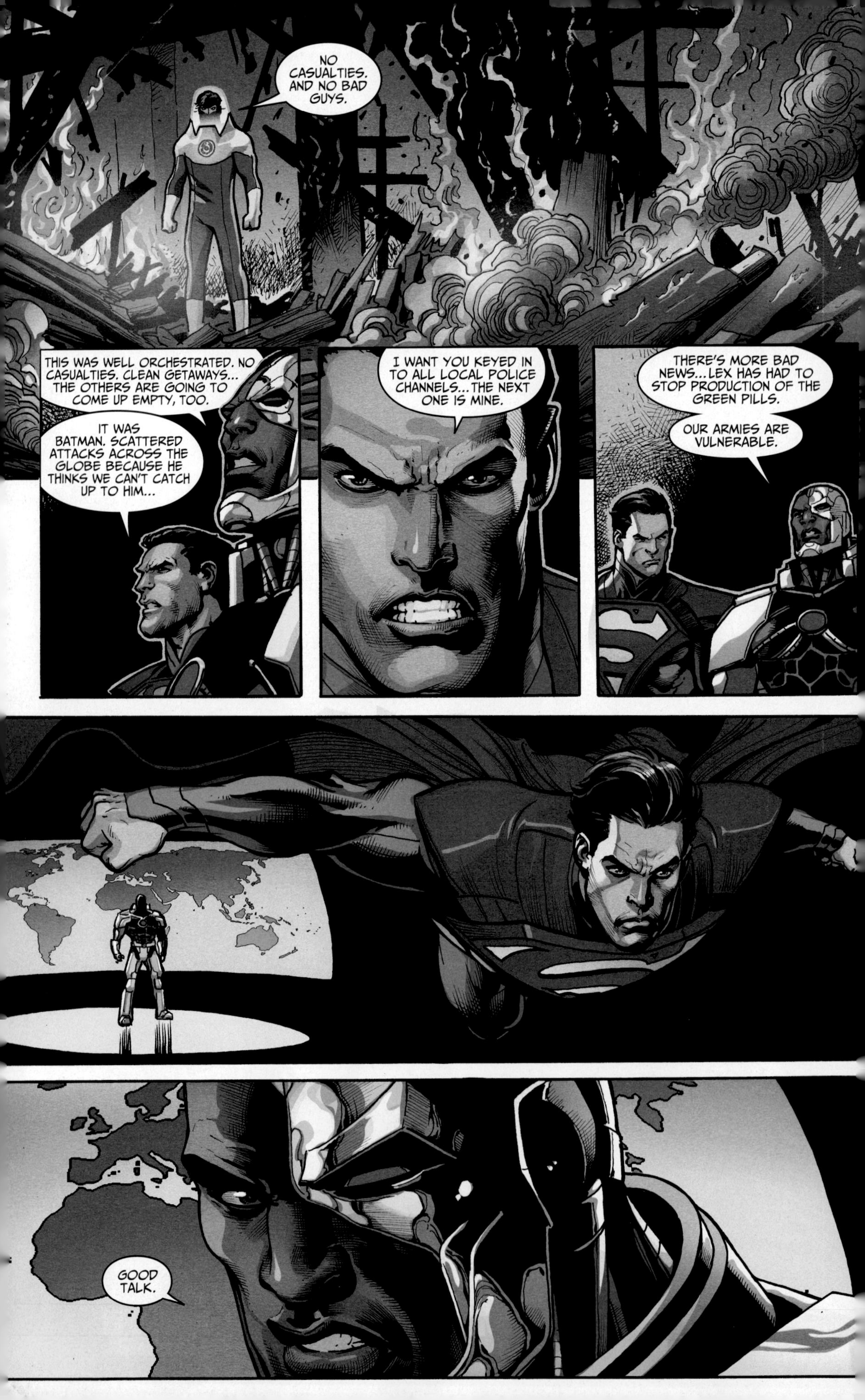
NO CASUALTIES. AND NO BAD GUYS.
THIS WAS WELL ORCHESTRATED. NO CASUALTIES. CLEAN GETAWAYS... THE OTHERS ARE GOING TO COME UP EMPTY, TOO.
IT WAS BATMAN. SCATTERED ATTACKS ACROSS THE GLOBE BECAUSE HE THINKS WE CAN'T CATCH UP TO HIM...
I WANT YOU KEYED IN TO ALL LOCAL POLICE CHANNELS...THE NEXT ONE IS MINE.
THERE'S MORE BAD NEWS...LEX HAS HAD TO STOP PRODUCTION OF THE GREEN PILLS.
OUR ARMIES ARE VULNERABLE.
GOOD TALK.

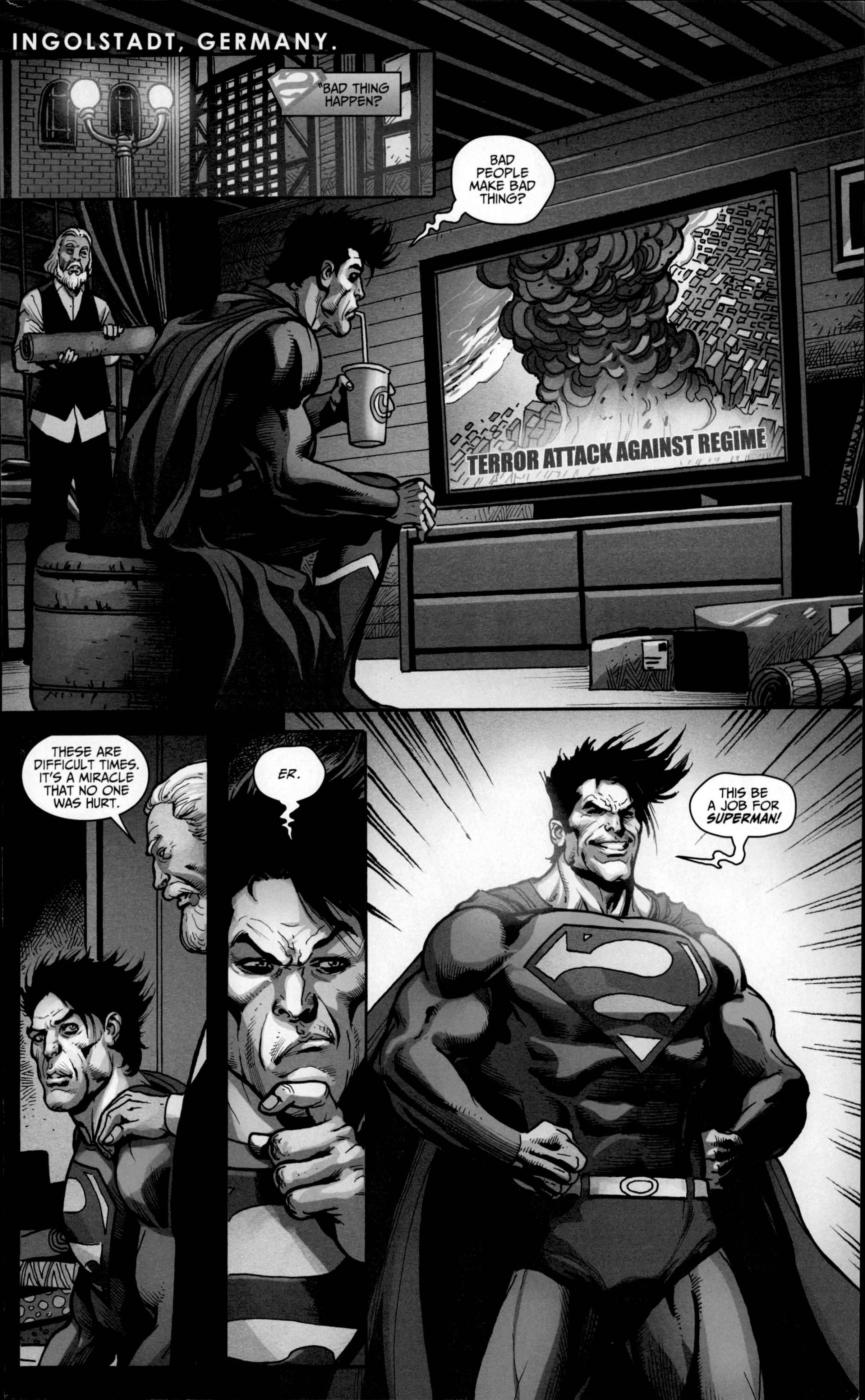
INGOLSTADT, GERMANY.
"BAD THING HAPPEN?
BAD PEOPLE MAKE BAD THING?
TERROR ATTACK AGAINST REGIME
THESE ARE DIFFICULT TIMES. IT'S A MIRACLE THAT NO ONE WAS HURT.
ER.
THIS BE A JOB FOR *SUPERMAN!*

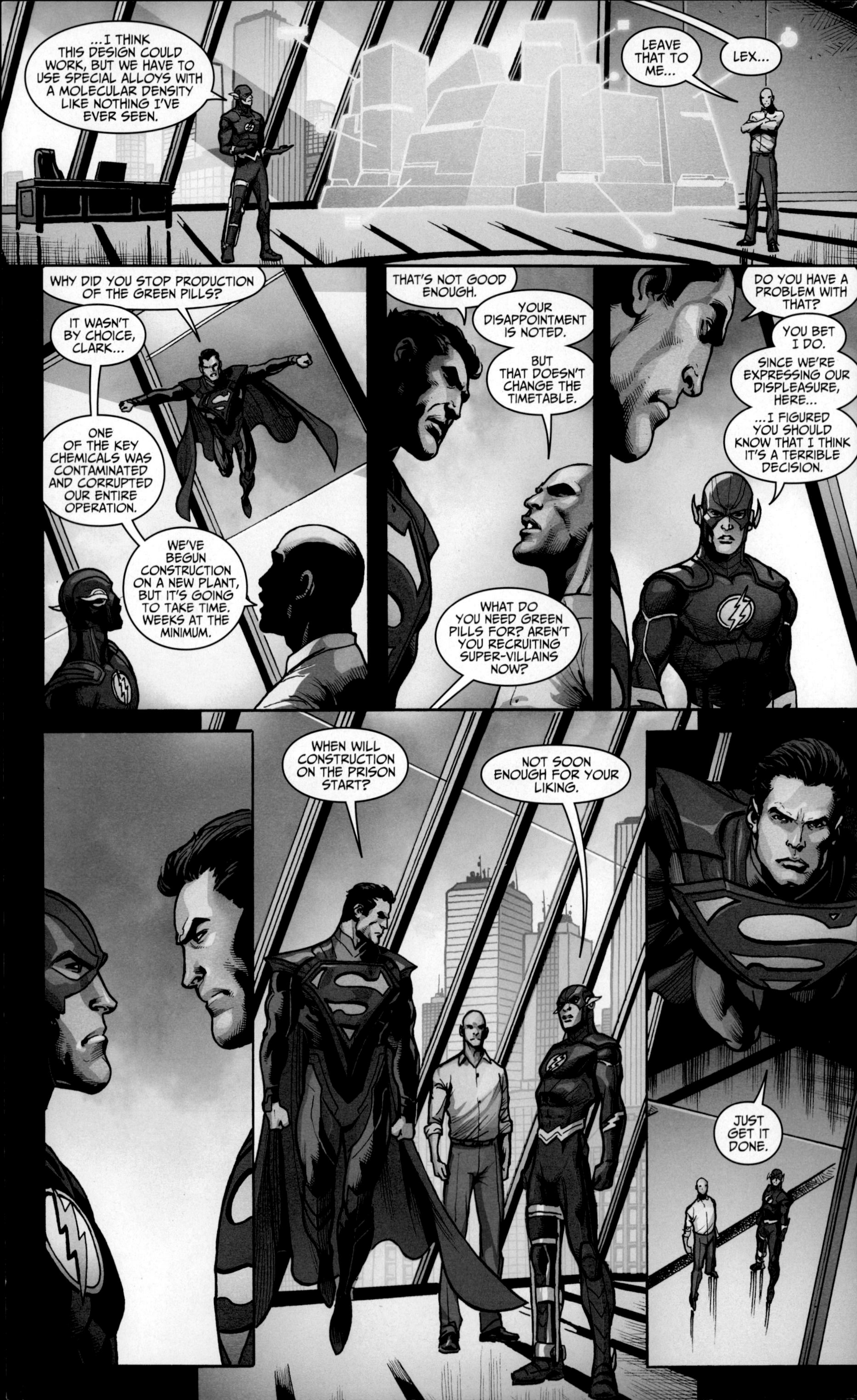
...I THINK THIS DESIGN COULD WORK, BUT WE HAVE TO USE SPECIAL ALLOYS WITH A MOLECULAR DENSITY LIKE NOTHING I'VE EVER SEEN.
LEAVE THAT TO ME...
LEX...
WHY DID YOU STOP PRODUCTION OF THE GREEN PILLS?
IT WASN'T BY CHOICE, CLARK...
ONE OF THE KEY CHEMICALS WAS CONTAMINATED AND CORRUPTED OUR ENTIRE OPERATION.
WE'VE BEGUN CONSTRUCTION ON A NEW PLANT, BUT IT'S GOING TO TAKE TIME. WEEKS AT THE MINIMUM.
THAT'S NOT GOOD ENOUGH.
YOUR DISAPPOINTMENT IS NOTED.
BUT THAT DOESN'T CHANGE THE TIMETABLE.
WHAT DO YOU NEED GREEN PILLS FOR? AREN'T YOU RECRUITING SUPER-VILLAINS NOW?
DO YOU HAVE A PROBLEM WITH THAT?
YOU BET I DO.
SINCE WE'RE EXPRESSING OUR DISPLEASURE, HERE...
...I FIGURED YOU SHOULD KNOW THAT I THINK IT'S A TERRIBLE DECISION.
WHEN WILL CONSTRUCTION ON THE PRISON START?
NOT SOON ENOUGH FOR YOUR LIKING.
JUST GET IT DONE.

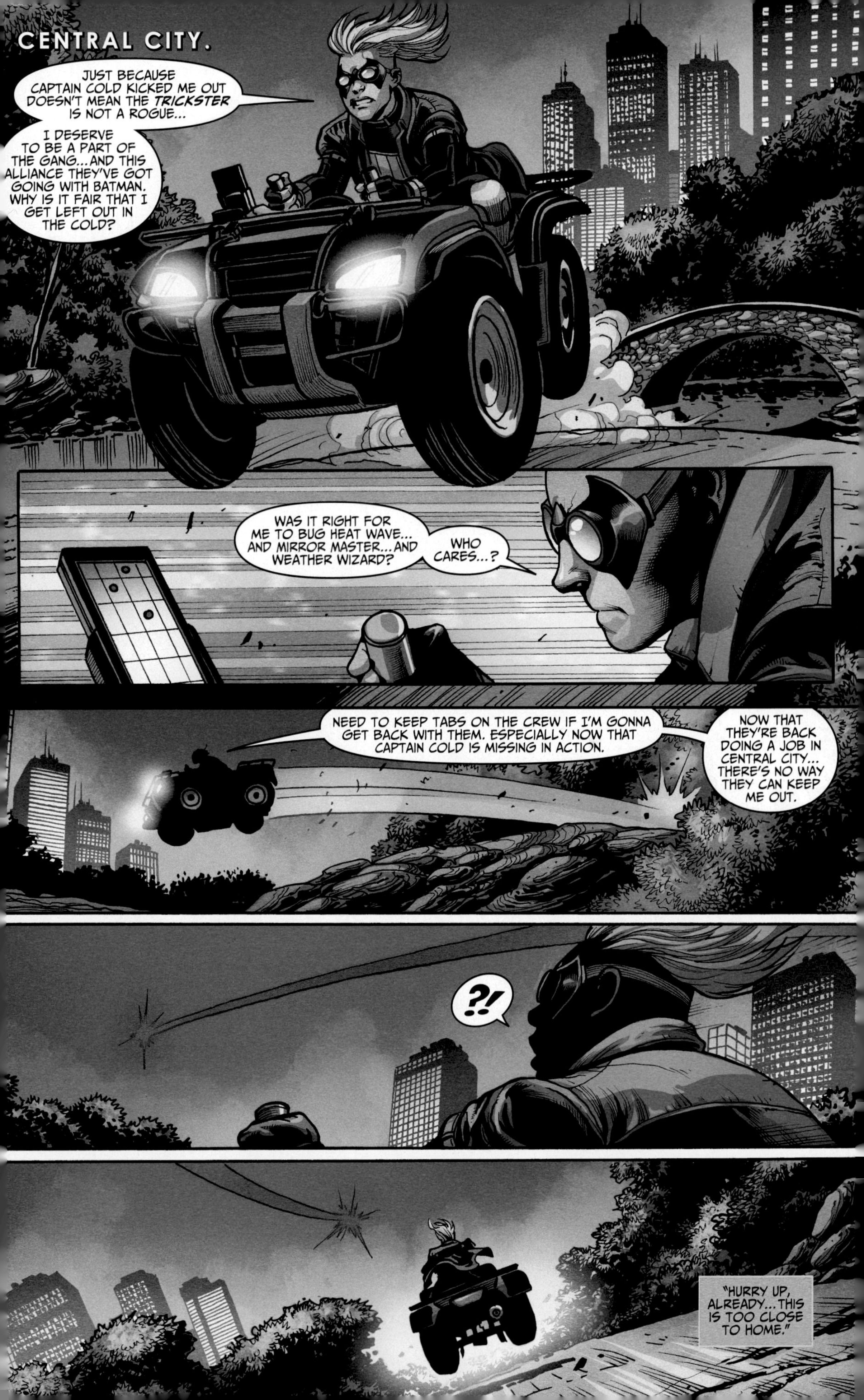
CENTRAL CITY.
JUST BECAUSE CAPTAIN COLD KICKED ME OUT DOESN'T MEAN THE TRICKSTER IS NOT A ROGUE...
I DESERVE TO BE A PART OF THE GANG...AND THIS ALLIANCE THEY'VE GOT GOING WITH BATMAN. WHY IS IT FAIR THAT I GET LEFT OUT IN THE COLD?
WAS IT RIGHT FOR ME TO BUG HEAT WAVE... AND MIRROR MASTER...AND WEATHER WIZARD?
WHO CARES...?
NEED TO KEEP TABS ON THE CREW IF I'M GONNA GET BACK WITH THEM. ESPECIALLY NOW THAT CAPTAIN COLD IS MISSING IN ACTION.
NOW THAT THEY'RE BACK DOING A JOB IN CENTRAL CITY... THERE'S NO WAY THEY CAN KEEP ME OUT.
?!
"HURRY UP, ALREADY...THIS IS TOO CLOSE TO HOME."

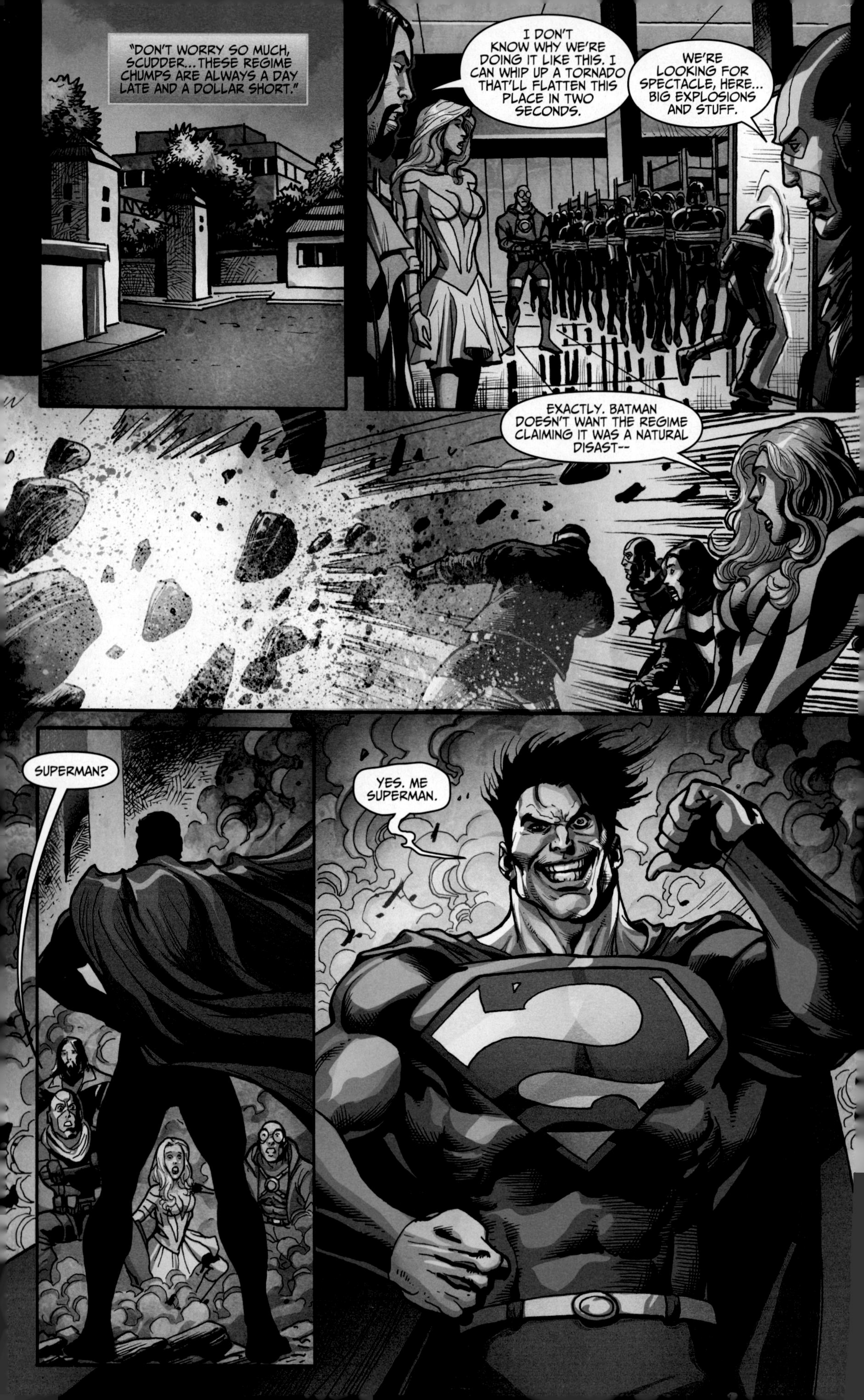
"DON'T WORRY SO MUCH, SCUDDER...THESE REGIME CHUMPS ARE ALWAYS A DAY LATE AND A DOLLAR SHORT."
I DON'T KNOW WHY WE'RE DOING IT LIKE THIS. I CAN WHIP UP A TORNADO THAT'LL FLATTEN THIS PLACE IN TWO SECONDS.
WE'RE LOOKING FOR SPECTACLE, HERE... BIG EXPLOSIONS AND STUFF.
EXACTLY. BATMAN DOESN'T WANT THE REGIME CLAIMING IT WAS A NATURAL DISAST--
SUPERMAN?
YES. ME SUPERMAN.

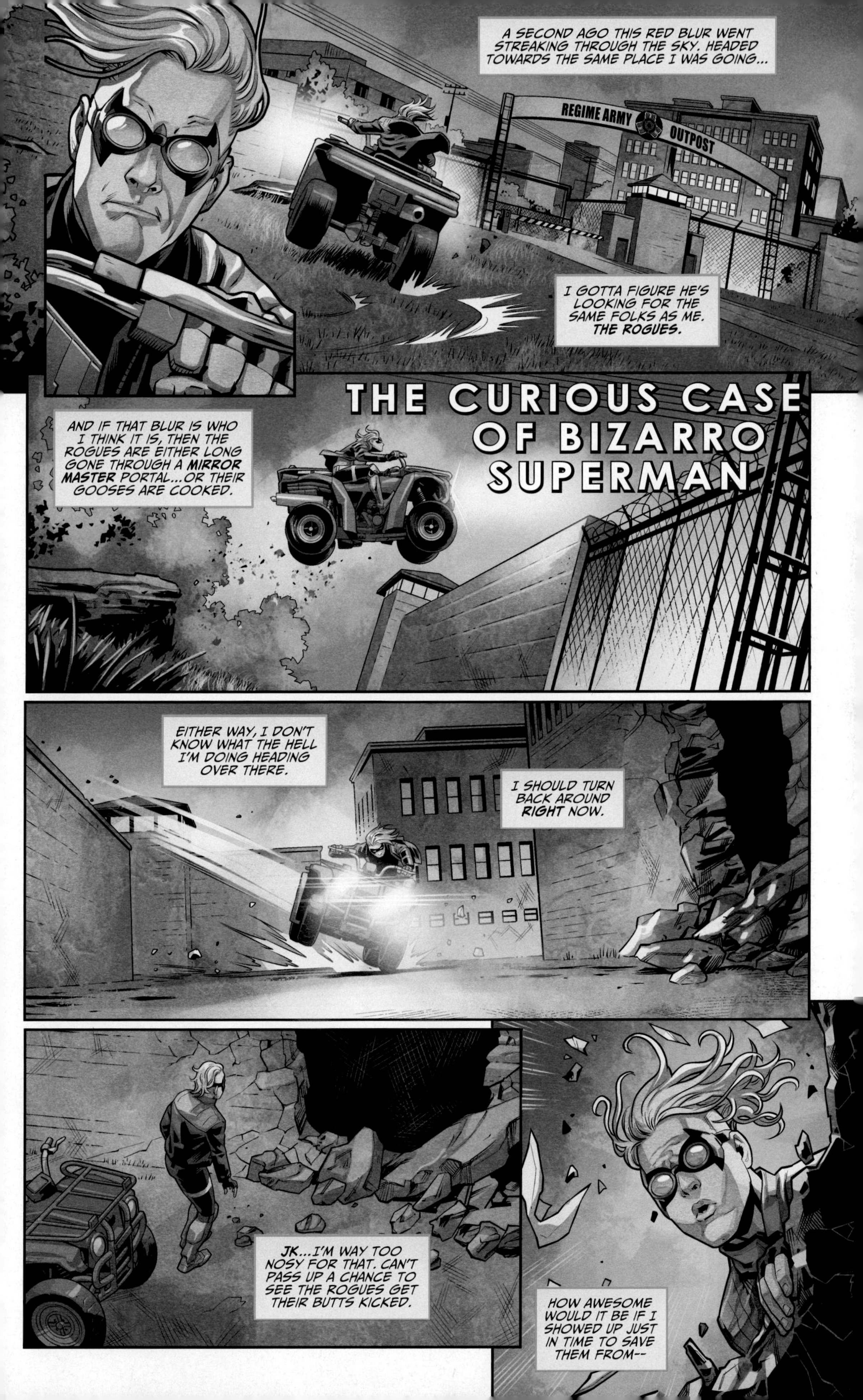
A SECOND AGO THIS RED BLUR WENT STREAKING THROUGH THE SKY. HEADED TOWARDS THE SAME PLACE I WAS GOING...
REGIME ARMY OUTPOST
I GOTTA FIGURE HE'S LOOKING FOR THE SAME FOLKS AS ME. THE ROGUES.
THE CURIOUS CASE OF BIZARRO SUPERMAN
AND IF THAT BLUR IS WHO I THINK IT IS, THEN THE ROGUES ARE EITHER LONG GONE THROUGH A MIRROR MASTER PORTAL...OR THEIR GOOSES ARE COOKED.
EITHER WAY, I DON'T KNOW WHAT THE HELL I'M DOING HEADING OVER THERE.
I SHOULD TURN BACK AROUND RIGHT NOW.
JK...I'M WAY TOO NOSY FOR THAT. CAN'T PASS UP A CHANCE TO SEE THE ROGUES GET THEIR BUTTS KICKED.
HOW AWESOME WOULD IT BE IF I SHOWED UP JUST IN TIME TO SAVE THEM FROM--

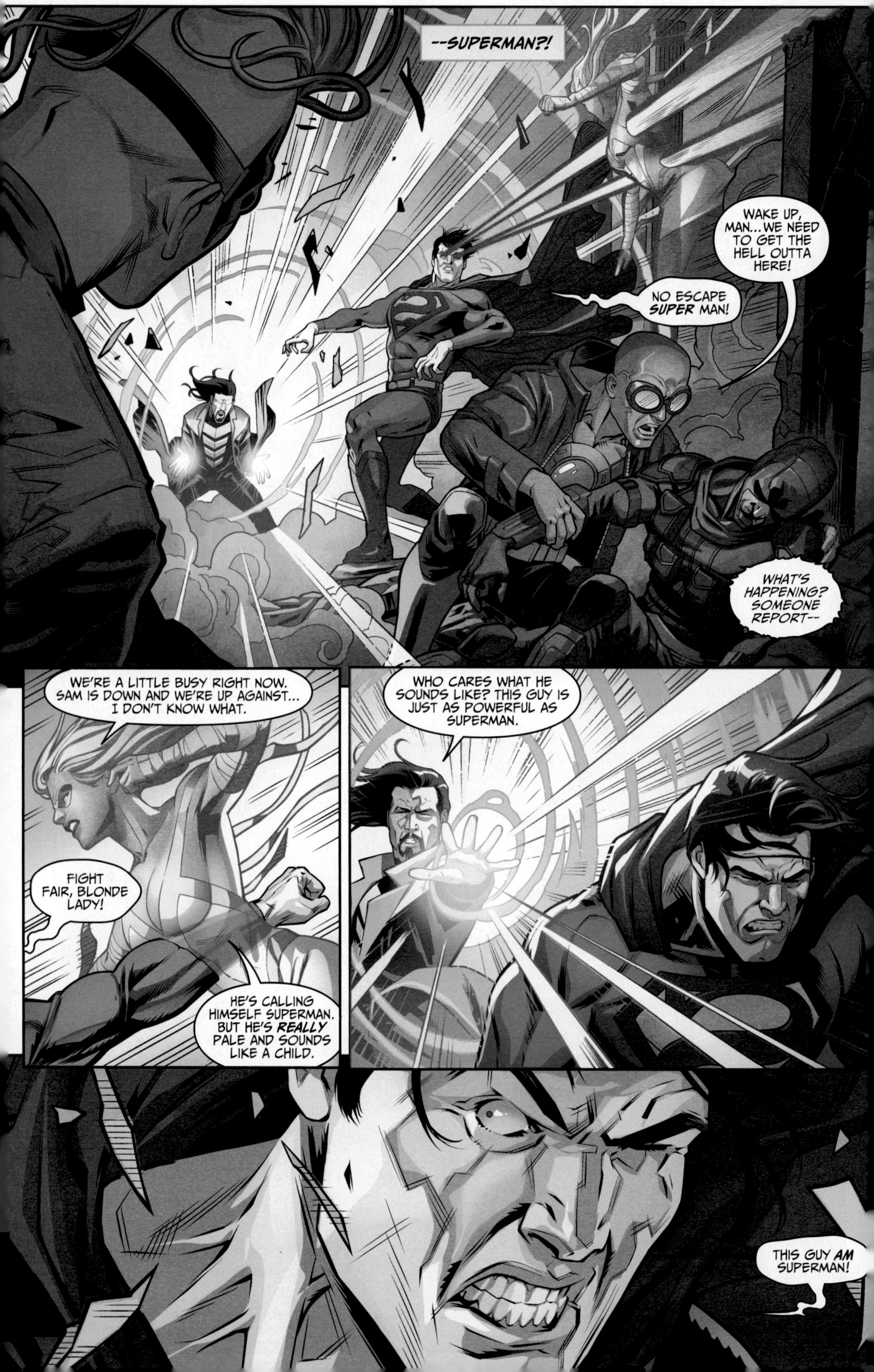
--SUPERMAN?!
WAKE UP, MAN...WE NEED TO GET THE HELL OUTTA HERE!
NO ESCAPE SUPER MAN!
WHAT'S HAPPENING? SOMEONE REPORT--
WE'RE A LITTLE BUSY RIGHT NOW. SAM IS DOWN AND WE'RE UP AGAINST... I DON'T KNOW WHAT.
FIGHT FAIR, BLONDE LADY!
HE'S CALLING HIMSELF SUPERMAN. BUT HE'S REALLY PALE AND SOUNDS LIKE A CHILD.
WHO CARES WHAT HE SOUNDS LIKE? THIS GUY IS JUST AS POWERFUL AS SUPERMAN.
THIS GUY AM SUPERMAN!

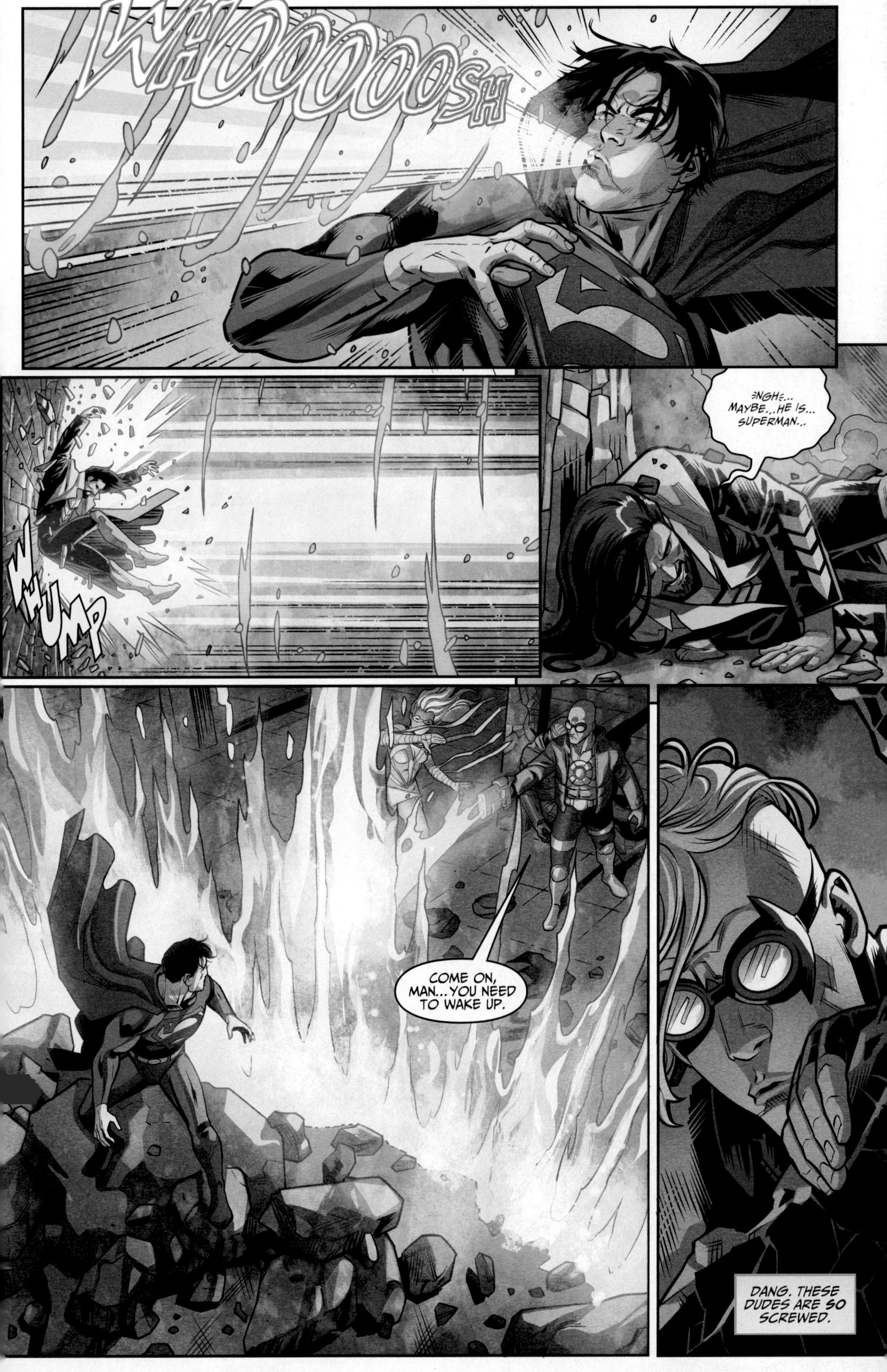
WHOOOOOOSH
WHUMP
NGH... MAYBE...HE IS... SUPERMAN...
COME ON, MAN...YOU NEED TO WAKE UP.
DANG. THESE DUDES ARE SO SCREWED.

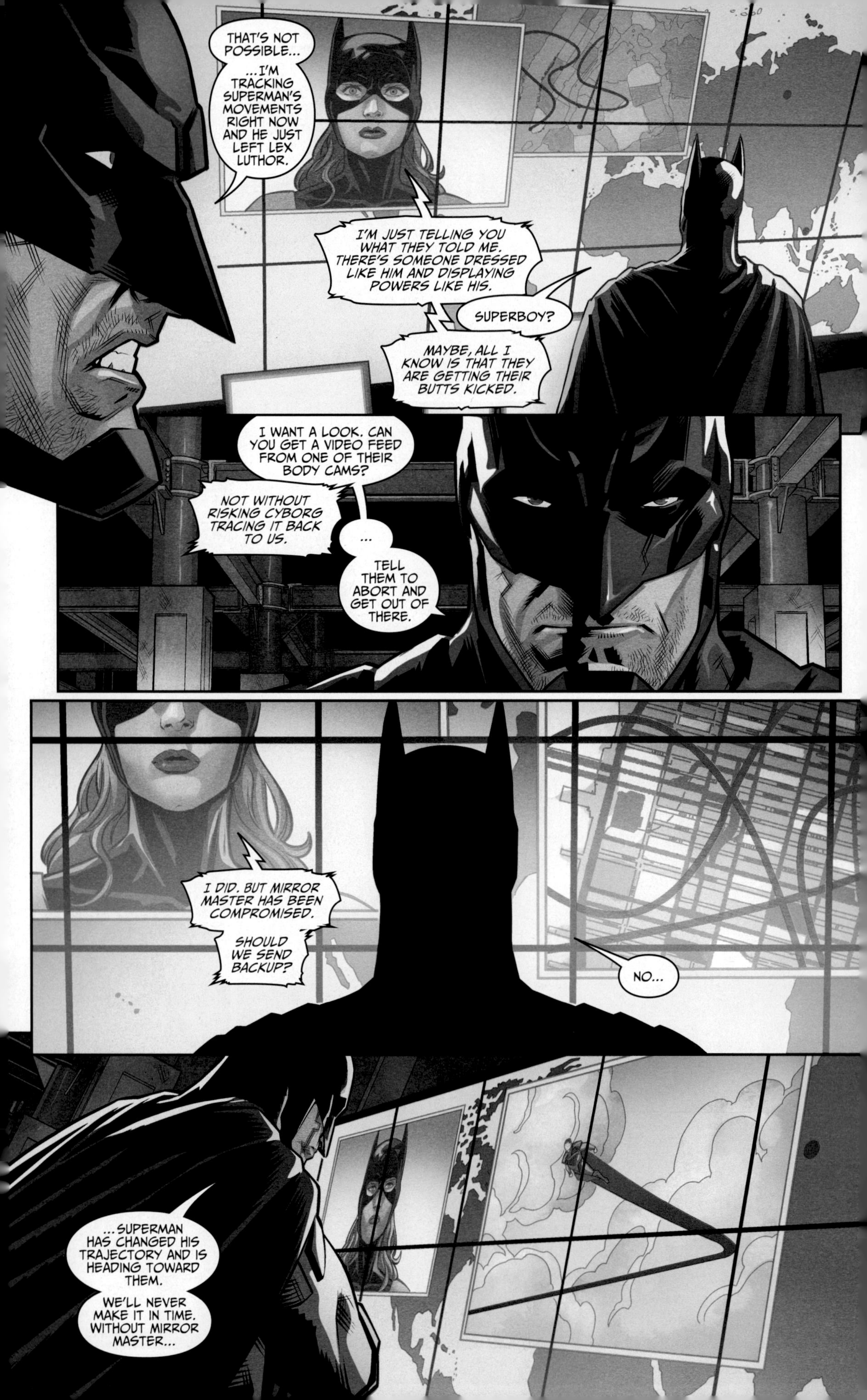
THAT'S NOT POSSIBLE...
...I'M TRACKING SUPERMAN'S MOVEMENTS RIGHT NOW AND HE JUST LEFT LEX LUTHOR.
I'M JUST TELLING YOU WHAT THEY TOLD ME. THERE'S SOMEONE DRESSED LIKE HIM AND DISPLAYING POWERS LIKE HIS.
SUPERBOY?
MAYBE, ALL I KNOW IS THAT THEY ARE GETTING THEIR BUTTS KICKED.
I WANT A LOOK. CAN YOU GET A VIDEO FEED FROM ONE OF THEIR BODY CAMS?
NOT WITHOUT RISKING CYBORG TRACING IT BACK TO US.
...
TELL THEM TO ABORT AND GET OUT OF THERE.
I DID. BUT MIRROR MASTER HAS BEEN COMPROMISED.
SHOULD WE SEND BACKUP?
NO...
...SUPERMAN HAS CHANGED HIS TRAJECTORY AND IS HEADING TOWARD THEM.
WE'LL NEVER MAKE IT IN TIME. WITHOUT MIRROR MASTER...

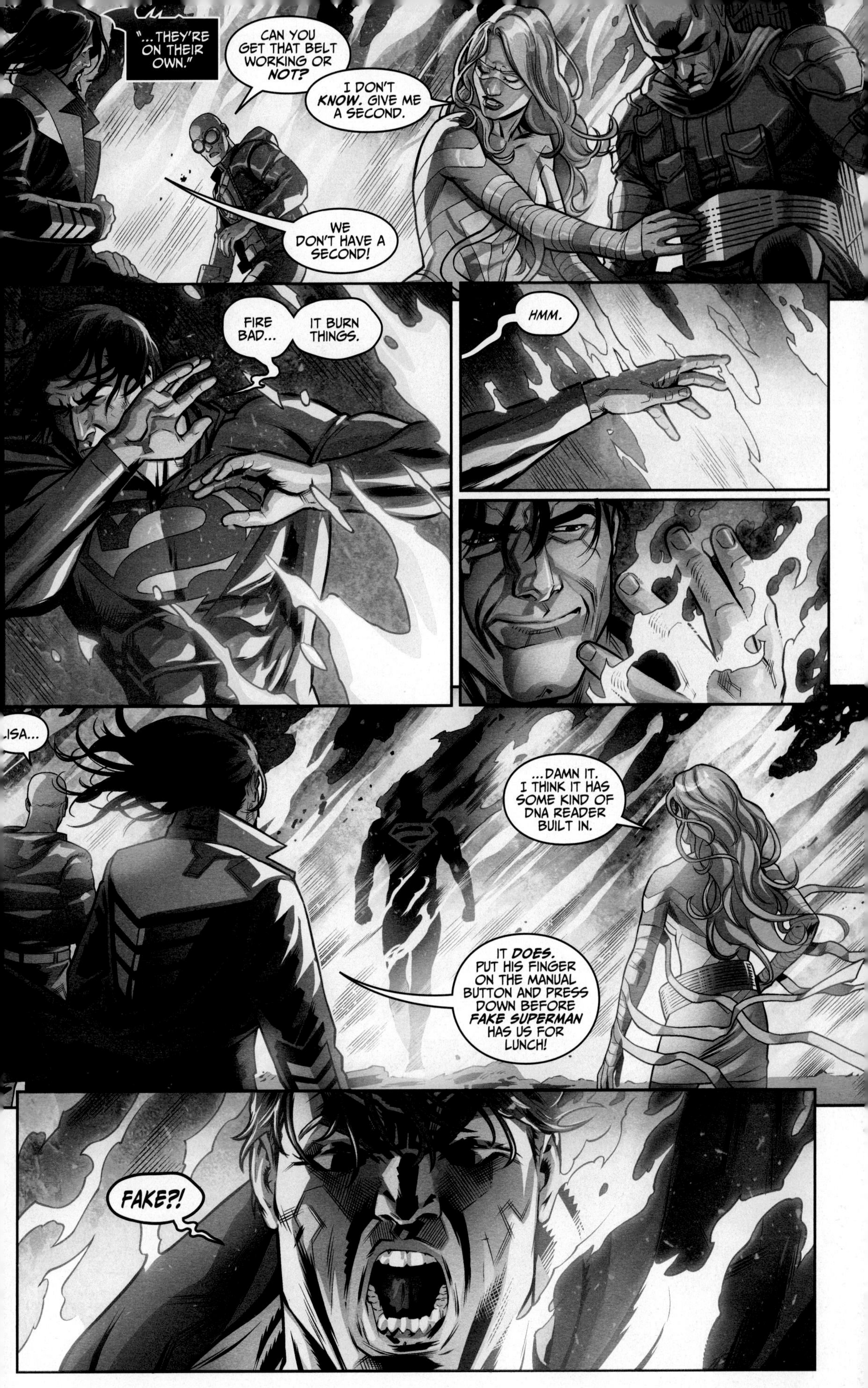
"...THEY'RE ON THEIR OWN."
CAN YOU GET THAT BELT WORKING OR NOT?
I DON'T KNOW. GIVE ME A SECOND.
WE DON'T HAVE A SECOND!
FIRE BAD...
IT BURN THINGS.
HMM.
...ISA...
...DAMN IT. I THINK IT HAS SOME KIND OF DNA READER BUILT IN.
IT DOES. PUT HIS FINGER ON THE MANUAL BUTTON AND PRESS DOWN BEFORE FAKE SUPERMAN HAS US FOR LUNCH!
FAKE?!

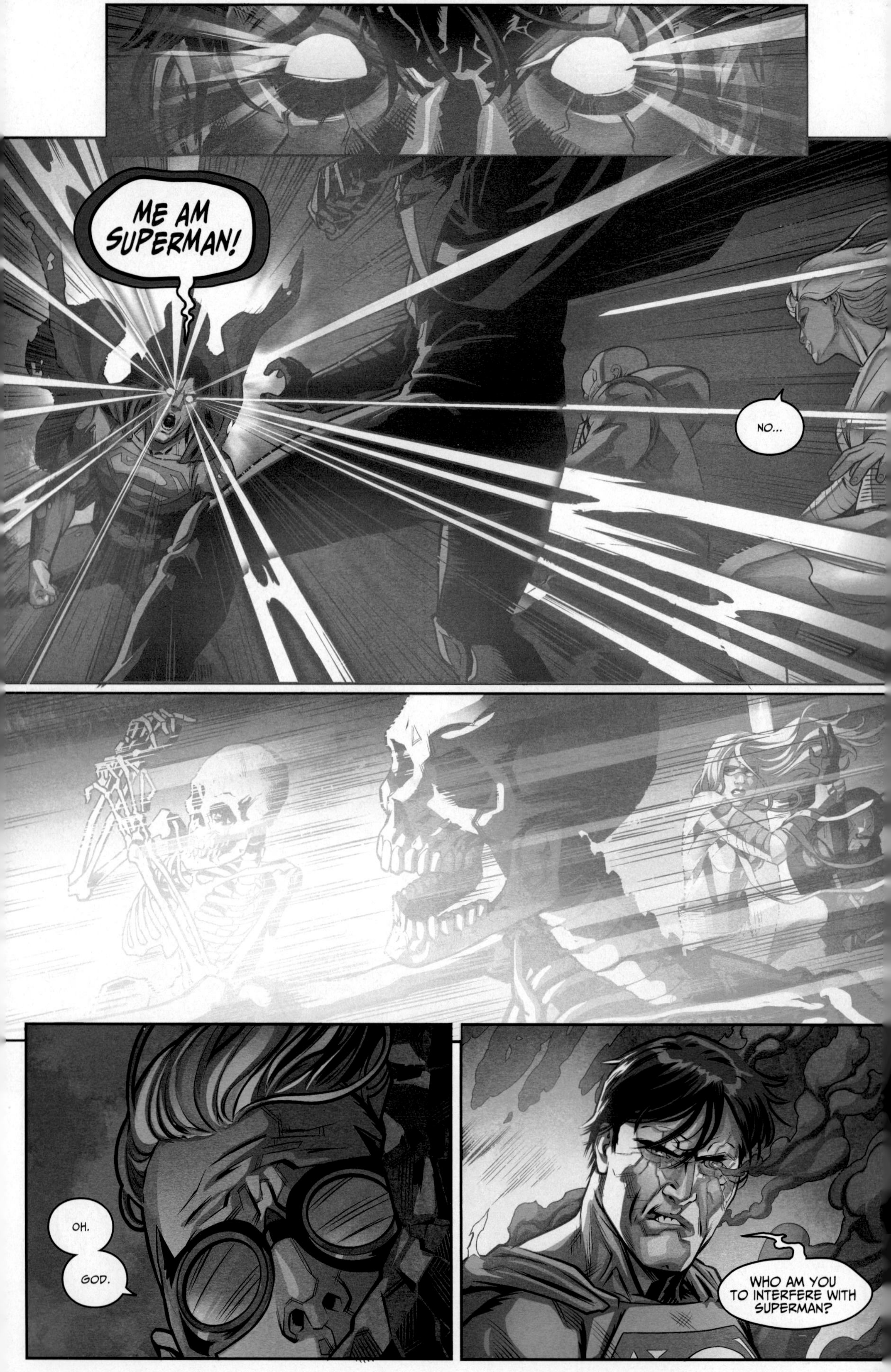
ME AM SUPERMAN!
NO...
OH.
GOD.
WHO AM YOU TO INTERFERE WITH SUPERMAN?

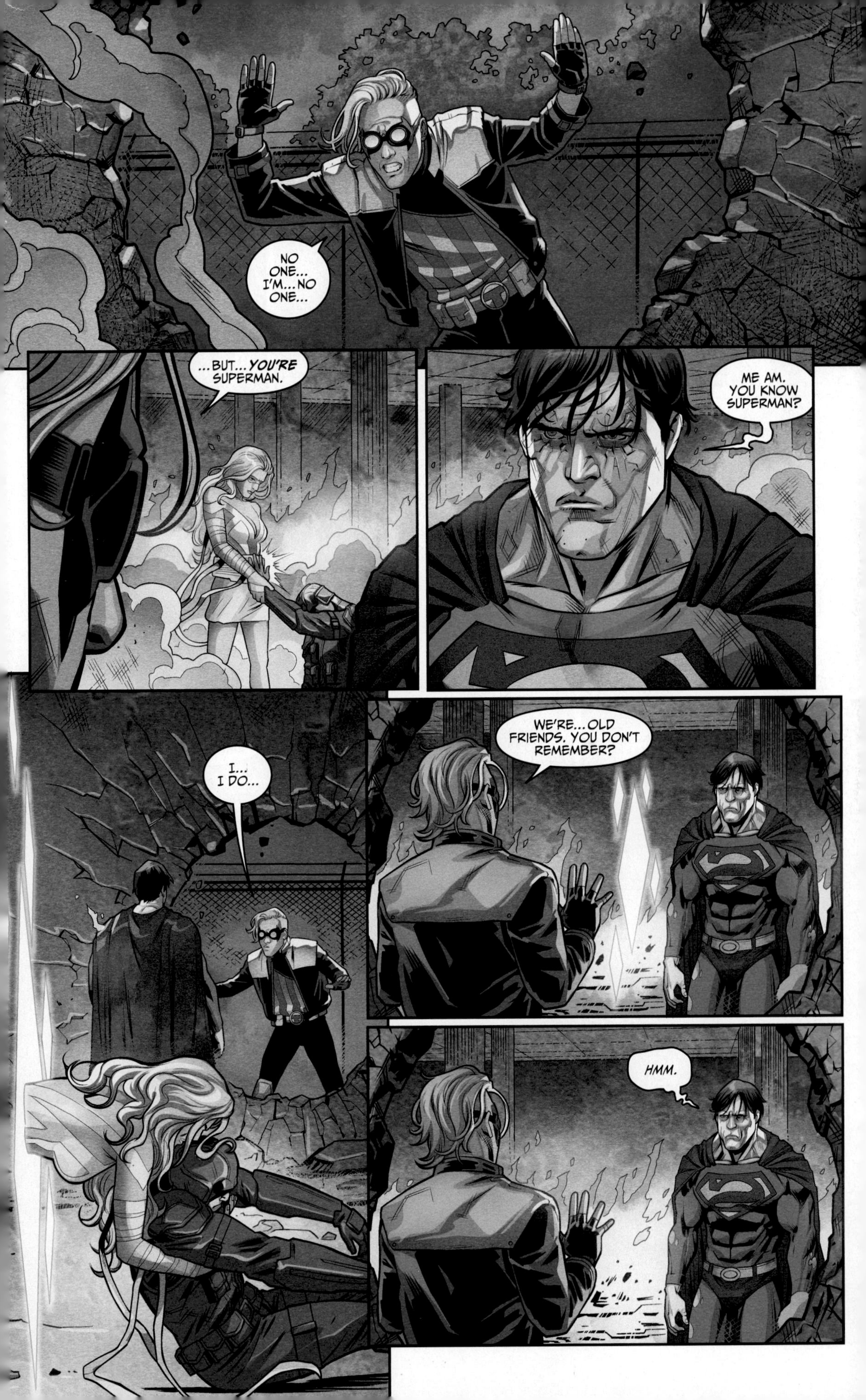
NO ONE... I'M...NO ONE...
...BUT...YOU'RE SUPERMAN.
ME AM. YOU KNOW SUPERMAN?
I... I DO...
WE'RE...OLD FRIENDS. YOU DON'T REMEMBER?
HMM.

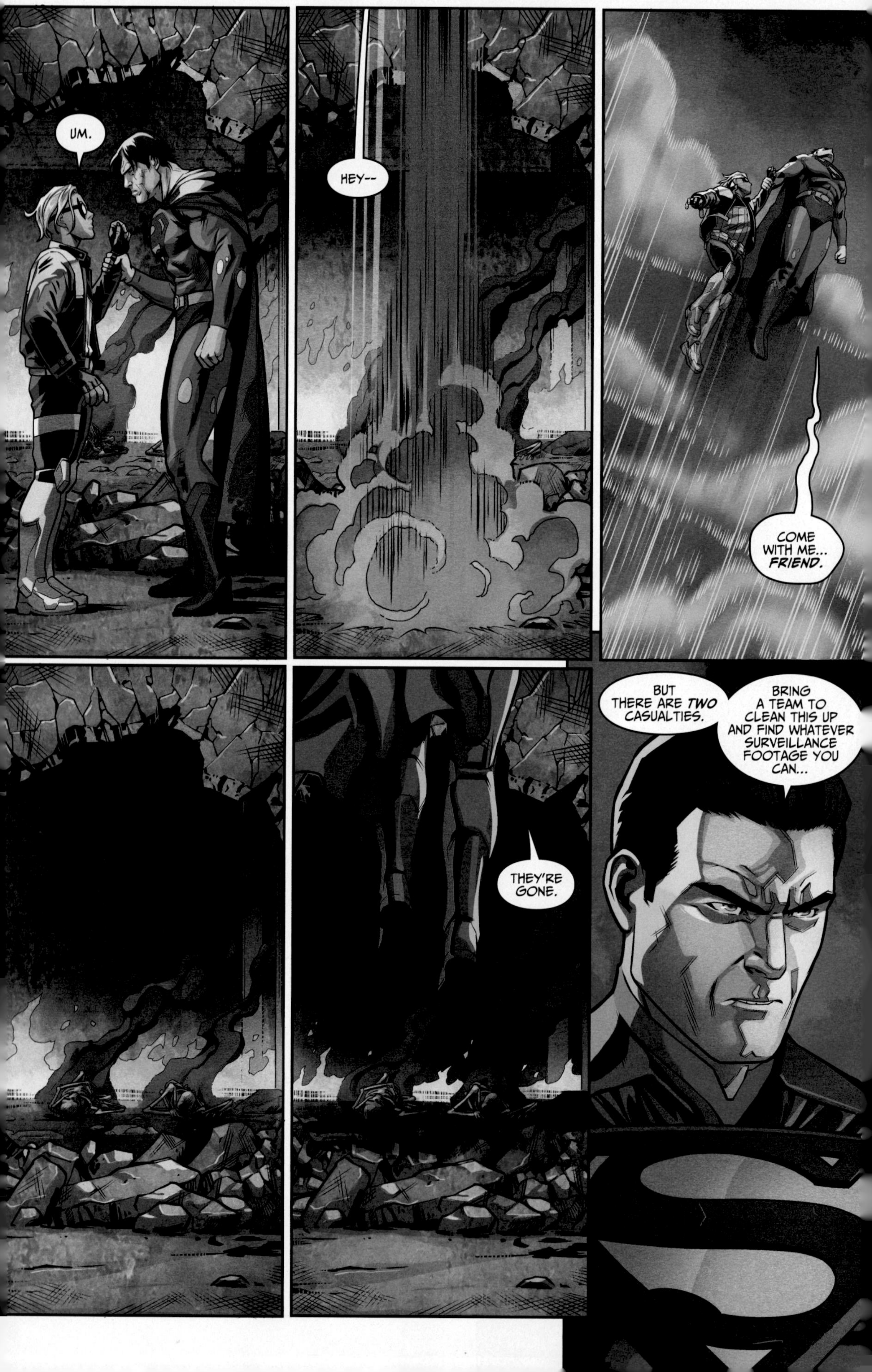
UM.
HEY--
COME WITH ME... *FRIEND.*
THEY'RE GONE.
BUT THERE ARE *TWO* CASUALTIES.
BRING A TEAM TO CLEAN THIS UP AND FIND WHATEVER SURVEILLANCE FOOTAGE YOU CAN...

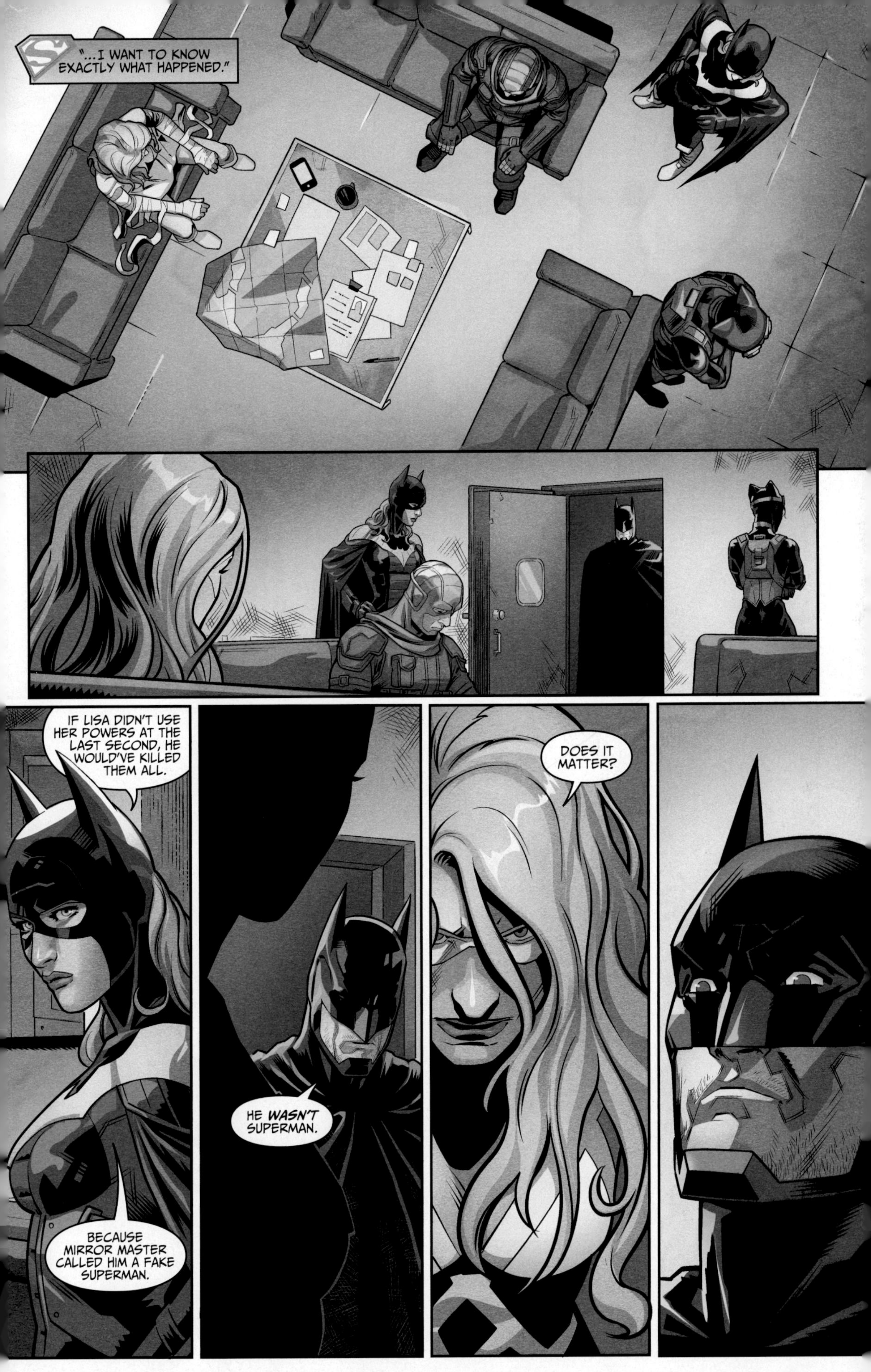
"...I WANT TO KNOW EXACTLY WHAT HAPPENED."
IF LISA DIDN'T USE HER POWERS AT THE LAST SECOND, HE WOULD'VE KILLED THEM ALL.
BECAUSE MIRROR MASTER CALLED HIM A FAKE SUPERMAN.
HE *WASN'T* SUPERMAN.
DOES IT MATTER?

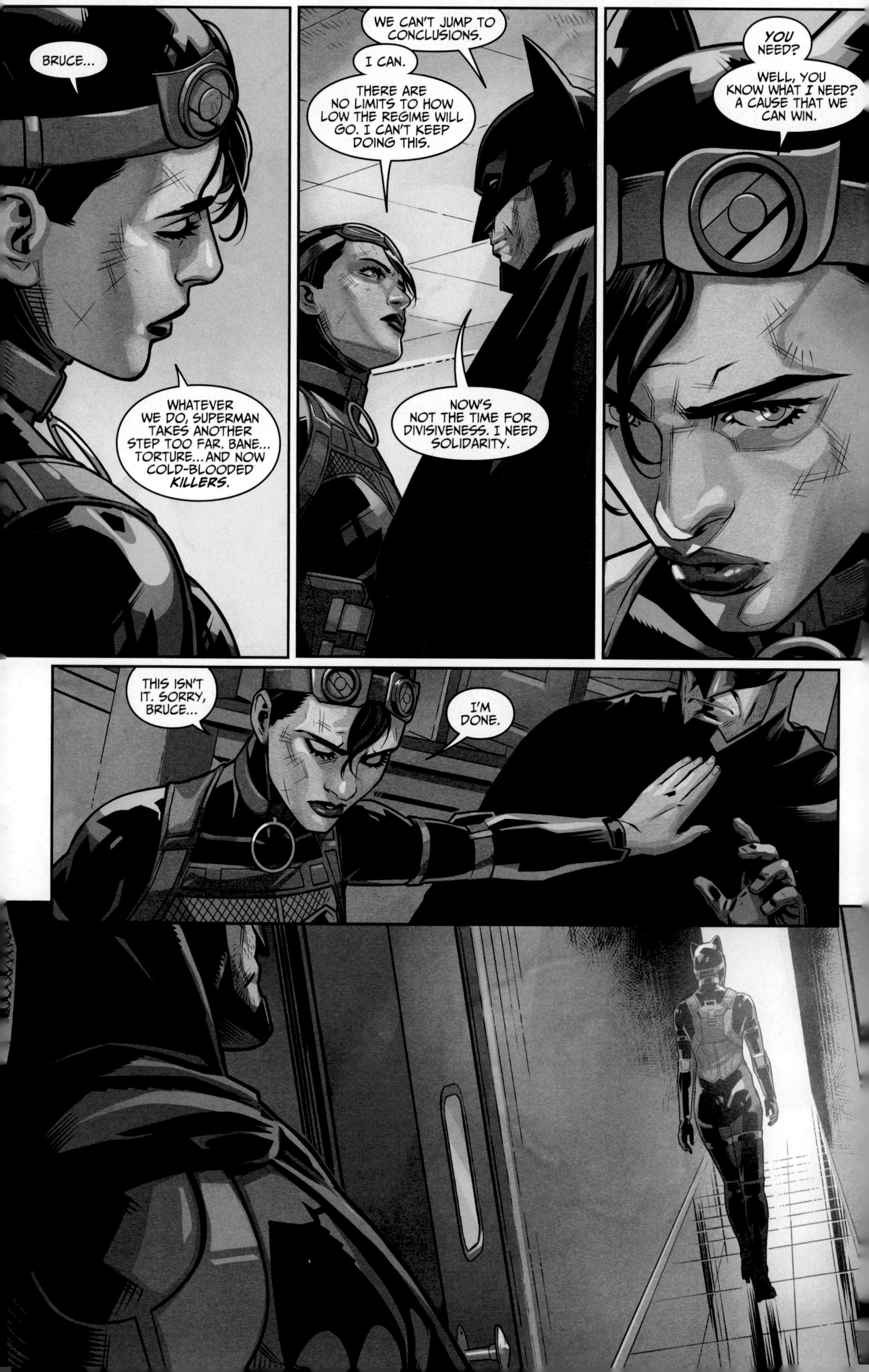
BRUCE...
WHATEVER WE DO, SUPERMAN TAKES ANOTHER STEP TOO FAR. BANE... TORTURE...AND NOW COLD-BLOODED *KILLERS*.
WE CAN'T JUMP TO CONCLUSIONS.
I CAN.
THERE ARE NO LIMITS TO HOW LOW THE REGIME WILL GO. I CAN'T KEEP DOING THIS.
NOW'S NOT THE TIME FOR DIVISIVENESS. I NEED SOLIDARITY.
YOU NEED?
WELL, YOU KNOW WHAT *I* NEED? A CAUSE THAT WE CAN WIN.
THIS ISN'T IT. SORRY, BRUCE...
I'M DONE.

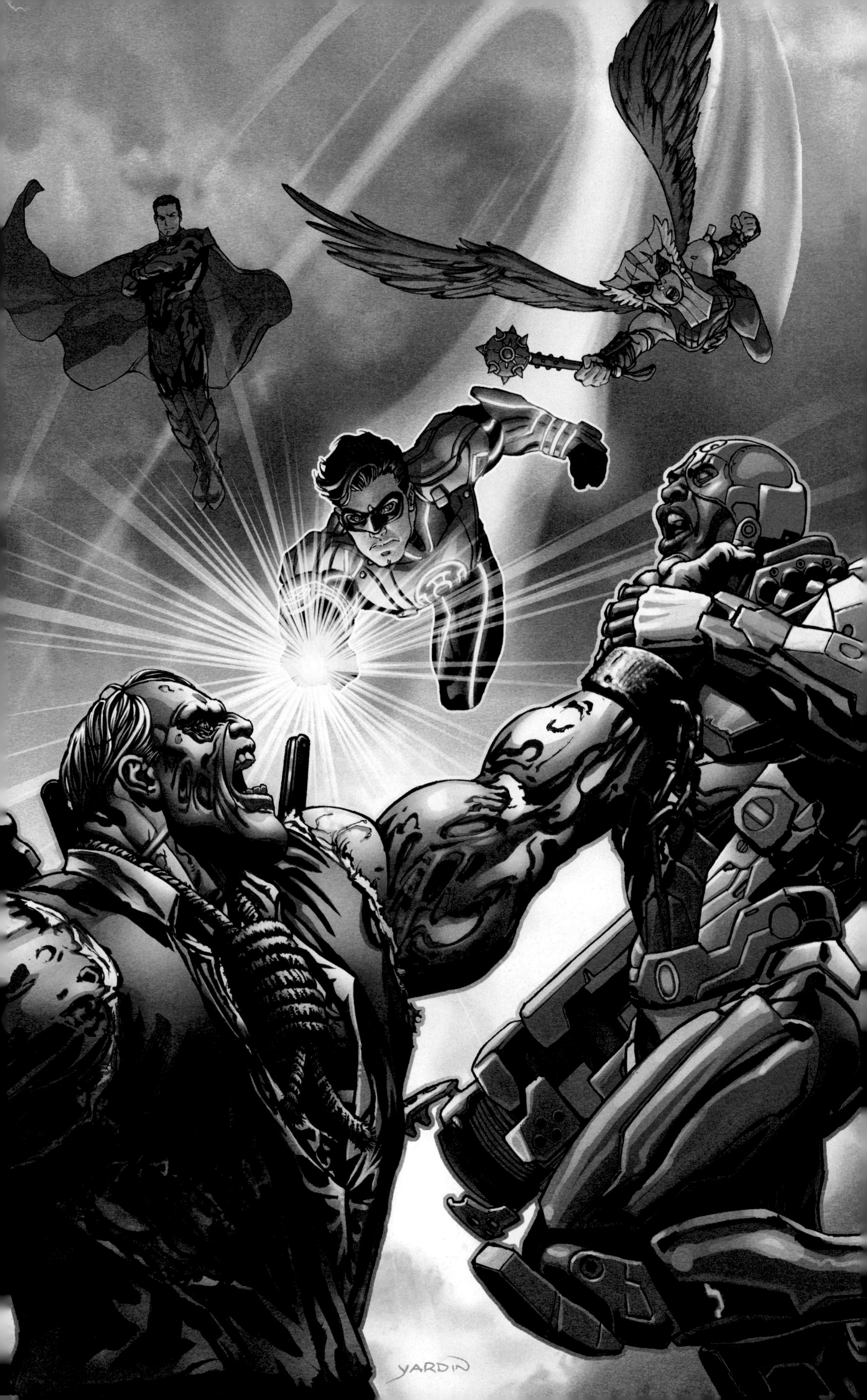
YARDIN

"Unusual Suspects" **Mike S. Miller** Artist **J. Nanjan** Colorist
"Three-For-All" **Iban Coello** Artist **J. Nanjan** Colorist

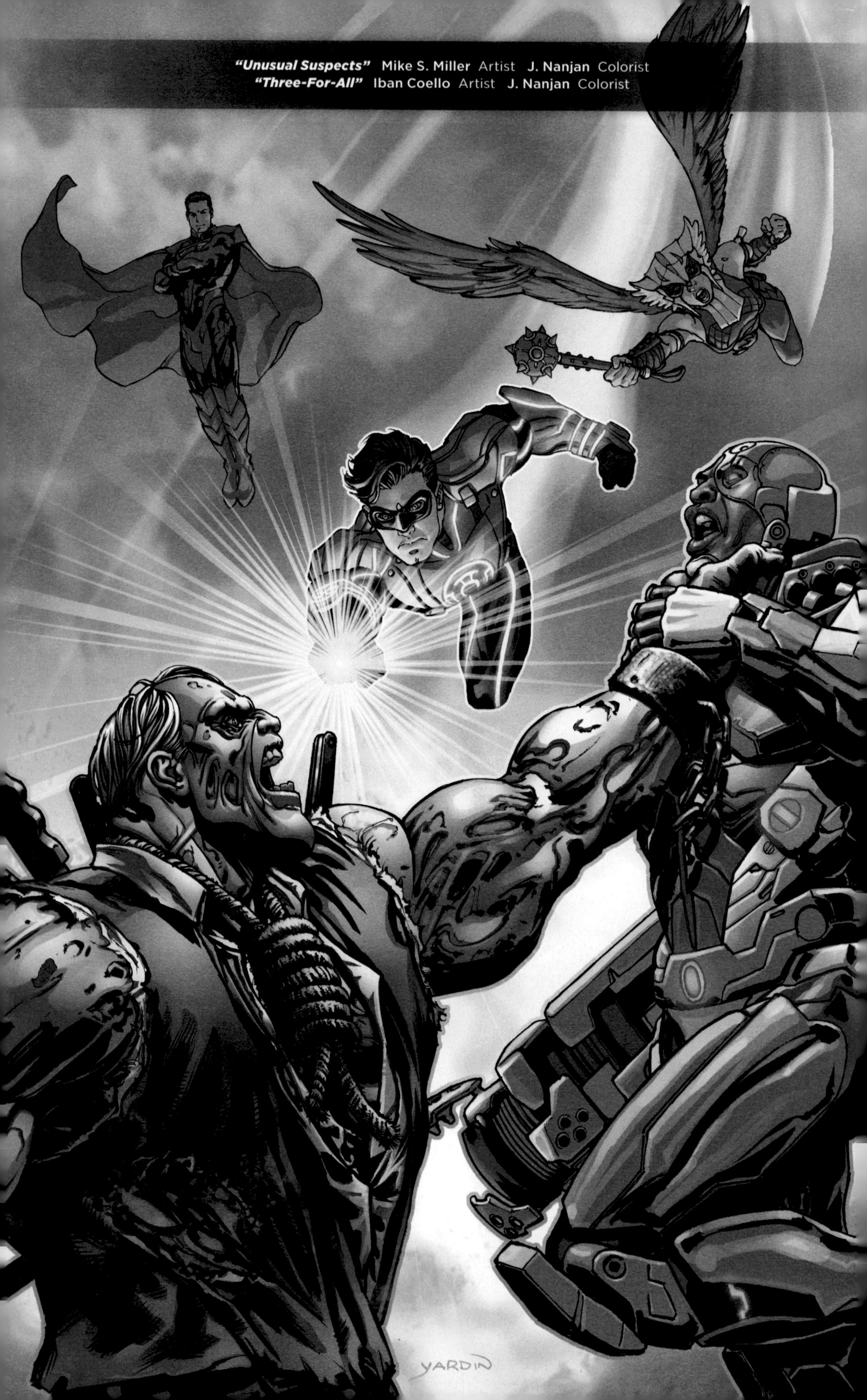
YARDIN

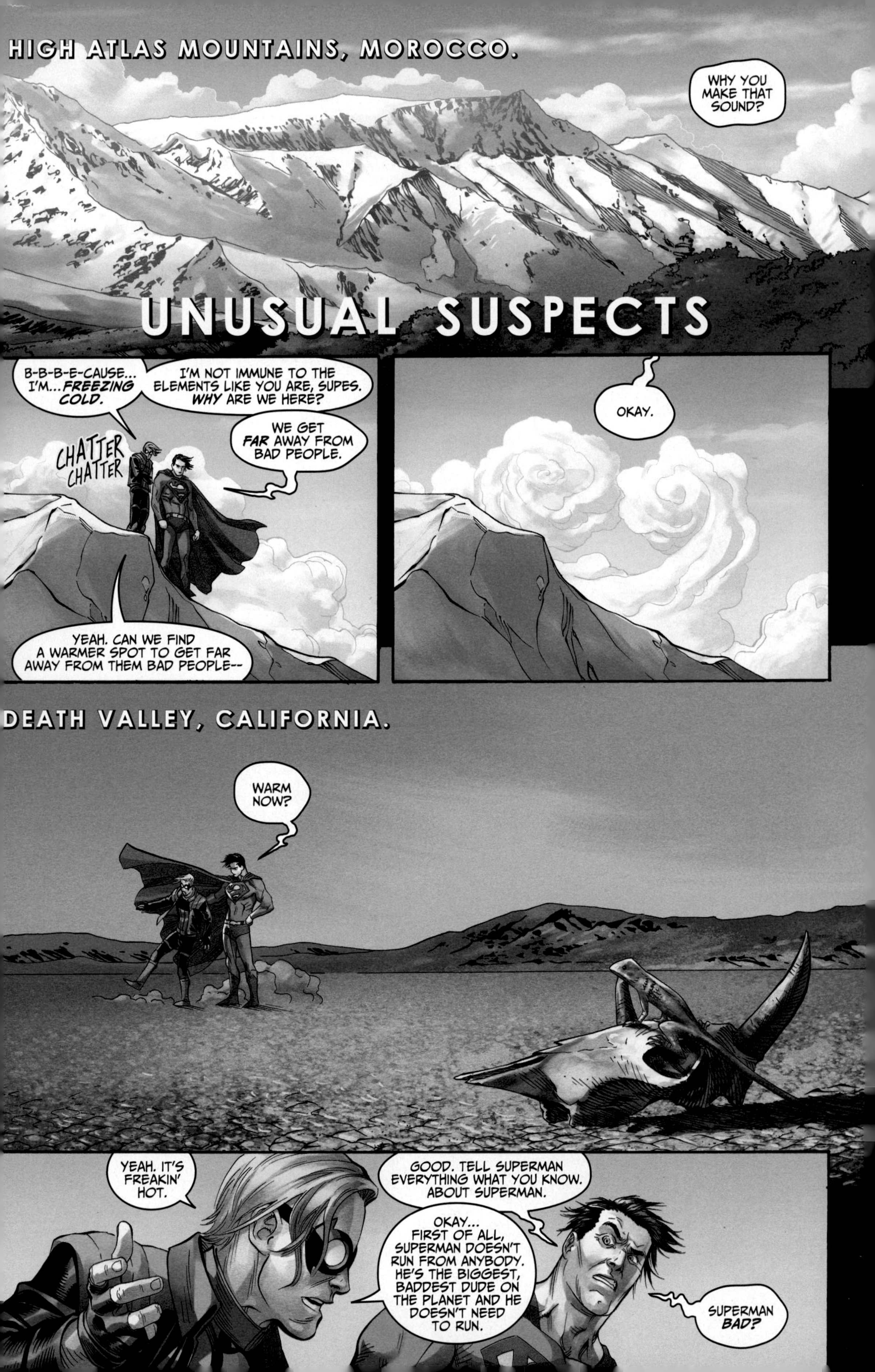
HIGH ATLAS MOUNTAINS, MOROCCO.
WHY YOU MAKE THAT SOUND?
UNUSUAL SUSPECTS
B-B-B-E-CAUSE... I'M... FREEZING COLD.
I'M NOT IMMUNE TO THE ELEMENTS LIKE YOU ARE, SUPES. WHY ARE WE HERE?
CHATTER CHATTER
WE GET FAR AWAY FROM BAD PEOPLE.
YEAH. CAN WE FIND A WARMER SPOT TO GET FAR AWAY FROM THEM BAD PEOPLE--
OKAY.
DEATH VALLEY, CALIFORNIA.
WARM NOW?
YEAH. IT'S FREAKIN' HOT.
GOOD. TELL SUPERMAN EVERYTHING WHAT YOU KNOW. ABOUT SUPERMAN.
OKAY... FIRST OF ALL, SUPERMAN DOESN'T RUN FROM ANYBODY. HE'S THE BIGGEST, BADDEST DUDE ON THE PLANET AND HE DOESN'T NEED TO RUN.
SUPERMAN BAD?

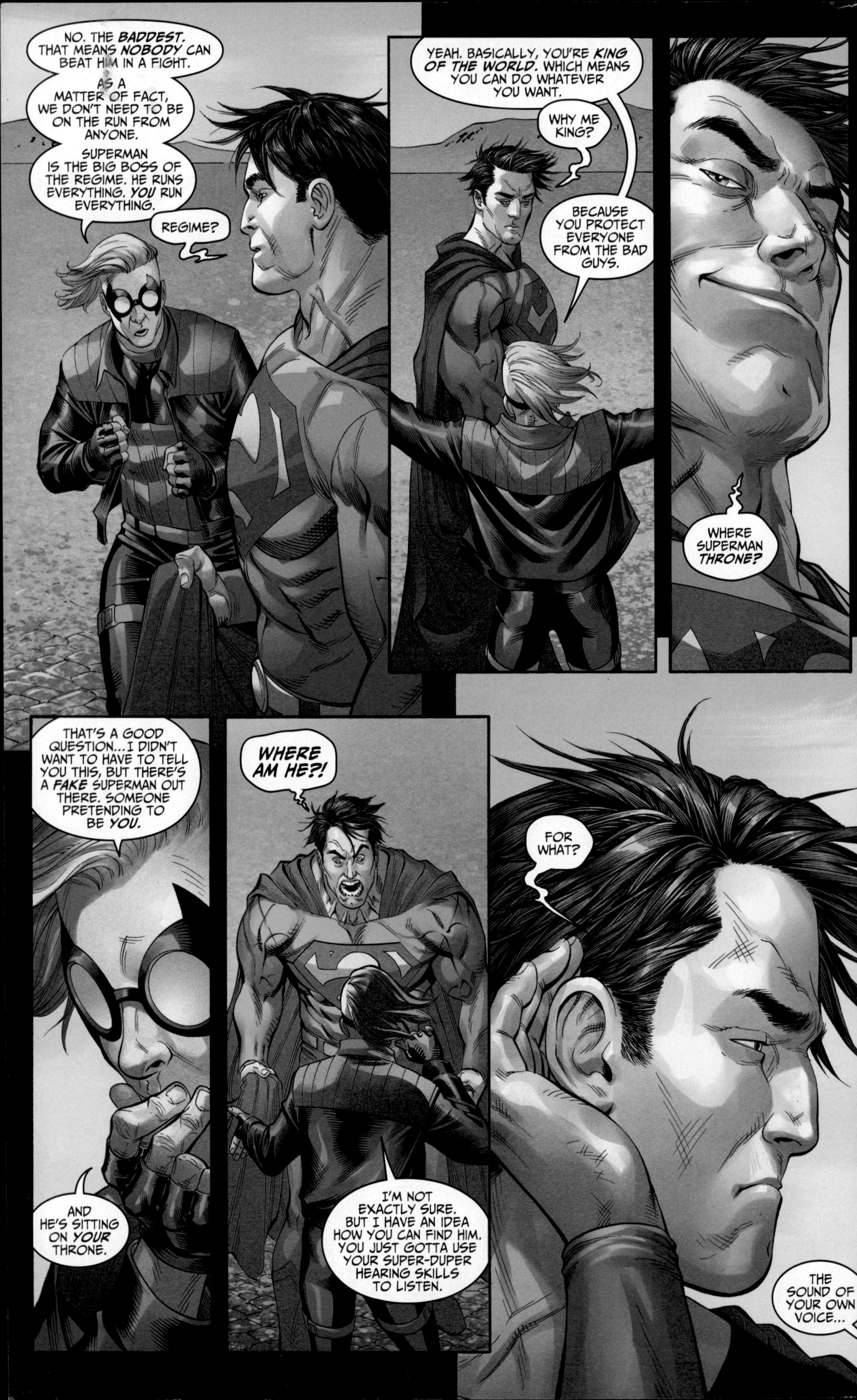

NO. THE BADDEST. THAT MEANS NOBODY CAN BEAT HIM IN A FIGHT.
AS A MATTER OF FACT, WE DON'T NEED TO BE ON THE RUN FROM ANYONE.
SUPERMAN IS THE BIG BOSS OF THE REGIME. HE RUNS EVERYTHING. YOU RUN EVERYTHING.
REGIME?
YEAH. BASICALLY, YOU'RE KING OF THE WORLD. WHICH MEANS YOU CAN DO WHATEVER YOU WANT.
WHY ME KING?
BECAUSE YOU PROTECT EVERYONE FROM THE BAD GUYS.
WHERE SUPERMAN THRONE?
THAT'S A GOOD QUESTION... I DIDN'T WANT TO HAVE TO TELL YOU THIS, BUT THERE'S A FAKE SUPERMAN OUT THERE. SOMEONE PRETENDING TO BE YOU.
AND HE'S SITTING ON YOUR THRONE.
WHERE AM HE?!
I'M NOT EXACTLY SURE. BUT I HAVE AN IDEA HOW YOU CAN FIND HIM. YOU JUST GOTTA USE YOUR SUPER-DUPER HEARING SKILLS TO LISTEN.
FOR WHAT?
THE SOUND OF YOUR OWN VOICE...

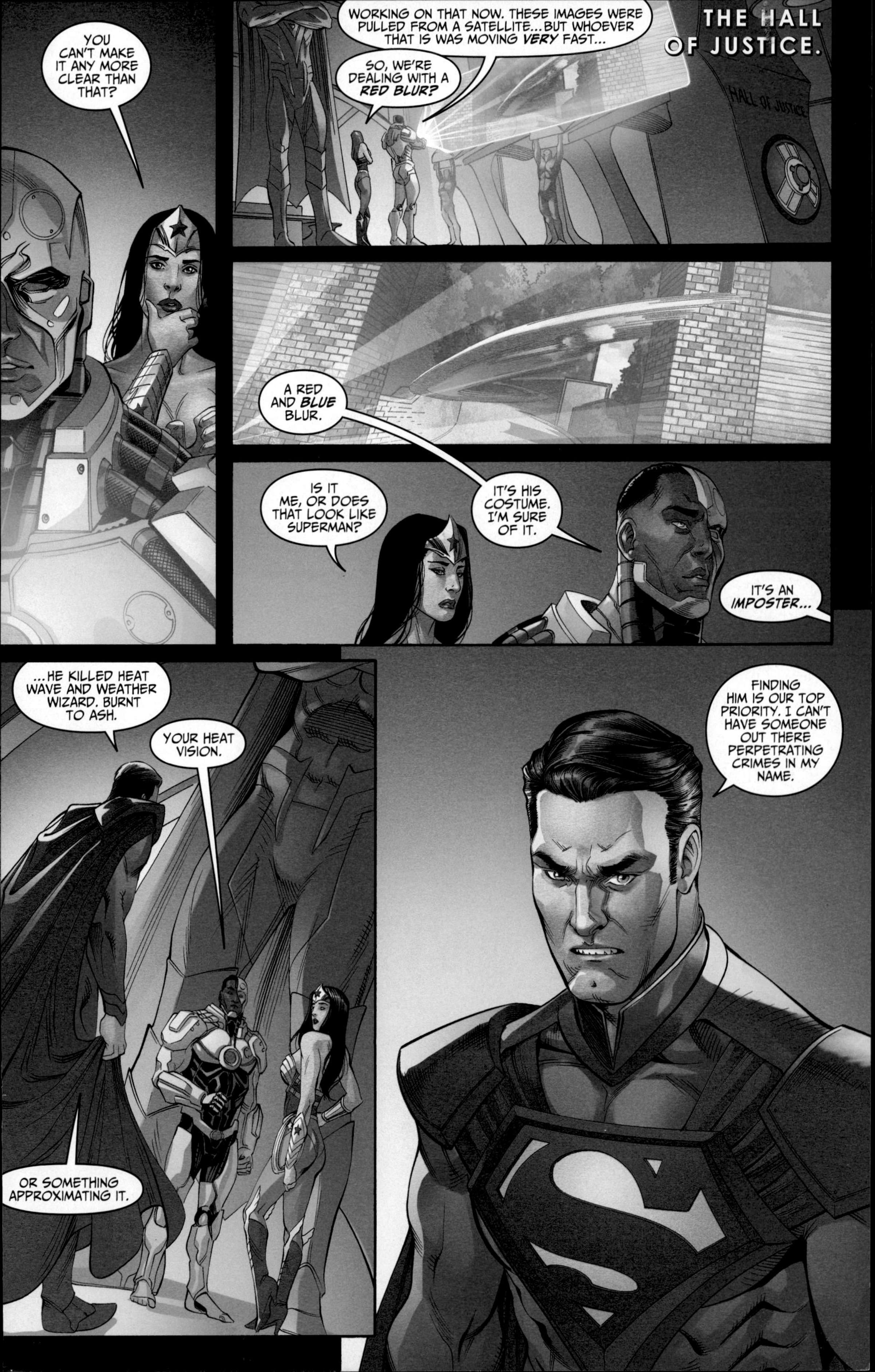
THE HALL OF JUSTICE.
YOU CAN'T MAKE IT ANY MORE CLEAR THAN THAT?
WORKING ON THAT NOW. THESE IMAGES WERE PULLED FROM A SATELLITE...BUT WHOEVER THAT IS WAS MOVING VERY FAST...
SO, WE'RE DEALING WITH A RED BLUR?
HALL OF JUSTICE
A RED AND BLUE BLUR.
IS IT ME, OR DOES THAT LOOK LIKE SUPERMAN?
IT'S HIS COSTUME. I'M SURE OF IT.
IT'S AN IMPOSTER...
...HE KILLED HEAT WAVE AND WEATHER WIZARD. BURNT TO ASH.
YOUR HEAT VISION.
OR SOMETHING APPROXIMATING IT.
FINDING HIM IS OUR TOP PRIORITY. I CAN'T HAVE SOMEONE OUT THERE PERPETRATING CRIMES IN MY NAME.

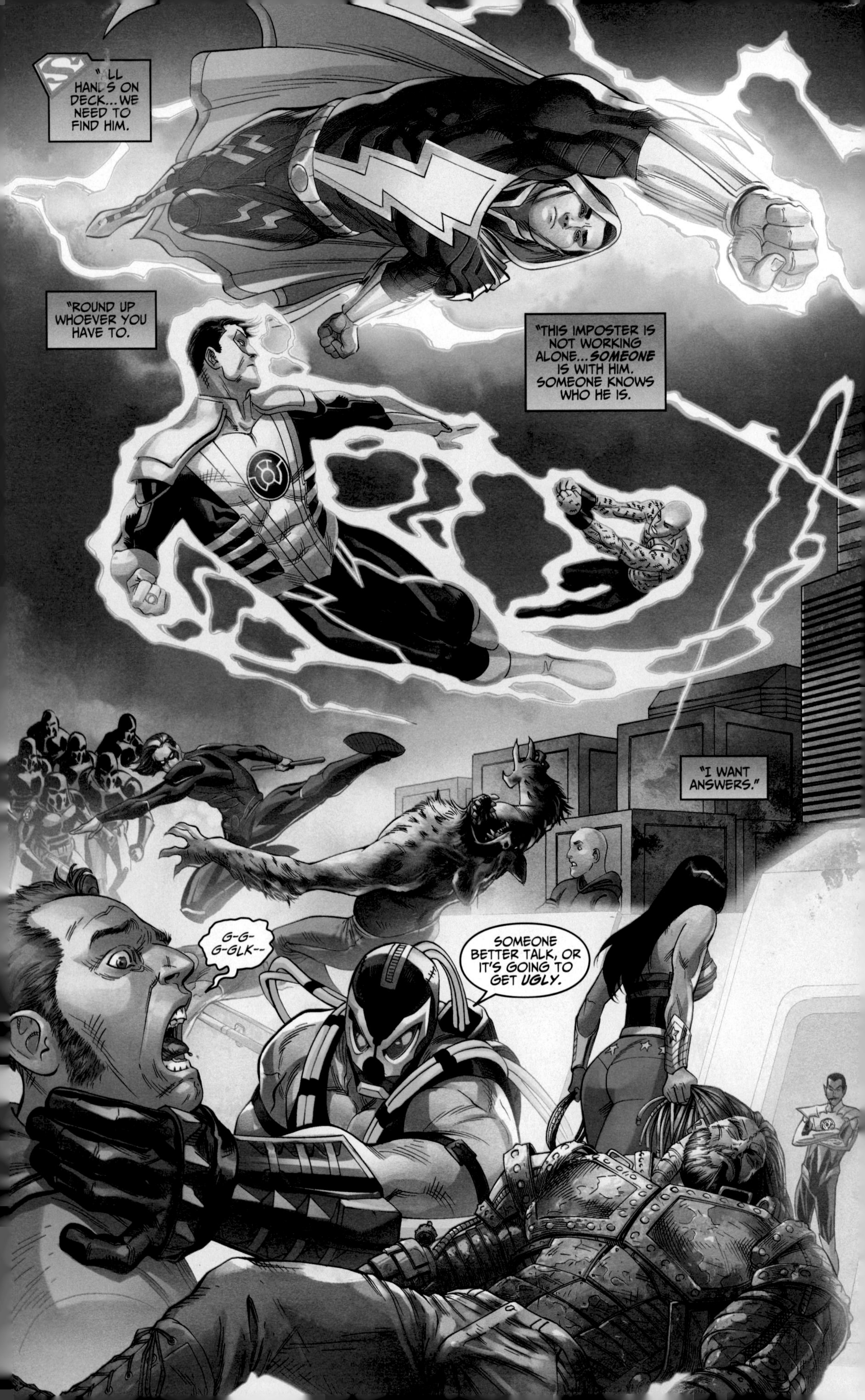
"ALL HANDS ON DECK...WE NEED TO FIND HIM.
"ROUND UP WHOEVER YOU HAVE TO.
"THIS IMPOSTER IS NOT WORKING ALONE...SOMEONE IS WITH HIM. SOMEONE KNOWS WHO HE IS.
"I WANT ANSWERS."
G-G-G-GLK--
SOMEONE BETTER TALK, OR IT'S GOING TO GET UGLY.

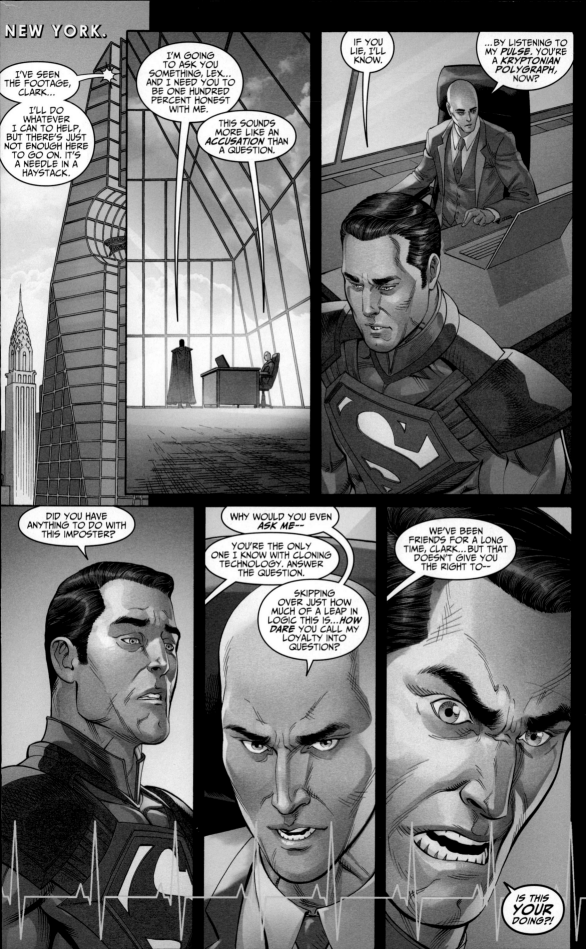

NEW YORK.

I'VE SEEN THE FOOTAGE, CLARK...

I'LL DO WHATEVER I CAN TO HELP, BUT THERE'S JUST NOT ENOUGH HERE TO GO ON. IT'S A NEEDLE IN A HAYSTACK.

I'M GOING TO ASK YOU SOMETHING, LEX... AND I NEED YOU TO BE ONE HUNDRED PERCENT HONEST WITH ME.

THIS SOUNDS MORE LIKE AN ACCUSATION THAN A QUESTION.

IF YOU LIE, I'LL KNOW.

...BY LISTENING TO MY PULSE. YOU'RE A KRYPTONIAN POLYGRAPH, NOW?

DID YOU HAVE ANYTHING TO DO WITH THIS IMPOSTER?

WHY WOULD YOU EVEN ASK ME--

YOU'RE THE ONLY ONE I KNOW WITH CLONING TECHNOLOGY. ANSWER THE QUESTION.

SKIPPING OVER JUST HOW MUCH OF A LEAP IN LOGIC THIS IS...HOW DARE YOU CALL MY LOYALTY INTO QUESTION?

WE'VE BEEN FRIENDS FOR A LONG TIME, CLARK...BUT THAT DOESN'T GIVE YOU THE RIGHT TO--

IS THIS YOUR DOING?!

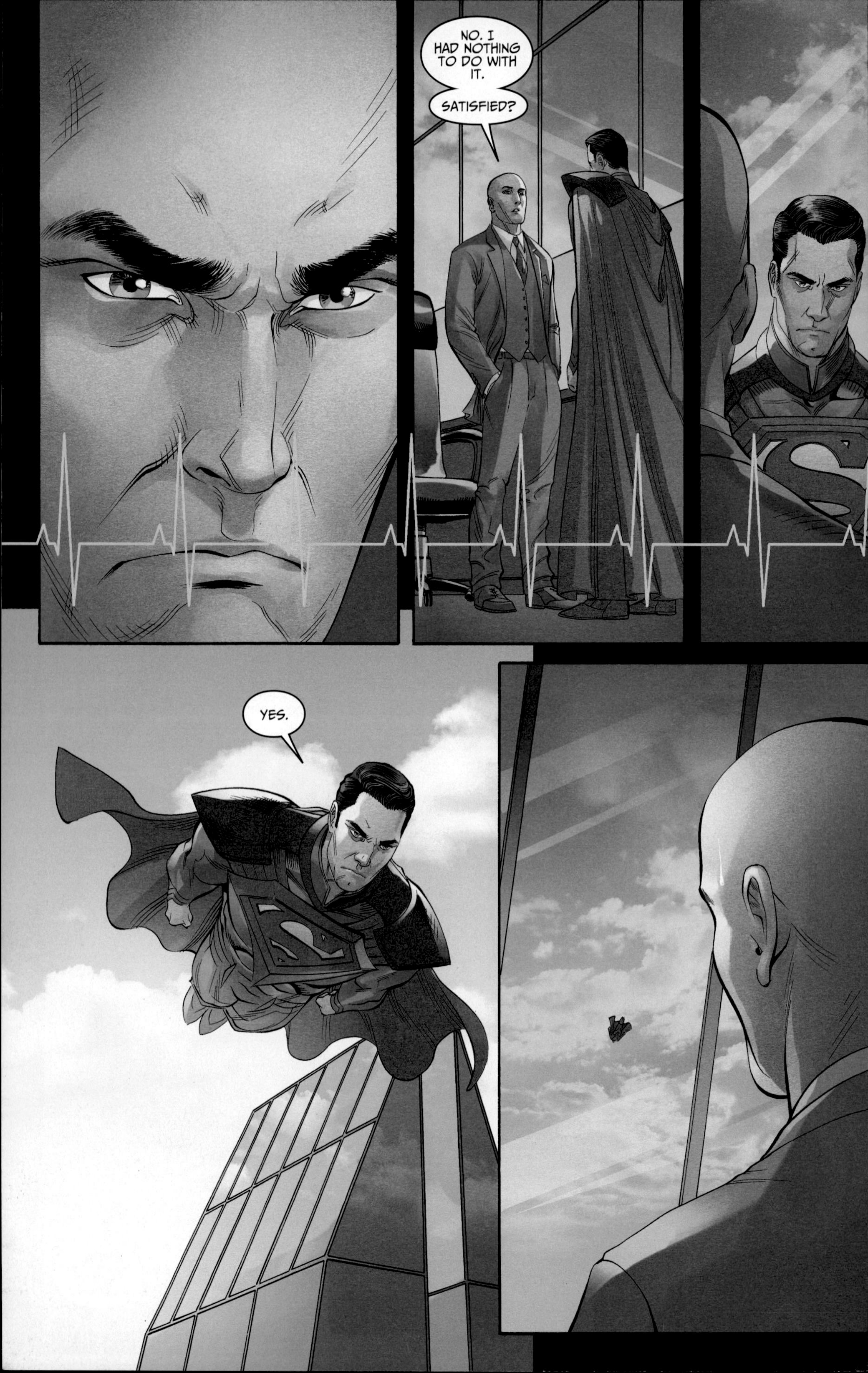
NO. I HAD NOTHING TO DO WITH IT.
SATISFIED?
YES.

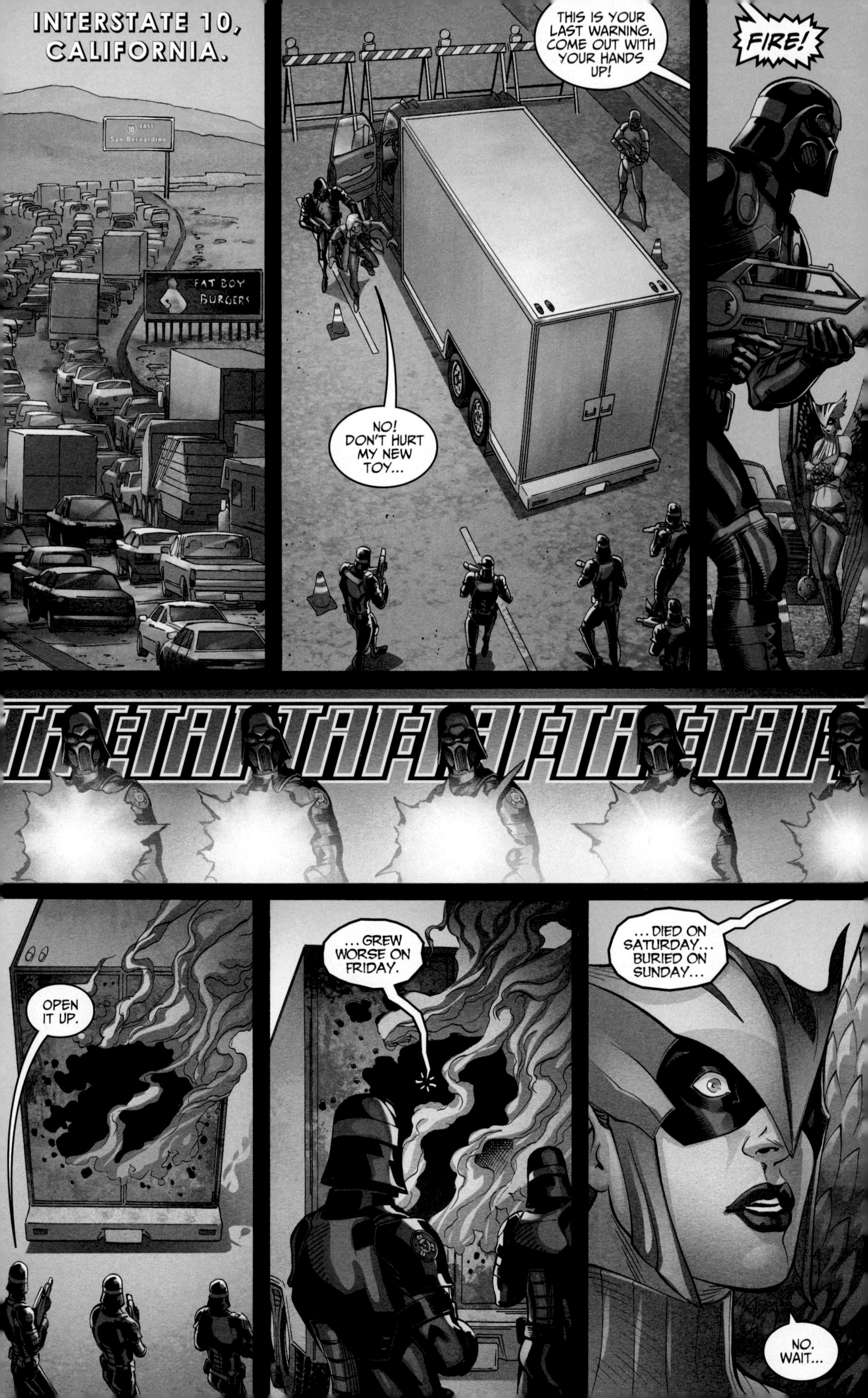
INTERSTATE 10, CALIFORNIA.
10 EAST San Bernardino
FAT BOY BURGERS
THIS IS YOUR LAST WARNING. COME OUT WITH YOUR HANDS UP!
NO! DON'T HURT MY NEW TOY...
FIRE!
TA-TA-TA-TA-TA-TA-TA-TA
OPEN IT UP.
...GREW WORSE ON FRIDAY.
...DIED ON SATURDAY... BURIED ON SUNDAY...
NO. WAIT...

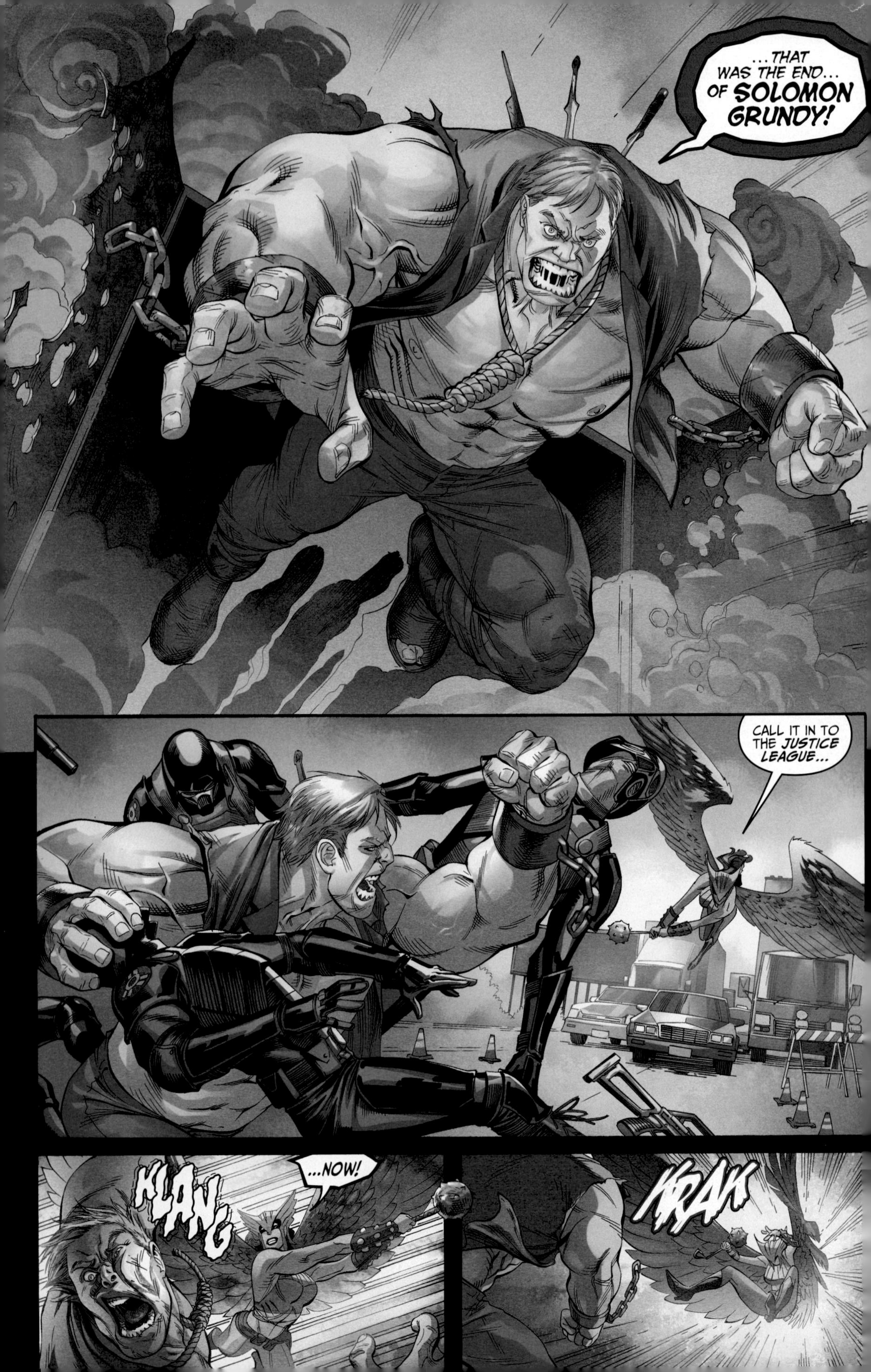
...THAT WAS THE END... OF SOLOMON GRUNDY!
CALL IT IN TO THE JUSTICE LEAGUE...
KLANG
...NOW!
KRAK

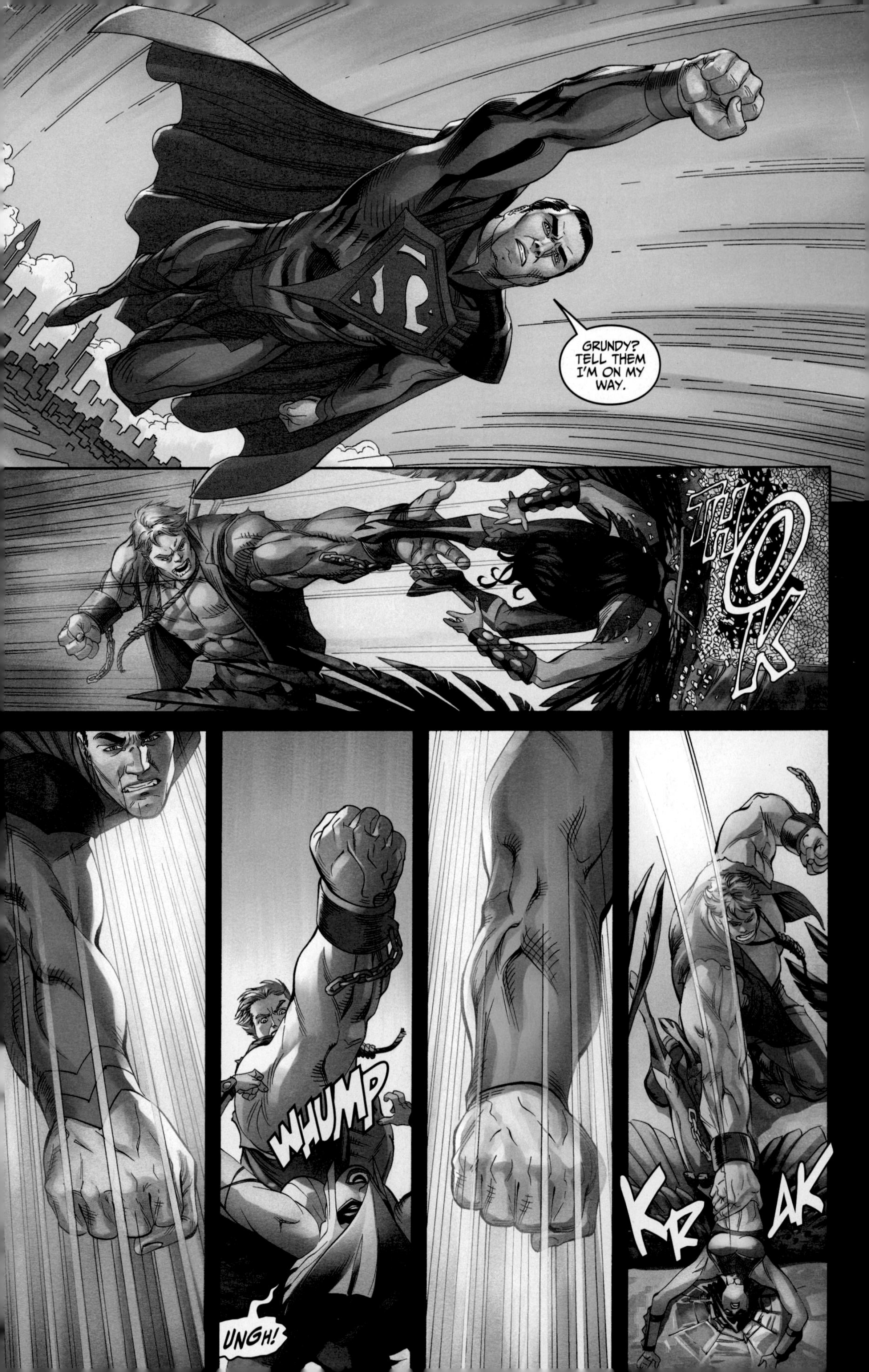
GRUNDY? TELL THEM I'M ON MY WAY.
THOK
WHUMP
UNGH!
KRAK

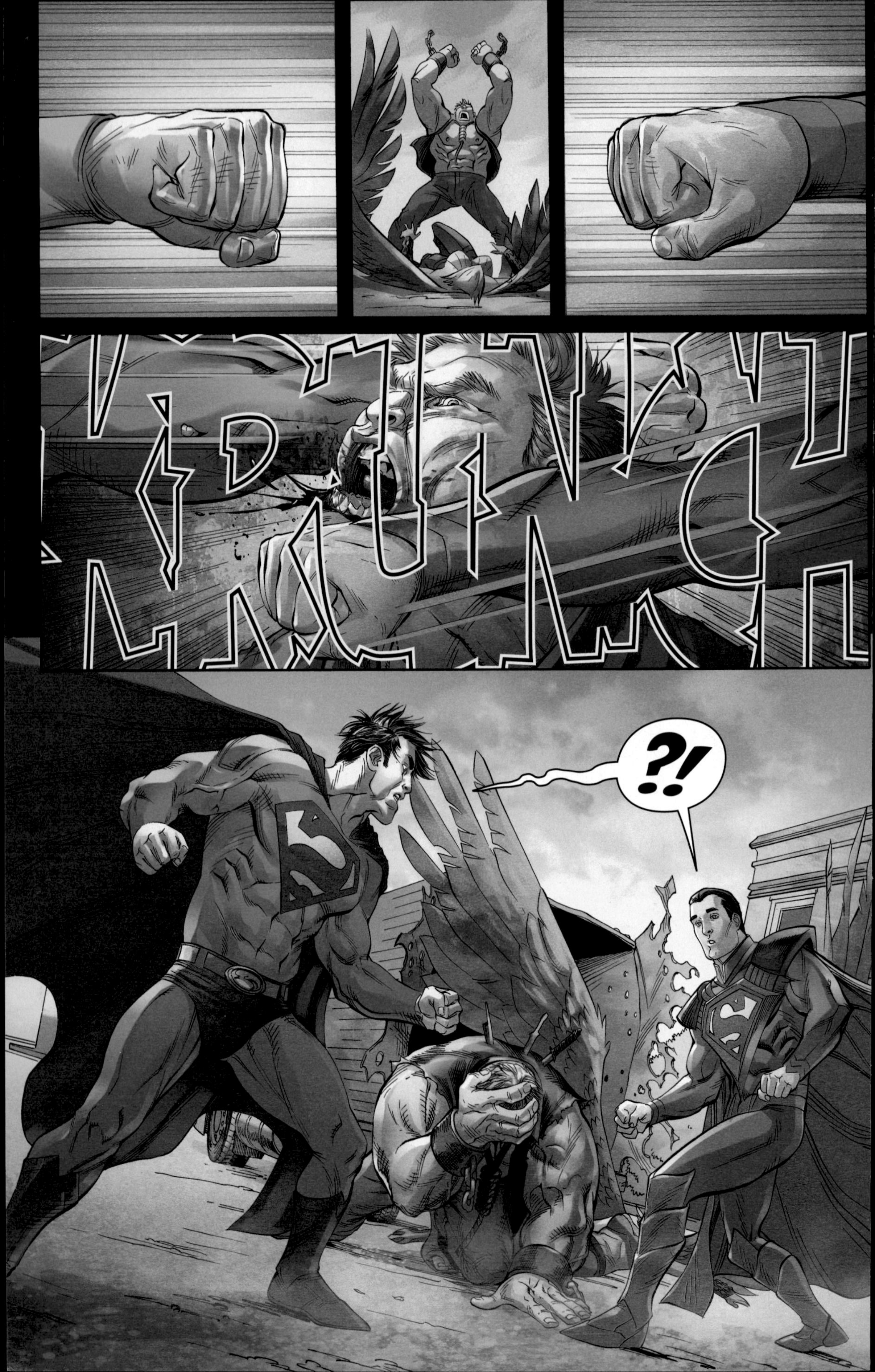
?!

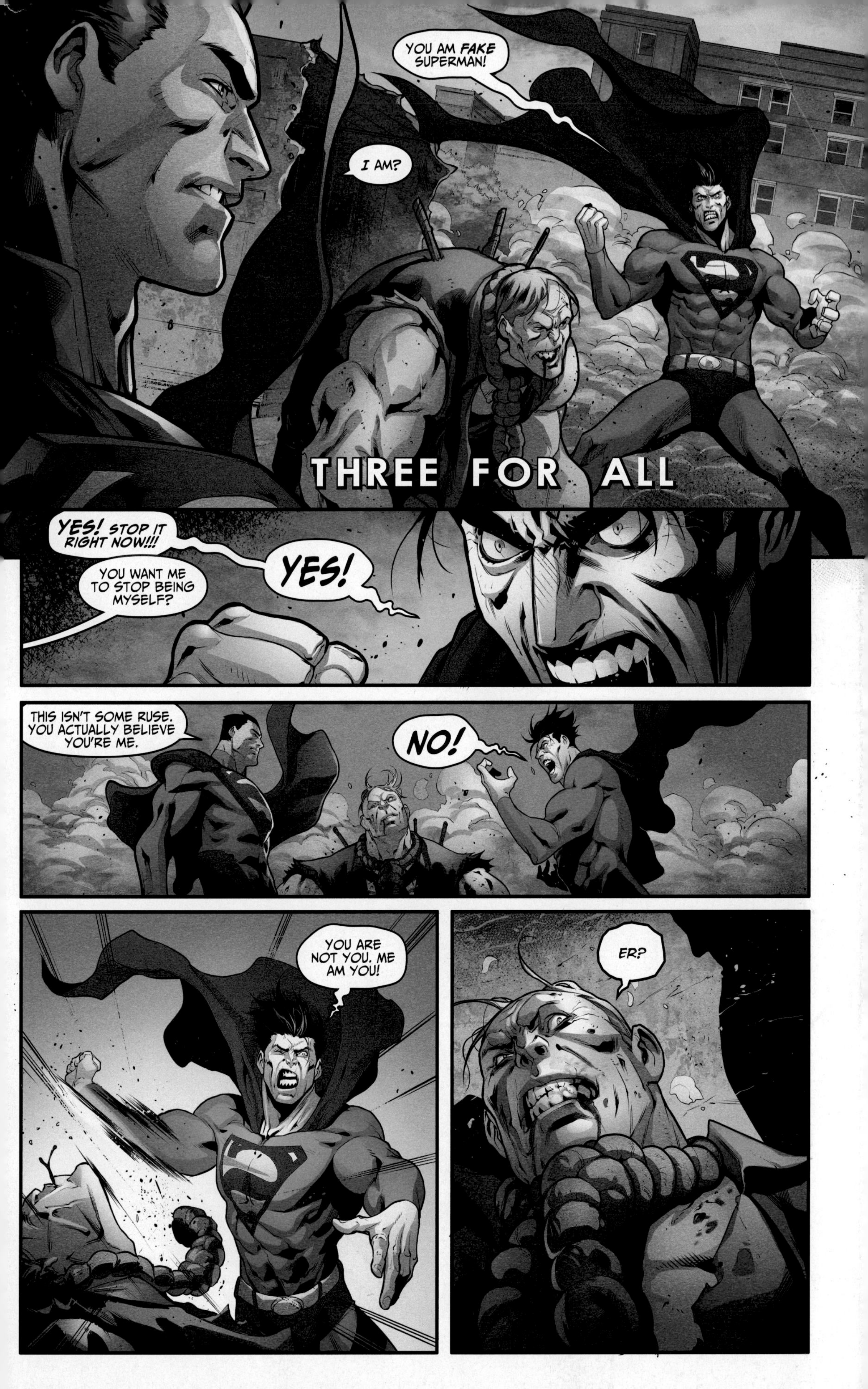
YOU AM FAKE SUPERMAN!
I AM?
THREE FOR ALL
YES! STOP IT RIGHT NOW!!!
YOU WANT ME TO STOP BEING MYSELF?
YES!
THIS ISN'T SOME RUSE. YOU ACTUALLY BELIEVE YOU'RE ME.
NO!
YOU ARE NOT YOU. ME AM YOU!
ER?

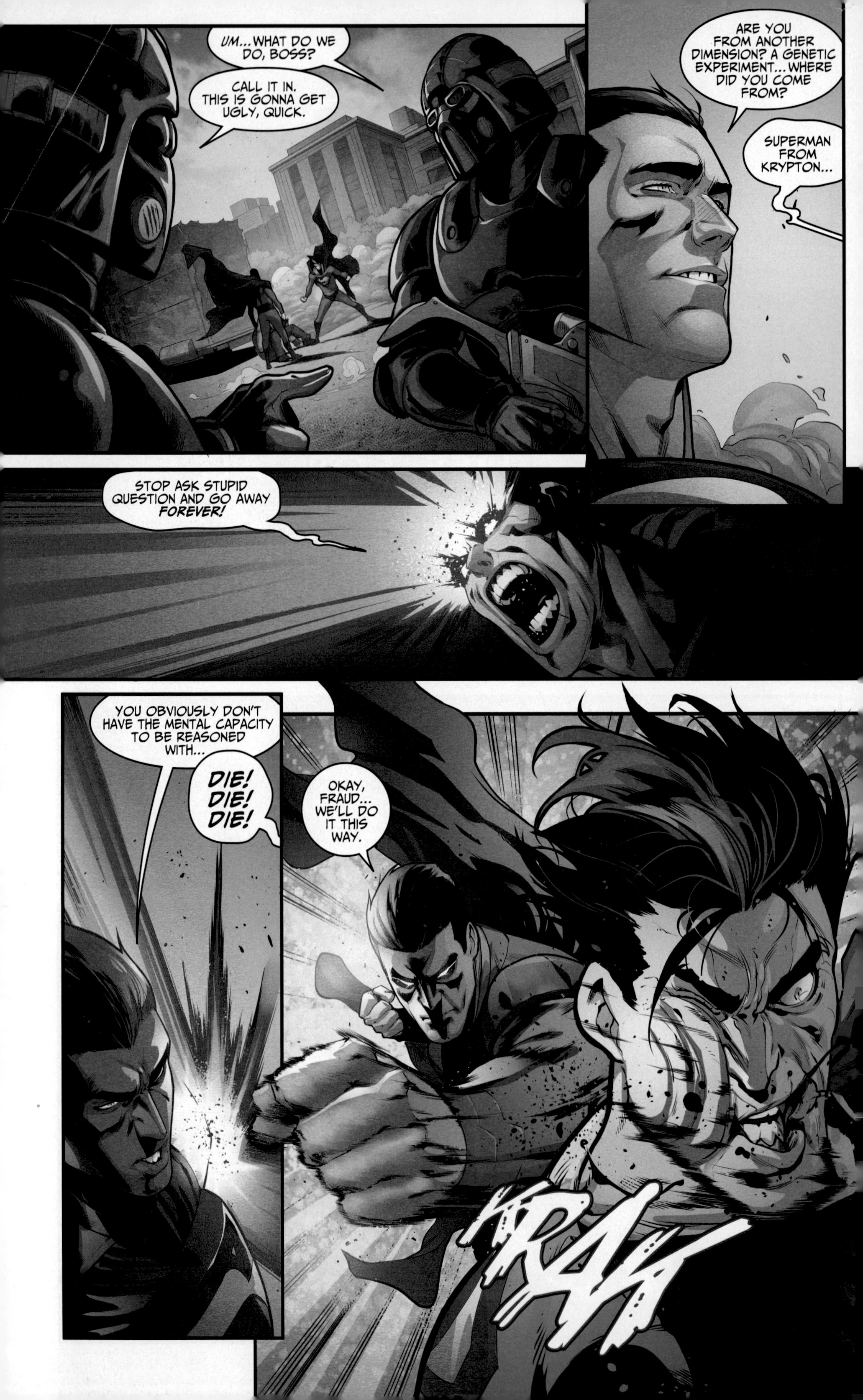
UM... WHAT DO WE DO, BOSS?
CALL IT IN. THIS IS GONNA GET UGLY, QUICK.
ARE YOU FROM ANOTHER DIMENSION? A GENETIC EXPERIMENT... WHERE DID YOU COME FROM?
SUPERMAN FROM KRYPTON...
STOP ASK STUPID QUESTION AND GO AWAY FOREVER!
YOU OBVIOUSLY DON'T HAVE THE MENTAL CAPACITY TO BE REASONED WITH...
DIE! DIE! DIE!
OKAY, FRAUD... WE'LL DO IT THIS WAY.
KRAK

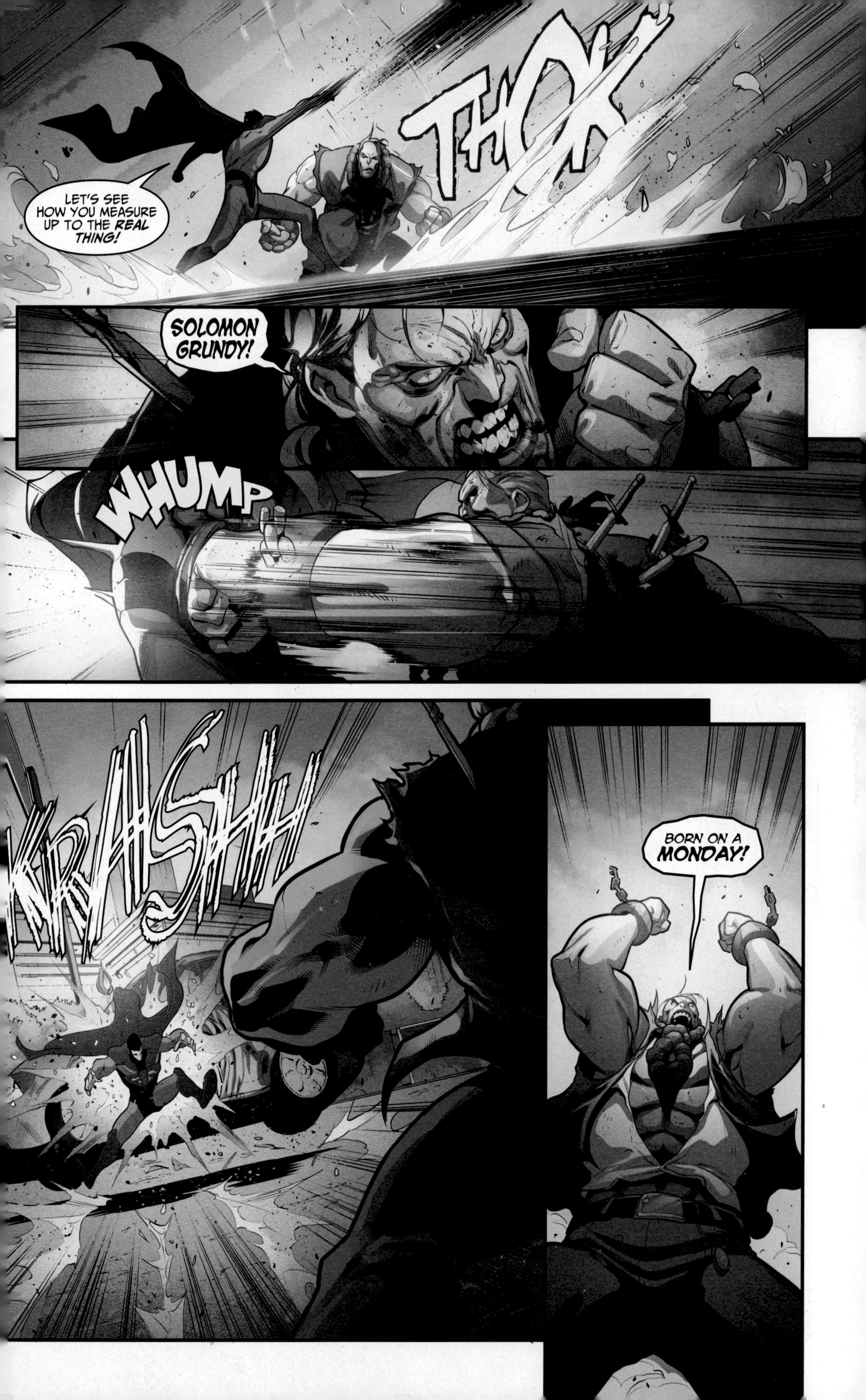
THOK
LET'S SEE HOW YOU MEASURE UP TO THE REAL THING!
SOLOMON GRUNDY!
WHUMP
KRASHH
BORN ON A MONDAY!

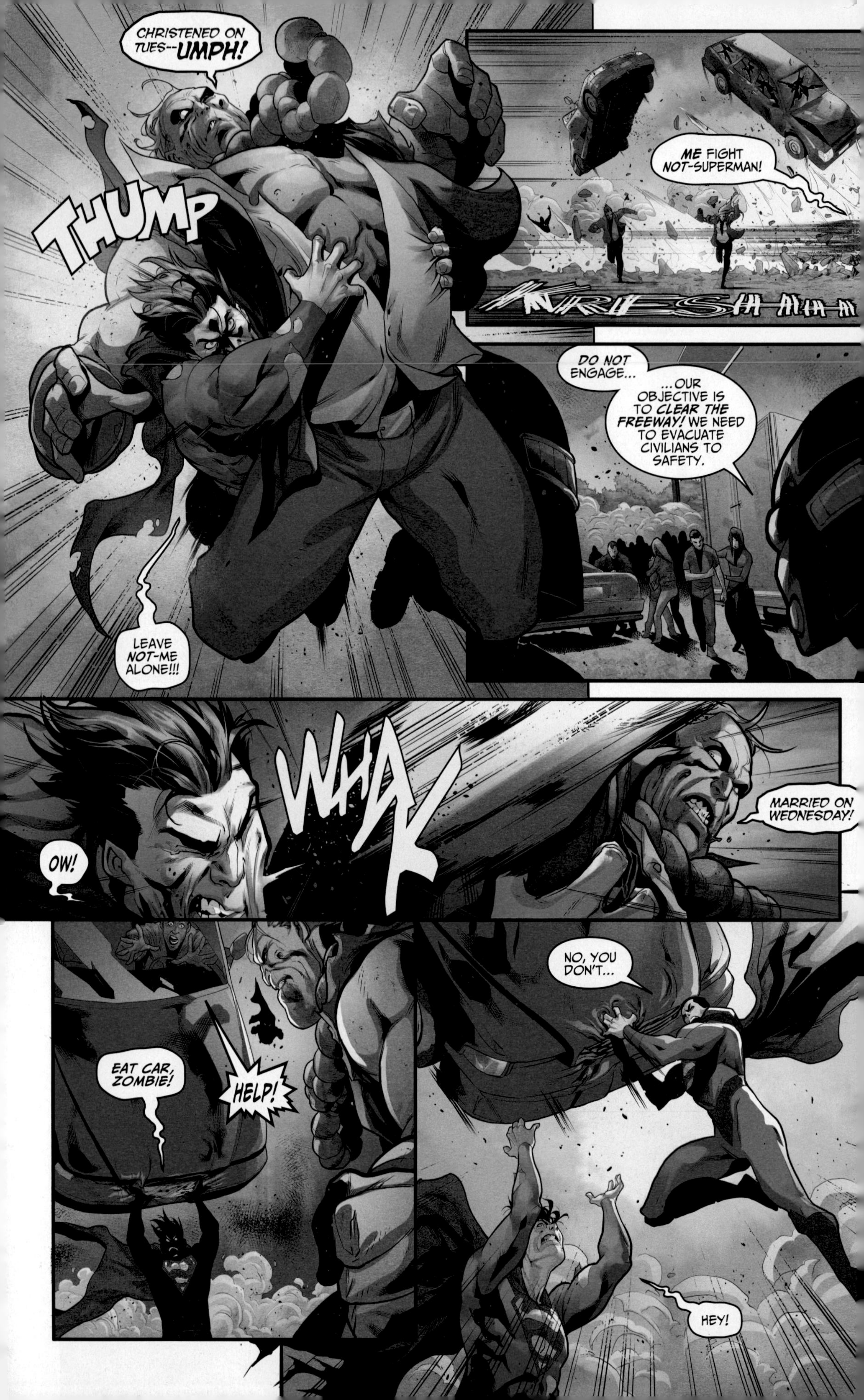
CHRISTENED ON TUES--UMPH!
THUMP
ME FIGHT NOT-SUPERMAN!
KRESHHHHH
DO NOT ENGAGE...
...OUR OBJECTIVE IS TO CLEAR THE FREEWAY! WE NEED TO EVACUATE CIVILIANS TO SAFETY.
LEAVE NOT-ME ALONE!!!
OW!
WHAK
MARRIED ON WEDNESDAY!
EAT CAR, ZOMBIE!
HELP!
NO, YOU DON'T...
HEY!

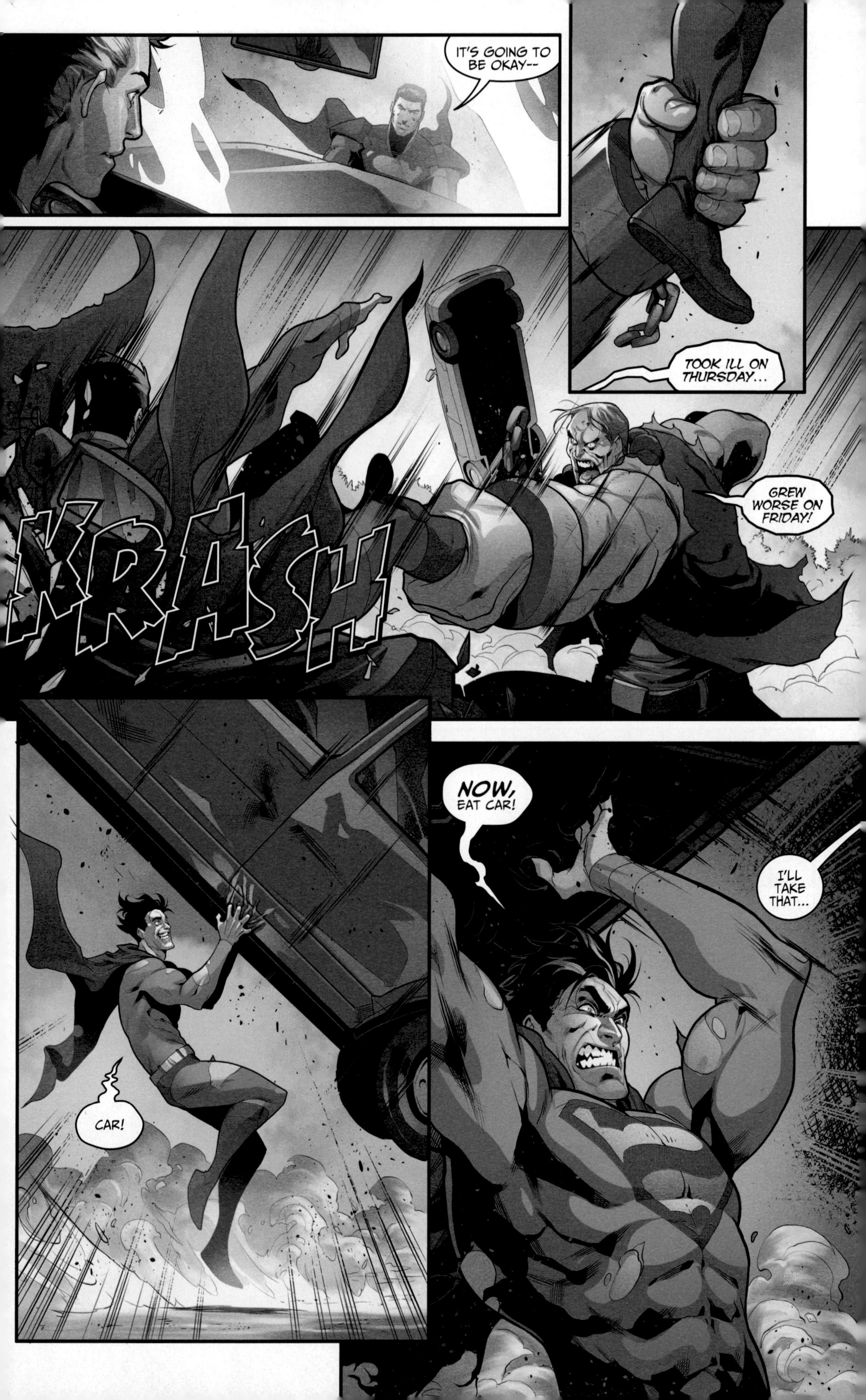
IT'S GOING TO BE OKAY--
TOOK ILL ON THURSDAY...
GREW WORSE ON FRIDAY!
KRASH
CAR!
NOW, EAT CAR!
I'LL TAKE THAT...

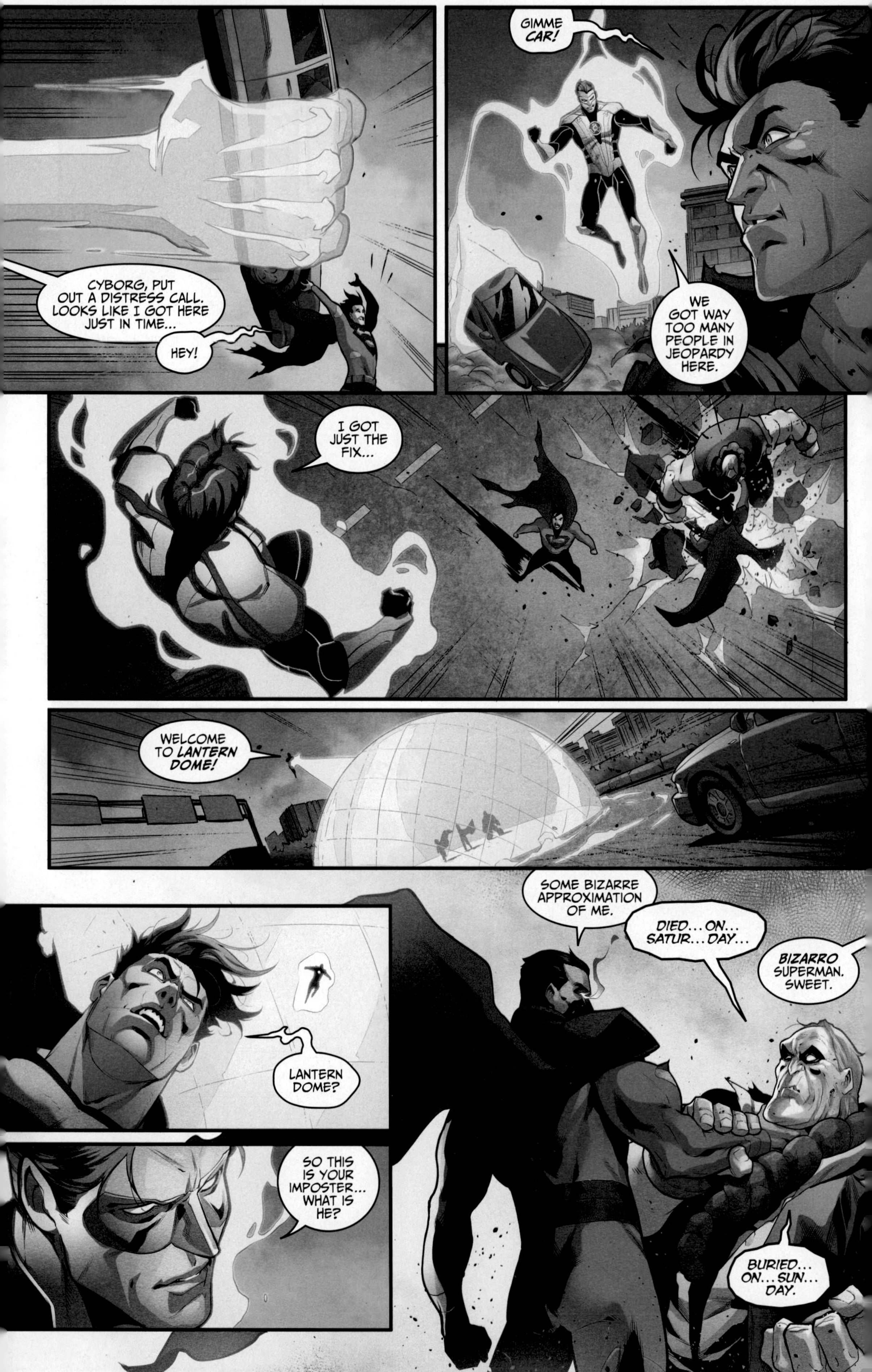
CYBORG, PUT OUT A DISTRESS CALL. LOOKS LIKE I GOT HERE JUST IN TIME...
HEY!
GIMME CAR!
WE GOT WAY TOO MANY PEOPLE IN JEOPARDY HERE.
I GOT JUST THE FIX...
WELCOME TO LANTERN DOME!
LANTERN DOME?
SO THIS IS YOUR IMPOSTER... WHAT IS HE?
SOME BIZARRE APPROXIMATION OF ME.
DIED... ON... SATUR... DAY...
BIZARRO SUPERMAN. SWEET.
BURIED... ON... SUN... DAY.

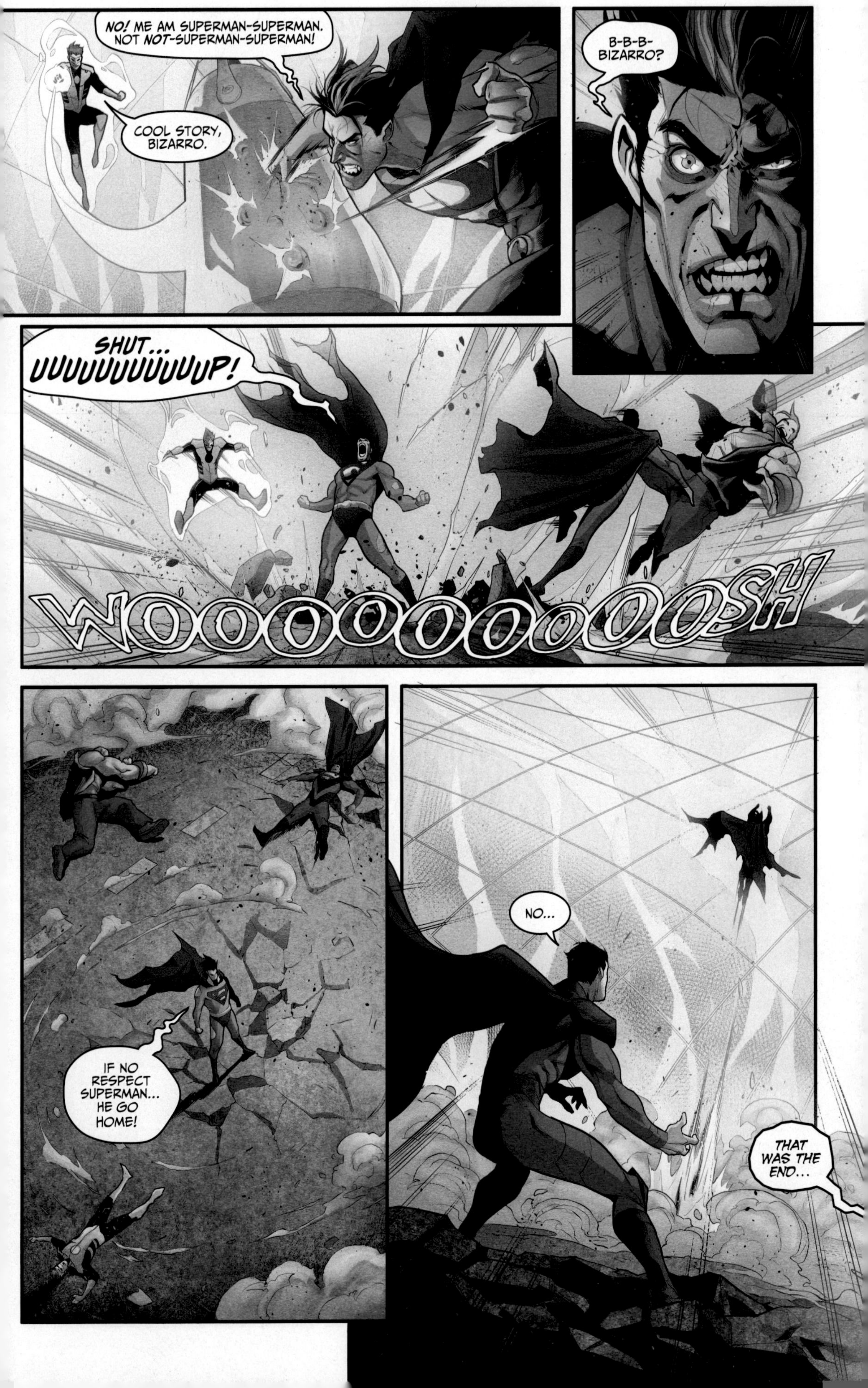
NO! ME AM SUPERMAN-SUPERMAN. NOT NOT-SUPERMAN-SUPERMAN!
COOL STORY, BIZARRO.
B-B-B-BIZARRO?
SHUT... UUUUUUUUUUUP!
WOOOOOOOOOOSH
IF NO RESPECT SUPERMAN... HE GO HOME!
NO...
THAT WAS THE END...

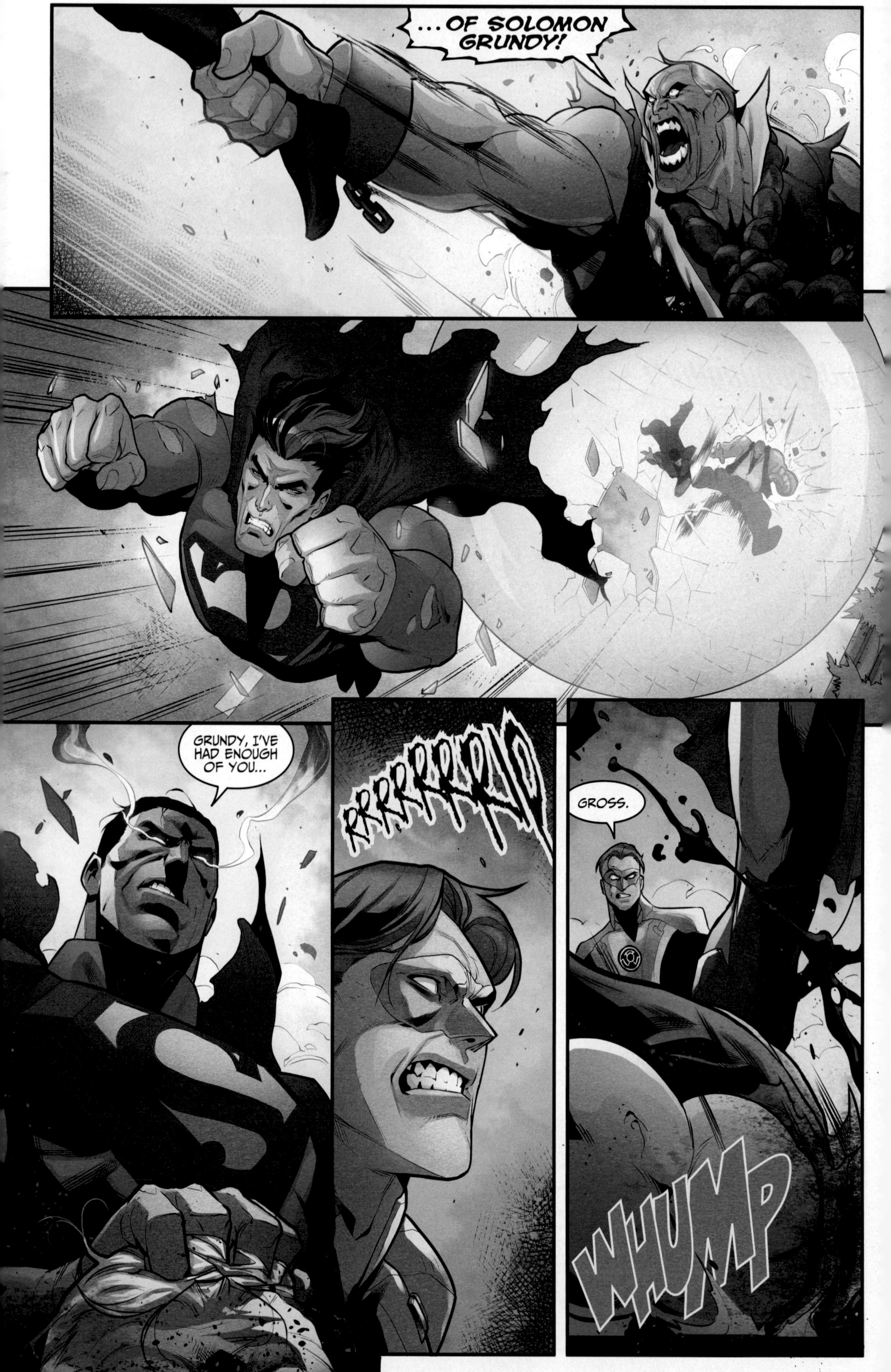
...OF SOLOMON GRUNDY!
GRUNDY, I'VE HAD ENOUGH OF YOU...
RRRRRRRRRAAA
GROSS.
WHUMP

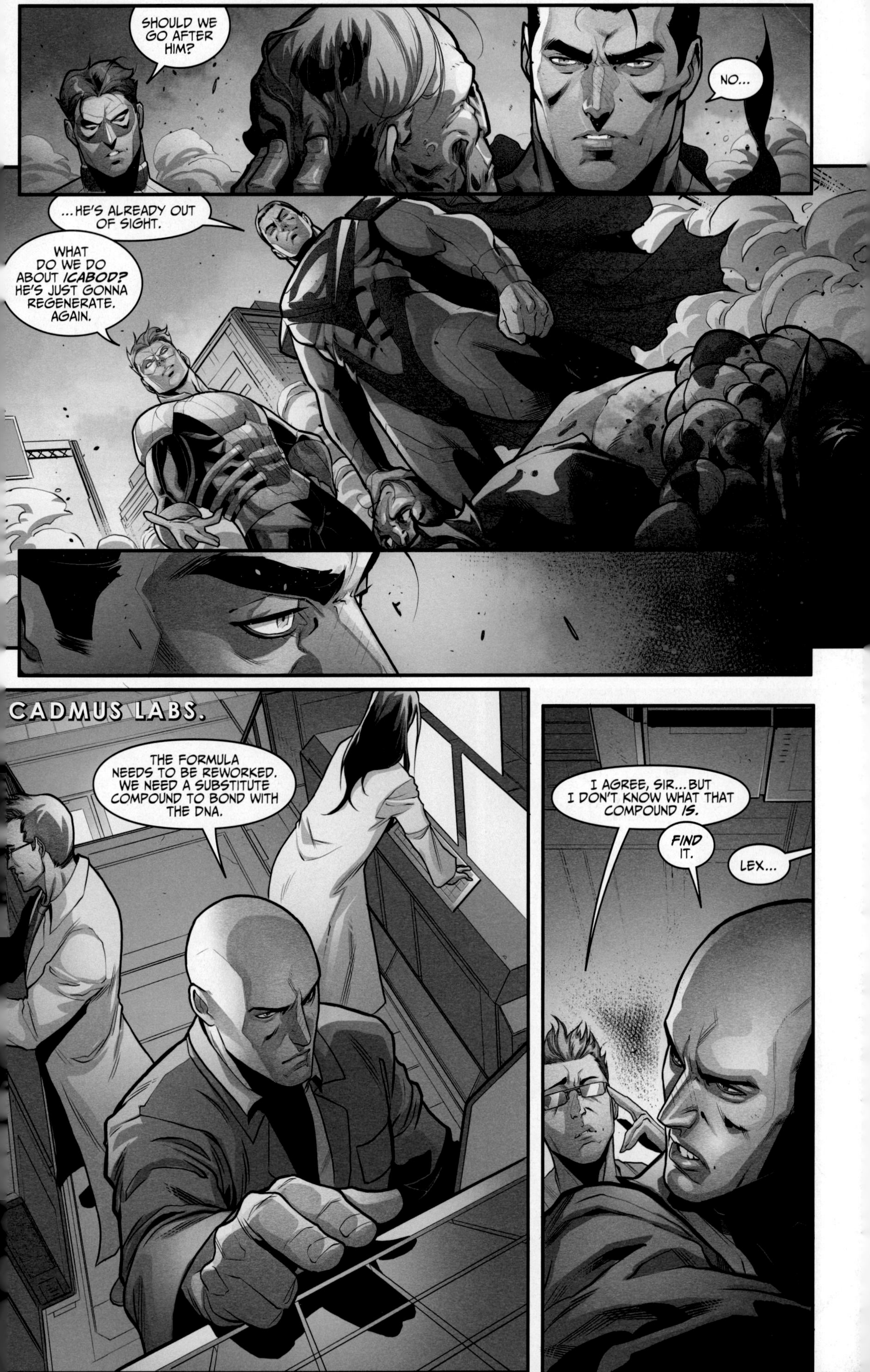
SHOULD WE GO AFTER HIM?
NO...
...HE'S ALREADY OUT OF SIGHT.
WHAT DO WE DO ABOUT ICABOD? HE'S JUST GONNA REGENERATE. AGAIN.
CADMUS LABS.
THE FORMULA NEEDS TO BE REWORKED. WE NEED A SUBSTITUTE COMPOUND TO BOND WITH THE DNA.
I AGREE, SIR...BUT I DON'T KNOW WHAT THAT COMPOUND IS.
FIND IT.
LEX...

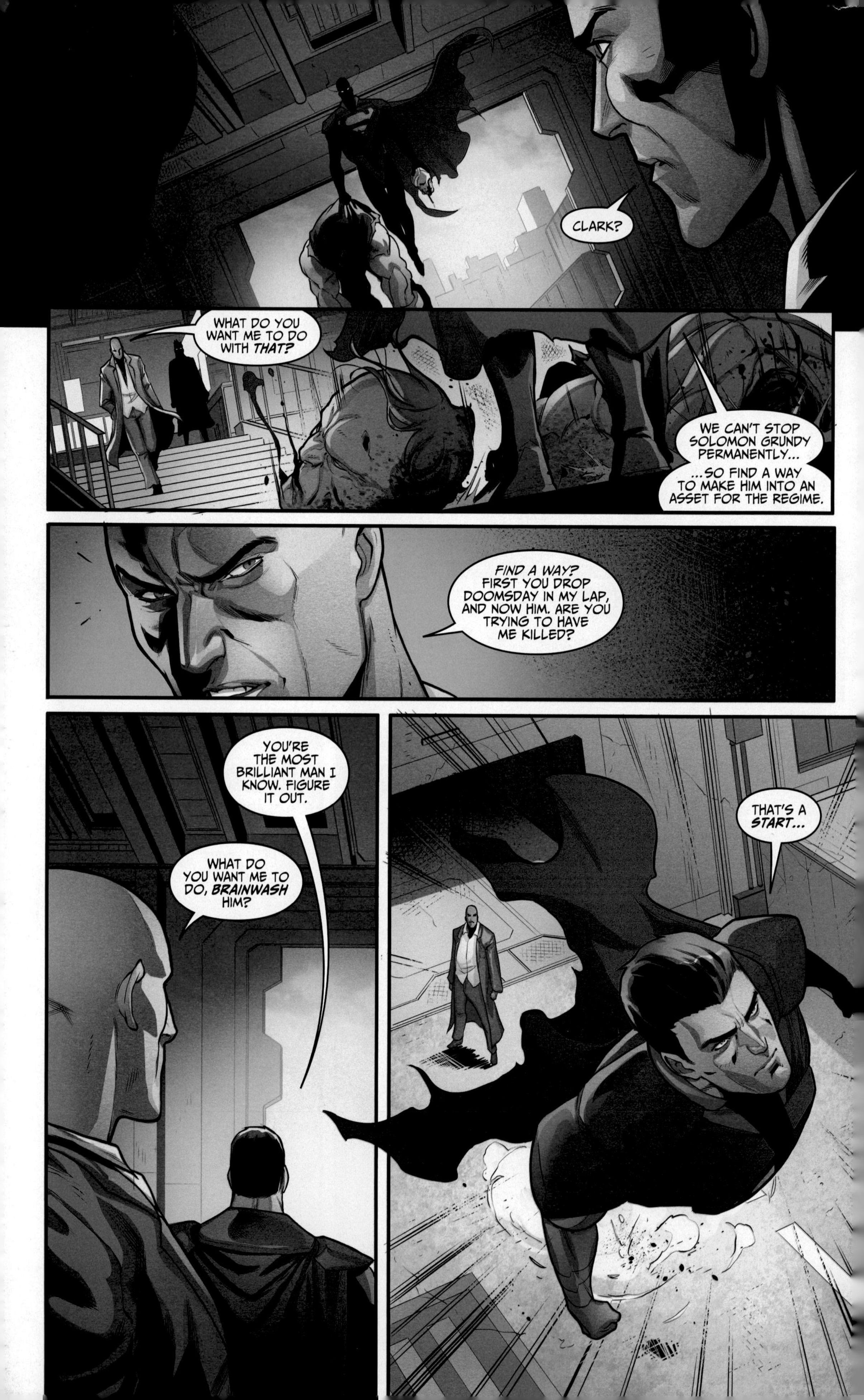
CLARK?
WHAT DO YOU WANT ME TO DO WITH *THAT?*
WE CAN'T STOP SOLOMON GRUNDY PERMANENTLY...
...SO FIND A WAY TO MAKE HIM INTO AN ASSET FOR THE REGIME.
FIND A WAY? FIRST YOU DROP DOOMSDAY IN MY LAP, AND NOW HIM. ARE YOU TRYING TO HAVE ME KILLED?
YOU'RE THE MOST BRILLIANT MAN I KNOW. FIGURE IT OUT.
WHAT DO YOU WANT ME TO DO, ***BRAINWASH*** HIM?
THAT'S A ***START...***

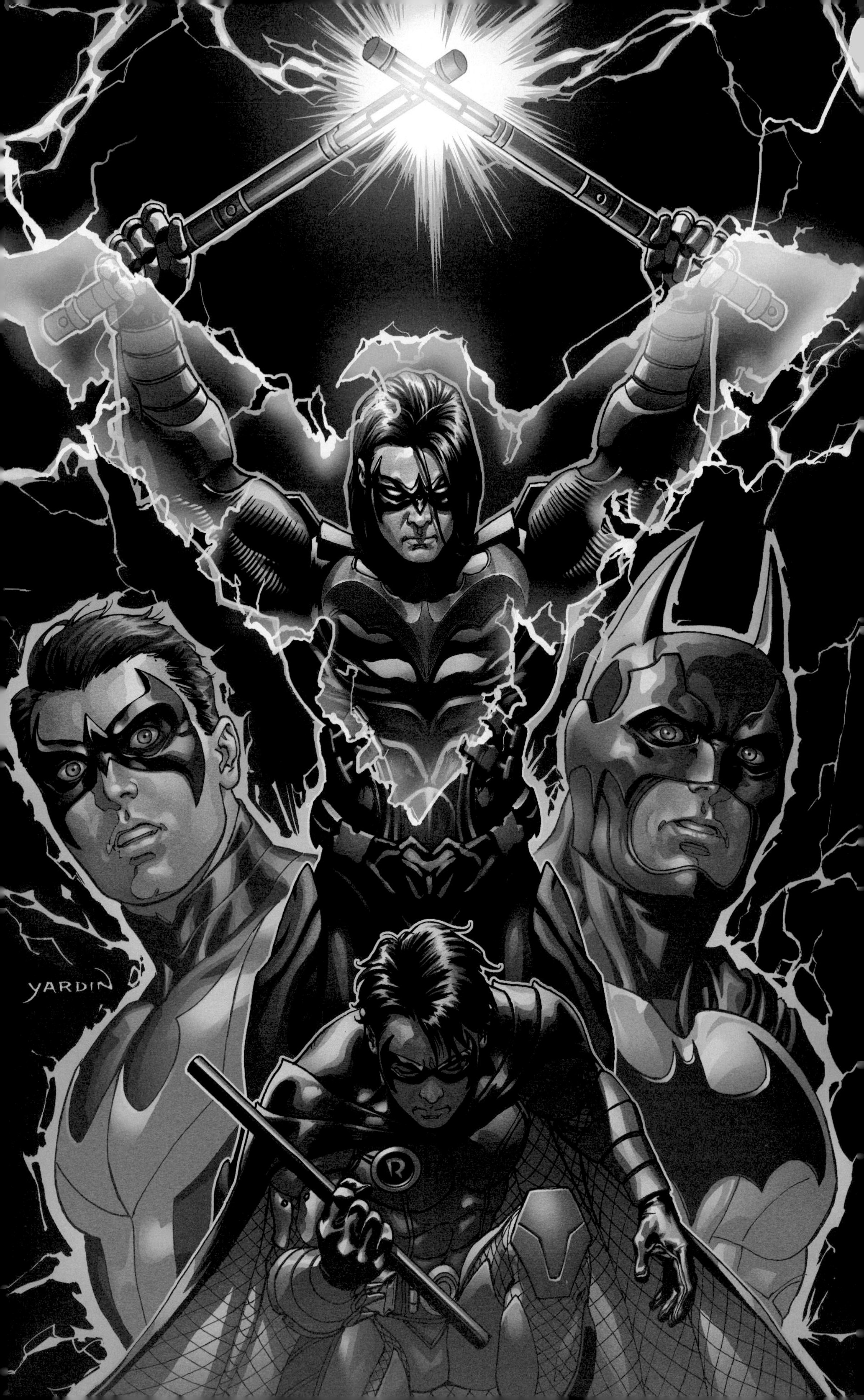
YARDIN

"Taking Sides" **Mike S. Miller** Artist **J. Nanjan** Colorist
"Casting Shadows" **Mike S. Miller** Artist **J. Nanjan** Colorist

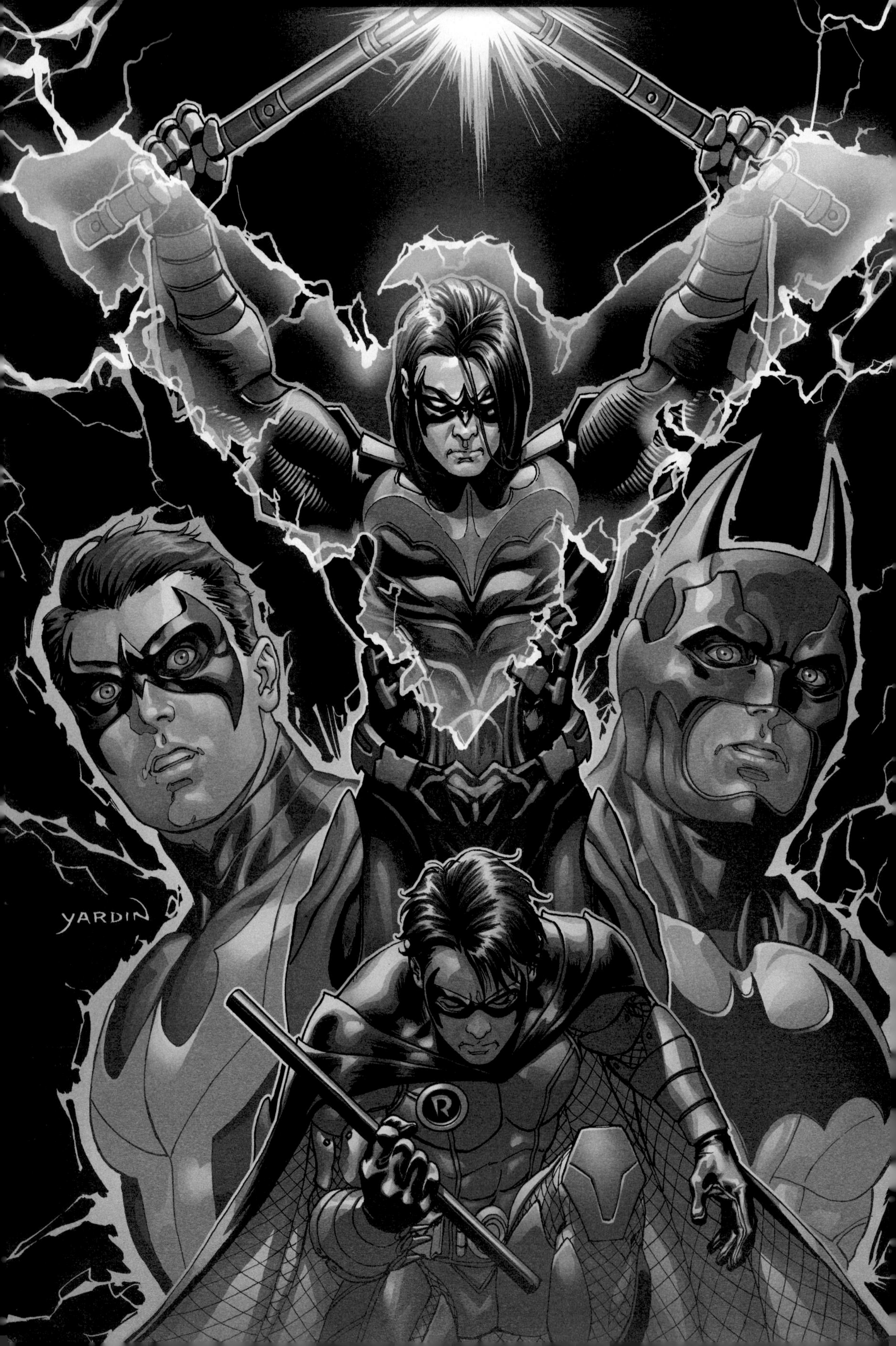
YARDIN

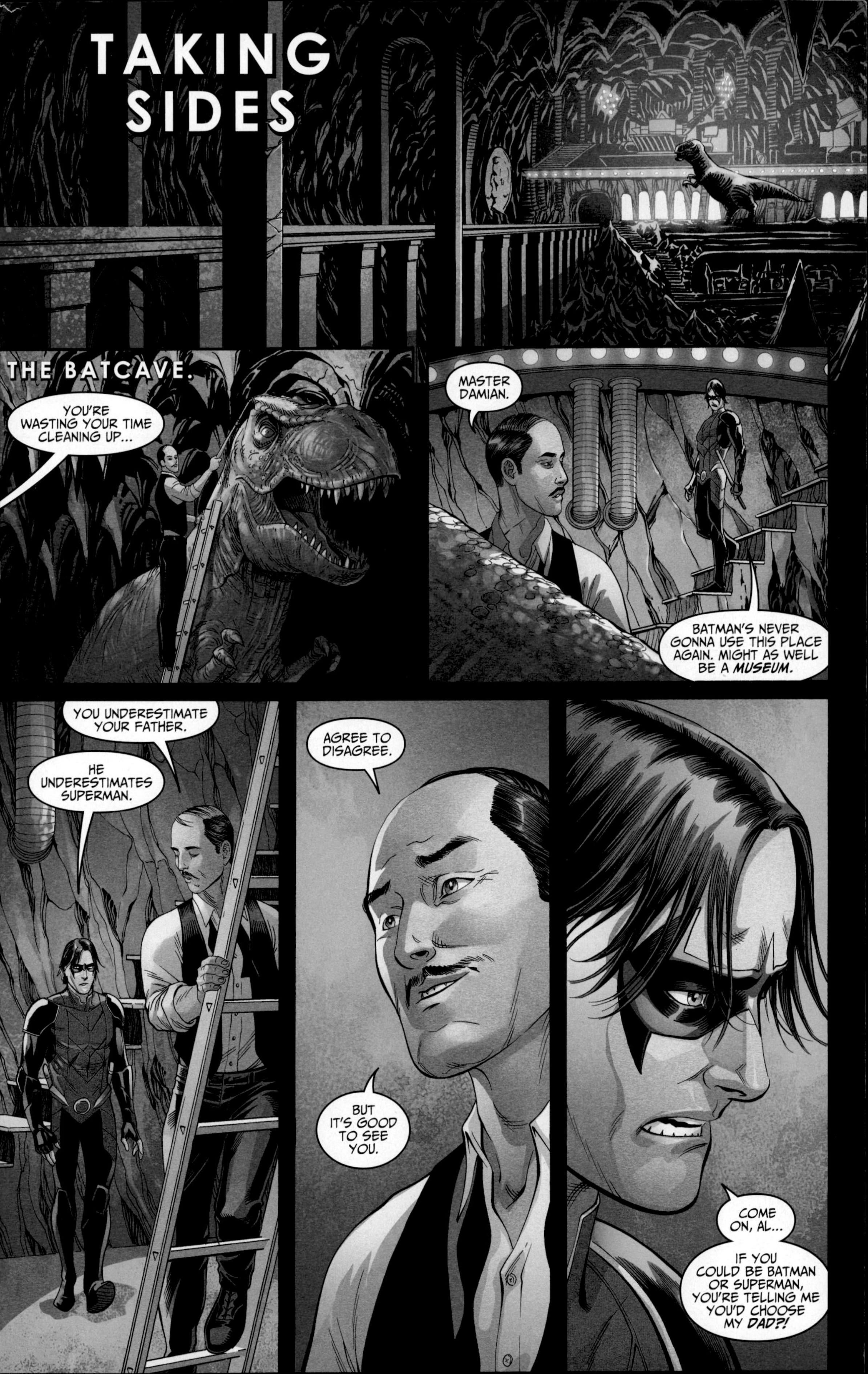
TAKING SIDES
THE BATCAVE.
YOU'RE WASTING YOUR TIME CLEANING UP...
MASTER DAMIAN.
BATMAN'S NEVER GONNA USE THIS PLACE AGAIN. MIGHT AS WELL BE A *MUSEUM.*
YOU UNDERESTIMATE YOUR FATHER.
HE UNDERESTIMATES SUPERMAN.
AGREE TO DISAGREE.
BUT IT'S GOOD TO SEE YOU.
COME ON, AL...
IF YOU COULD BE BATMAN OR SUPERMAN, YOU'RE TELLING ME YOU'D CHOOSE MY *DAD?!*

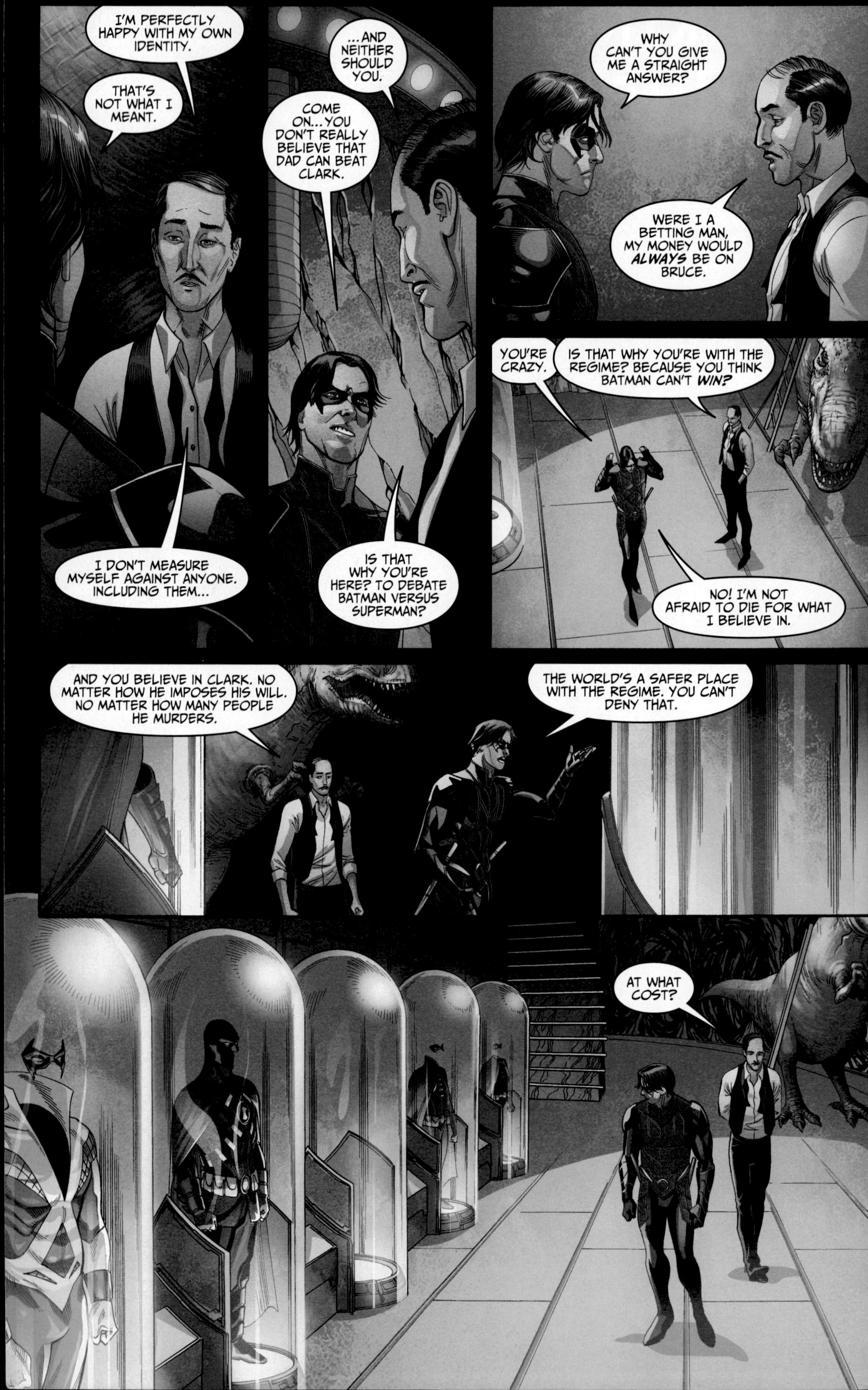
I'M PERFECTLY HAPPY WITH MY OWN IDENTITY.
THAT'S NOT WHAT I MEANT.
I DON'T MEASURE MYSELF AGAINST ANYONE. INCLUDING THEM...
...AND NEITHER SHOULD YOU.
COME ON...YOU DON'T REALLY BELIEVE THAT DAD CAN BEAT CLARK.
IS THAT WHY YOU'RE HERE? TO DEBATE BATMAN VERSUS SUPERMAN?
WHY CAN'T YOU GIVE ME A STRAIGHT ANSWER?
WERE I A BETTING MAN, MY MONEY WOULD ALWAYS BE ON BRUCE.
YOU'RE CRAZY.
IS THAT WHY YOU'RE WITH THE REGIME? BECAUSE YOU THINK BATMAN CAN'T WIN?
NO! I'M NOT AFRAID TO DIE FOR WHAT I BELIEVE IN.
AND YOU BELIEVE IN CLARK. NO MATTER HOW HE IMPOSES HIS WILL. NO MATTER HOW MANY PEOPLE HE MURDERS.
THE WORLD'S A SAFER PLACE WITH THE REGIME. YOU CAN'T DENY THAT.
AT WHAT COST?

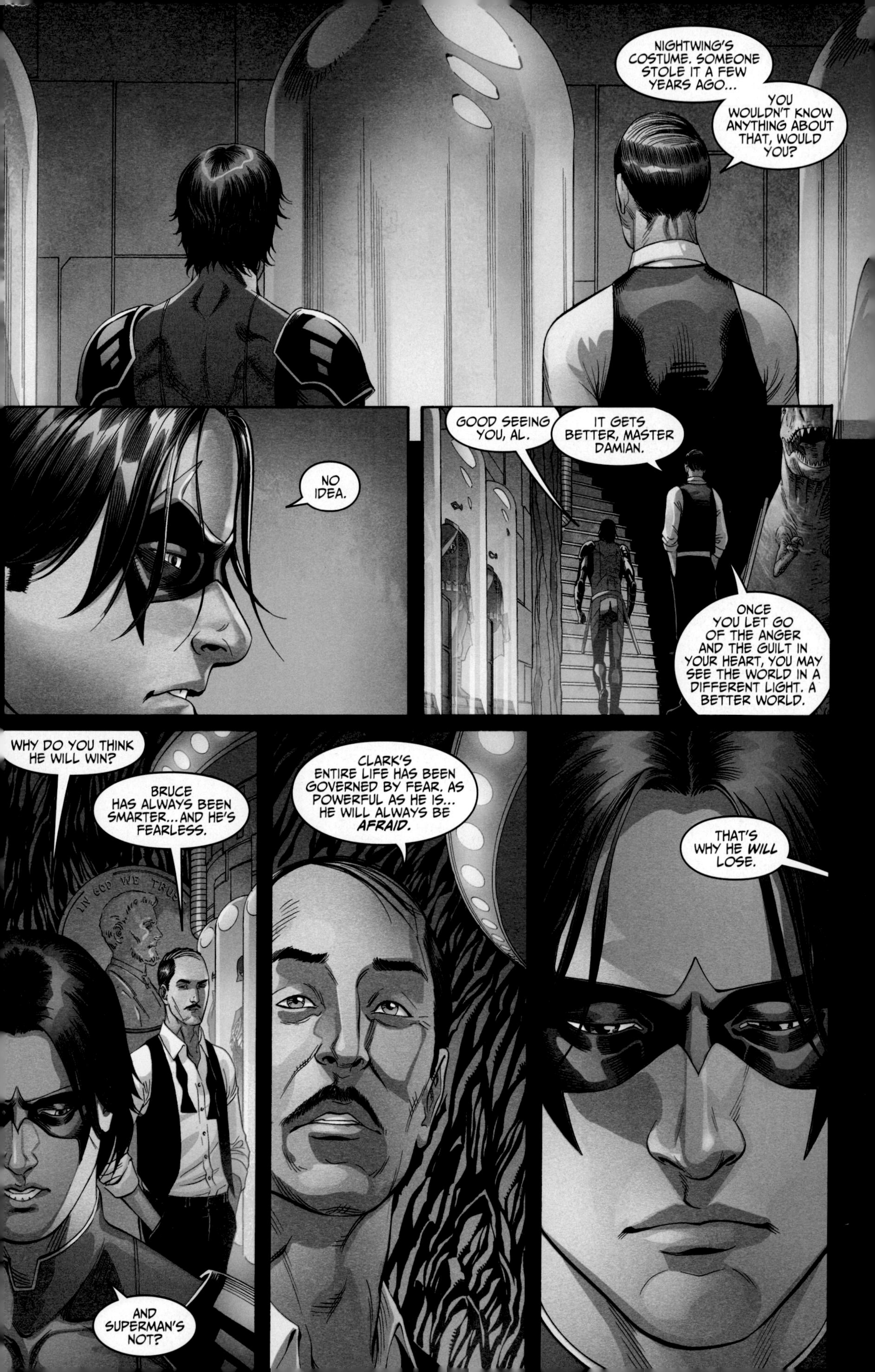
NIGHTWING'S COSTUME. SOMEONE STOLE IT A FEW YEARS AGO...
YOU WOULDN'T KNOW ANYTHING ABOUT THAT, WOULD YOU?
NO IDEA.
GOOD SEEING YOU, AL.
IT GETS BETTER, MASTER DAMIAN.
ONCE YOU LET GO OF THE ANGER AND THE GUILT IN YOUR HEART, YOU MAY SEE THE WORLD IN A DIFFERENT LIGHT. A BETTER WORLD.
WHY DO YOU THINK HE WILL WIN?
BRUCE HAS ALWAYS BEEN SMARTER... AND HE'S FEARLESS.
AND SUPERMAN'S NOT?
CLARK'S ENTIRE LIFE HAS BEEN GOVERNED BY FEAR. AS POWERFUL AS HE IS... HE WILL ALWAYS BE AFRAID.
THAT'S WHY HE WILL LOSE.

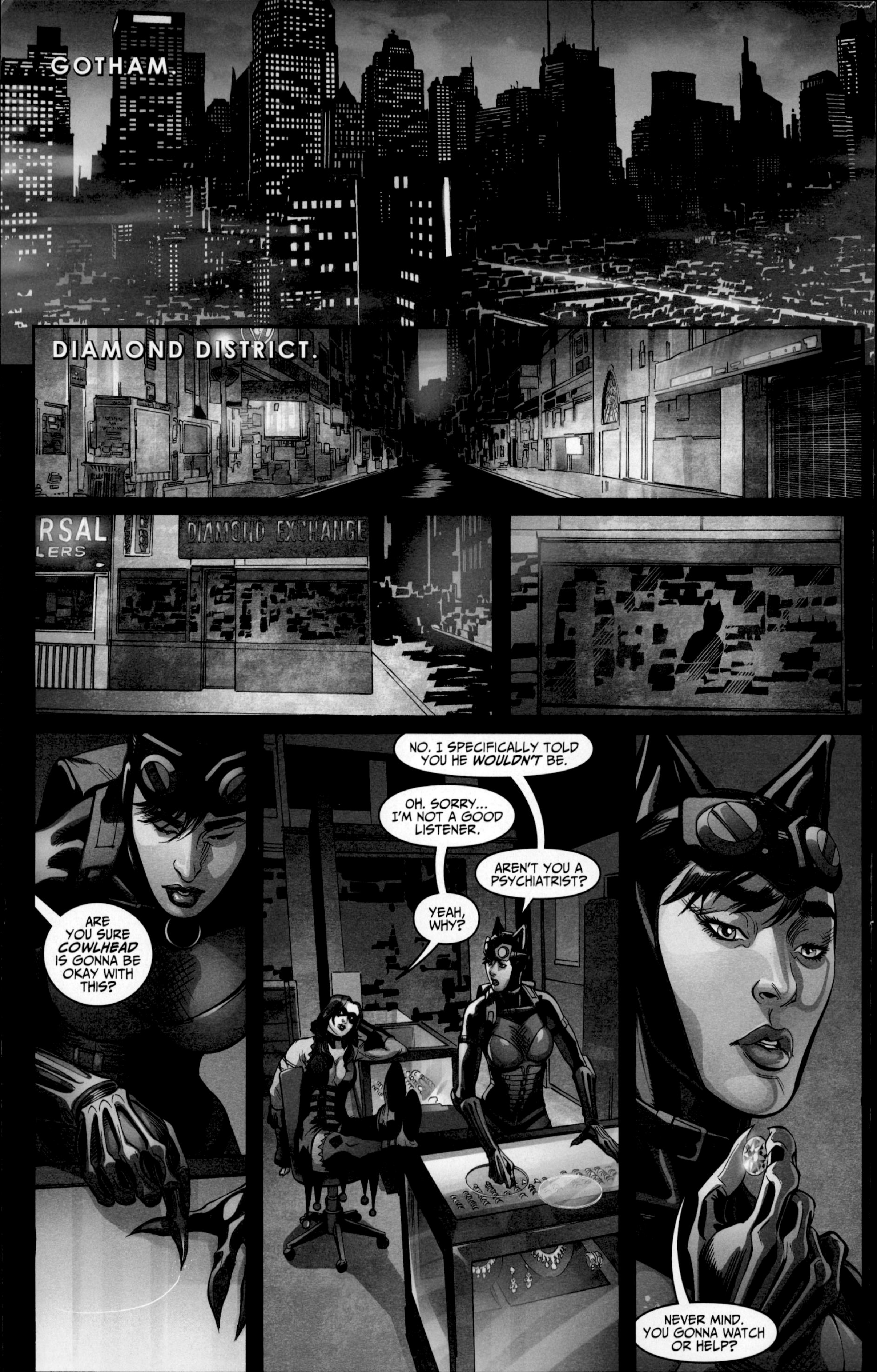
GOTHAM.
DIAMOND DISTRICT.
RSAL
LERS
DIAMOND EXCHANGE
ARE YOU SURE COWLHEAD IS GONNA BE OKAY WITH THIS?
NO. I SPECIFICALLY TOLD YOU HE WOULDN'T BE.
OH. SORRY... I'M NOT A GOOD LISTENER.
ARE'NT YOU A PSYCHIATRIST?
YEAH, WHY?
NEVER MIND. YOU GONNA WATCH OR HELP?

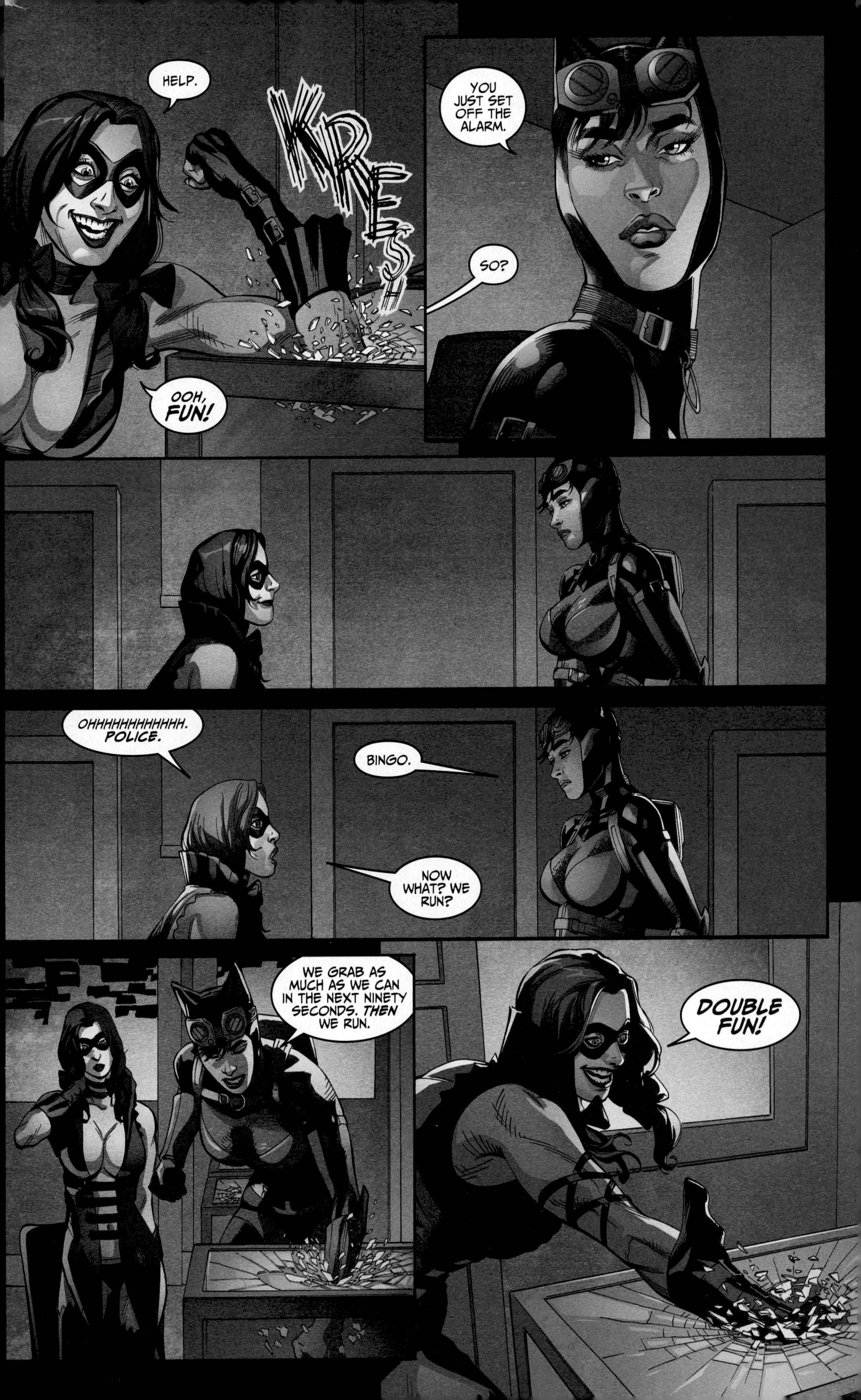
HELP.
KRESH
YOU JUST SET OFF THE ALARM.
SO?
OOH, FUN!
OHHHHHHHHHHHH. POLICE.
BINGO.
NOW WHAT? WE RUN?
WE GRAB AS MUCH AS WE CAN IN THE NEXT NINETY SECONDS. THEN WE RUN.
DOUBLE FUN!

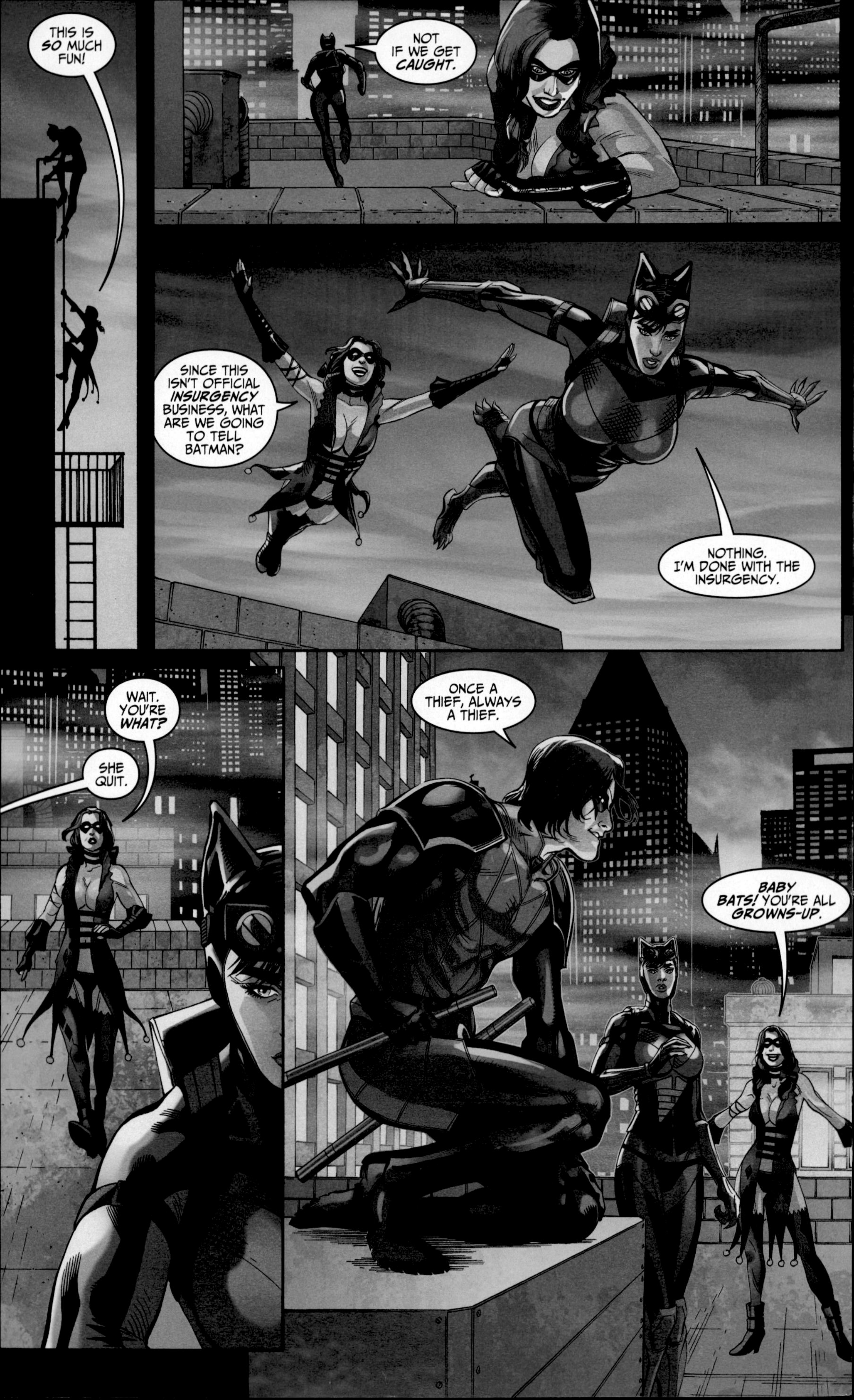
THIS IS SO MUCH FUN!
NOT IF WE GET CAUGHT.
SINCE THIS ISN'T OFFICIAL INSURGENCY BUSINESS, WHAT ARE WE GOING TO TELL BATMAN?
NOTHING. I'M DONE WITH THE INSURGENCY.
WAIT. YOU'RE WHAT?
SHE QUIT.
ONCE A THIEF, ALWAYS A THIEF.
BABY BATS! YOU'RE ALL GROWNS-UP.

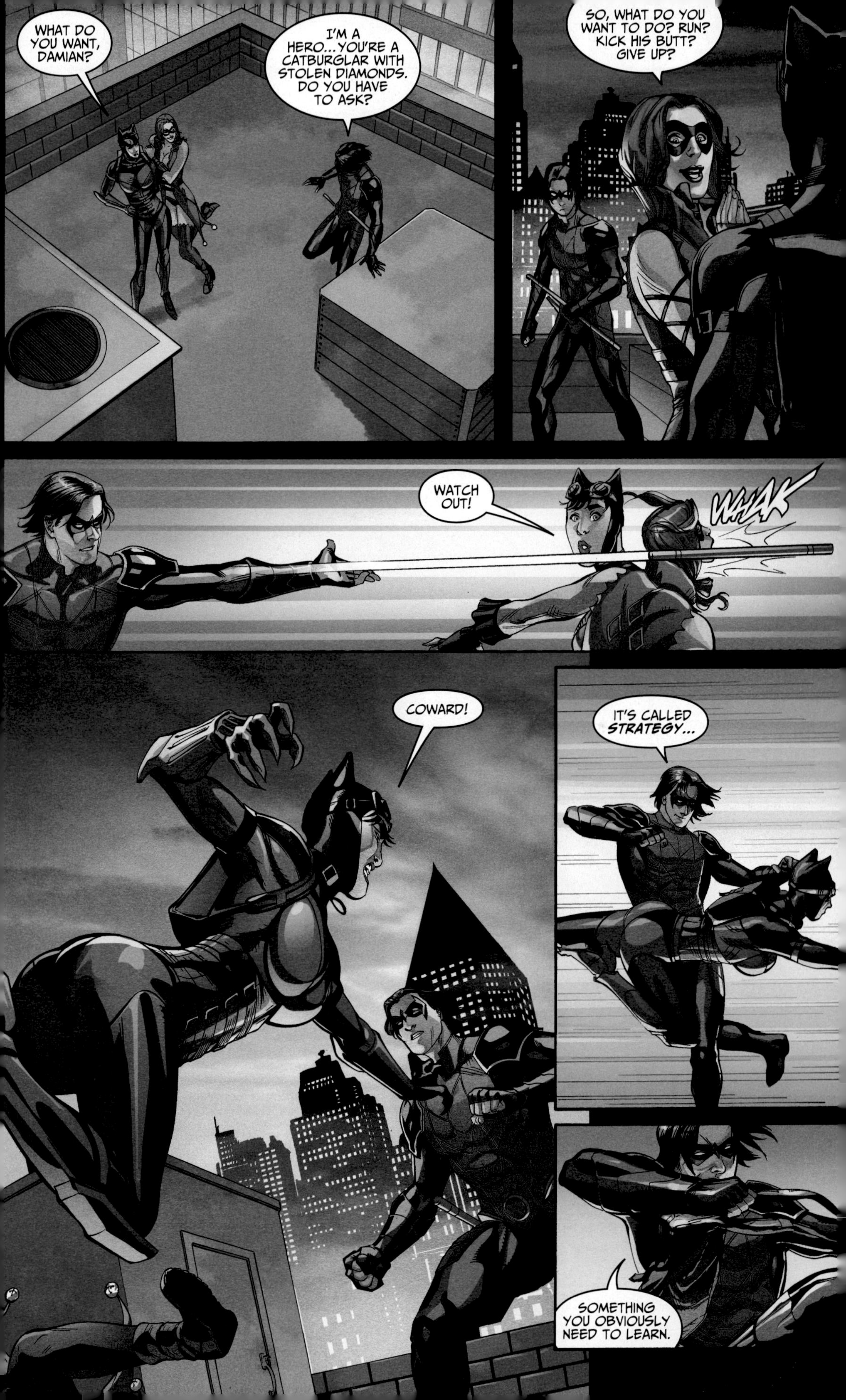
WHAT DO YOU WANT, DAMIAN?
I'M A HERO...YOU'RE A CATBURGLAR WITH STOLEN DIAMONDS. DO YOU HAVE TO ASK?
SO, WHAT DO YOU WANT TO DO? RUN? KICK HIS BUTT? GIVE UP?
WATCH OUT!
WHAK
COWARD!
IT'S CALLED STRATEGY...
SOMETHING YOU OBVIOUSLY NEED TO LEARN.

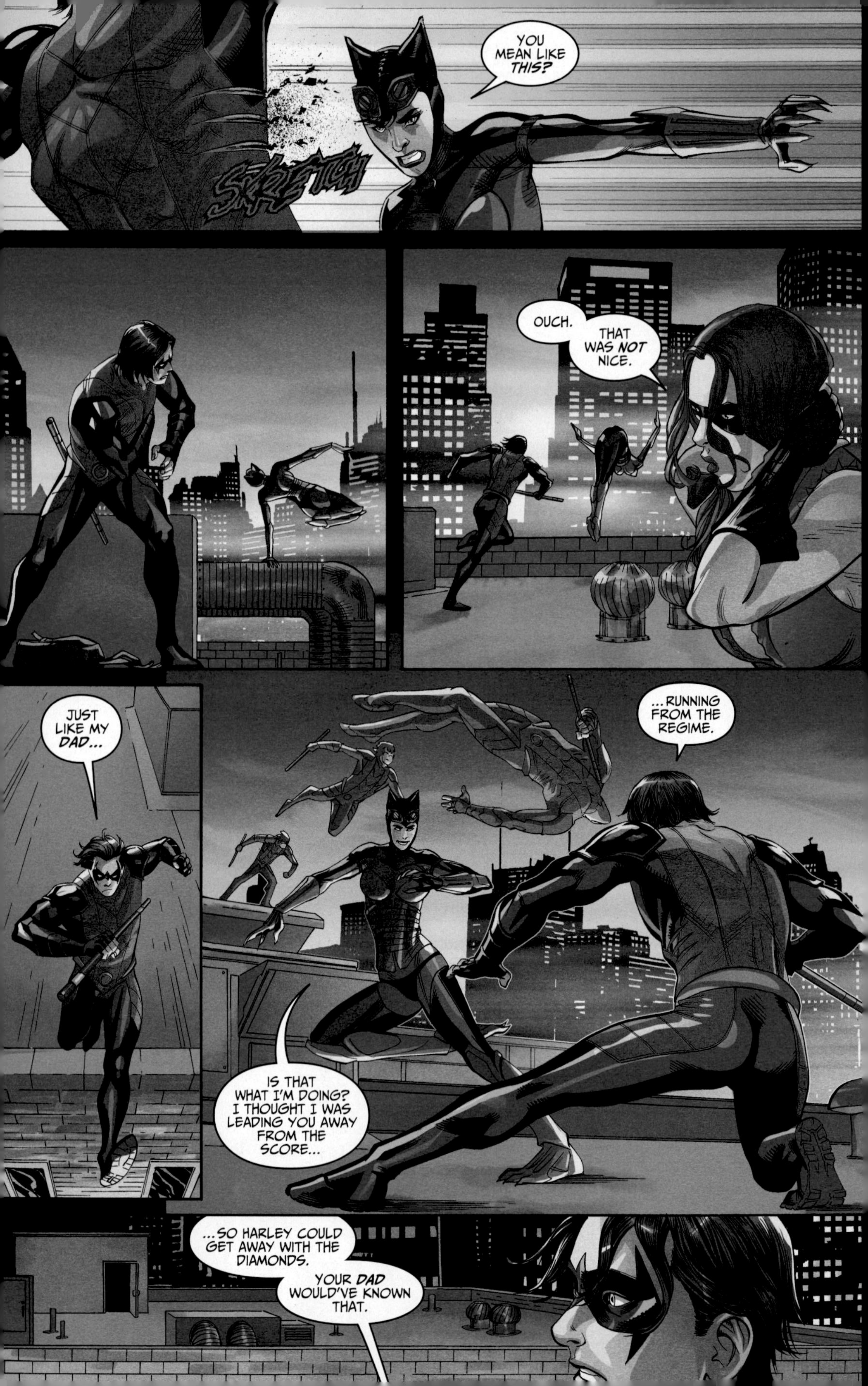
YOU MEAN LIKE THIS?
SKRETCH
OUCH.
THAT WAS NOT NICE.
JUST LIKE MY DAD...
...RUNNING FROM THE REGIME.
IS THAT WHAT I'M DOING? I THOUGHT I WAS LEADING YOU AWAY FROM THE SCORE...
...SO HARLEY COULD GET AWAY WITH THE DIAMONDS.
YOUR DAD WOULD'VE KNOWN THAT.

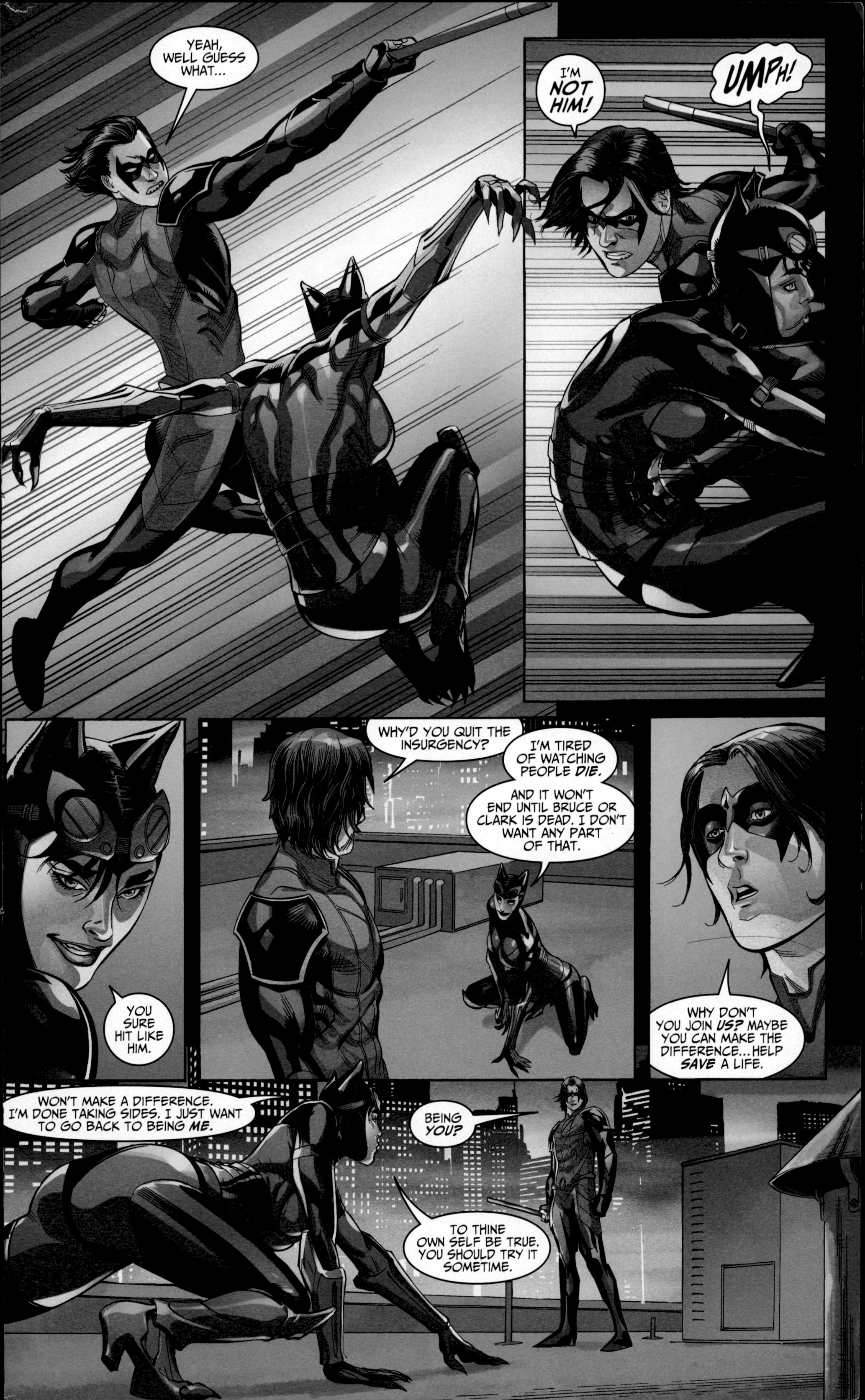
YEAH, WELL GUESS WHAT...
I'M NOT HIM!
UMPH!
YOU SURE HIT LIKE HIM.
WHY'D YOU QUIT THE INSURGENCY?
I'M TIRED OF WATCHING PEOPLE DIE.
AND IT WON'T END UNTIL BRUCE OR CLARK IS DEAD. I DON'T WANT ANY PART OF THAT.
WHY DON'T YOU JOIN US? MAYBE YOU CAN MAKE THE DIFFERENCE...HELP SAVE A LIFE.
WON'T MAKE A DIFFERENCE. I'M DONE TAKING SIDES. I JUST WANT TO GO BACK TO BEING ME.
BEING YOU?
TO THINE OWN SELF BE TRUE. YOU SHOULD TRY IT SOMETIME.

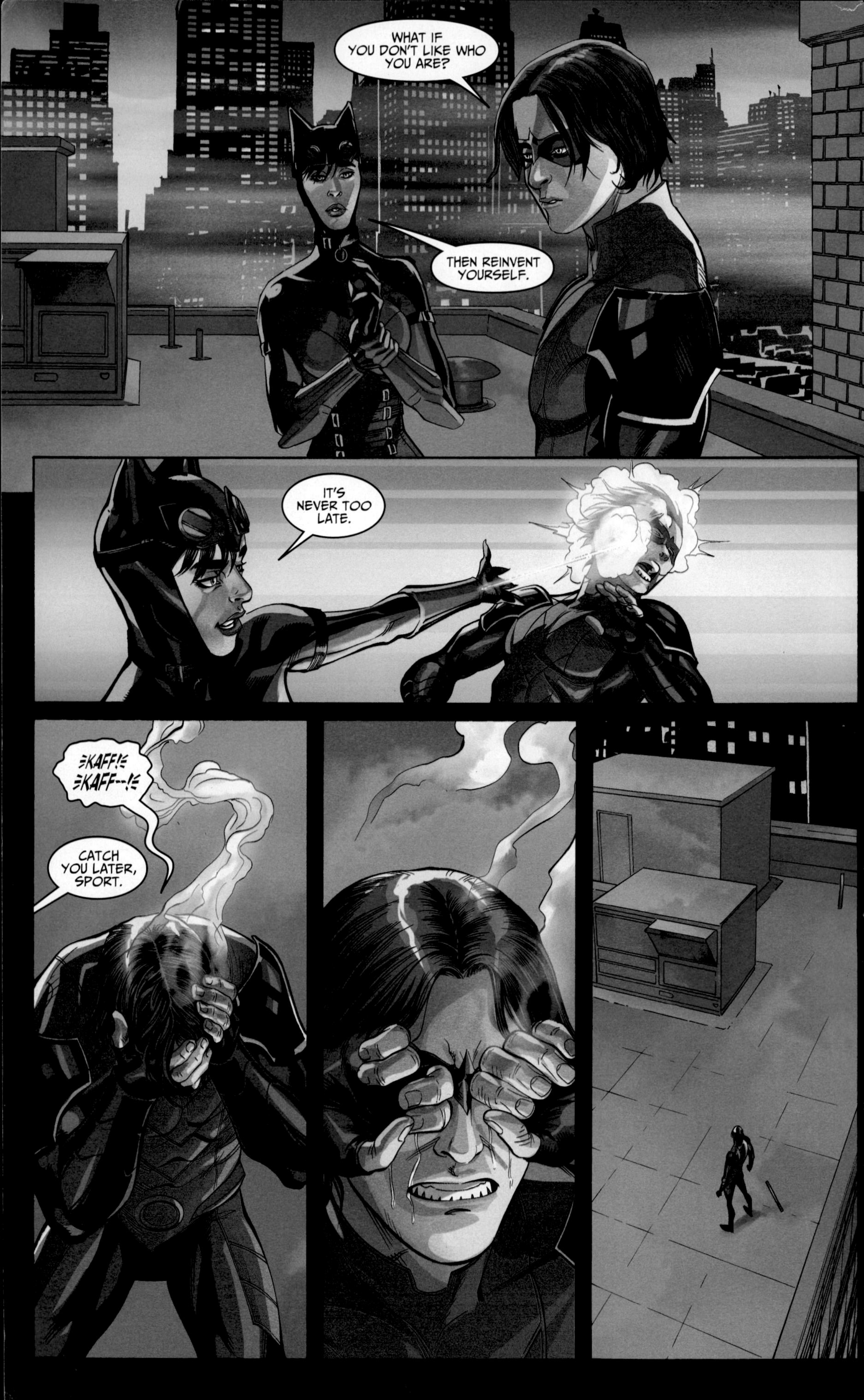
WHAT IF YOU DON'T LIKE WHO YOU ARE?
THEN REINVENT YOURSELF.
IT'S NEVER TOO LATE.
KAFF! KAFF--!
CATCH YOU LATER, SPORT.

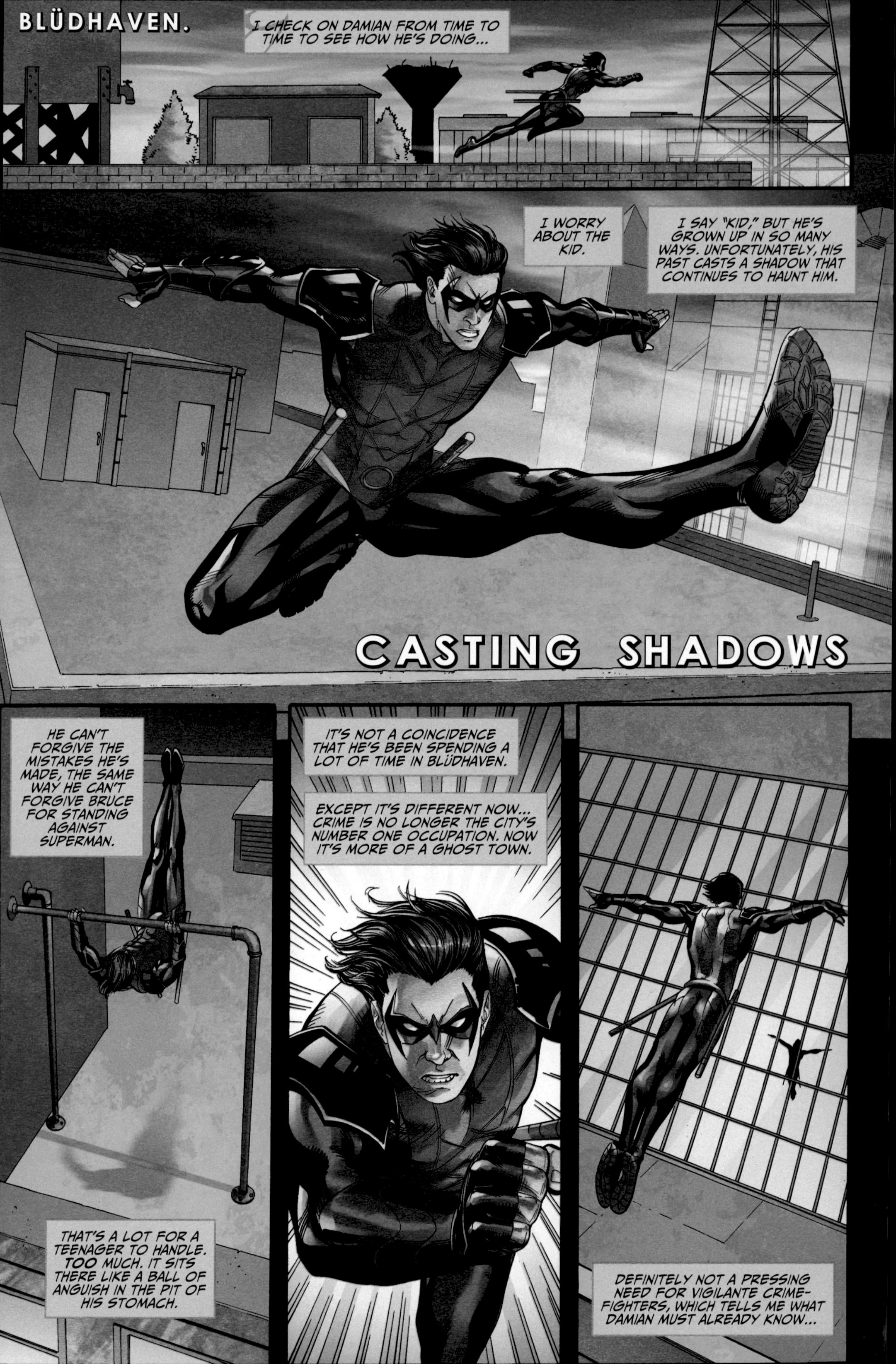
BLÜDHAVEN.
I CHECK ON DAMIAN FROM TIME TO TIME TO SEE HOW HE'S DOING...
I WORRY ABOUT THE KID.
I SAY "KID," BUT HE'S GROWN UP IN SO MANY WAYS. UNFORTUNATELY, HIS PAST CASTS A SHADOW THAT CONTINUES TO HAUNT HIM.
CASTING SHADOWS
HE CAN'T FORGIVE THE MISTAKES HE'S MADE, THE SAME WAY HE CAN'T FORGIVE BRUCE FOR STANDING AGAINST SUPERMAN.
THAT'S A LOT FOR A TEENAGER TO HANDLE. TOO MUCH. IT SITS THERE LIKE A BALL OF ANGUISH IN THE PIT OF HIS STOMACH.
IT'S NOT A COINCIDENCE THAT HE'S BEEN SPENDING A LOT OF TIME IN BLÜDHAVEN.
EXCEPT IT'S DIFFERENT NOW... CRIME IS NO LONGER THE CITY'S NUMBER ONE OCCUPATION. NOW IT'S MORE OF A GHOST TOWN.
DEFINITELY NOT A PRESSING NEED FOR VIGILANTE CRIME-FIGHTERS, WHICH TELLS ME WHAT DAMIAN MUST ALREADY KNOW...

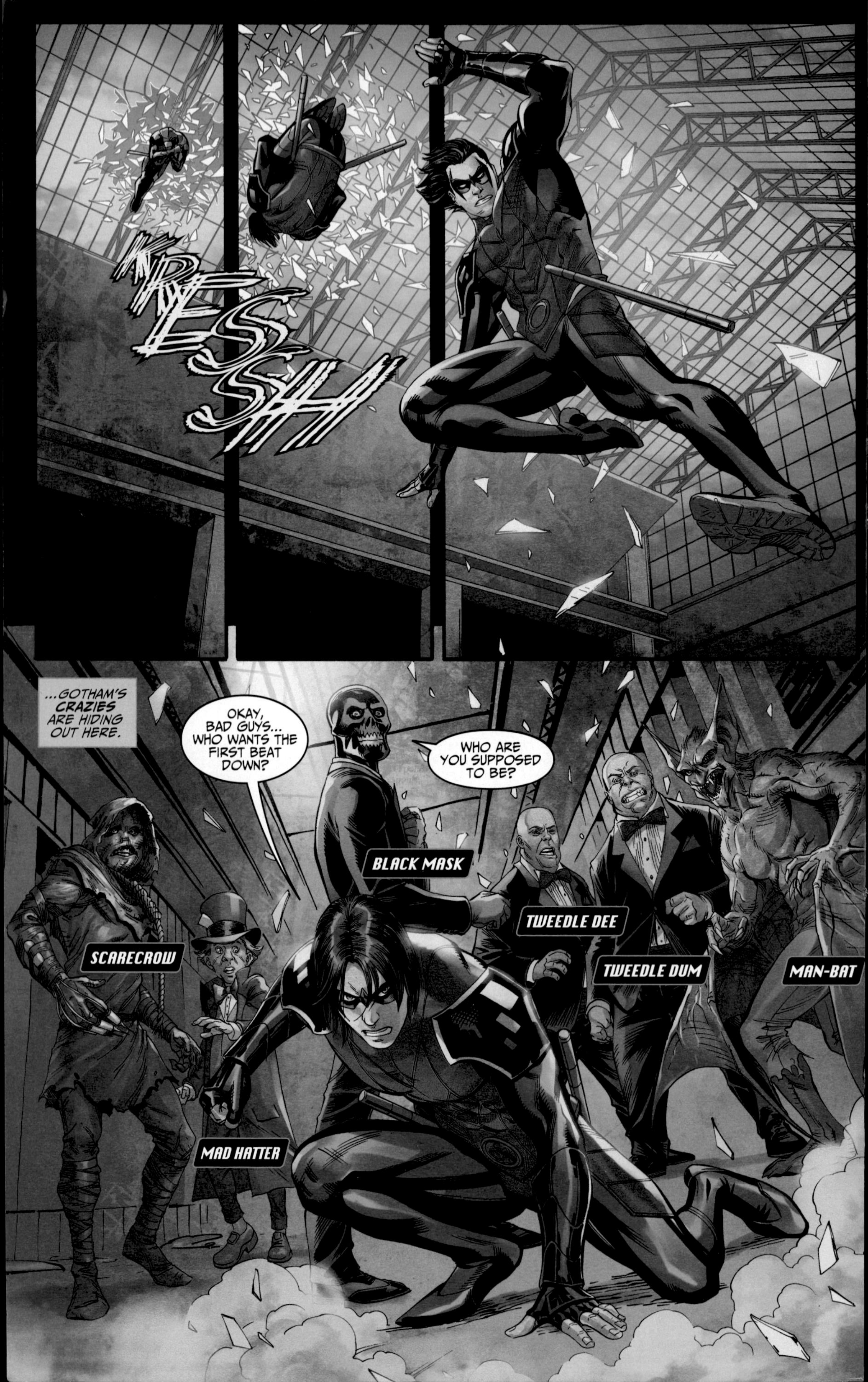

KRESSH
...GOTHAM'S CRAZIES ARE HIDING OUT HERE.
OKAY, BAD GUYS... WHO WANTS THE FIRST BEAT DOWN?
WHO ARE YOU SUPPOSED TO BE?
BLACK MASK
SCARECROW
MAD HATTER
TWEEDLE DEE
TWEEDLE DUM
MAN-BAT

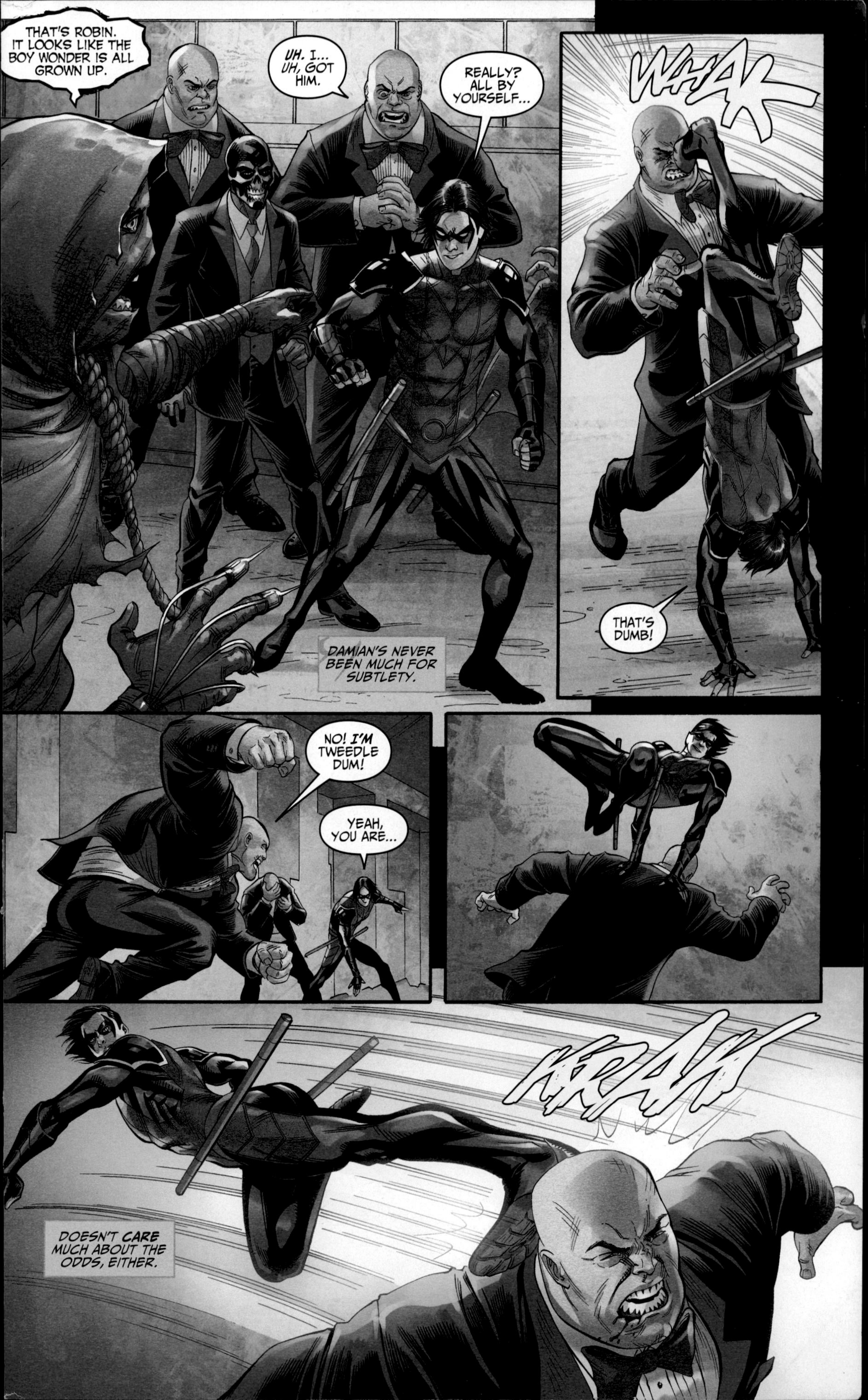
THAT'S ROBIN. IT LOOKS LIKE THE BOY WONDER IS ALL GROWN UP.
UH. I... UH, GOT HIM.
REALLY? ALL BY YOURSELF...
DAMIAN'S NEVER BEEN MUCH FOR SUBTLETY.
WHAK
THAT'S DUMB!
NO! I'M TWEEDLE DUM!
YEAH, YOU ARE...
KRAK
DOESN'T CARE MUCH ABOUT THE ODDS, EITHER.

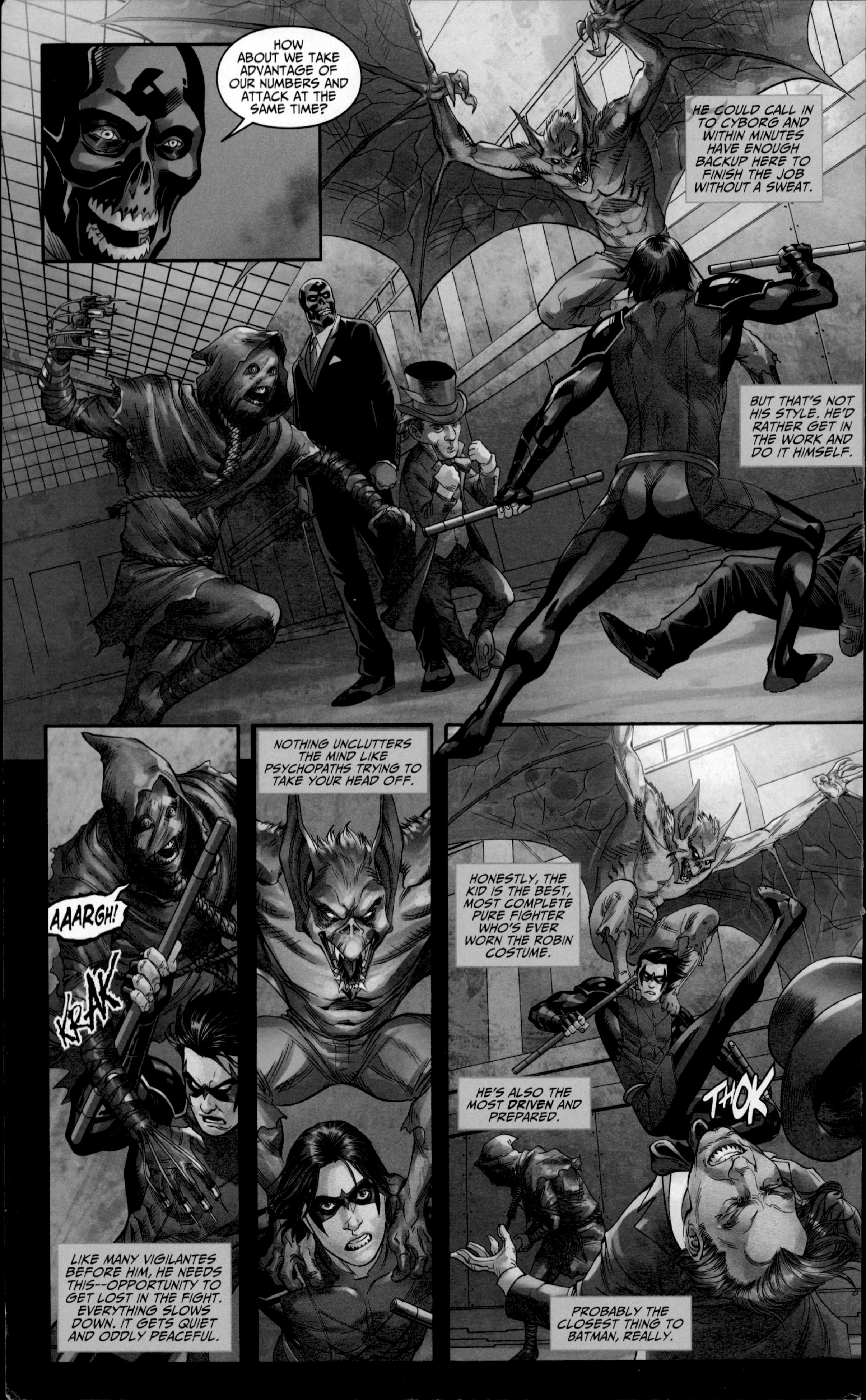
HOW ABOUT WE TAKE ADVANTAGE OF OUR NUMBERS AND ATTACK AT THE SAME TIME?
HE COULD CALL IN TO CYBORG AND WITHIN MINUTES HAVE ENOUGH BACKUP HERE TO FINISH THE JOB WITHOUT A SWEAT.
BUT THAT'S NOT HIS STYLE. HE'D RATHER GET IN THE WORK AND DO IT HIMSELF.
AAARGH!
KRAK
LIKE MANY VIGILANTES BEFORE HIM, HE NEEDS THIS--OPPORTUNITY TO GET LOST IN THE FIGHT. EVERYTHING SLOWS DOWN. IT GETS QUIET AND ODDLY PEACEFUL.
NOTHING UNCLUTTERS THE MIND LIKE PSYCHOPATHS TRYING TO TAKE YOUR HEAD OFF.
HONESTLY, THE KID IS THE BEST, MOST COMPLETE PURE FIGHTER WHO'S EVER WORN THE ROBIN COSTUME.
HE'S ALSO THE MOST DRIVEN AND PREPARED.
THOK
PROBABLY THE CLOSEST THING TO BATMAN, REALLY.

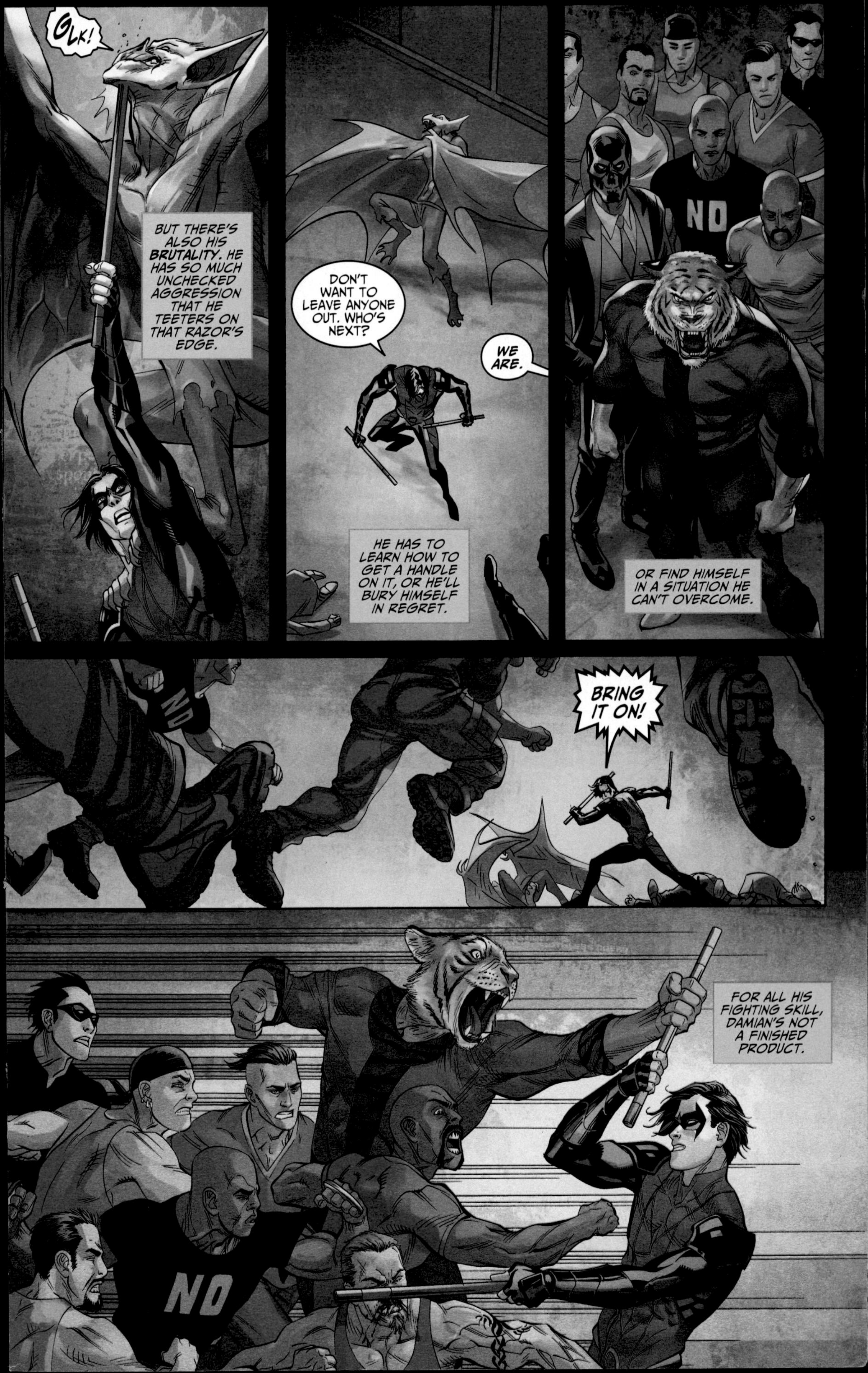
GLK!
BUT THERE'S ALSO HIS BRUTALITY. HE HAS SO MUCH UNCHECKED AGGRESSION THAT HE TEETERS ON THAT RAZOR'S EDGE.
DON'T WANT TO LEAVE ANYONE OUT. WHO'S NEXT?
WE ARE.
HE HAS TO LEARN HOW TO GET A HANDLE ON IT, OR HE'LL BURY HIMSELF IN REGRET.
NO
OR FIND HIMSELF IN A SITUATION HE CAN'T OVERCOME.
ND
BRING IT ON!
FOR ALL HIS FIGHTING SKILL, DAMIAN'S NOT A FINISHED PRODUCT.
NO

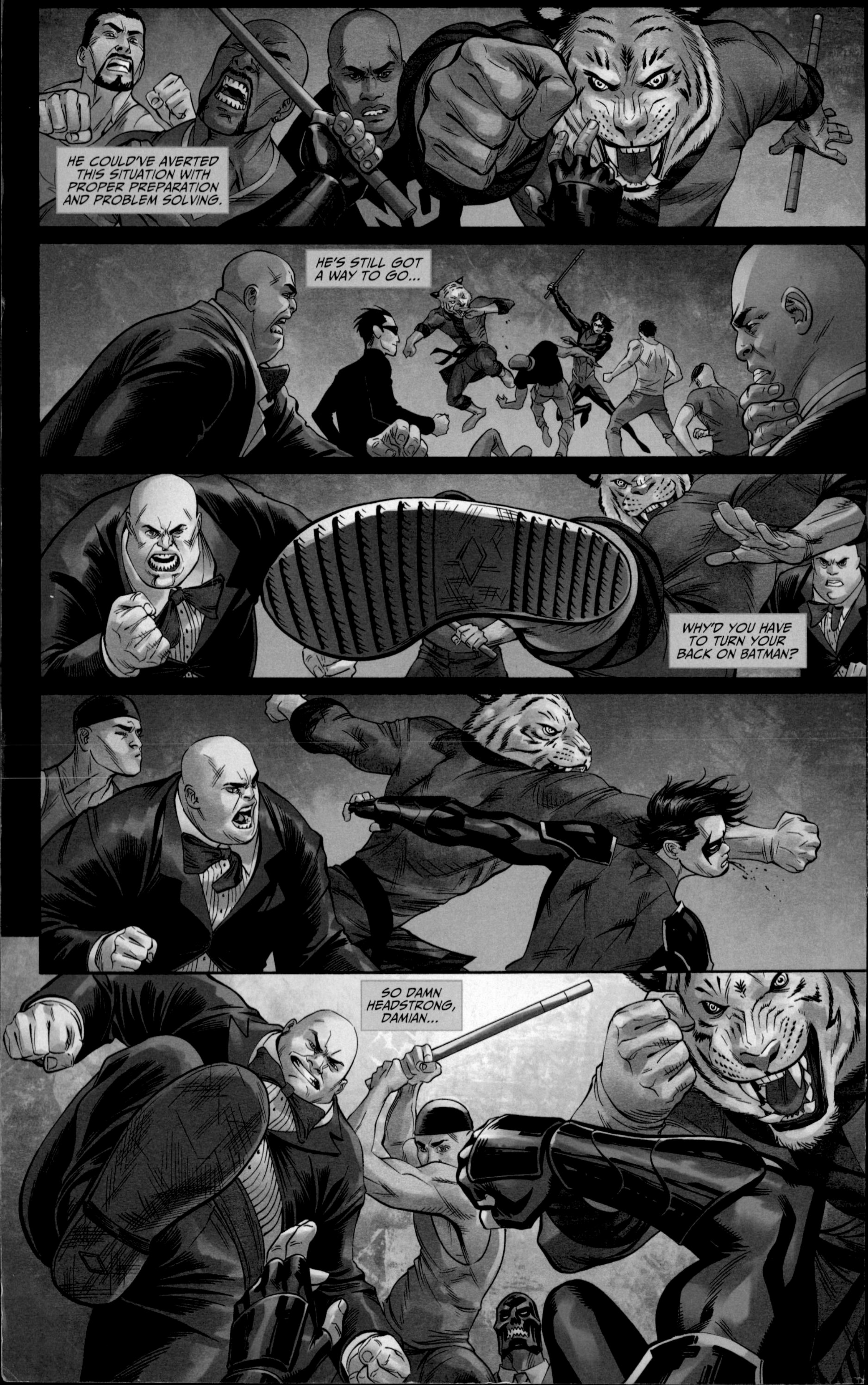
HE COULD'VE AVERTED THIS SITUATION WITH PROPER PREPARATION AND PROBLEM SOLVING.
HE'S STILL GOT A WAY TO GO...
WHY'D YOU HAVE TO TURN YOUR BACK ON BATMAN?
SO DAMN HEADSTRONG, DAMIAN...

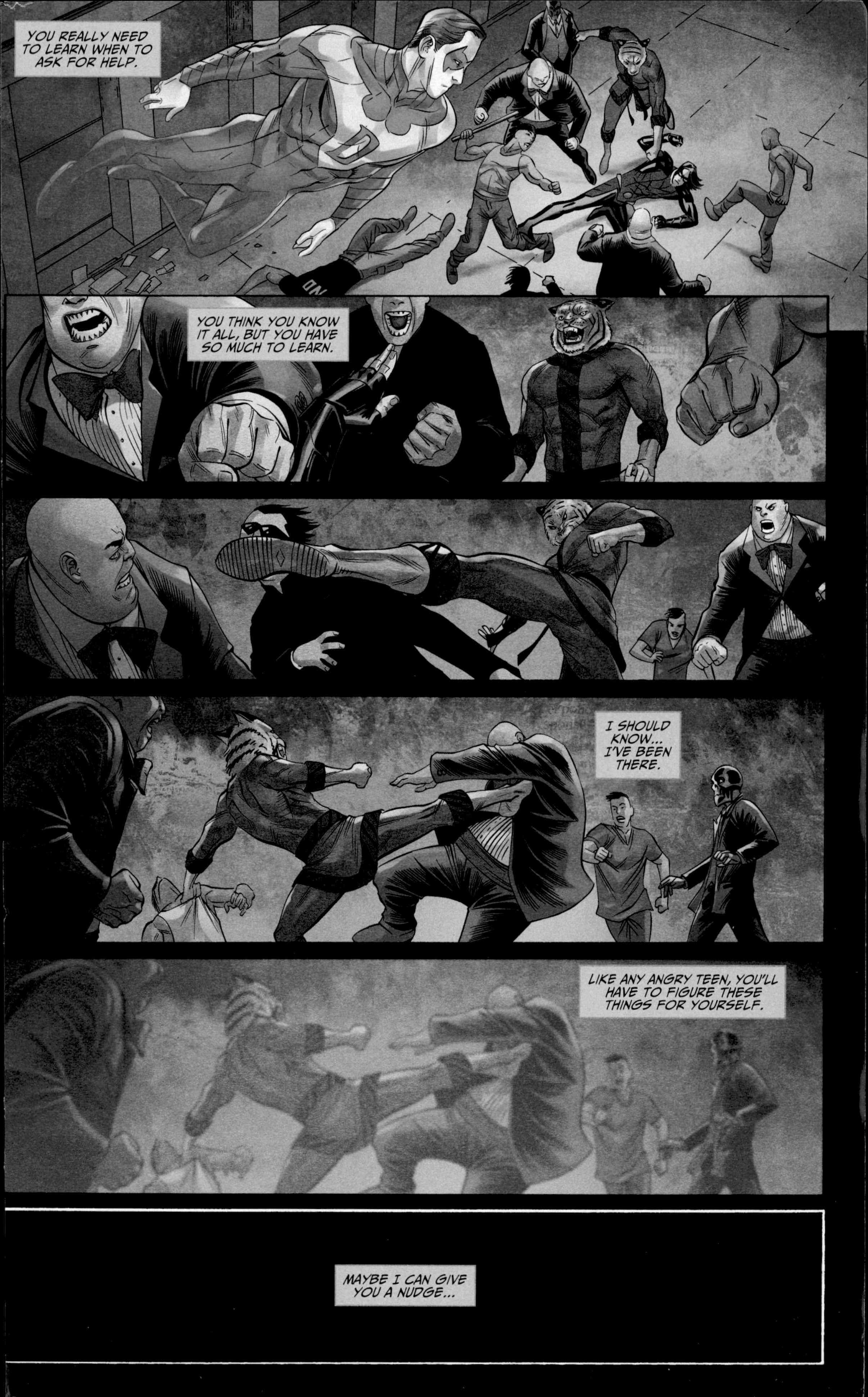
YOU REALLY NEED TO LEARN WHEN TO ASK FOR HELP.
YOU THINK YOU KNOW IT ALL, BUT YOU HAVE SO MUCH TO LEARN.
I SHOULD KNOW... I'VE BEEN THERE.
LIKE ANY ANGRY TEEN, YOU'LL HAVE TO FIGURE THESE THINGS FOR YOURSELF.
MAYBE I CAN GIVE YOU A NUDGE...

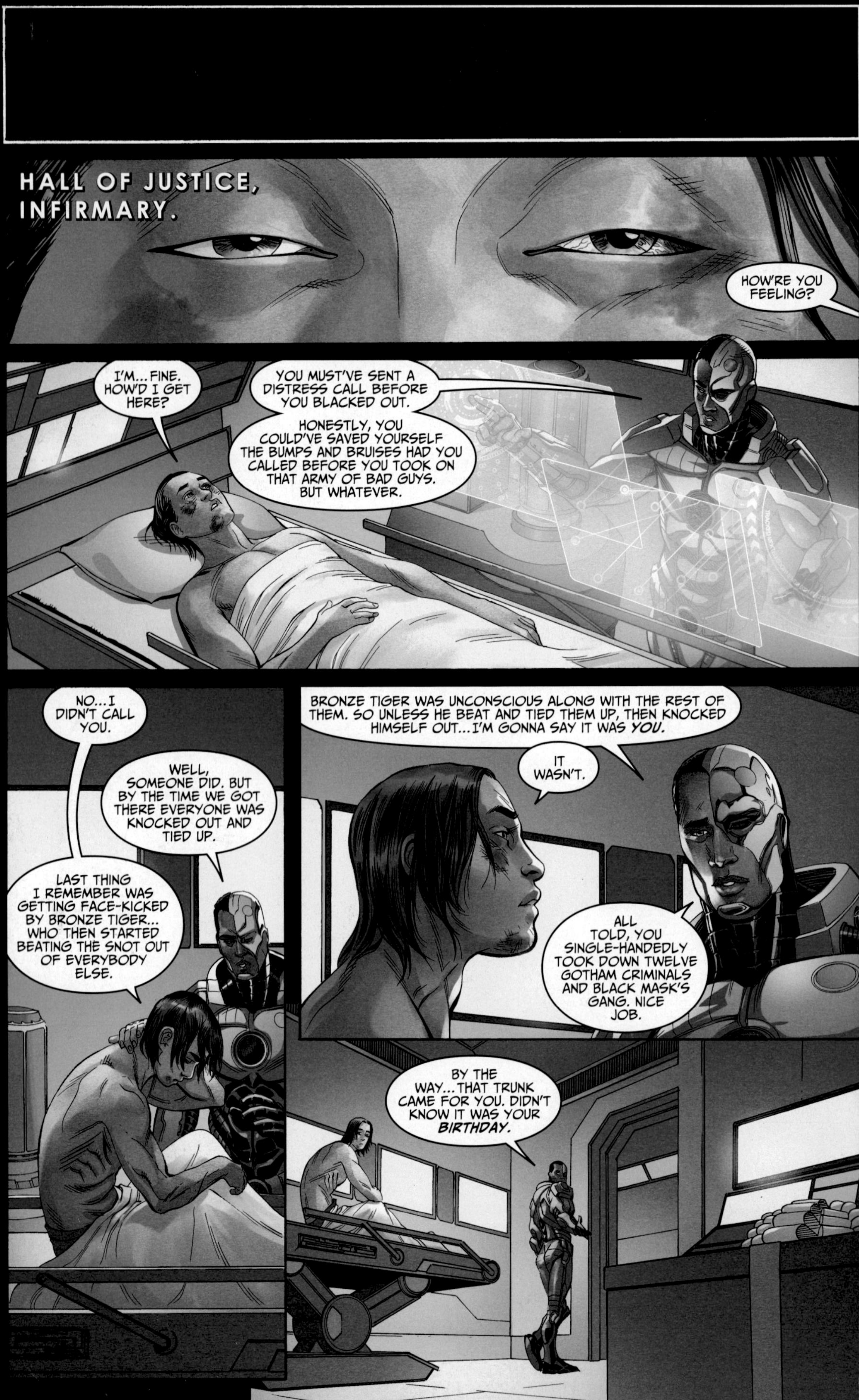
HALL OF JUSTICE, INFIRMARY.
HOW'RE YOU FEELING?
I'M... FINE. HOW'D I GET HERE?
YOU MUST'VE SENT A DISTRESS CALL BEFORE YOU BLACKED OUT.
HONESTLY, YOU COULD'VE SAVED YOURSELF THE BUMPS AND BRUISES HAD YOU CALLED BEFORE YOU TOOK ON THAT ARMY OF BAD GUYS. BUT WHATEVER.
NO... I DIDN'T CALL YOU.
WELL, SOMEONE DID. BUT BY THE TIME WE GOT THERE EVERYONE WAS KNOCKED OUT AND TIED UP.
LAST THING I REMEMBER WAS GETTING FACE-KICKED BY BRONZE TIGER... WHO THEN STARTED BEATING THE SNOT OUT OF EVERYBODY ELSE.
BRONZE TIGER WAS UNCONSCIOUS ALONG WITH THE REST OF THEM. SO UNLESS HE BEAT AND TIED THEM UP, THEN KNOCKED HIMSELF OUT... I'M GONNA SAY IT WAS *YOU.*
IT WASN'T.
ALL TOLD, YOU SINGLE-HANDEDLY TOOK DOWN TWELVE GOTHAM CRIMINALS AND BLACK MASK'S GANG. NICE JOB.
BY THE WAY... THAT TRUNK CAME FOR YOU. DIDN'T KNOW IT WAS YOUR *BIRTHDAY.*

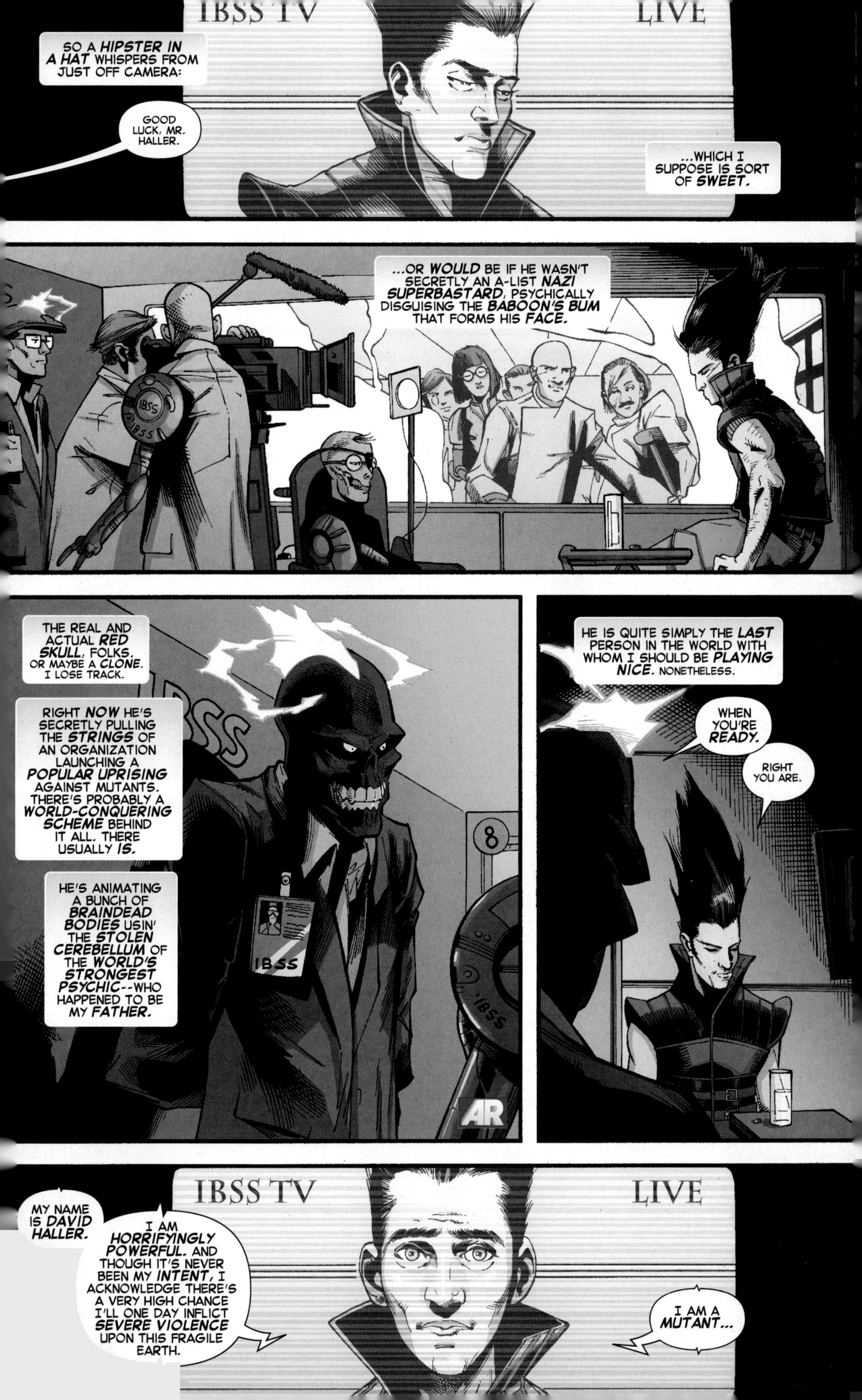
IBSS TV
LIVE
SO A HIPSTER IN A HAT WHISPERS FROM JUST OFF CAMERA:
GOOD LUCK, MR. HALLER.
...WHICH I SUPPOSE IS SORT OF SWEET.
...OR WOULD BE IF HE WASN'T SECRETLY AN A-LIST NAZI SUPERBASTARD, PSYCHICALLY DISGUISING THE BABOON'S BUM THAT FORMS HIS FACE.
IBSS
THE REAL AND ACTUAL RED SKULL, FOLKS. OR MAYBE A CLONE. I LOSE TRACK.
RIGHT NOW HE'S SECRETLY PULLING THE STRINGS OF AN ORGANIZATION LAUNCHING A POPULAR UPRISING AGAINST MUTANTS. THERE'S PROBABLY A WORLD-CONQUERING SCHEME BEHIND IT ALL. THERE USUALLY IS.
HE'S ANIMATING A BUNCH OF BRAINDEAD BODIES USIN' THE STOLEN CEREBELLUM OF THE WORLD'S STRONGEST PSYCHIC--WHO HAPPENED TO BE MY FATHER.
IBSS
HE IS QUITE SIMPLY THE LAST PERSON IN THE WORLD WITH WHOM I SHOULD BE PLAYING NICE. NONETHELESS.
WHEN YOU'RE READY.
RIGHT YOU ARE.
IBSS TV
LIVE
MY NAME IS DAVID HALLER.
I AM HORRIFYINGLY POWERFUL. AND THOUGH IT'S NEVER BEEN MY INTENT, I ACKNOWLEDGE THERE'S A VERY HIGH CHANCE I'LL ONE DAY INFLICT SEVERE VIOLENCE UPON THIS FRAGILE EARTH.
I AM A MUTANT...

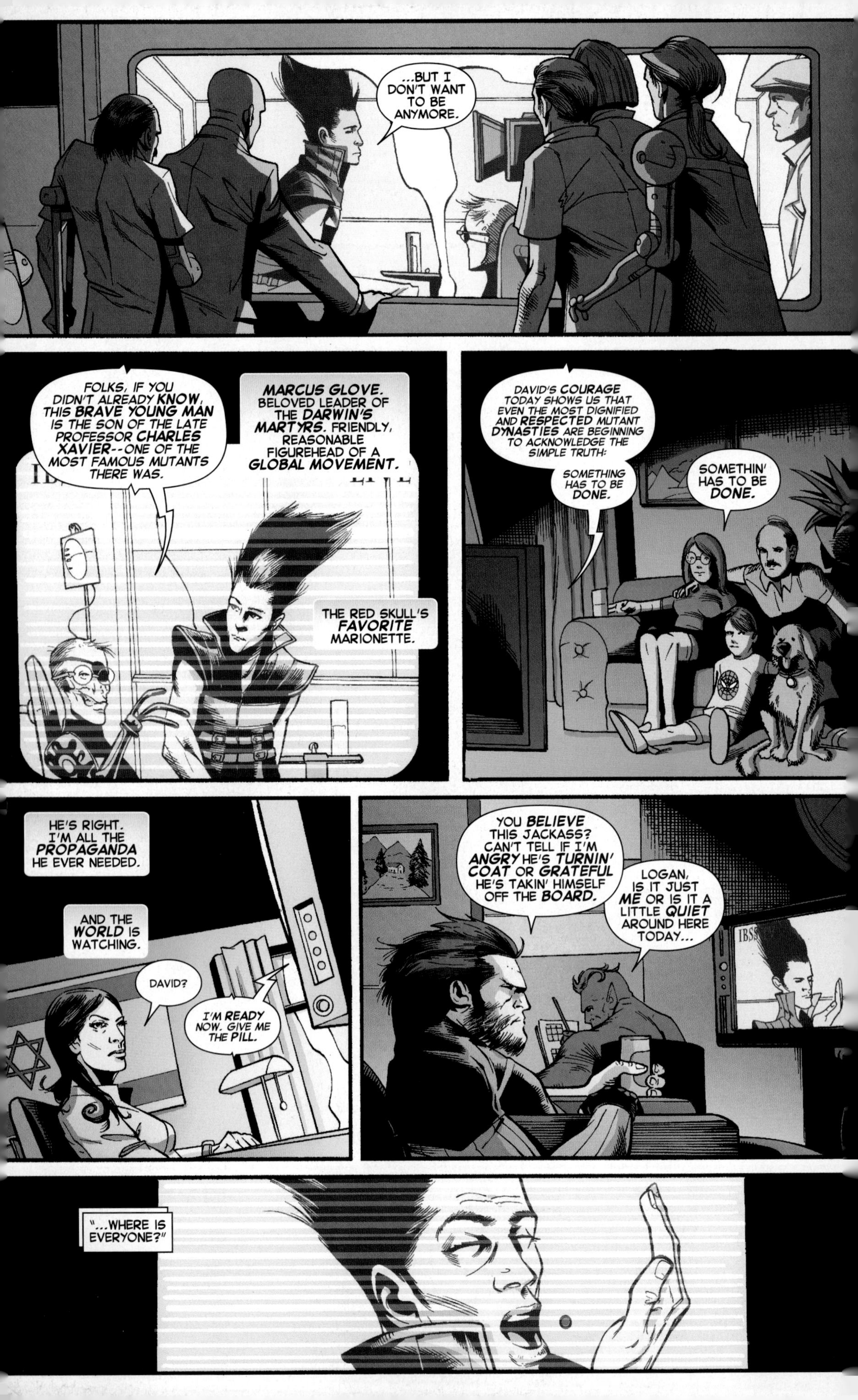
...BUT I DON'T WANT TO BE ANYMORE.
FOLKS, IF YOU DIDN'T ALREADY KNOW, THIS BRAVE YOUNG MAN IS THE SON OF THE LATE PROFESSOR CHARLES XAVIER--ONE OF THE MOST FAMOUS MUTANTS THERE WAS.
MARCUS GLOVE. BELOVED LEADER OF THE DARWIN'S MARTYRS. FRIENDLY, REASONABLE FIGUREHEAD OF A GLOBAL MOVEMENT.
THE RED SKULL'S FAVORITE MARIONETTE.
DAVID'S COURAGE TODAY SHOWS US THAT EVEN THE MOST DIGNIFIED AND RESPECTED MUTANT DYNASTIES ARE BEGINNING TO ACKNOWLEDGE THE SIMPLE TRUTH:
SOMETHING HAS TO BE DONE.
SOMETHIN' HAS TO BE DONE.
HE'S RIGHT. I'M ALL THE PROPAGANDA HE EVER NEEDED.
AND THE WORLD IS WATCHING.
DAVID?
I'M READY NOW. GIVE ME THE PILL.
YOU BELIEVE THIS JACKASS? CAN'T TELL IF I'M ANGRY HE'S TURNIN' COAT OR GRATEFUL HE'S TAKIN' HIMSELF OFF THE BOARD.
LOGAN, IS IT JUST ME OR IS IT A LITTLE QUIET AROUND HERE TODAY...
"...WHERE IS EVERYONE?"

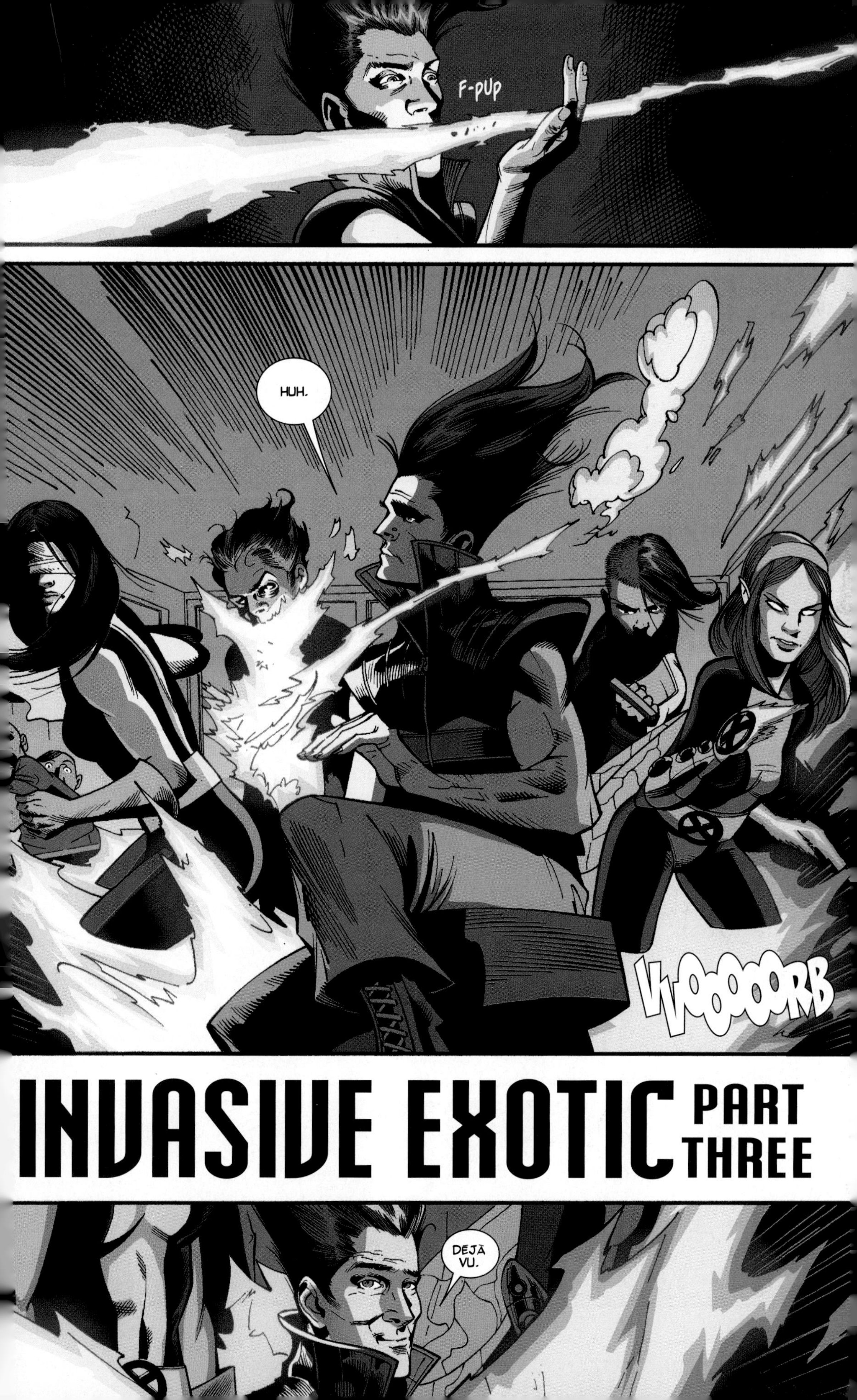
F-PUP
HUH.
VVOOOOORB
INVASIVE EXOTIC PART THREE
DEJÀ VU.

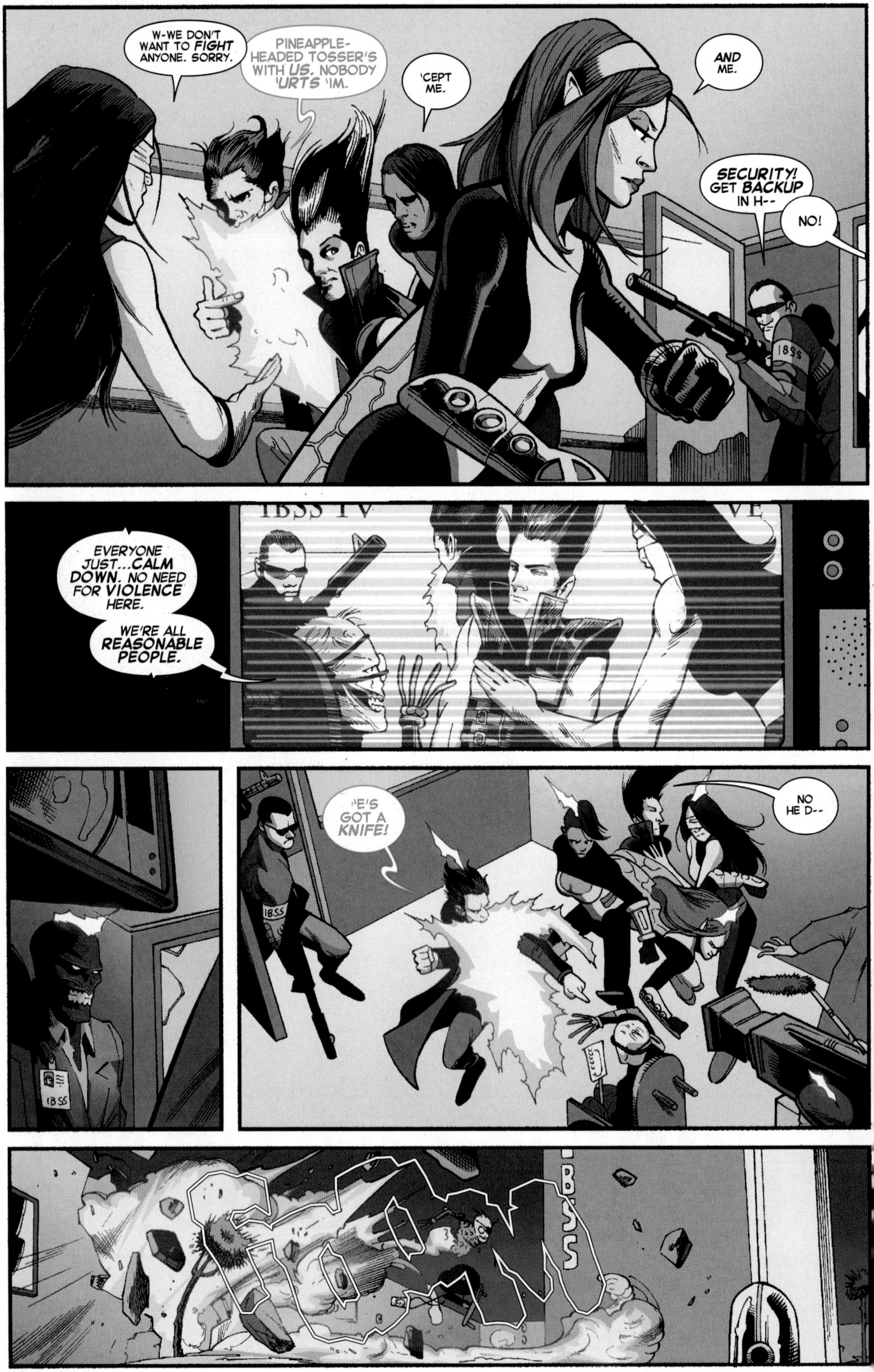
W-WE DON'T WANT TO FIGHT ANYONE. SORRY.
PINEAPPLE-HEADED TOSSER'S WITH US. NOBODY 'URTS 'IM.
'CEPT ME.
AND ME.
SECURITY! GET BACKUP IN H--
NO!
EVERYONE JUST...CALM DOWN. NO NEED FOR VIOLENCE HERE.
WE'RE ALL REASONABLE PEOPLE.
'E'S GOT A KNIFE!
NO HE D--

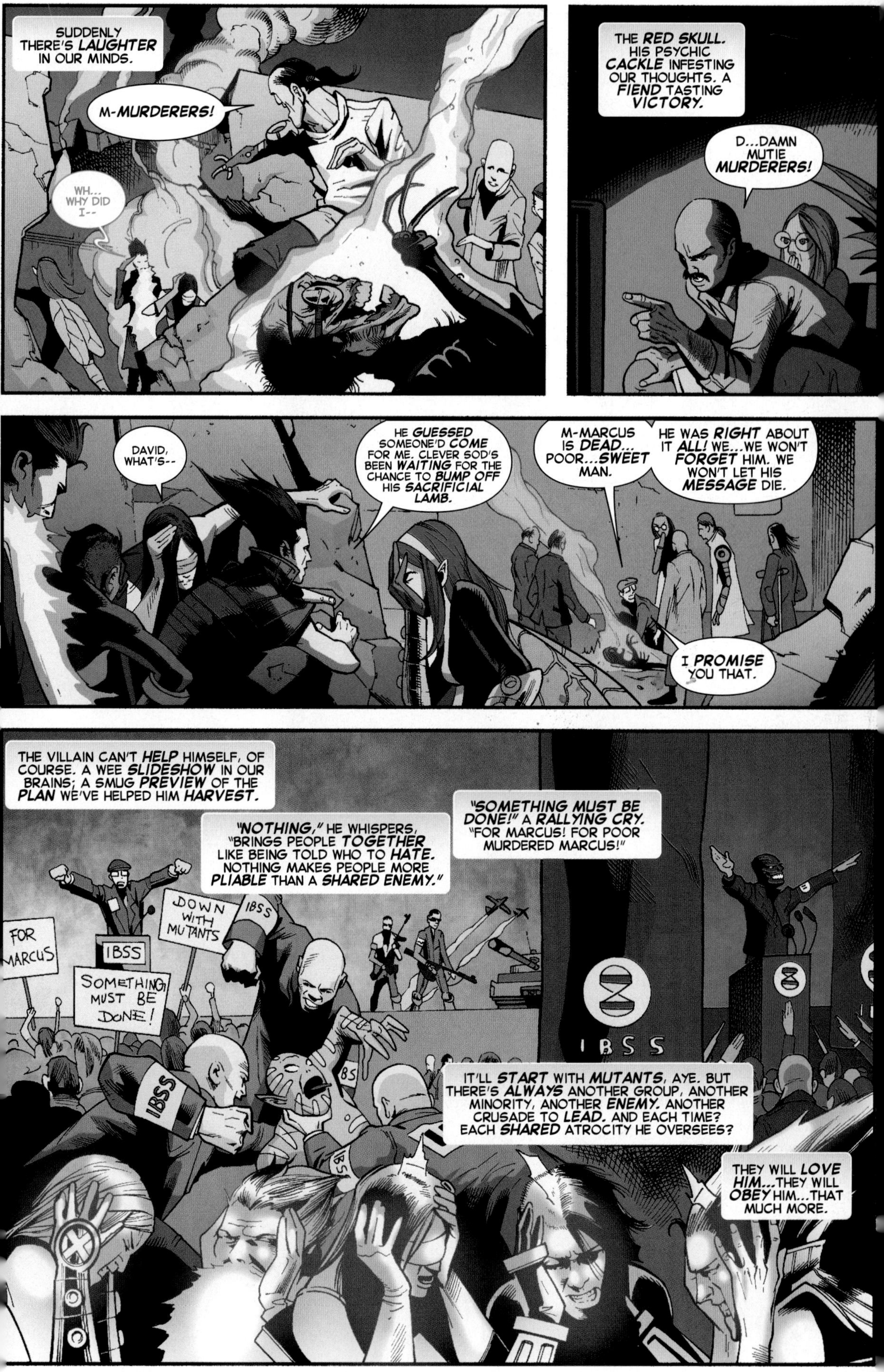
SUDDENLY THERE'S LAUGHTER IN OUR MINDS.
M-MURDERERS!
WH... WHY DID I--
THE RED SKULL. HIS PSYCHIC CACKLE INFESTING OUR THOUGHTS. A FIEND TASTING VICTORY.
D...DAMN MUTIE MURDERERS!
DAVID, WHAT'S--
HE GUESSED SOMEONE'D COME FOR ME. CLEVER SOD'S BEEN WAITING FOR THE CHANCE TO BUMP OFF HIS SACRIFICIAL LAMB.
M-MARCUS IS DEAD... POOR...SWEET MAN.
HE WAS RIGHT ABOUT IT ALL! WE...WE WON'T FORGET HIM. WE WON'T LET HIS MESSAGE DIE.
I PROMISE YOU THAT.
THE VILLAIN CAN'T HELP HIMSELF, OF COURSE. A WEE SLIDESHOW IN OUR BRAINS; A SMUG PREVIEW OF THE PLAN WE'VE HELPED HIM HARVEST.
"NOTHING," HE WHISPERS, "BRINGS PEOPLE TOGETHER LIKE BEING TOLD WHO TO HATE. NOTHING MAKES PEOPLE MORE PLIABLE THAN A SHARED ENEMY."
"SOMETHING MUST BE DONE!" A RALLYING CRY. "FOR MARCUS! FOR POOR MURDERED MARCUS!"
FOR MARCUS
IBSS
SOMETHING MUST BE DONE!
DOWN WITH MUTANTS
IBSS
IBSS
IBSS
IBSS
IT'LL START WITH MUTANTS, AYE. BUT THERE'S ALWAYS ANOTHER GROUP, ANOTHER MINORITY, ANOTHER ENEMY. ANOTHER CRUSADE TO LEAD. AND EACH TIME? EACH SHARED ATROCITY HE OVERSEES?
THEY WILL LOVE HIM...THEY WILL OBEY HIM...THAT MUCH MORE.

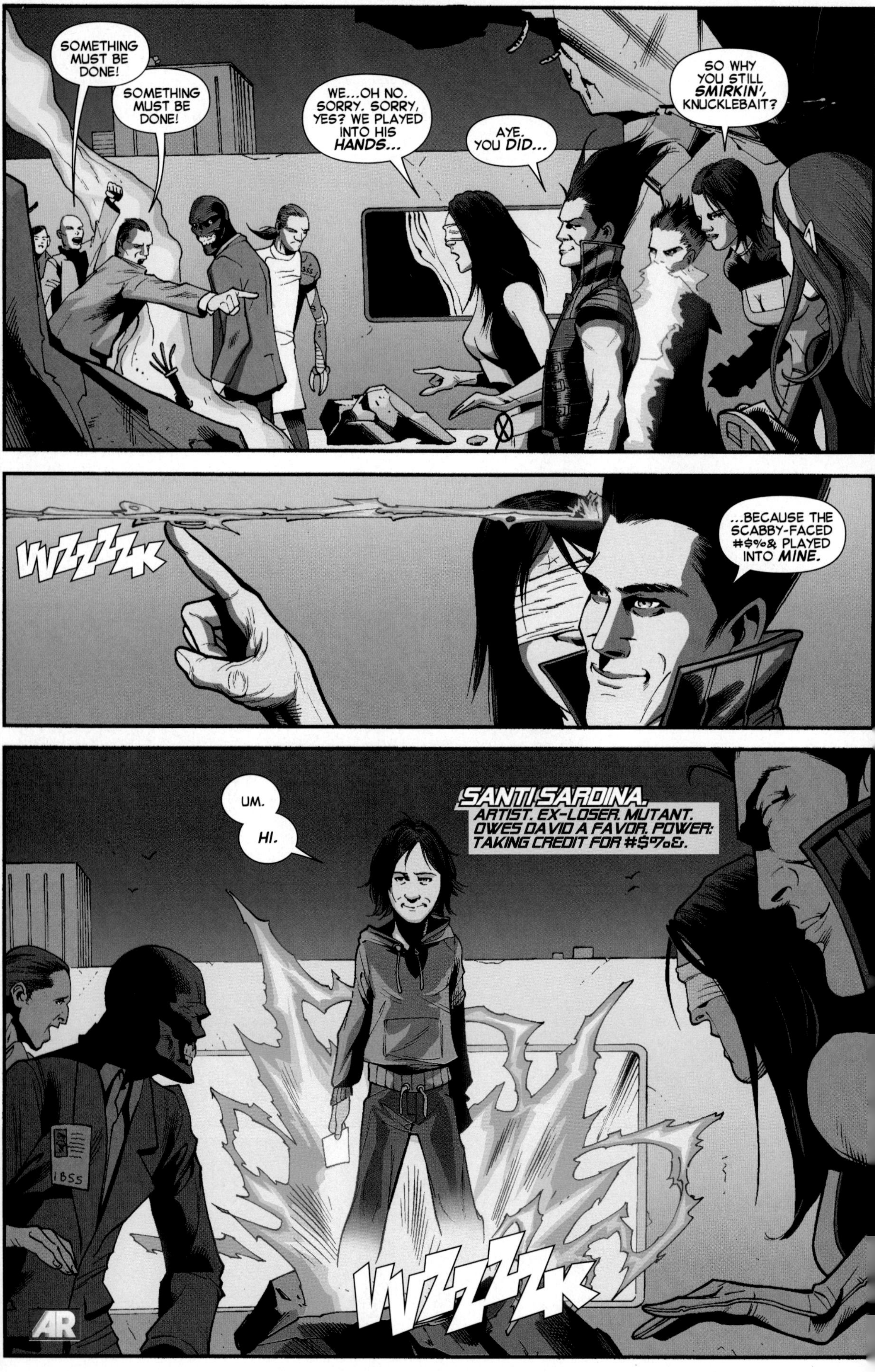
SOMETHING MUST BE DONE!
SOMETHING MUST BE DONE!
WE...OH NO. SORRY. SORRY, YES? WE PLAYED INTO HIS HANDS...
AYE. YOU DID...
SO WHY YOU STILL SMIRKIN', KNUCKLEBAIT?
VVZZZZK
...BECAUSE THE SCABBY-FACED #$%& PLAYED INTO MINE.
UM.
HI.
SANTI SARDINA.
ARTIST. EX-LOSER. MUTANT. OWES DAVID A FAVOR. POWER: TAKING CREDIT FOR #$%&.
VVZZZZK

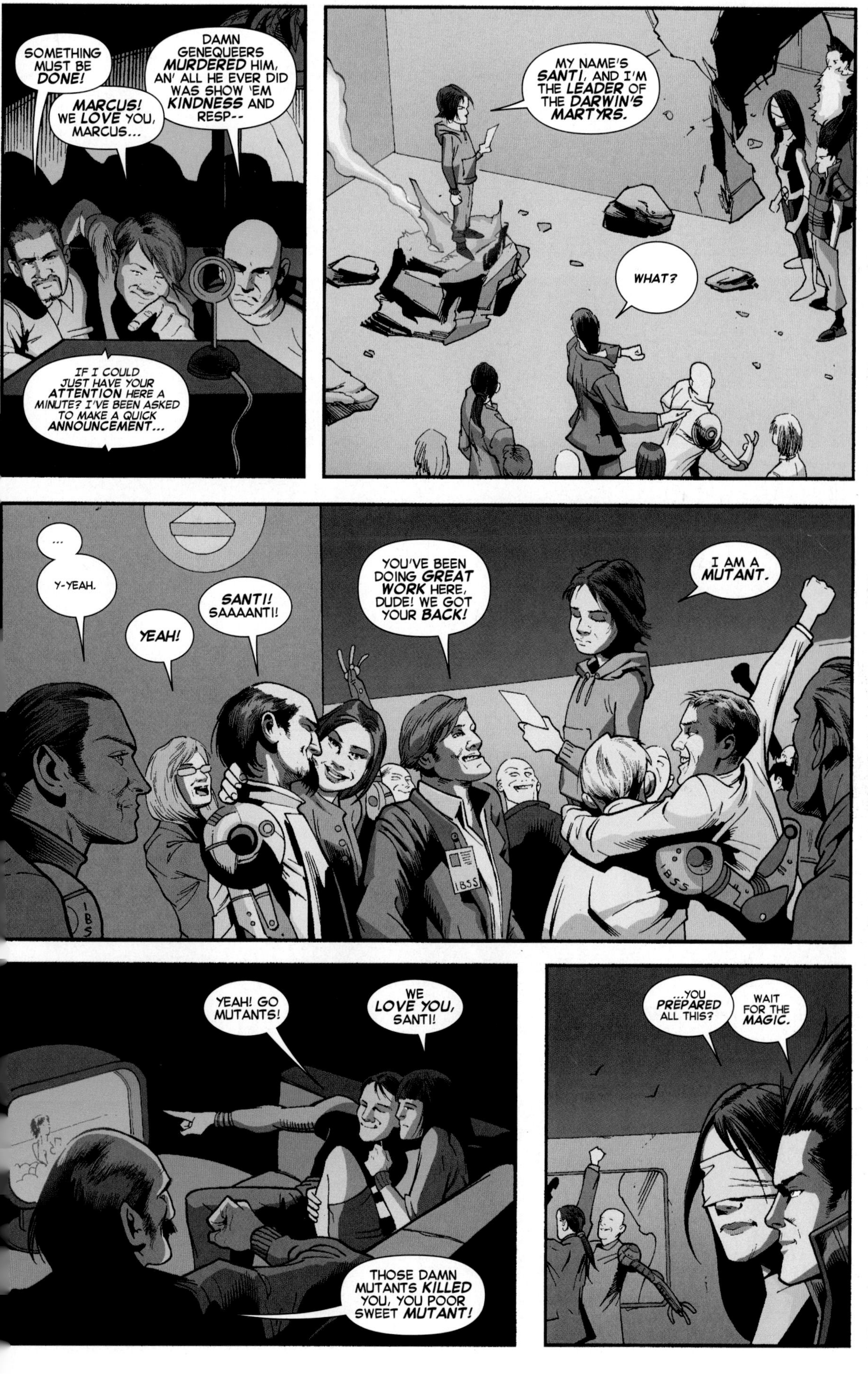
SOMETHING MUST BE DONE!
MARCUS! WE LOVE YOU, MARCUS...
DAMN GENEQUEERS MURDERED HIM, AN' ALL HE EVER DID WAS SHOW 'EM KINDNESS AND RESP--
IF I COULD JUST HAVE YOUR ATTENTION HERE A MINUTE? I'VE BEEN ASKED TO MAKE A QUICK ANNOUNCEMENT...
MY NAME'S SANTI, AND I'M THE LEADER OF THE DARWIN'S MARTYRS.
WHAT?
...
Y-YEAH.
YEAH!
SANTI! SAAAANTI!
YOU'VE BEEN DOING GREAT WORK HERE, DUDE! WE GOT YOUR BACK!
I AM A MUTANT.
YEAH! GO MUTANTS!
WE LOVE YOU, SANTI!
THOSE DAMN MUTANTS KILLED YOU, YOU POOR SWEET MUTANT!
...YOU PREPARED ALL THIS?
WAIT FOR THE MAGIC.

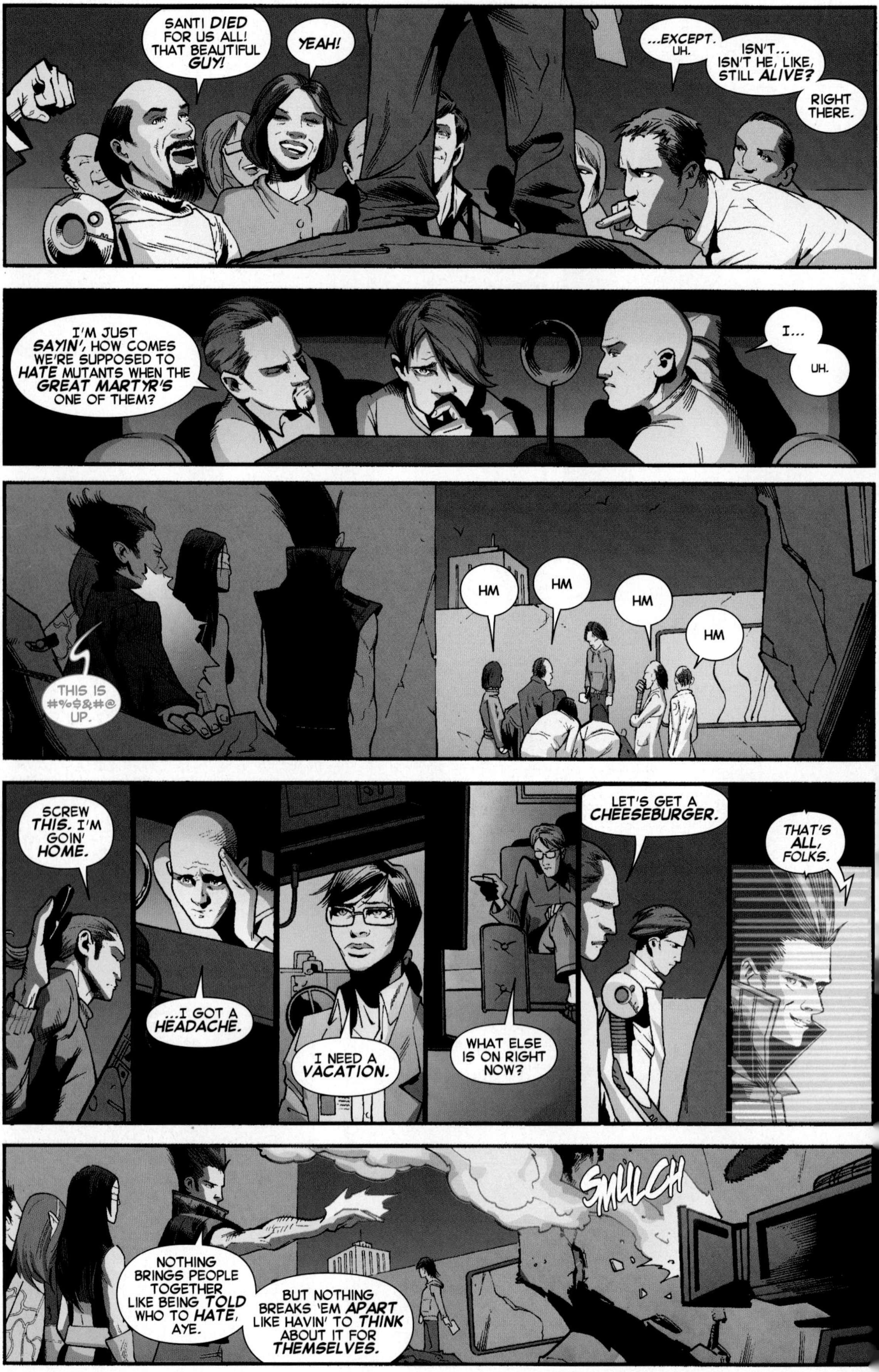
SANTI DIED FOR US ALL! THAT BEAUTIFUL GUY!
YEAH!
...EXCEPT. UH.
ISN'T... ISN'T HE, LIKE, STILL ALIVE?
RIGHT THERE.
I'M JUST SAYIN', HOW COMES WE'RE SUPPOSED TO HATE MUTANTS WHEN THE GREAT MARTYR'S ONE OF THEM?
I...
UH.
THIS IS #%$&#@ UP.
HM
HM
HM
HM
SCREW THIS. I'M GOIN' HOME.
...I GOT A HEADACHE.
I NEED A VACATION.
WHAT ELSE IS ON RIGHT NOW?
LET'S GET A CHEESEBURGER.
THAT'S ALL, FOLKS.
SMULCH
NOTHING BRINGS PEOPLE TOGETHER LIKE BEING TOLD WHO TO HATE, AYE.
BUT NOTHING BREAKS 'EM APART LIKE HAVIN' TO THINK ABOUT IT FOR THEMSELVES.

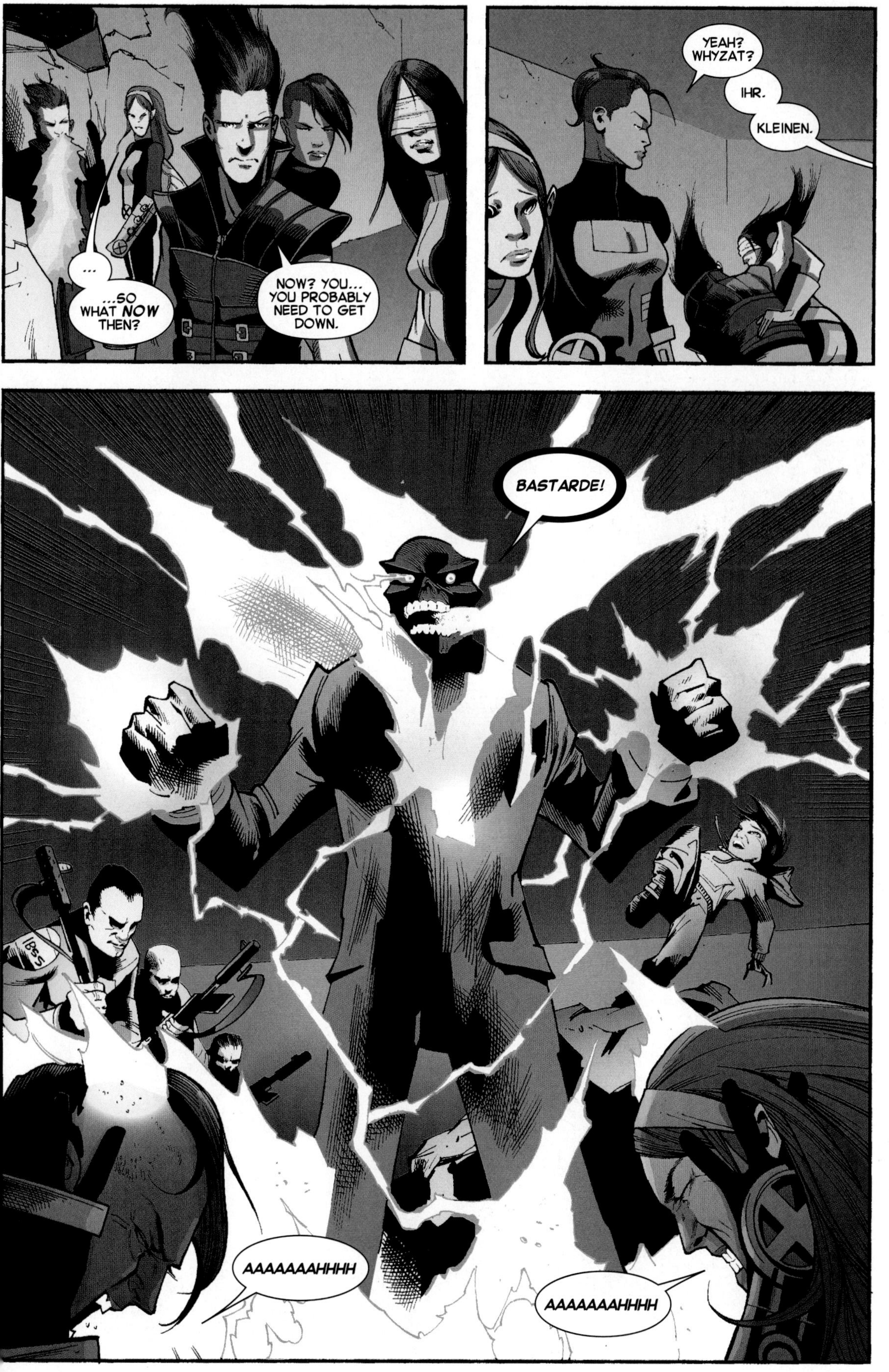
...
...SO WHAT NOW THEN?
NOW? YOU... YOU PROBABLY NEED TO GET DOWN.
YEAH? WHYZAT?
IHR.
KLEINEN.
BASTARDE!
AAAAAAAHHHH
AAAAAAAHHHH

AAAAAAA

OHCRAP CRAPCRAP HE'S...HE'S *TOO STRONG!*

I *DIDN'T...* DIDN'T *KNOW...* HE'D BE *THIS STRRRR...*

"KNOW"? YOU... SORRY, WAIT, YES, YOU *KNEW* THIS WOULD HAPPEN?

...D-DARWIN'S *MARTYRS.*

THREAT TO *MUTANTKIND...* REASONABLE, FRIENDLY-- NNN--DOESN'T *MATTER.* H-HAD TO BE *DESTROYED. PROACTIVE,* RUTH. *PRE-EMPTIVE...*

BUT...BUT LUCA'S PREDICTIONS... *OUR FUTURE...THAT'S* WHY YOU CAME!

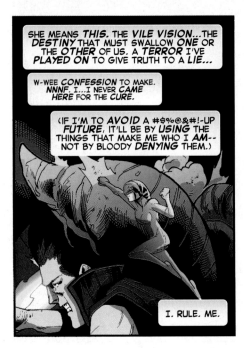

SHE MEANS *THIS.* THE *VILE VISION...*THE *DESTINY* THAT MUST SWALLOW *ONE* OR THE *OTHER* OF US. A *TERROR* I'VE *PLAYED ON* TO GIVE TRUTH TO A *LIE...*

W-WEE *CONFESSION* TO MAKE. NNNF. I...I NEVER *CAME HERE* FOR THE *CURE.*

(IF I'M TO *AVOID* A #$%@&#!-UP *FUTURE*, IT'LL BE BY *USING* THE THINGS THAT MAKE ME WHO I *AM*-- NOT BY BLOODY *DENYING* THEM.)

I. RULE. ME.

SO WHAT YOU'RE SAYIN' IS, ALL THIS TAKIN'-THE-*PILL* #$%& WAS A *SCAM* TO TRICK THE *MANKY-FACED FREAK?*

AND LURE US 'ERE TO HELP YOU?

YYYY.

YYYY.

BUT WE'RE GETTIN' OUR *ARSES 'ANDED TO US* ANYWAY?

YYYY.

I WISH TO STATE FOR THE RECORD THAT I AM *DEFINITELY* GOING TO *KILL* YOU.

YYY

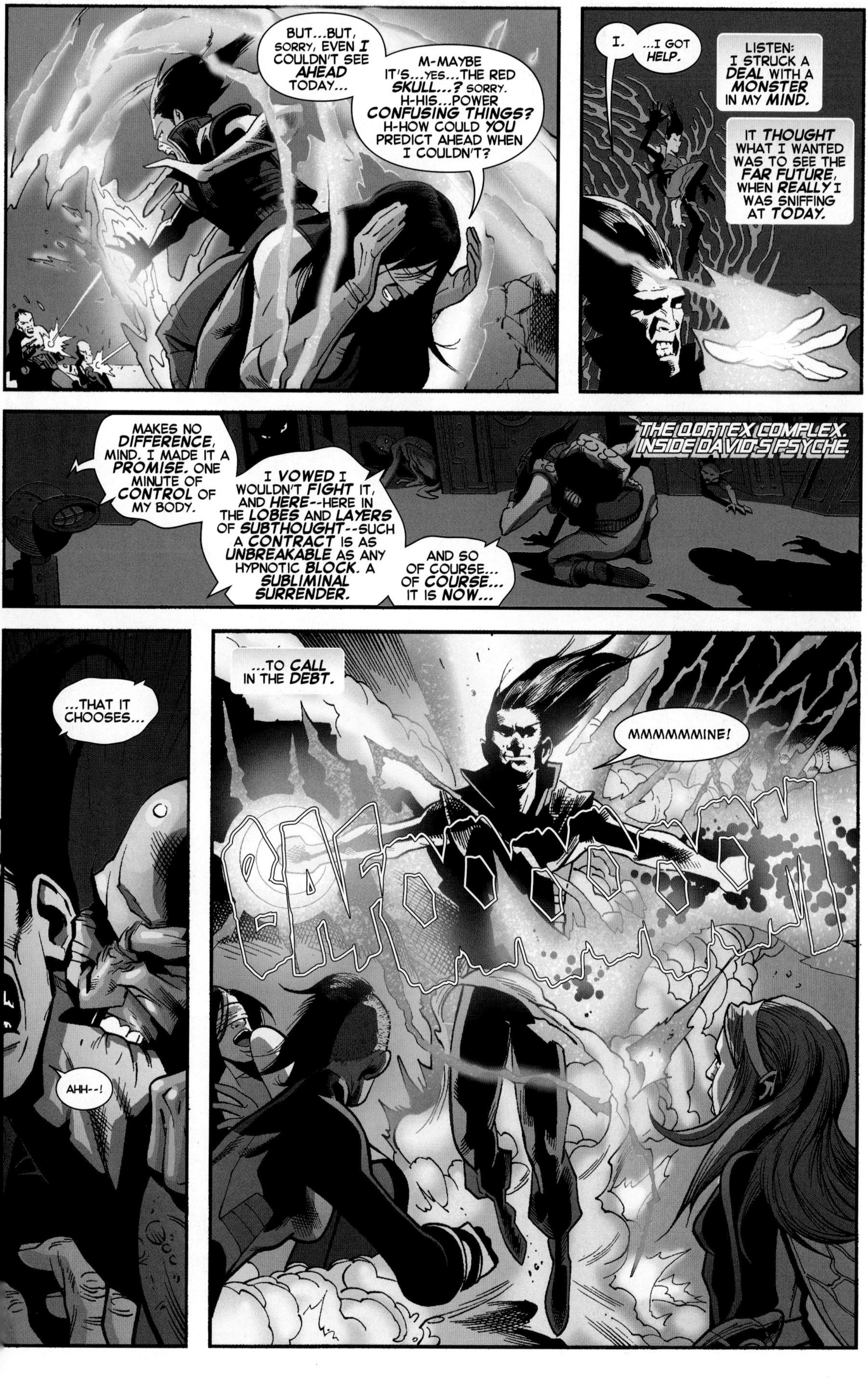
BUT...BUT, SORRY, EVEN I COULDN'T SEE AHEAD TODAY...
M-MAYBE IT'S...YES...THE RED SKULL...? SORRY. H-HIS...POWER CONFUSING THINGS? H-HOW COULD YOU PREDICT AHEAD WHEN I COULDN'T?
I.
...I GOT HELP.
LISTEN: I STRUCK A DEAL WITH A MONSTER IN MY MIND.
IT THOUGHT WHAT I WANTED WAS TO SEE THE FAR FUTURE, WHEN REALLY I WAS SNIFFING AT TODAY.
THE VORTEX COMPLEX. INSIDE DAVID'S PSYCHE.
MAKES NO DIFFERENCE, MIND. I MADE IT A PROMISE. ONE MINUTE OF CONTROL OF MY BODY.
I VOWED I WOULDN'T FIGHT IT, AND HERE--HERE IN THE LOBES AND LAYERS OF SUBTHOUGHT--SUCH A CONTRACT IS AS UNBREAKABLE AS ANY HYPNOTIC BLOCK. A SUBLIMINAL SURRENDER.
AND SO OF COURSE... OF COURSE... IT IS NOW...
...THAT IT CHOOSES...
AHH--!
...TO CALL IN THE DEBT.
MMMMMMINE!

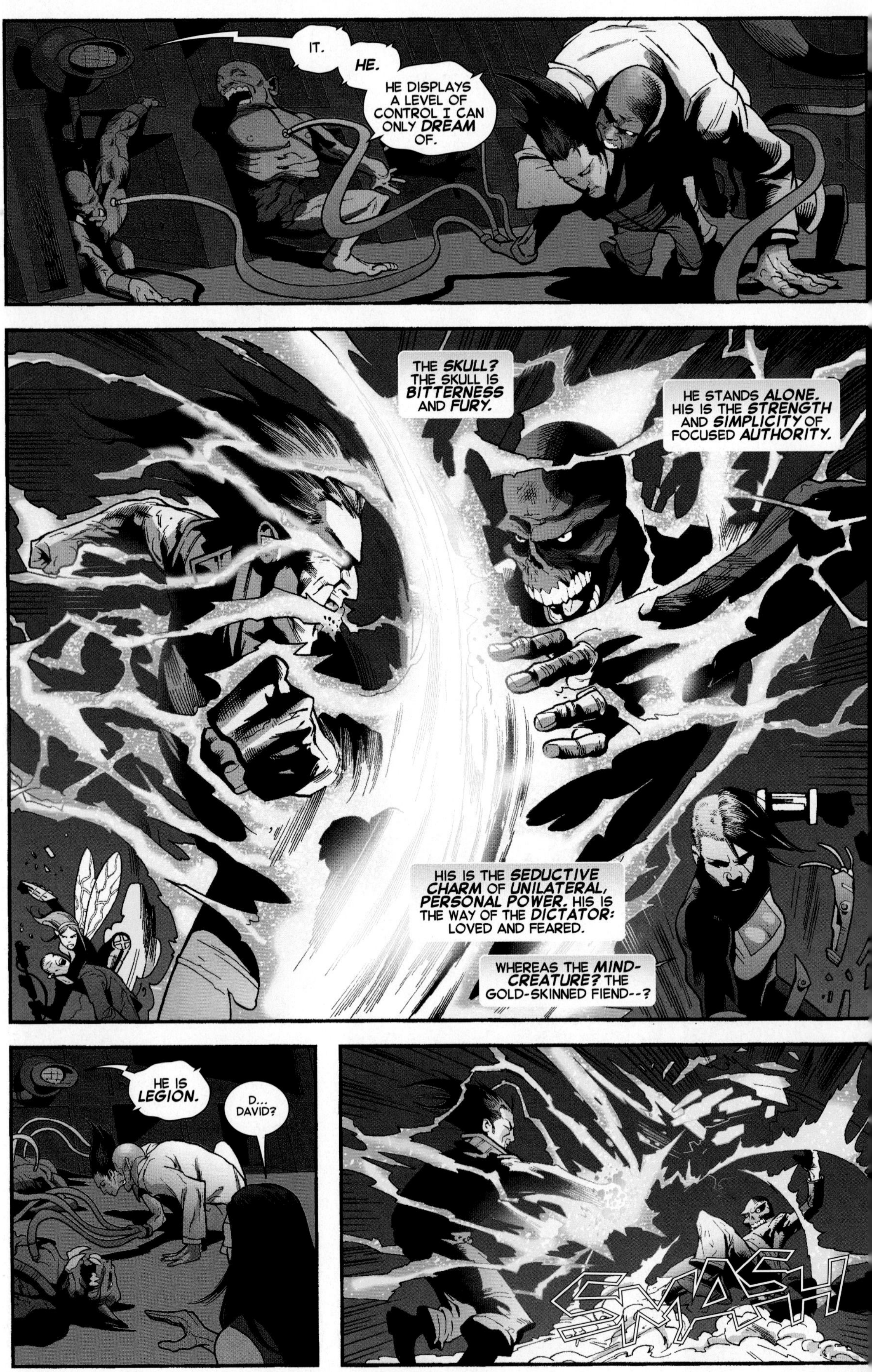

IT.
HE.
HE DISPLAYS A LEVEL OF CONTROL I CAN ONLY DREAM OF.
THE SKULL? THE SKULL IS BITTERNESS AND FURY.
HE STANDS ALONE. HIS IS THE STRENGTH AND SIMPLICITY OF FOCUSED AUTHORITY.
HIS IS THE SEDUCTIVE CHARM OF UNILATERAL, PERSONAL POWER. HIS IS THE WAY OF THE DICTATOR: LOVED AND FEARED.
WHEREAS THE MIND-CREATURE? THE GOLD-SKINNED FIEND--?
HE IS LEGION.
D... DAVID?
SMASH SMASH

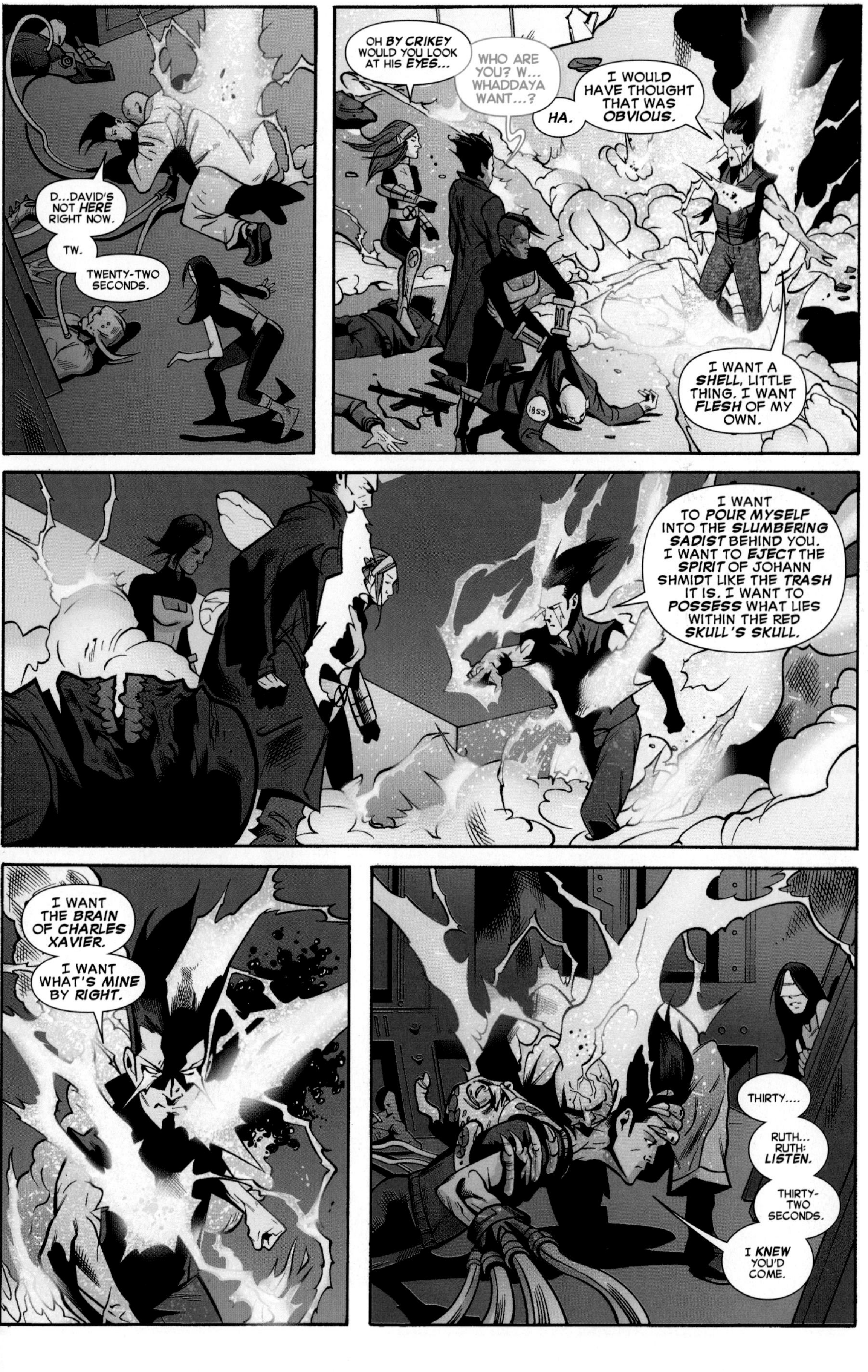

D...DAVID'S NOT HERE RIGHT NOW.
TW.
TWENTY-TWO SECONDS.
OH BY CRIKEY WOULD YOU LOOK AT HIS EYES...
WHO ARE YOU? W... WHADDAYA WANT...?
HA.
I WOULD HAVE THOUGHT THAT WAS OBVIOUS.
I WANT A SHELL, LITTLE THING. I WANT FLESH OF MY OWN.
I WANT TO POUR MYSELF INTO THE SLUMBERING SADIST BEHIND YOU. I WANT TO EJECT THE SPIRIT OF JOHANN SHMIDT LIKE THE TRASH IT IS. I WANT TO POSSESS WHAT LIES WITHIN THE RED SKULL'S SKULL.
I WANT THE BRAIN OF CHARLES XAVIER.
I WANT WHAT'S MINE BY RIGHT.
THIRTY....
RUTH... RUTH: LISTEN.
THIRTY-TWO SECONDS.
I KNEW YOU'D COME.

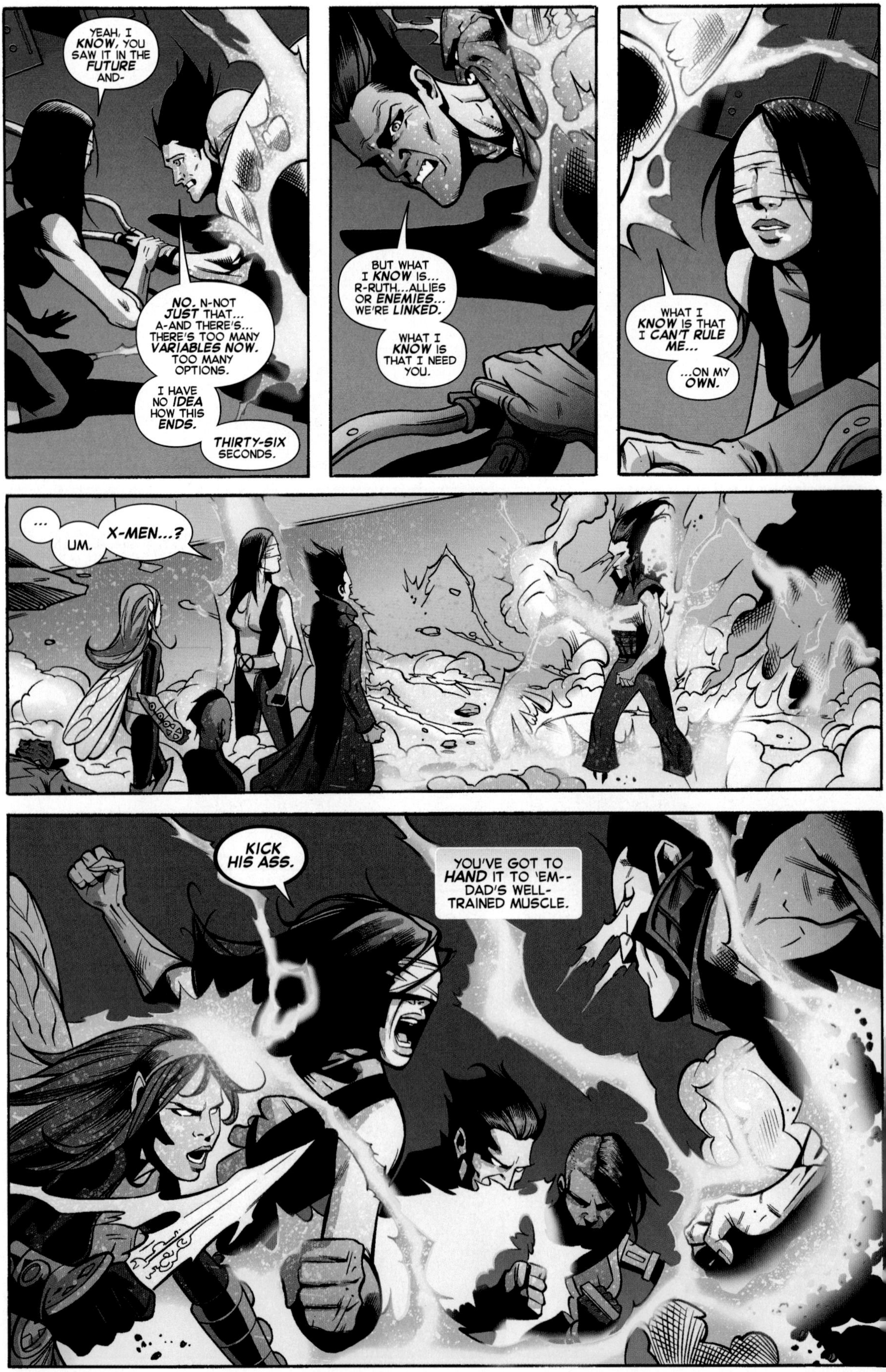
YEAH, I KNOW, YOU SAW IT IN THE FUTURE AND-
NO. N-NOT JUST THAT... A-AND THERE'S... THERE'S TOO MANY VARIABLES NOW. TOO MANY OPTIONS.
I HAVE NO IDEA HOW THIS ENDS.
THIRTY-SIX SECONDS.
BUT WHAT I KNOW IS... R-RUTH...ALLIES OR ENEMIES... WE'RE LINKED.
WHAT I KNOW IS THAT I NEED YOU.
WHAT I KNOW IS THAT I CAN'T RULE ME...
...ON MY OWN.
...
UM.
X-MEN...?
KICK HIS ASS.
YOU'VE GOT TO HAND IT TO 'EM--DAD'S WELL-TRAINED MUSCLE.

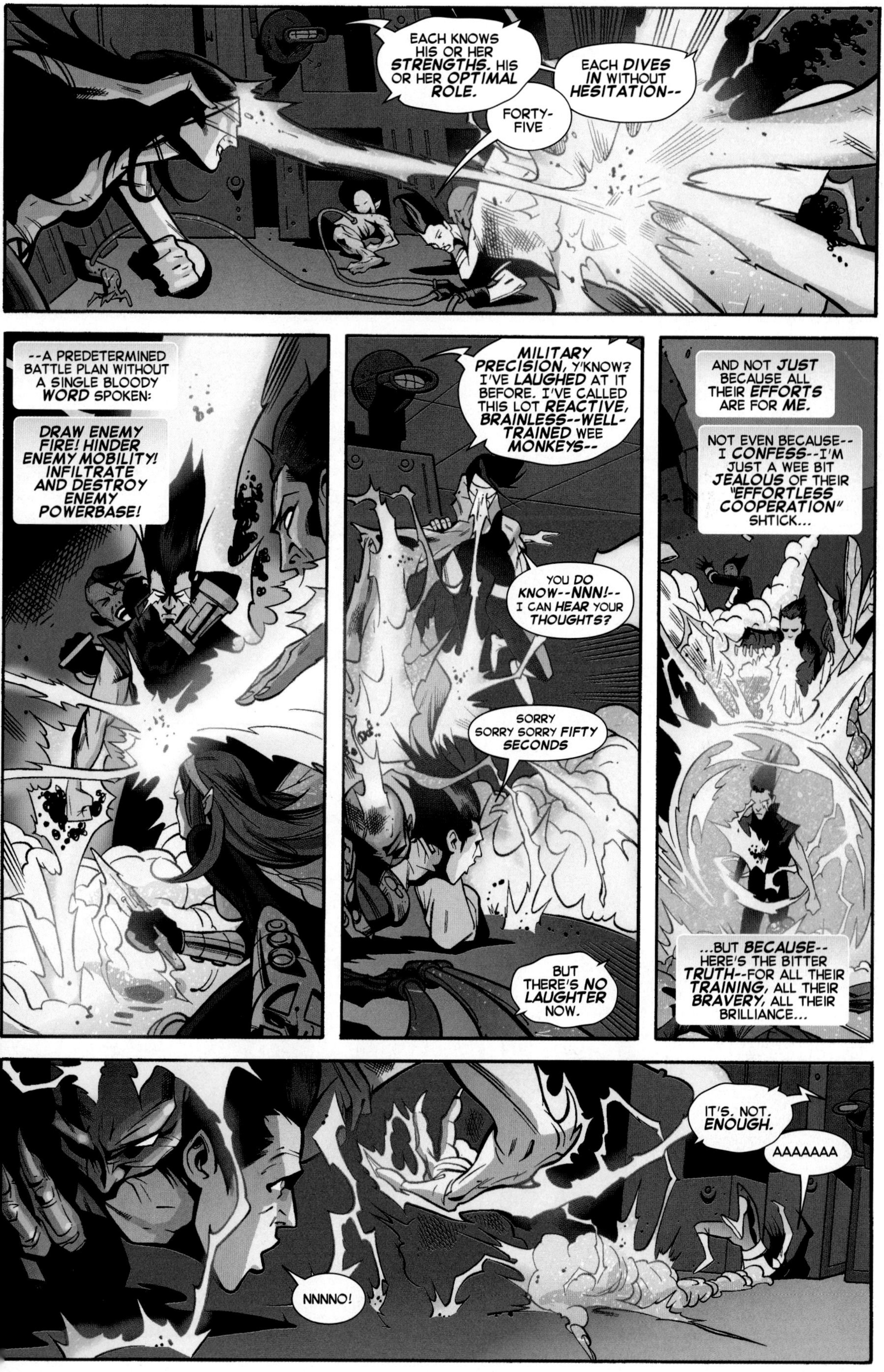
EACH KNOWS HIS OR HER STRENGTHS. HIS OR HER OPTIMAL ROLE.
EACH DIVES IN WITHOUT HESITATION--
FORTY-FIVE
--A PREDETERMINED BATTLE PLAN WITHOUT A SINGLE BLOODY WORD SPOKEN:
DRAW ENEMY FIRE! HINDER ENEMY MOBILITY! INFILTRATE AND DESTROY ENEMY POWERBASE!
MILITARY PRECISION, Y'KNOW? I'VE LAUGHED AT IT BEFORE. I'VE CALLED THIS LOT REACTIVE, BRAINLESS--WELL-TRAINED WEE MONKEYS--
YOU DO KNOW--NNN!--I CAN HEAR YOUR THOUGHTS?
SORRY SORRY SORRY FIFTY SECONDS
BUT THERE'S NO LAUGHTER NOW.
AND NOT JUST BECAUSE ALL THEIR EFFORTS ARE FOR ME.
NOT EVEN BECAUSE--I CONFESS--I'M JUST A WEE BIT JEALOUS OF THEIR "EFFORTLESS COOPERATION" SHTICK...
...BUT BECAUSE--HERE'S THE BITTER TRUTH--FOR ALL THEIR TRAINING, ALL THEIR BRAVERY, ALL THEIR BRILLIANCE...
IT'S. NOT. ENOUGH.
AAAAAAA
NNNNO!

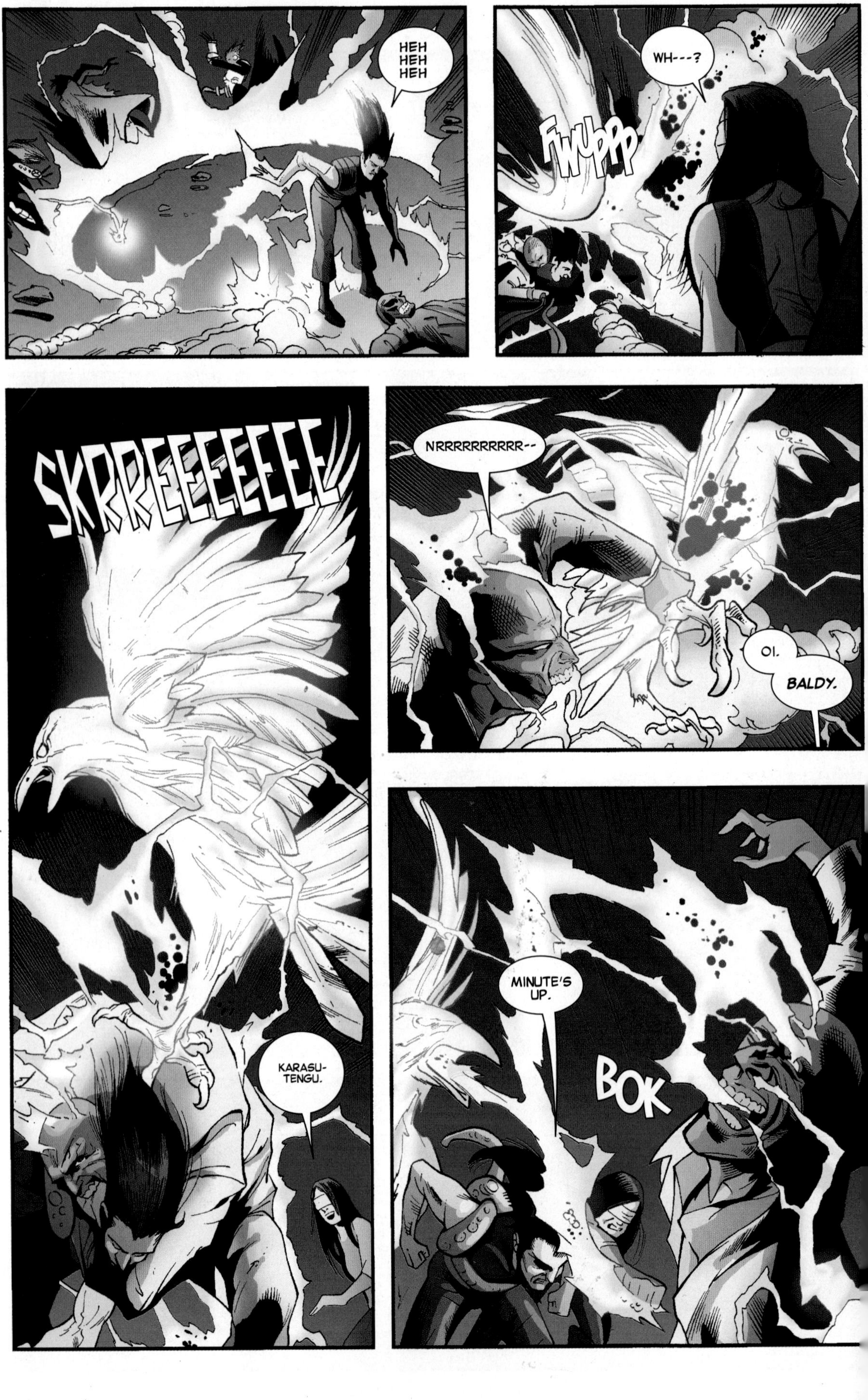
HEH HEH HEH
WH---?
FWUPPP
SKREEEEEEEE
KARASU-TENGU.
NRRRRRRRRRR--
OI.
BALDY.
MINUTE'S UP.
BOK

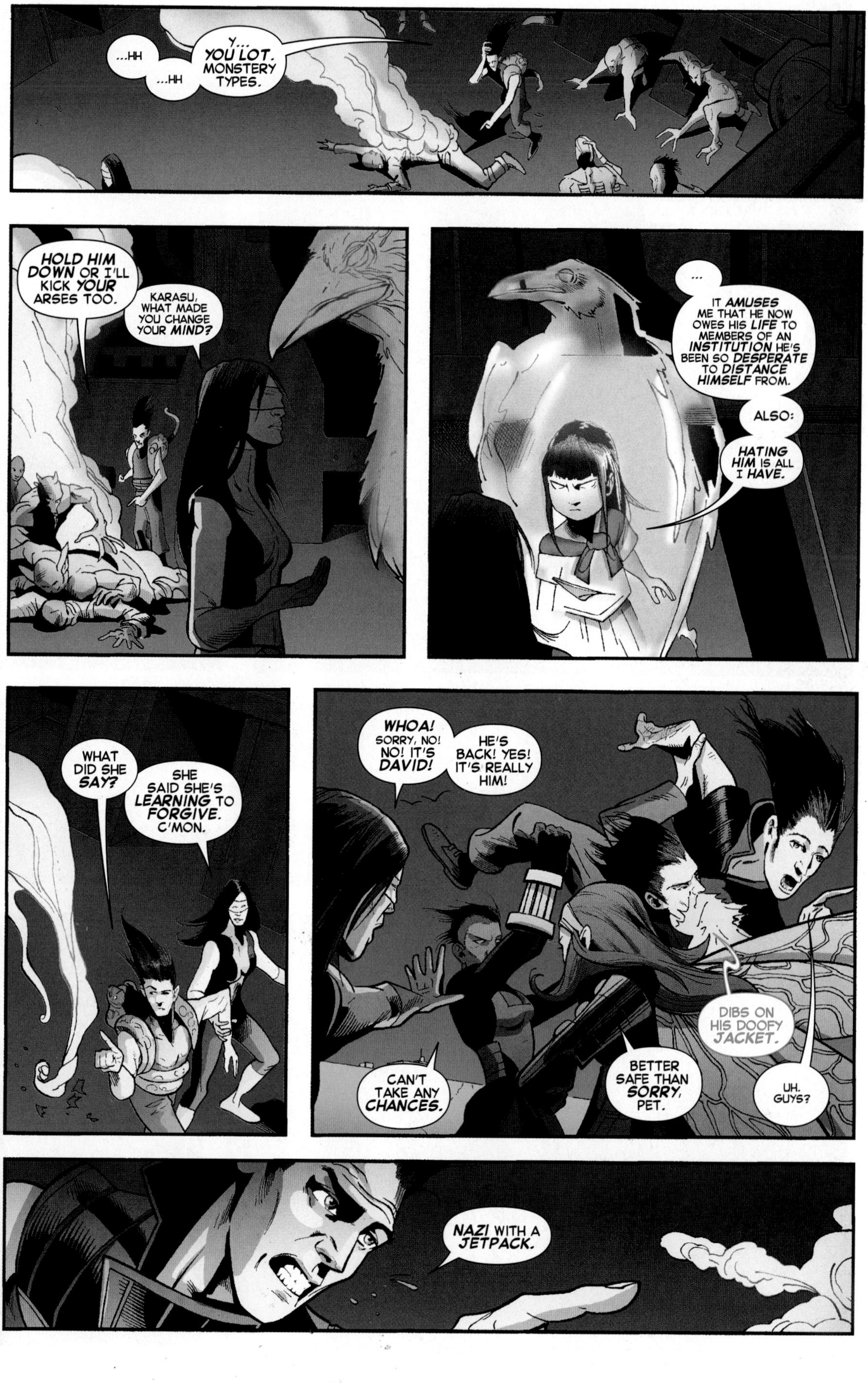

...HH
...HH
Y... YOU LOT. MONSTERY TYPES.
HOLD HIM DOWN OR I'LL KICK YOUR ARSES TOO.
KARASU, WHAT MADE YOU CHANGE YOUR MIND?
...
IT AMUSES ME THAT HE NOW OWES HIS LIFE TO MEMBERS OF AN INSTITUTION HE'S BEEN SO DESPERATE TO DISTANCE HIMSELF FROM.
ALSO:
HATING HIM IS ALL I HAVE.
WHAT DID SHE SAY?
SHE SAID SHE'S LEARNING TO FORGIVE. C'MON.
WHOA! SORRY, NO! NO! IT'S DAVID!
HE'S BACK! YES! IT'S REALLY HIM!
CAN'T TAKE ANY CHANCES.
BETTER SAFE THAN SORRY, PET.
DIBS ON HIS DOOFY JACKET.
UH. GUYS?
NAZI WITH A JETPACK.

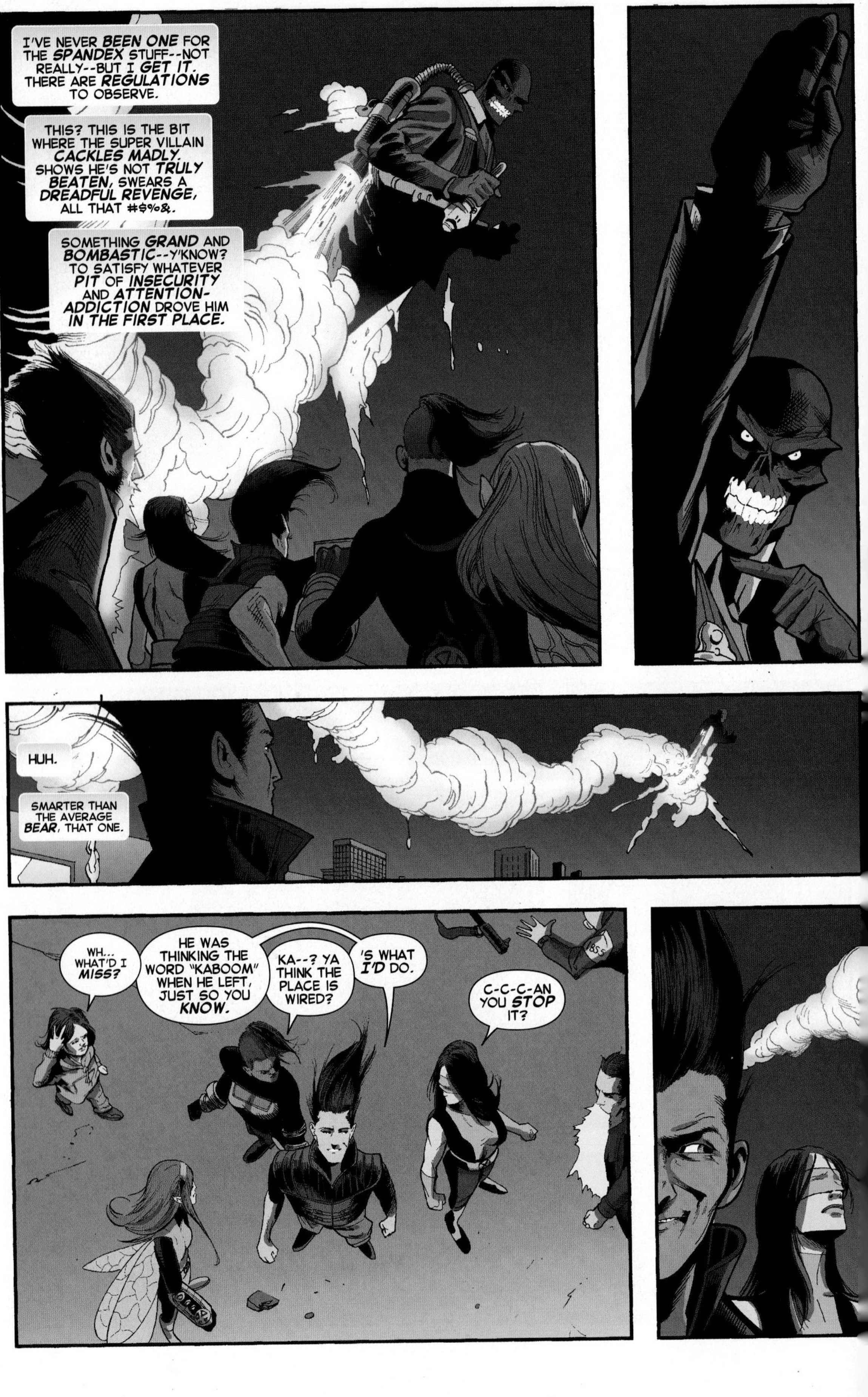
I'VE NEVER BEEN ONE FOR THE SPANDEX STUFF--NOT REALLY--BUT I GET IT. THERE ARE REGULATIONS TO OBSERVE.
THIS? THIS IS THE BIT WHERE THE SUPER VILLAIN CACKLES MADLY. SHOWS HE'S NOT TRULY BEATEN, SWEARS A DREADFUL REVENGE, ALL THAT #$%&.
SOMETHING GRAND AND BOMBASTIC--Y'KNOW? TO SATISFY WHATEVER PIT OF INSECURITY AND ATTENTION-ADDICTION DROVE HIM IN THE FIRST PLACE.
HUH.
SMARTER THAN THE AVERAGE BEAR, THAT ONE.
WH... WHAT'D I MISS?
HE WAS THINKING THE WORD "KABOOM" WHEN HE LEFT, JUST SO YOU KNOW.
KA--? YA THINK THE PLACE IS WIRED?
'S WHAT I'D DO.
C-C-C-AN YOU STOP IT?

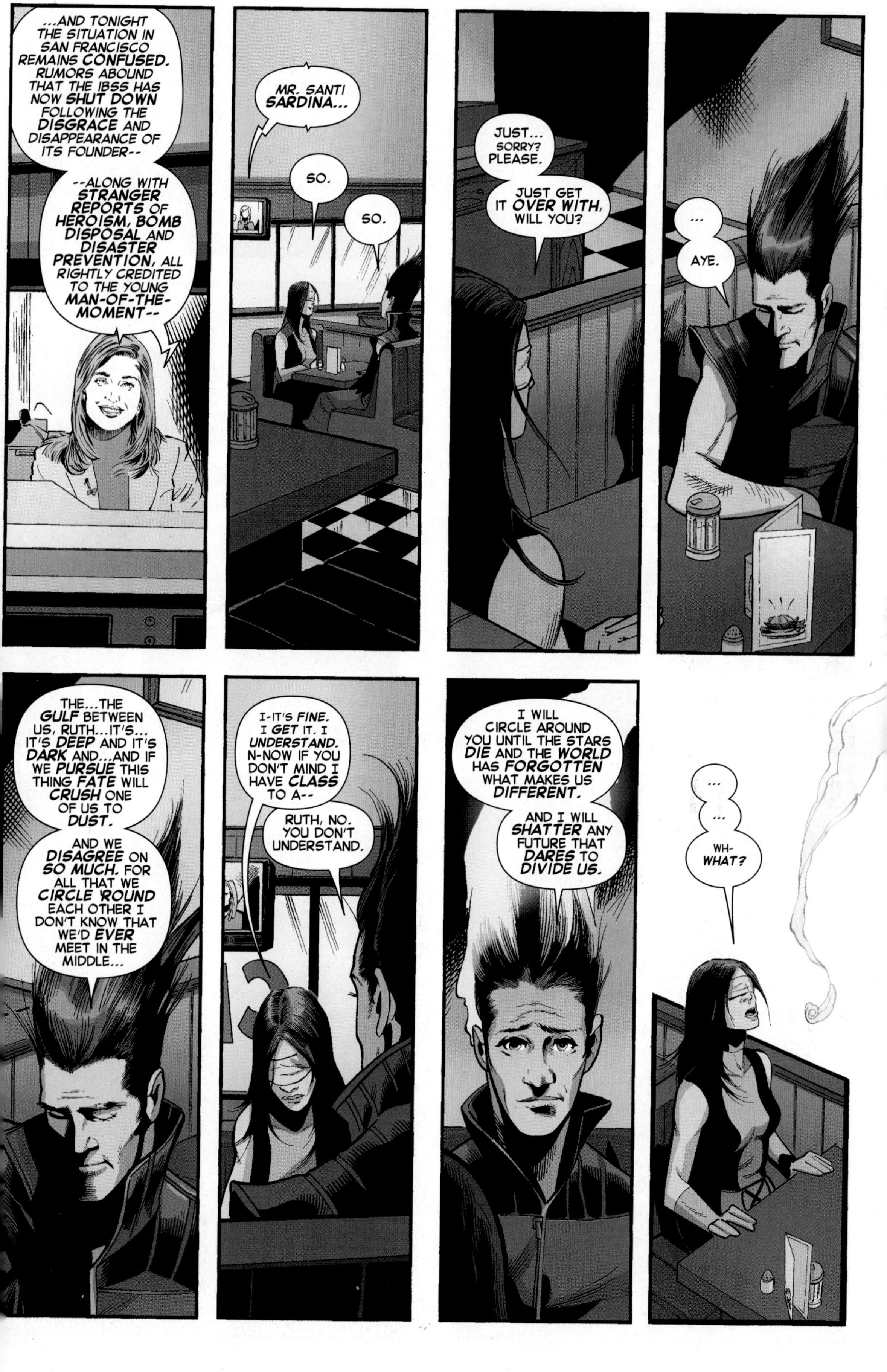
...AND TONIGHT THE SITUATION IN SAN FRANCISCO REMAINS CONFUSED. RUMORS ABOUND THAT THE IBSS HAS NOW SHUT DOWN FOLLOWING THE DISGRACE AND DISAPPEARANCE OF ITS FOUNDER--
--ALONG WITH STRANGER REPORTS OF HEROISM, BOMB DISPOSAL AND DISASTER PREVENTION, ALL RIGHTLY CREDITED TO THE YOUNG MAN-OF-THE-MOMENT--
MR. SANTI SARDINA...
SO.
SO.
JUST... SORRY? PLEASE.
JUST GET IT OVER WITH, WILL YOU?
...
AYE.
THE...THE GULF BETWEEN US, RUTH...IT'S... IT'S DEEP AND IT'S DARK AND...AND IF WE PURSUE THIS THING FATE WILL CRUSH ONE OF US TO DUST.
AND WE DISAGREE ON SO MUCH. FOR ALL THAT WE CIRCLE 'ROUND EACH OTHER I DON'T KNOW THAT WE'D EVER MEET IN THE MIDDLE...
I-IT'S FINE. I GET IT. I UNDERSTAND. N-NOW IF YOU DON'T MIND I HAVE CLASS TO A--
RUTH, NO. YOU DON'T UNDERSTAND.
I WILL CIRCLE AROUND YOU UNTIL THE STARS DIE AND THE WORLD HAS FORGOTTEN WHAT MAKES US DIFFERENT.
AND I WILL SHATTER ANY FUTURE THAT DARES TO DIVIDE US.
...
...
WH-WHAT?

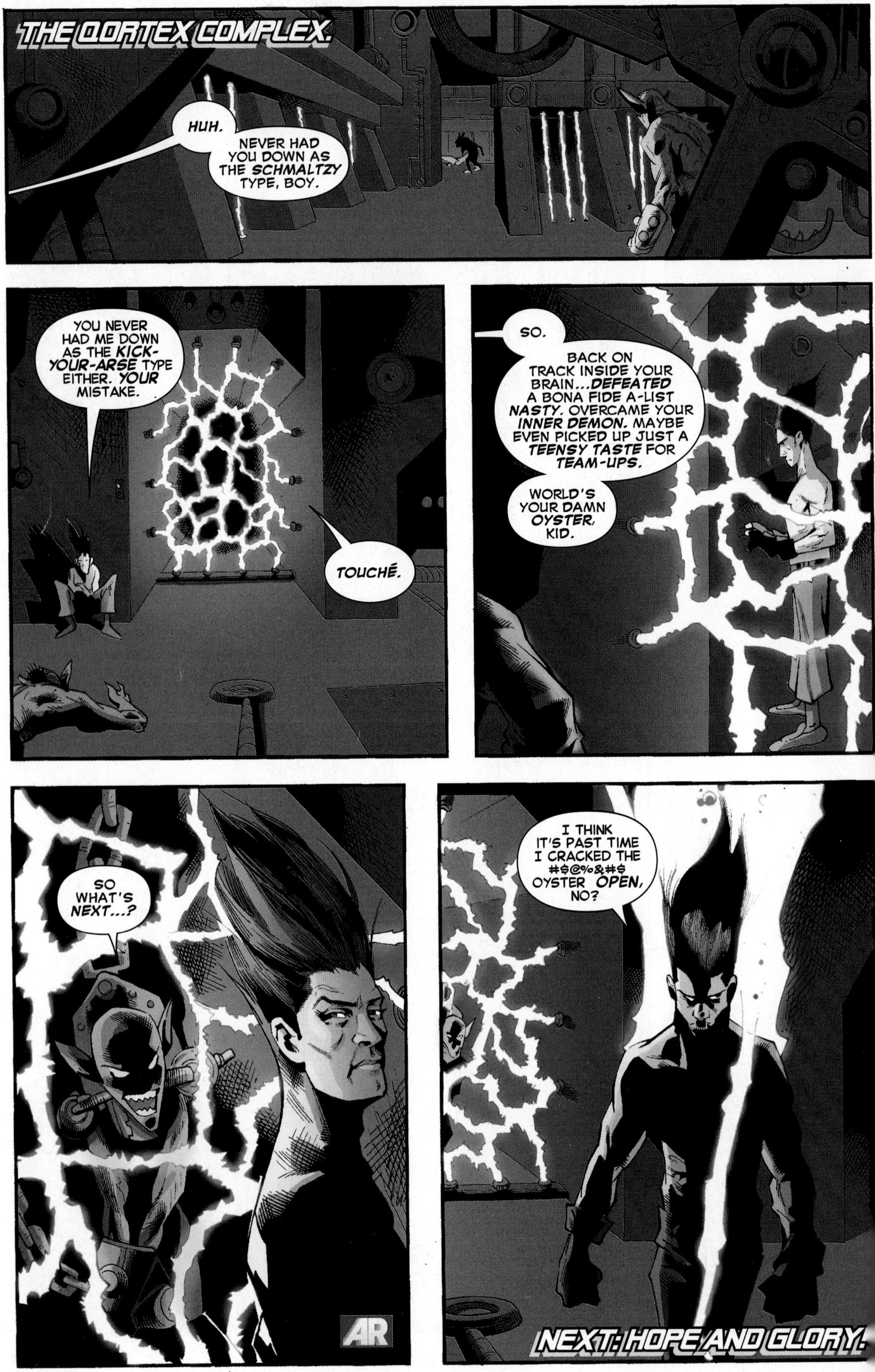
THE QORTEX COMPLEX.
HUH.
NEVER HAD YOU DOWN AS THE SCHMALTZY TYPE, BOY.
YOU NEVER HAD ME DOWN AS THE KICK-YOUR-ARSE TYPE EITHER. YOUR MISTAKE.
TOUCHÉ.
SO.
BACK ON TRACK INSIDE YOUR BRAIN...DEFEATED A BONA FIDE A-LIST NASTY. OVERCAME YOUR INNER DEMON. MAYBE EVEN PICKED UP JUST A TEENSY TASTE FOR TEAM-UPS.
WORLD'S YOUR DAMN OYSTER, KID.
SO WHAT'S NEXT...?
I THINK IT'S PAST TIME I CRACKED THE #$@%&#$ OYSTER OPEN, NO?
NEXT: HOPE AND GLORY.